BUSINESS AND
GENERAL
REFERENCE
BOOK SERIES
FROM IDG

Wine For Dummies™

W9-BVS-774

Quick Reference Card

Ten Most Useful Wine Descriptors

1. **Aroma or Bouquet:** The smell of the wine. Aroma generally applies to younger wines, and bouquet applies to older wines.

2. **Body:** The apparent weight of a wine in your mouth (light, medium, or full)

3. **Crisp:** A wine with refreshing acidity

4. **Dry:** Not sweet

5. **Finish:** The impression a wine leaves as you swallow it

6. **Flavor intensity:** How strong or weak the flavors of a wine are

7. **Fruity:** A wine that has aromas and flavors of fruit; does *not* imply sweetness

8. **Oaky:** A wine that has oak flavors

9. **Soft:** A wine that is smooth and not crisp

10. **Tannic:** A red wine that is firm and leaves the mouth feeling dry

Quick Pronunciation Guide to Common Wine Names

Auslese	*OUSE lay seh*
Beaujolais	*boh jhoe lay*
Bourgogne	*bor guh nyeh*
Cabernet Sauvignon	*cab er nay saw vee nyon*
Chardonnay	*shar dohn nay*
Châteauneuf-du-Pape	*shah toe nuf-doo-pahp*
Gewürztraminer	*gah VERTZ trah mee ner*
Haut-Brion	*oh bree yon*
Loire	*lwahr*
Mâcon	*mah kon*
Merlot	*mer loh*
Meursault	*muhr so*
Moët	*moh ett*
Montepulciano d'Abruzzo	*mon tay pul CHA noh dah BREWTZ zoh*
Mosel-Saar-Ruwer	*MOH zel-zar-ROO ver*
Pauillac	*poy yac*
Perrier-Jouët	*per ree yay-joo ett*
Pinot Grigio	*pee noh GREE joe*
Pinot Noir	*pee noh nwahr*
Pouilly-Fuissé	*pwee fwee say*
Riesling	*REESE ling*
Rioja	*ree OH hah*
Sancerre	*sahn sehr*
Spätlese	*SHPATE lay seh*
Vosne Romanée	*vone roh mah nay*

The stressed syllable in each word is capitalized; if no syllable is capitalized, all syllables carry equal weight.

... For Dummies™: The Best Selling Book Series

Guide to Wine Vintages

Like any vintage wine chart, this must be considered only a rough guide. Many wines will be exceptions to the vintage's rating.

Wine Region	1985	1986	1987	1988	1989	1990	1991	1992	1993
Bordeaux: Médoc, Graves	90b	90a	75c	85a	90a	95a	75b	75b	80a
Bordeaux: Pomerol, St Emilion	85b	85a	75c	85a	90a	95a	65c	75b	80a
Côte de Nuits- Red Burgundy	85c	75d	85c	90b	85b	95a	85a	75b	85a
Côte Beaune- Red Burgundy	85c	70d	80d	90b	85b	90b	70b	80b	85a
Burgundy, White	85c	90c	80c	80c	90b	85c	70c	90b	70c

Tear out this card and carry it in your wallet as a handy guide to picking out the best wines!

Wine For Dummies™

BUSINESS AND GENERAL REFERENCE BOOK SERIES FROM IDG

Quick Reference Card

Instant Wine Identifier

Wine Name	Grape or Place	Wine Color
Bardolino	Place/Italy	Red
Beaujolais	Place/France	Red
Bordeaux	Place/France	Red or white
Burgundy (Bourgogne)	Place/France	Red or white
Cabernet Sauvignon	Grape	Red
Chablis	Place/France	White
Champagne	Place/France	White or rosé
Chardonnay	Grape	White
Chianti	Place/Italy	Red
Côtes du Rhône	Place/France	Red
Merlot	Grape	Red
Mosel	Place/Germany	White
Pinot Grigio/Pinot Gris	Grape	White
Pinot Noir	Grape	Red
Port (Porto)	Place/Portugal	Red (fortified)
Pouilly-Fuissé	Place/France	White
Rhine (Rheingau, Rheinhessen)	Place/Germany	White
Riesling	Grape	White
Rioja	Place/Spain	Red or white
Sancerre	Place/France	White
Sauternes	Place/France	White (dessert)
Sauvignon Blanc	Grape	White
Sherry	Place/Spain	White (fortified)
Soave	Place/Italy	White
Syrah/Shiraz	Grape	Red
Valpolicella	Place/Italy	Red
Zinfandel	Grape	Red or rosé

Positive Thinking for Wine Shoppers

No one in the world knows everything about wine.

Smart people aren't afraid to ask "dumb" questions.

The purpose of wine is to be enjoyed.

Expensive doesn't necessarily mean better.

I am my own best judge of wine quality.

Most wines *are* good wines.

Experimentation is fun.

Advice is free for the asking.

Every bottle of wine is a live performance.

I'll never know... until I try it!

Wine Region	1985	1986	1987	1988	1989	1990	1991	1992	1993
Northern Rhône	90c	80b	75c	90c	90b	90a	90b	75c	65c
Southern Rhône	80c	75c	60d	85c	95a	95b	70c	75c	80b
Germany	85c	75c	65c	85c	90b	95b	80b	85c	85c
Rioja (Spain)	80c	80c	80c	85b	90b	85c	75c	85b	85b
Piedmont	95b	85c	80c	90a	95a	95a	75c	70c	85b
Tuscany	95c	85c	75c	90a	70c	90b	75c	70c	75c
Calif. N. Coast Cab. Sauvignon	90b	80c	85c	75c	80c	95b	95a	90b	90a
Calif. N. Coast Chardonnay	85c	90c	75d	85c	75d	90c	85c	90c	90b

Vintage Key:
- 100 = Outstanding
- 95 = Excellent
- 90 = Very Good
- 85 = Good
- 80 = Fairly Good
- 75 = Average
- 70 = Below Average
- 65 = Poor
- 50 – 60 = Very Poor

a = Too young to drink   b = Can be consumed now, but will improve with time
c = Ready to drink   d = May be too old

IDG BOOKS WORLDWIDE

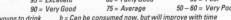

Praise for Wine For Dummies . . .

"A delightfully formatted compendium of everything you need to know about wine. . . . This book will appeal to all wine drinkers, from the occasional drinker to the seasoned pro."

> — Piero Antinori, Proprietor
> Marchesi Antinori Winery
> Florence, Italy

"This is the best news about wine since *60 Minutes* broadcast its story on the so-called French Paradox which linked red wine consumption to cardiovascular benefits. McCarthy & Mulligan's book will, finally and forever, eliminate the intimidation surrounding the enjoyment of wine. Oenophiles . . . you can now call yourself 'Wine Lovers.' Drop the pretense and drink up!!!"

> — Dr. Steven Berglas
> Department of Psychiatry
> Harvard Medical School

"*Wine For Dummies* is comprehensive, it is efficient, uncomplicated, logical, unpretentious but serious, and entirely appropriate as the book of first choice for any person interested in taking the first steps on the journey towards the wonderful world of wine. . . .the best book of its kind."

> — John W. Gay, President
> Rosemount Estates winery, Australia

"A great book for wine lovers!"

> — Bengt Marnfeld
> President, IDG Sweden

"A big, full-bodied, voluptuous read, chock full of brain-coating wit and wisdom. Written with finesse, elegance, and fine breeding."

> — Tom Mathews
> Wine collector

"If this *Dummies* book were a wine, I would describe it as full-bodied with tons of information, written with great clarity, in a style that's not overly complex. Although fully mature and ready to be enjoyed now, it has the staying power to last for years. Order it by the case to give to anyone who enjoys wine. Overall rating: 100+!"

> — Allan H.Weitzman
> Attorney and wine lover

Praise for Ed McCarthy and Mary Ewing-Mulligan

""The [International Wine] center has been the site of hundreds of tastings, judgings, and trade shows. . . . It has also been a training ground for numerous members of the wine trade. . ."
— *The New York Times*

". . . Mary is straightforward, direct, with a good sense of humor."
—*The Philadelphia Daily News*

"Mulligan is New York's wine educator par excellence, knowledgeable, approachable, affable, and up to her elbows in credentials."
— *Avenue* magazine

"She's very informative but she has no airs," says one of the students, Bronx accountant Vincent Altieri. "She wants you to appreciate wine, but she doesn't put you down if you say something silly."
— *Daily News* (New York)

"The International Wine Center . . . is a sort of mecca for wine lovers. It offers down-to-earth wine courses. . ."
— *Staten Island Advance*

"The International Wine Center is a devoted group of wine nuts."
— W. Reed Foster, Ravenswood Winery
Letter to the editor of *The Wine Spectator*

Praise from students for International Wine Center

"I'll never be afraid to order the wine again."

"Snobs they're not!"

"He debunks the myths without killing the magic of wine."

"Terrific personal anecdotes bring the subject alive."

"A wonderful, knowledge-gaining experience and a great time. Most rewarding."

"He has a real passion for wine — and it's contagious."

BUSINESS AND GENERAL REFERENCE BOOK SERIES FROM IDG

References for the Rest of Us

Do you find that traditional reference books are overloaded with technical details and advice you'll never use? Do you postpone important life decisions because you just don't want to deal with them? Then our ...*For Dummies*™ business and general reference book series is for you.

... *For Dummies* business and general reference books are written for those frustrated and hard-working souls who know they aren't dumb, but find that the myriad of personal and business issues and the accompanying horror stories make them feel helpless. ...*For Dummies* books use a lighthearted approach, a down-to-earth style, and even cartoons and humorous icons to diffuse fears and build confidence. Lighthearted but not lightweight, these books are perfect survival guides to solve your everyday personal and business problems.

"More than a publishing phenomenon, 'Dummies' is a sign of the times."
— The New York Times

"A world of detailed and authoritative information is packed into them..."
— U.S. News and World Report

"... you won't go wrong buying them."
— Walter Mossberg, Wall Street Journal, on IDG's ...For Dummies™ books

Already, hundreds of thousands of satisfied readers agree. They have made ...*For Dummies* the #1 introductory level computer book series and a best-selling business book series. They have written asking for more. So if you're looking for the best and easiest way to learn about business and other general reference topics, look to ...*For Dummies* to give you a helping hand.

IDG BOOKS WORLDWIDE

WINE FOR DUMMIES™

by Ed McCarthy
and Mary Ewing-Mulligan, MW

Foreword by
Piero Antinori
Proprietor, Marchesi Antinori Winery
Florence, Italy

IDG BOOKS WORLDWIDE

IDG Books Worldwide, Inc.
An International Data Group Company

Foster City, CA ◆ Chicago, IL ◆ Indianapolis, IN ◆ Braintree, MA ◆ Dallas, TX

Wine For Dummies™

Published by
IDG Books Worldwide, Inc.
An International Data Group Company
919 E. Hillsdale Blvd.
Suite 400
Foster City, CA 94404

Developed and produced by Steve Ettlinger Ettlinger Editorial Projects, New York.

Library of Congress Catalog Card No.: 95-78777

ISBN: 1-56884-390-9

Printed in the United States of America

10 9 8 7 6 5 4 3 2 1

1B/SZ/QY/ZV

Distributed in the United States by IDG Books Worldwide, Inc.

Distributed by Macmillan Canada for Canada; by Computer and Technical Books for the Caribbean Basin; by Contemporanea de Ediciones for Venezuela; by Distribuidora Cuspide for Argentina; by CITEC for Brazil; by Ediciones ZETA S.C.R. Ltda. for Peru; by Editorial Limusa SA for Mexico; by Transworld Publishers Limited in the United Kingdom and Europe; by Al-Maiman Publishers & Distributors for Saudi Arabia; by Simron Pty. Ltd. for South Africa; by IDG Communications (HK) Ltd. for Hong Kong; by Toppan Company Ltd. for Japan; by Addison Wesley Publishing Company for Korea; by Longman Singapore Publishers Ltd. for Singapore, Malaysia, Thailand, and Indonesia; by Unalis Corporation for Taiwan; by WS Computer Publishing Company, Inc. for the Philippines; by WoodsLane Pty. Ltd. for Australia; by WoodsLane Enterprises Ltd. for New Zealand.

For general information on IDG Books Worldwide's books in the U.S., please call our Consumer Customer Service department at 800-762-2974. For reseller information, including discounts and premium sales, please call our Reseller Customer Service department at 800-434-3422.

For information on where to purchase IDG Books Worldwide's books outside the U.S., contact IDG Books Worldwide at 415-655-3021 or fax 415-655-3295.

For information on translations, contact Marc Jeffrey Mikulich, Director, Foreign & Subsidiary Rights, at IDG Books Worldwide, 415-655-3018 or fax 415-655-3295.

For sales inquiries and special prices for bulk quantities, write to the address above or call IDG Books Worldwide at 415-655-3200.

For information on using IDG Books Worldwide's books in the classroom, or ordering examination copies, contact Jim Kelly at 800-434-2086.

For authorization to photocopy items for corporate, personal, or educational use, please contact Copyright Clearance Center, 222 Rosewood Drive, Danvers, MA 01923, or fax 508-750-4470.

 is a trademark under exclusive license to IDG Books Worldwide, Inc., from International Data Group, Inc.

About the Authors

Ed McCarthy and Mary Ewing-Mulligan

Ed McCarthy and Mary Ewing-Mulligan are two wine lovers who met at an Italian wine tasting in New York's Chinatown in 1981 and formally merged their wine libraries and cellars when they married in 1983.

At the time of that fateful meeting, Mary had worked in the wine trade for ten years and had directed the Italian government's wine information bureau for the U.S. She grew up in Pennsylvania and studied English literature at the University of Pennsylvania.

Although employed full-time as an English teacher, Ed held part-time jobs in wine shops to satisfy his passion for wine and to subsidize his rapidly expanding wine collection. Born and raised in New York City, he earned a master's degree in psychology from City University of NY.

Today, Mary is co-owner and director of International Wine Center, a wine school in Manhattan. She and Ed teach classes at the Center — solo and jointly — for wine lovers and for individuals employed in the wine trade. Retired from teaching English, Ed now devotes all of his time to wine, writing articles for *Wine Enthusiast Magazine* and *The Wine Journal,* consulting, and moonlighting at his favorite wine shop.

In 1993, Mary culminated five years of independent study in wine by becoming the only American woman who is a Master of Wine. She earned the title by passing a rigorous professional examination given by London's Institute of Masters of Wine. There are only 195 Masters of Wine in the world, including 13 in America.

When they are not teaching or writing about wine, Mary and Ed take busman's holidays to the wine regions of the world. They admit to living thoroughly unbalanced lives in which their only non-wine pursuits are hiking in the Italian Alps, running, unwinding to Neil Young music, and spending quiet time with Sherry, La Tache, Leoville, Pinot Grigio, Brunello and Dolcetto — their cats.

Welcome to the world of IDG Books Worldwide.

IDG Books Worldwide, Inc., is a subsidiary of International Data Group, the world's largest publisher of computer-related information and the leading global provider of information services on information technology. IDG was founded more than 25 years ago and now employs more than 7,500 people worldwide. IDG publishes more than 235 computer publications in 67 countries (see listing below). More than 60 million people read one or more IDG publications each month.

Launched in 1990, IDG Books Worldwide is today the #1 publisher of best-selling computer books in the United States. We are proud to have received 8 awards from the Computer Press Association in recognition of editorial excellence, and our best-selling ...For Dummies™ series has more than 17 million copies in print with translations in 25 languages. IDG Books Worldwide, through a recent joint venture with IDG's Hi-Tech Beijing, became the first U.S. publisher to publish a computer book in the People's Republic of China. In record time, IDG Books Worldwide has become the first choice for millions of readers around the world who want to learn how to better manage their businesses.

Our mission is simple: Every one of our books is designed to bring extra value and skill-building instructions to the reader. Our books are written by experts who understand and care about our readers. The knowledge base of our editorial staff comes from years of experience in publishing, education, and journalism — experience which we use to produce books for the '90s. In short, we care about books, so we attract the best people. We devote special attention to details such as audience, interior design, use of icons, and illustrations. And because we use an efficient process of authoring, editing, and desktop publishing our books electronically, we can spend more time ensuring superior content and spend less time on the technicalities of making books.

You can count on our commitment to deliver high-quality books at competitive prices on topics consumers want to read about. At IDG Books Worldwide, we value quality, and we have been delivering quality for more than 25 years. You'll find no better book on a subject than an IDG book.

John J. Kilcullen

John Kilcullen
President and CEO
IDG Books Worldwide, Inc.

IDG Books Worldwide, Inc., is a subsidiary of International Data Group, the world's largest publisher of computer-related information and the leading global provider of information services on information technology. International Data Group publishes over 235 computer publications in 67 countries. More than sixty million people read one or more International Data Group publications each month. The officers are Patrick J. McGovern, Founder and Board Chairman; Kelly Conlin, President; Jim Casella, Chief Operating Officer. International Data Group's publications include: **ARGENTINA'S** Computerworld Argentina, Infoworld Argentina; **AUSTRALIA'S** Computerworld Australia, Computer Living, Australian PC World, Australian Macworld, Network World, Mobile Business Australia, Publish!, Reseller, IDG Sources; **AUSTRIA'S** Computerwelt Oesterreich, PC Test; **BELGIUM'S** Data News (CW); **BOLIVIA'S** Computerworld; **BRAZIL'S** Computerworld, Connections, Game Power, Mundo Unix, PC World, Publish, Super Game; **BULGARIA'S** Computerworld Bulgaria, PC & Mac World Bulgaria, Network World Bulgaria; **CANADA'S** CIO Canada, Computerworld Canada, InfoCanada, Network World Canada, Reseller; **CHILE'S** Computerworld Chile, Informatica; **COLOMBIA'S** Computerworld Colombia, PC World; **COSTA RICA'S** PC World; **CZECH REPUBLIC'S** Computerworld, Elektronika, PC World; **DENMARK'S** Communications World, Computerworld Denmark, Computerworld Focus, Macintosh Produktkatalog, Macworld Danmark, PC World Danmark, PC Produktguide, Tech World, Windows World; **ECUADOR'S** PC World Ecuador; **EGYPT'S** Computerworld (CW) Middle East, PC World Middle East; **FINLAND'S** MikroPC, Tietoviikko, Tietoverkko; **FRANCE'S** Distributique, GOLDEN MAC, InfoPC, Le Guide du Monde Informatique, Le Monde Informatique, Telecoms & Reseaux; **GERMANY'S** Computerwoche, Computerwoche Focus, Computerwoche Extra, Electronic Entertainment, Gamepro, Information Management, Macwelt, Netzwelt, PC Welt, Publish, Publish; **GREECE'S** Publish & Macworld; **HONG KONG'S** Computerworld Hong Kong, PC World Hong Kong; **HUNGARY'S** Computerworld SZT, PC World; **INDIA'S** Computers & Communications; **INDONESIA'S** Info Komputer; **IRELAND'S** ComputerScope; **ISRAEL'S** Beyond Windows, Computerworld Israel, Multimedia, PC World Israel; **ITALY'S** Computerworld Italia, Lotus Magazine, Macworld Italia, Networking Italia, PC Shopping Italy, PC World Italia; **JAPAN'S** Computerworld Today, Information Systems World, Macworld Japan, Nikkei Personal Computing, SunWorld Japan, Windows World; **KENYA'S** East African Computer News; **KOREA'S** Computerworld Korea, Macworld Korea, PC World Korea; **LATIN AMERICA'S** GamePro; **MALAYSIA'S** Computerworld Malaysia, PC World Malaysia; **MEXICO'S** Compu Edicion, Compu Manufactura, Computacion/Punto de Venta, Computerworld Mexico, MacWorld, Mundo Unix, PC World, Windows; **THE NETHERLANDS'** Computer! Totaal, Computable (CW), LAN Magazine, Lotus Magazine, MacWorld; **NEW ZEALAND'S** Computer Buyer, Computerworld New Zealand, Network World, New Zealand PC World; **NIGERIA'S** PC World Africa; **NORWAY'S** Computerworld Norge, Lotusworld Norge, Macworld Norge, Maxi Data, Networld, PC World Ekspress, PC World Nettverk, PC World Norge, PC World's Produktguide, Publish& Multimedia World, Student Data, Unix World, Windowsworld; **PAKISTAN'S** PC World Pakistan; **PANAMA'S** PC World Panama; **PERU'S** Computerworld Peru, PC World; **PEOPLE'S REPUBLIC OF CHINA'S** China Computerworld, China Infoworld, China PC Info Magazine, Computer Fan, PC World China, Electronics International, Electronics Today/Multimedia World, Electronic Product World, China Network World, Software World Magazine, Telecom Product World; **PHILIPPINES'** Computerworld Philippines, PC Digest (PCW); **POLAND'S** Computerworld Poland, Computerworld Special Report, Networld, PC World/Komputer, Sunworld; **PORTUGAL'S** Cerebro/PC World, Correio Informatico/Computerworld, MacIn; **ROMANIA'S** Computerworld, PC World, Telecom Romania; **RUSSIA'S** Computerworld-Moscow, Mir - PK (PCW), Sety (Networks); **SINGAPORE'S** Computerworld Southeast Asia, PC World Singapore; **SOUTH AFRICA'S** Computer Mail (CIO), Computing S.A., Network World S.A., Software World; **SPAIN'S** Advanced Systems, Amiga World, Computerworld Espana, Communicaciones World, Macworld Espana, NeXTWORLD, Super Juegos Magazine (GamePro), PC World Espana, Publish; **SWEDEN'S** Attack, ComputerSweden, Corporate Computing, Macworld, Mikrodatorn, Natverk & Kommunikation, PC World, CAP & Design, Datalngenjoren, Maxi Data, Windows World; **SWITZERLAND'S** Computerworld Schweiz, Macworld Schweiz, PC Tip; **TAIWAN'S** Computerworld Taiwan, PC World Taiwan; **THAILAND'S** Thai Computerworld; **TURKEY'S** Computerworld Monitor, Macworld Turkiye, PC World Turkiye; **UKRAINE'S** Computerworld, Computers+Software Magazine; **UNITED KINGDOM'S** Computing/Computerworld, Connexion/Network World, Lotus Magazine, Macworld, Open Computing/Sunworld; **UNITED STATES'** Advanced Systems, AmigaWorld, Cable in the Classroom, CD Review, CIO, Computerworld, Computerworld Client/Server Journal, Digital Video, DOS World, Electronic Entertainment Magazine (E2), Federal Computer Week, Game Hits, GamePro, IDG Books Worldwide, Infoworld, Laser Event, Macworld, Maximize, Multimedia World, Network World, PC Letter, PC World, Publish, SWATPro, Video Event; **URUGUAY'S** PC World Uruguay; **VENEZUELA'S** Computerworld Venezuela, PC World; **VIETNAM'S** PC World Vietnam.
08/15/95

Dedication

We dedicate this book to the members of the International Wine Club, past and present — our favorite wine-tasting companions and partners in learning — and to Mouton.

Acknowledgments

As we wrote this book, we were very conscious of being part of a team of people all dedicated to making the book happen. We acknowledge everyone at IDG Books Worldwide who was part of the team at various stages — John Kilcullen, Milissa Koloski, Kathy Welton, Stacy Collins, Sarah Kennedy, and especially Colleen Rainsberger, our best student.

We thank Steve Ettlinger for his constant advice and support closer to home. We acknowledge Peter Leslie with appreciation for his key role in making this book happen and author David Pogue, whose brilliant *Macs For Dummies* first planted the seed of this book in our minds.

Thanks, too, to Jane Barrett, Len Benjamin, Richard Carras, Akira Chiwaki, Mark Lawless, Bernie Fradin of Quality House Liquors — our first wine teacher — and Daniel Oliveros, whose extraordinary generosity has enabled us to enjoy more bottles of legendary wine than any two people deserve in a lifetime. Our gratitude extends to all our friends who are present namelessly throughout the book in anecdote, and to our winemaker friends whose wonderful wines have inspired and fed our passion for the subject. Thanks also to Elise, E.J., and Lucinda McCarthy for their support and enthusiasm.

Book producer and agent Steve Ettlinger would like to thank David Pogue for his inspiration, advice, and encouragement.

(The Publisher would like to give special thanks to Patrick J. McGovern and Bill Murphy, without whom this book would not have been possible.)

Credits

Vice President and Publisher
Kathleen A. Welton

Executive Editor
Sarah Kennedy

Managing Editor
Stephanie Britt

Brand Manager
Stacy S. Collins

Executive Assistant
Jamie Klobuchar

Production Director
Beth Jenkins

**Supervisor of
Project Coordination**
Cindy L. Phipps

Supervisor of Page Layout
Kathie S. Schnorr

Pre-Press Coordinator
Steve Peake

**Associate
Pre-Press Coordinator**
Tony Augsburger

Media/Archive Coordinator
Paul Belcastro

Project Editor
Colleen Rainsberger

Editors
Suzanne Packer
Tamara S. Castleman
Diana R. Conover
Diane L. Giangrossi
Shannon Lesley Ross
Michael Simsic

Technical Reviewers
François Chaussonniere
Bengt Marnfeldt
Tom Mathews
David Pogue

Associate Project Coordinators
J. Tyler Connor
Sherry Gomoll

Production Staff
Gina Scott
Carla C. Radzikinas
Patricia R. Reynolds
Melissa D. Buddendeck
Dwight Ramsey
Robert Springer
Theresa Sánchez-Baker
Dominique DeFelice
Maridee V. Ennis
Angela F. Hunckler
Mark C. Owens

Proofreader
Alys Caviness

Indexer
Sherry Massey

Cover Design
Kavish + Kavish

Contents at a Glance

Cartoons at a Glance

By Rich Tennant

Table of Contents

Foreword

· ·

*I*t is my privilege to have been asked to write the foreword to Ed McCarthy and Mary Ewing-Mulligan's book. I've known them for twenty years and can wholeheartedly vouch for their knowledge, their enthusiasm, and their pure pleasure in the joy of wine. I honestly can't think of anyone whose talents are better suited to *Wine For Dummies*.

I consider it particularly appropriate that wine is among the first . . . *For Dummies* books written for a subject other than computers, since many people consider winespeak as foreign and intimidating as computerese. Ed and his wife Mary prove in this down-to-earth, humorous yet thorough book that nothing could be further from the truth.

In everyday language (something missing from most wine literature), they explain all that you ever wanted to know about wine: where and how to buy it, how to read wine labels and speak the language of wine; how to taste wine, how to recognize a bad one, how to navigate restaurant wine lists, and even how to open a bottle. They cover every topic from the most basic to the more advanced. Truly a delightfully formatted compendium of everything you need to know about wine. And its timing is perfect.

These days wine production is at an all-time high, as is wine quality. More varieties of wine are coming from more regions than ever before, creating more confusion in consumers' minds (though I hope that my wines, from Italy's regions of Tuscany and Umbria, do not add to that confusion!) Anyway, we now have the spirited and personal assistance of *Wine For Dummies*.

Wine is for everyone, after all, and we should not treat it as if it were something reserved for a mystical elite. Producers such as myself must support the effort to help the uninitiated and the intimidated.

This book will appeal to all wine drinkers, from the occasional drinker to the seasoned pro. Whether you read this book from cover to cover, dip into it for an occasional bit of knowledge, or turn to it in a moment of crisis, you will be rewarded with the wit and wisdom of two expert teachers. To your health!

Piero Antinori, Proprietor
Marchesi Antinori Winery
Florence, Italy

Piero Antinori's family has been making wine since 1385; his wines are prized by connoisseurs the world over. He also owns Atlas Peak winery in Napa, California and an interest in a Hungarian winery. He has been honored by many of the leading international wine organizations and has often acted as a spokesman for the Italian wine industry.

Introduction

*I*n some parts of the world, people have a very interesting attitude toward wine. They just drink it.

The servers in neighborhood restaurants don't hand the guest a wine list with unrecognizable names on it that he is expected to know (assuming he is the least bit intelligent and sensitive to the finer things in life). They just ask, "Will you be having white or red?" Then they bring a bottle or a carafe of wine, and everyone drinks it. Sometimes guests even drink it out of squat little glasses that we would use only for orange juice. If the guests talk about the wine at all, they use fancy words like *good* to describe it.

Somehow, all that has gotten lost in the translation.

Sophisticates, information addicts, and seekers of status have made wine so complicated that many people are too confused to drink it. The jumble of wine types, brands, vintages, and scores is dizzying to anyone who presumes to buy a bottle of wine without first seeking the counsel of a personal trainer.

Of course, if there weren't some incredibly fabulous wines that are as much art as beverage, the intellectualization and complication of wine would never have happened. The fact is that some wines inspire passion and enthusiasm; that's why some people spend all their leisure time collecting wine, comparing vintages, visiting winemakers, and reading the latest reviews. *But not all wine has to be taken so seriously.*

Wine can be complicated, sure, but the good news is that you really don't have to know very much in order to enjoy it. And if you learn just a little and decide that wine is fascinating, it can become a wonderful hobby.

How to Use This Book

We consider this book a wine textbook of sorts, a user's manual, and a reference book, all in one.

We have included very basic information about wine for readers who know nothing (or next to nothing) about wine, but we have also included tips, suggestions, and more sophisticated information for seasoned wine drinkers who want to take their interest to a more advanced level. Depending on where you fall on the wine-knowledge gradient, different chapters will be relevant to you.

Part I: If You Are a Total Novice

The six chapters that comprise Part I are designed to get you up-and-sipping even if you have never tasted a wine before in your life.

Chapter 1 explains what wine is and the major categories into which all the wines of the world are divided. **Chapter 2** explains how to taste a wine and what you are likely to find when you do taste it. It also tackles the tricky subject of wine quality — how can someone else tell you what you're supposed to like? — and introduces the basic vocabulary used to describe wine's taste and quality. If you drink wine now and then but aren't very comfortable with what you're doing, a quick review of both of these chapters should be helpful.

Chapter 3 takes you behind the scenes of winemaking and reveals the hidden meaning of the winemaking jargon you hear.

Chapters 4 and **5** tell you what you'll find when you head out to buy wine in a shop or restaurant. They offer tips for getting the type of wine you want and moral support for your encounters with snooty wine clerks or servers.

Chapter 6 discusses the nuts and bolts — or rather the corkscrews and glassware — of wine drinking. You'll discover which gadgets make opening a bottle of wine easier, and which are unnecessary. And we take you through the process of removing the cork from the bottle, step by painless step.

Part II: If You Are An Occasional Imbiber

This section is the heart of the book for readers who already feel comfortable buying and serving wine but want to know more about the different types of wine in the world.

In Chapter 7, you get a clear explanation of how wines are named and what you can learn from the name of a wine. In case you've ever wondered what all those words and phrases on wine labels mean, you'll find the answer in **Chapter 8.** (Did you know that some phrases mean *nothing* — that they're just designed to impress you?!) **Chapter 9** brings you down to earth — literally — in a discussion of the grapevine and the fruit of the vine with a description of the main wine grapes.

Chapters 10, 11, and 12 describe the major wine regions of the world and the most important wines produced in each of them. **Chapters 13** and **14** do the same for sparkling wines and dessert wines, respectively — along with explaining just how sparkling wines and dessert wines are made and the differences in quality and style among them. All five chapters provide handy references as you taste your way through the huge universe of wines.

Part III: When You've Caught the Bug

Intermediate to advanced readers will find a wealth of practical advice and recommendations in this section.

In **Chapter 15**, we steer you toward purchasing the types of wine and the quantities of wine that suit your needs and advise you how to store your wines so that they don't get old before their time. **Chapter 16** reveals where and how you can buy wine beyond the outlets already available where you live. Continuing education is the topic of **Chapter 17:** where you can go and what you can do to keep learning about wine. A vacation in wine country, anyone?

The ever-elusive language of wine will frustrate you less after you read **Chapter 18**; in fact, you'll find yourself taking wine notes like a pro! **Chapter 19** gives advice on wine and food pairings and other practical issues of serving wine to yourself or to guests.

For advanced readers who are serious about experiencing the ultimate enjoyment of wine, **Chapter 20** provides specific recommendations on buying and drinking older wines.

Part IV: The Part of Tens

What ...*For Dummies* book would be complete without this final section? It's a synopsis of interesting tips and recommendations about wine to reinforce our suggestions earlier in the book. We're particularly happy to debunk ten prevalent myths about wine so that you can become a savvier consumer and a more contented wine drinker.

Part V: Appendixes

In this part, you can check out a vintage chart and find out more about the wines in the 1855 classification of Bordeaux.

Icons Used in This Book

This odd little guy is a bit like the two-year-old who constantly insists on knowing "Why, Mommy, why?" But he knows that you might not have the same level of curiosity that he has. Where you see him, feel free to skip over the technical information that follows. Wine will still taste just as delicious.

Advice and information that will make you a wiser wine drinker is marked by this bull's-eye so that you won't miss it.

There's very little you can do in the course of moderate wine consumption that can land you in jail — but you could spoil an expensive bottle and sink into a deep depression over your loss. This symbol will warn you about common pitfalls.

Some issues in wine are so fundamental that they bear repeating. Just so you don't think we repeated ourselves without realizing it, we'll mark the repetitions with this symbol.

Wine snobs practice all sorts of affectations designed to make other wine drinkers feel inferior. But you won't be intimidated by their snobbery if you see it for what it is. (And you can learn how to impersonate a wine snob!)

Look for the Dummies Approved check mark when you need advice on specific wines to try. We recommend various wines throughout the book.

Wine Is for Everyone

Because we hate to think that wine, which has brought so much pleasure into our lives, could be the source of anxiety for anyone, we want to help you feel more comfortable around wine. Some knowledge of wine, gleaned from the pages of this book and from our shared experiences, will go a long way toward increasing your comfort level.

But ironically, what will _really_ make you feel comfortable about wine is accepting the fact that you'll never know it all — and that you've got _plenty_ of company.

You see, once you really get a handle on wine, you discover that _no one_ knows everything there is to know about wine. There is just too much information, and it's always changing. And when you know that, you can just relax and enjoy the stuff.

Part I

If You Are a Total Novice

The 5th Wave — By Rich Tennant

"ALL RIGHT, LET'S TRY THIS ONE MORE TIME. IT'S NOT THAT DIFFICULT—YOU JUST WIGGLE THE CORK WITH YOUR THUMBS UNTIL IT SLIPS GENTLY FROM THE BOTTLE."

In this part...

To grasp the material in this part of the book, it helps to have some preliminary knowledge: what a grape is, where your tongue and nose are located, what a shop is, and what a restaurant is.

If you've got those bases covered, you're ready to begin understanding and enjoying wine — even if you've never tasted wine before in your life. We'll start slowly so that you can enjoy the scenery along the way.

Chapter 1

Wine 101

- -

In This Chapter

▶ What wine is

▶ Fifty-cent words like *fermentation* and *sulfites*

▶ What red wine has that white wine doesn't

▶ The blushing truth about rosés

▶ The legalese of table wines, sparkling wines, and fortified wines

- -

*W*e visit wineries all the time, and when we do, we usually end up talking with the winemaker about how he makes his wine. One of us is thrilled by these conversations because they're opportunities to learn more about why wines taste the way they do. But the other one very quickly gets bored; who cares how wine is made, as long as it's wonderful?

It seems that there are two types of wine lovers in the world: the *hedonists,* who just want to enjoy wine and find more and more wines they can enjoy; and the *thinkers,* who are fascinated by how wine happens. (The hedonists call the thinkers *wine nerds.*) Our family has one of each.

If you're a thinker, you'll enjoy discovering what's behind the differences in wines; and if you're a hedonist, a little knowledge can help you discover more wines that you'll enjoy. Of course, this is the thinker speaking.

How Wine Happens

The recipe for turning fruit into wine goes something like this:

1. **Pick a large quantity of ripe grapes from grapevines.**

   You could substitute raspberries or any other fruit, but 99.9 percent of all the wine in the world is made from grapes.

2. **Put the grapes into a clean container that doesn't leak.**

3. Crush the grapes somehow to release their juice.

Once upon a time, feet performed this step.

4. Wait.

In its most basic form, winemaking is that simple. After the grapes are crushed, *yeasts* (tiny one-celled organisms that exist naturally in the vineyard and, therefore, on the grapes) come into contact with the sugar in the grapes' juice and gradually convert that sugar into alcohol. Yeasts also produce carbon dioxide, which evaporates into the air. When the yeasts are done working, your grape juice is wine. The sugar that was in the juice is no longer there — alcohol is present instead. (The riper and sweeter the grapes, the more alcohol there will be in the wine.) This process is called *fermentation*.

What could be more natural?

Fermentation is a totally natural process that doesn't require man's participation at all, except to put the grapes in a container and release the juice from the grapes. (And the grapes could even do that second step themselves, by crushing themselves with their own weight.) Fermentation occurs in fresh apple cider left too long in your refrigerator, too, without any help from you. In fact we read that milk, which contains another sort of sugar, develops small amounts of alcohol if left on the kitchen table all day.

Speaking of milk, Louis Pasteur is the man credited with discovering fermentation in the nineteenth century. That's discovering, not inventing. Some of those apples in the Garden of Eden probably fermented long before Pasteur came along. (Well, we don't think it could have been much of an Eden without wine.)

Modern wrinkles in winemaking

Now if every winemaker actually made wine as crudely as we just described, we'd be drinking some pretty rough stuff that would hardly inspire us to write a book about wine.

But today's winemakers have a bag of tricks as big as George Foreman's appetite. That's one reason why no two wines will ever taste exactly the same. The men and women who make wine can control the type of container they use for the fermentation process (stainless steel and oak are the two main types), as well as the size of the container and the temperature of the juice during fermentation — and every one of these choices can make a big difference in the flavor or quality of the wine. After the fermentation, they can choose how long to let the wine *mature* (a stage when the wine sort of gets its act together) and in what kind of container. Fermentation can last three days or three weeks, and the wine can then mature for a couple of months or a couple of years or anything in between. If you have trouble making decisions, don't ever become a winemaker.

The main ingredient

Obviously, one of the biggest factors making one wine different from the next is the nature of the grape juice. Besides the fact that riper, sweeter grapes make a more alcoholic wine, different *varieties* of grapes (Chardonnay, Cabernet Sauvignon, or Merlot, for example) make different wines. Grapes are the main ingredient in wine, and everything the winemaker does, he does to the particular grape juice he has. Chapter 9 covers specific grapes and the kinds of wine they make, but this chapter takes a broader view.

Contains sulfites

Sulfur dioxide, a compound formed from sulfur and oxygen, is produced naturally during fermentation, in very small quantities. Winemakers add it, too. Sulfur dioxide is to wine what aspirin and vitamin E combined are to humans — the wonder drug that cures all sorts of afflictions and prevents others. Sulfur dioxide is an antibacterial, preventing the wine from turning to vinegar. It inhibits yeasts, preventing sweet wines from refermenting in the bottle. It's an antioxidant, keeping the wine fresh and untainted by the demon *oxygen*. Despite these magic properties, winemakers try to use as little sulfur dioxide as possible because most of them share a belief that the less you add to wine, the better — just as many people prefer to ingest as little medication as possible.

Now here's a bit of irony for you:

Today — when winemaking is so advanced that winemakers need to rely on sulfur dioxide's help less than ever before — wine labels in America say "Contains Sulfites" (meaning sulfur dioxide). That's because in 1988, Congress passed a law requiring that the phrase be included on the label. So now you might think that there is *more* sulfur in the wine than there used to be; but, in reality, sulfur dioxide use is probably at an all-time low.

Approximately five percent of asthmatics are extremely sensitive to sulfites. To protect them, Congress passed the law requiring that any wine containing more than 10 parts per million of sulfites carry the "Contains Sulfites" phrase on its label. Considering that 10 to 20 parts per million occur naturally in wine, that just about covers every wine.

Actual sulfite levels range from about 100 to 150 parts per million, and the legal max (in the U.S.) is 350. White dessert wines have the most sulfur — followed by medium-sweet white wines and blush wines — because those types of wine need it more. Dry white wines generally have less, and dry red wines have the least.

What Color Is Your Appetite?

Your inner child will be happy to know that when it comes to wine, it's okay to like some colors more than others. You can't get away with saying, "I don't like green food!" beyond your sixth birthday, but you can express a general preference for white wine, red wine, or pink wine for all your adult years.

What white wine is

Whoever named white wine was color blind. All you have to do is look at it to see that it's not white, it's yellow. But we've all gotten used to the expression by now, and so *white wine* it is. (Let's hope that person didn't live in a snowy city.)

White wine is wine without any red color (or pink color, which is in the red family). This means that *White Zinfandel,* a popular pink wine, isn't white wine. But yellow wine, golden wine, and wine that's pale as water are all white wines.

Wine becomes white wine in one of two ways. First, white wine can be made from white grapes — which, by the way, are not white. (Did you see that one coming?) *White* grapes are greenish, greenish yellow, golden yellow, or sometimes even pinkish yellow. Basically, white grapes include all the grape types which are not dark red or bluish. If you make a wine from white grapes, it's a white wine.

The second way a wine can become white is a little more complicated. The process involves using red grapes — but only the *juice* of red grapes, not the grape skins. The reason this makes a white wine is that the juice has no red pigmentation — only the skins do. So a wine made with only the juice of a red grape can be a white wine. In practice, though, very few white wines are made from red grapes.

In case you're wondering, the skins are removed from the grapes by either *pressing* large quantities of grapes so that the juice flows out and the skins stay behind — sort of like squeezing the pulp out of grapes, the way kids do in the cafeteria — or *crushing* the grapes by putting them through a machine with a huge screw that breaks the skins, and then draining the juice away from the skins.

Does white go with everything?

You can drink white wine anytime you like — which for most people means as a drink without food or with lighter foods.

White wines are often considered *apéritif* wines, meaning a wine to have before dinner, in place of a cocktail, or at parties. If you ask U.S. or Canadian officials who busy themselves defining such things, an apéritif wine is a wine that has flavors added to it, as vermouth does. But unless you're in the business of writing wine labels for a living, don't worry about that. In common parlance, an apéritif wine is just what we said.

Lots of people like to drink white wines when the weather is hot because they are more refreshing than red wines, and they are usually drunk chilled (the wines, not the people).

 We serve white wines cool, but not ice-cold. Sometimes restaurants serve white wines too cold, and we actually have to wait a while for the wine to warm up before we drink it. If you like your wine cold, fine; but try drinking your favorite white wine a little less cold sometime, and we bet you'll discover it has more flavor that way.

White wine styles: There's no such thing as just plain white wine

There are three main taste categories of white wines, not counting sparkling wine or the really sweet white wine you drink with dessert (see Chapter 14). If the words we use to describe the taste categories sound weird, take heart — it's all explained in Chapter 2. Here are the three categories:

✔ Some white wines are *dry and crisp, with no sweetness and no oaky character.* (Turn to Chapter 3 for the lowdown on oak.) Most Italian white wines, like Soave and Pinot Grigio, and some French whites, like Sancerre and Chablis, fall into this category.

✔ And some white wines are *dry and full-bodied, with oaky character.* The more expensive Californian and French wines — like California Chardonnays selling for $12 a bottle on up in the U.S. or most white wines from the Burgundy region of France — fall into this group. (Those wines are more expensive because the oak is very expensive, for one thing.)

✔ Finally, some white wines are *medium-dry* (that is, not bone-dry). Good examples are the less expensive American wines (under $8 a bottle in the U.S.) as well as a lot of German wines, especially the least expensive ones like Liebfraumilch.

Red, red wine

In this case, the name is correct. Red wines really are red. They can be purple-red, or pale brick red, or ruby red, but they're red.

Red wines are made from grapes that are red or bluish in color. So guess what wine people call these grapes? Black grapes! We suppose that's because black is the opposite of white.

The most obvious difference between red wines and white wines is their color. The red color occurs when colorless juice sits in contact with the red grape skins during fermentation and absorbs the skins' color. Along with color, the grape skins give the wine *tannin*, a substance that is an important part of the way a red wine tastes. (See Chapter 2 for more about tannin.) The presence of tannin in red wines is actually the most important difference between red wines and white wines.

Red wines vary in style more than white wines do. This is partly because so many red grapes are very different from one another. But it's also because winemakers have more leverage in *styling* a red wine (that is, more leverage in adjusting their winemaking to achieve the kind of wine they want). For example, if winemakers leave the juice in contact with the skins for a long time, the wine becomes darker in color and more *tannic* (firmer in the mouth, like strong tea; tannic wines can make you pucker). If winemakers drain the juice off the skins sooner, the wine is softer and less tannic.

Red wines also tend to be more complex than white wines (which is logical when you consider that red wines have at least one more element than white wines do: tannin).

Red wine styles: There's no such thing as just plain red wine, either

Some common styles of red wines are

✔ *Light-bodied, fruity red wines* with not much tannin (like Beaujolais from France, most Australian reds under $8 a bottle, and any red under $10 from California)

✔ *Medium-bodied, moderately tannic red wines* (like less expensive wines from Bordeaux, in France; like Italian Chianti; and like some Merlots)

✔ *Full-bodied, tannic reds* (such as the best Bordeaux wines; the most expensive California Cabernets; Barolo, from Italy; and lots of other expensive reds)

You can find red wines to go with just about every type of food and every occasion when you want to drink wine (except the times when you want to drink a wine with bubbles, because most bubbly wines are white or pink). But it would be a mistake to assume that all red wines are the same and that any one of them will go as well as the next with your swordfish, your spicy Mexican food, or your Super Bowl party.

We'll give you some tips on matching red wine and food in Chapter 19. In the meantime, if you really force us to be specific, we'd say that red wine is consumed more often as part of a meal than as a drink on its own.

One sure way to spoil the fun in drinking most red wines is to drink them cold. Those tannins can taste really bitter when the wine is cold — just like in a cold cup of very strong tea. On the other hand, many restaurants serve red wines too warm. (Where do they store them? Next to the boiler?) If the bottle feels cool to your hand, that's a good temperature.

A rose is a rose, but a rosé is "white"

Rosé wines are pink wines. Although rosé wines are made from red grapes, the wines aren't red because the grape juice is left in contact with the red skins for a very short time — only a few hours, compared to days or weeks for red wines. Because this *skin contact* (the period when the juice and the skins intermingle) is brief, very little tannin is absorbed from the skins in rosé wines. Therefore, you can chill rosé wines and drink them as you would white wines.

Back in the late sixties and early seventies, rosé wines were very popular. Now, lots of people are drinking rosé again — only they're not calling them rosés.

Red wine sensitivities

Lots of people complain that they can't drink red wines without getting a headache or feeling ill. Usually, they blame the sulfites in the wine. We're not doctors or scientists, but we can tell you that red wines contain far less sulfur than white wines. That's because the tannin in red wines preserves the wine (one of the functions performed by sulfur in white wines). Red wines do contain histamines. But the level of histamines in wine is low enough that scientists doubt that the histamines could trigger an allergic reaction. Whatever the reason for the discomfort, it's probably not sulfur dioxide.

Ten occasions to drink rosé (and defy the snobs)

1. When she's having fish and he's having meat (or vice versa)

2. When a red wine just seems too heavy

3. With lunch — hamburger, grilled cheese sandwiches, and so on

4. On picnics on warm, sunny days

5. To wean your son/daughter, mate, friend (yourself?) off cola

6. With Sunday brunches or with egg dishes

7. To celebrate the arrival of spring or summer

8. With ham (hot or cold) or other pork dishes

9. When you feel like putting ice cubes in your wine

10. To accentuate a Valentine's Day dinner (or any other romantic occasion)

You see, the people who market wine in America have figured out that wines called *rosé* don't sell, so they invented the term *blush* wines. Lest someone figures out that *blush* is a synonym for *rosé,* the labels call the wine *white.* But even a child can see that White Zinfandel is really pink.

The blush wines that call themselves *white* are fairly sweet. Wines labeled rosé can be sweetish, but some wonderful rosés from Europe (and a few from America, too) are *dry* (not sweet).

Even if a wine called rosé is dry, most people will assume that it's sweet, because the common perception among Americans is that rosés are sweet. Yet lots of people who drink White Zinfandel believe that they're drinking a *dry* wine, because it's not called rosé. Go figure.

Although hard-core wine lovers hardly ever drink rosé wine, we love to drink them (the dry ones) in the summer. We'd probably drink rosés a lot more than we do if it were easier to find those dry ones. But everyone sells sweet blush wines today; hardly anyone sells dry rosés.

Other Ways of Categorizing Wine

There's a game we sometimes play with our friends. "Which wine," we ask them, "would you want to have with you if you were stranded on a desert island?" In other words, which wine could you drink for the rest of your life without getting tired of it? Our own answer is always Champagne, with a capital *C* (more on the capitalization in a few minutes).

In a way, it's an odd choice because, as much as we love Champagne, we don't drink it *every day* under normal circumstances. We welcome guests with it, we celebrate with it after successfully root-root-rooting for the home team, and we toast our cats with it on their birthdays. It doesn't take much to give us an excuse to drink Champagne, but it's not the type of wine we drink every night.

What we drink every night is regular wine — red, white, or pink — without bubbles. There are various names for these wines. In America, they are called *table* wines, and in Europe they're called *light* wines. Sometimes we refer to them as *still* wines, because they don't have bubbles moving around in them.

Can I serve table wine if I'm having a buffet?

Table wine, or light wine, is fermented grape juice whose alcohol content falls within a certain range defined by law. Furthermore, table wine is not bubbly. (Although some table wines have a very slight carbonation, the amount is not enough to disqualify them as table wines.) According to U.S. standards of identity, table wine may have an alcohol content that is no higher than 14 percent; in Europe, light wine must be within 8.5 percent and 14 percent alcohol by volume, generally speaking (with some minor exceptions). So unless a wine has more than 14 percent alcohol — which usually means that extra alcohol has been added — or it has bubbles, it's a table wine or a light wine.

The regulations-makers didn't get the number 14 by drawing it from a hat. When grapes that are more or less ripe are fermented, the percentage of alcohol that results is usually not more than 14 percent. In fact, the percentage is almost always between 12 and 13.5 percent. Most of the wine you drink is probably in that range.

You can learn the alcohol percentage of a wine by reading its label: Wineries are required by law to show the alcohol percentage on the label (again, with some minor exceptions). It can be expressed in *degrees*, like 12.5 degrees, or as a percentage, like 12.5 percent.

For wines sold within the U.S. — whether the wine is American or imported — there's a big catch. The labels are allowed to lie. U.S. regulations give wineries a 1.5 percent leeway in the accuracy of the alcohol level. If the alcohol level is actually 12.5 percent, the label can indicate a level as high as 14 percent or as low as 11 percent. The leeway does not entitle the wineries to exceed the 14 percent maximum, however.

If the alcohol percentage is stated as a number that is neither a full number nor a half-number — not 12 or 12.5, for example, but 12.8 or 13.2 — odds are it's precise. If the labels states "Alcohol by volume 11 to 14 percent," the alcohol level is anybody's guess.

Beyond table wines

Although table wine is by far the most popular type of wine, two other types have a strong following among some people (like us, with Champagne). The names for these other two types are *sparkling wines*, wines that have bubbles, and *dessert* or *liqueur wines*, wines that have more than 14 percent alcohol.

Dessert wines

If a wine has more than 14 percent alcohol, odds are that alcohol was added during or after the fermentation. That's an unusual way of making wine, but some parts of the world, like the Sherry region in Spain and the Port region in Portugal, have made quite a specialty of it.

Dessert wines is the legal U.S. terminology for these wines, probably because they're usually sweet and often enjoyed after dinner. We find that term misleading, because dessert wines are not *always* sweet and not *always* consumed after dinner. (Dry Sherry is categorized as a dessert wine, for example, but it's dry, and we drink it before dinner.) We prefer the term *fortified,* which suggests that the wine has been strengthened with additional alcohol. But until we get elected to run things, the term will have to be *dessert wine.*

In Europe, fortified wines are called *liqueur wines.* The wine authorities of the European Union have done such a thorough job of naming all the different types of wine that we find it tough to argue with them, but liqueur wine has the same connotation to us as dessert wine: sweet.

Sparkling wines (and a highly personal spelling lesson)

Sparkling wines are wines that have bubbles. The bubbles are carbon dioxide, a natural by-product of fermentation that winemakers sometimes decide to trap in the wine so that the wine bubbles.

In the U.S., Canada, and Europe, *sparkling wine* is the official name for the category of wines with bubbles. (Isn't it nice when everyone agrees?)

Champagne (with a capital C) is the most famous sparkling wine — and probably the most famous *wine*, for that matter. Champagne is a specific sparkling wine (made from certain grape varieties and produced in a certain way) that comes from a region in France called Champagne. It is the undisputed Grand Champion of Bubblies.

Unfortunately, for the people of Champagne, France, their wine is so famous that the name *champagne* has been borrowed again and again by producers elsewhere, until the word has become synonymous with practically the whole category of sparkling wines. In the U.S., for example, you can legally call a sparkling wine *champagne* — even with a capital C, if you want — as long as the carbonation was not added artificially. Winemakers in Canada and Australia are also permitted by local law to use the name *champagne* for their sparkling wine.

To the French, however, limiting the use of the name *champagne* to the wines of the Champagne region has become a *cause célèbre*. European Union regulations not only prevent any other member country from calling its sparkling wines *champagne* but also prohibit the use of terms that even *suggest* the word *champagne,* such as fine print on the label saying that a wine was made using the champagne method. What's more, bottles of sparkling wines from countries outside the European Union — such as the U.S. and Australia — that use the word champagne on the label are banned from sale in Europe. The French are that serious.

To us, this seems perfectly fair. You'll never catch us using the word *champagne* as a generic term for wine with bubbles. We have too much respect for the people and the traditions of Champagne, France, where the best sparkling wines in the world are made. That's why we stress the capital "C" when we say Champagne. *Those* are the wines we want on our desert island, not just any sparkling wine from anywhere that calls itself champagne.

When someone tries to impress you by serving a nominal Champagne (as opposed to a real one), don't be impressed. In places where it is legal to call sparkling wines champagne, usually just the least expensive, low quality wines actually use that name. Most of the top sparkling winemakers in America, for example, won't call their wines champagne — even though it's legal — out of respect for their French counterparts. (Many of California's top sparkling wine companies are actually owned by the French, so it's no surprise that *they* won't call their wines champagne — but many other companies won't, either.)

Ten common red wines

These are some of the most widely available red wines. You'll find descriptions and explanations of these wines all through this book.

1. **Cabernet Sauvignon:** Can come from California, Australia, France, and other places

2. **Merlot:** Can come from California, France, Washington, New York, Chile, and other places

3. **Pinot Noir:** Can come from California, France, Oregon, and other places

4. **Beaujolais:** Comes from France

5. **Valpolicella:** Comes from Italy

6. **Lambrusco:** Usually comes from Italy

7. **Chianti:** Comes from Italy

8. **Burgundy:** Comes from France

   (Completely different wines called "Burgundy" also come from California and other places.)

9. **Zinfandel:** Usually comes from California

10. **Bordeaux:** Comes from France

Ten common white wines

These are some of the most widely available white wines. You'll find descriptions and explanations of these wines all through this book.

1. **Chardonnay:** Can come from California, Australia, France, and other places

2. **Sauvignon Blanc:** Can come from California, France, New Zealand, South Africa, and other places

3. **Riesling:** Can come from Germany, California, New York, Washington, France, and other places

4. **Gewürztraminer:** Can come from France, California, Washington, Germany, and other places

5. **Pinot Grigio or Pinot Gris:** Can come from Italy, Oregon, France, and other places

6. **Soave:** Comes from Italy

7. **Pouilly-Fuissé:** Comes from France

8. **Liebfraumilch:** Comes from Germany

9. **Chablis:** Comes from France

   (Completely different wines called "Chablis" also come from California and other places.)

10. **Frascati:** Comes from Italy

Chapter 2
These Taste Buds Are for You

- -

In This Chapter
▶ How to slurp and gurgle
▶ Aromas you should smell in wine
▶ Aromas you shouldn't smell in wine
▶ The taste of acidity, tannin, and boysenberries
▶ Wine can have backbone and body
▶ Five mysterious concepts of wine quality

- -

*O*ur friends who are normal people (as opposed to our friends who are wine people) like to mock us when we do things like bring our own wine to a party or drive all the way from New York to Boston to go wine shopping. Most of the time, we don't even try to defend ourselves. We realize how ridiculous our behavior must seem.

In our early days as wine drinkers, we too used to think that all wines taste more or less the same. Wine was wine. We liked some better than others, but we couldn't exactly say why. All that changed when we started to taste wine the way the pros do.

The Special Technique for Tasting Wine

We know you're out there — the cynics who are saying right about now, "Hey, I already know how to taste. I do it every day, three to five times a day. All that wine-tasting humbug is just another way of making wine seem fancy."

And you know, in a way, those cynics are right. Anyone who can taste coffee or a hamburger can taste wine. All you need are a nose, taste buds, and a brain. Unless you're like our friend who lost his sense of smell from the permanent-wave solution he used every day as a cosmetology teacher back in the sixties, you, too, have all that it takes to taste wine properly.

You also have all that it takes to speak Mandarin. Having the ability to do something is different from knowing how to do it and applying that know-how in everyday life, however.

Two very complicated rules of wine tasting

Although you drink beverages every day, tasting them as they pass through your mouth, wine is a special case. Wine is much more complex than other beverages. Wine people believe that wine is *so* complex that it deserves to be looked at and smelled before it is even tasted.

One thing is for sure: The more slowly and attentively you taste wine, the more interesting it tastes. If you gulp wine quickly, the way you do soda pop, you'll only *get* ten or twenty percent of the wine's flavor.

And with that, we have two of the fundamental rules of wine tasting:

1. Slow down.
2. Pay attention.

The appearance of the wine

We get pleasure from looking at the wine in our glass, noticing how brilliant it is and the way it reflects the light, trying to decide precisely which shade of red it is and whether it will stain the tablecloth permanently if we tilt the glass too far. (One of the secret techniques of professional wine-tasters in differentiating between white wines and red wines is to look at the wine in the glass.)

Most books tell you that you look at the wine to determine whether it is clear (cloudiness generally indicates a flawed wine). That advice dates itself, though. Ever since high technology infiltrated the wine industry, especially for inexpensive and medium-priced wines, visual flaws in wine are as rare as a winning lottery ticket. You could probably drink wine every night for a year without encountering a cloudy wine.

But look at the wine for a moment, anyway. Tilt your (half-full) glass away from you and look at the color of the wine against a white background. Serious wine tasters prefer white tablecloths to colored ones so that they always have a white background handy. But a piece of white paper is just as good. Once at a black-tie dinner we even saw a distinguished fellow, who must have been a *very* serious wine lover, pull up his tuxedo sleeve and hold his glass against his white shirt to judge the color!

Look at the wine in your tilted glass and just notice how dark or how pale it is and what color it is, for the record. Eventually, you'll begin to notice differences from one wine to the next; but for now, just observe.

The nose knows

Now we get to the really fun part of tasting wine: swirling and sniffing. This is when you can let your imagination run wild, and no one will ever dare to contradict you. If you say that a wine smells like boysenberries to you, how can anyone prove that it doesn't?

To get the most out of your sniffing, swirl the wine in the glass first. But don't even *think* about swirling your wine if your glass is more than half full.

Keep your glass on the table and swirl it so that air becomes mixed in with the wine. Then bring the glass to your nose quickly. Stick your nose as far as it will go into the airspace of the glass without actually touching the wine and smell the wine. Free associate. Is the aroma fruity, woodsy, fresh, cooked, intense, light? Your nose tires quickly, but it recovers quickly, too. Wait just a moment and try again. Listen to your friends' comments and try to find the same things they find in the smell.

Tips for smelling wine

1. Be bold. Stick your nose right into the glass where all the aromas are captured in the air space.

2. Don't wear strong scent; it will compete with the smell of the wine.

3. Don't wear yourself out smelling a wine when there are strong food aromas around. The tomatoes you smell in the wine could really be the tomato in someone's pasta sauce.

4. Become a smeller. Smell every ingredient when you cook, everything you eat, the fresh fruits and vegetables you buy at the super-market, even the smells of your environment — like leather, wet earth, tar, grass, flowers, your wet dog, shoe polish, your medicine cabinet. Stuff your mental database with smells so that you'll have them at your disposal when you need them.

5. Try different techniques of sniffing. Some people like to take short, quick sniffs, while others like to inhale a deep whiff of the wine's smell. Keeping your mouth open a bit while you inhale can help. (Some people even hold one nostril closed and smell with the other, but we think that's a bit too kinky, especially in family restaurants.)

Wines have noses

With poetic license typical of wine tasters, someone once dubbed the smell of a wine its *nose*—and the expression took hold. If someone says that a wine has a huge nose, he means that the wine has a very strong smell. If he says that he detects strawberries *in the nose* or *on the nose*, he means that the wine smells like strawberries.

In fact, most wine tasters rarely use the word *smell* to describe how a wine smells because the word *smell* (like the word *odor*) seems pejorative. Wine tasters talk about the wine's *nose* or *aroma*. Sometimes they use the word *bouquet*, although that word seems to be falling out of fashion.

You can revitalize your nose more quickly by smelling something else, like your water, a piece of bread, or your shirt sleeve — but be prepared for the odd looks you'll get from everyone around you.

As you swirl, the aromas in the wine vaporize into the air, and you can smell them. Wine has so many *aromatic compounds* that whatever you find in the smell of a wine is probably not merely a figment of your imagination.

The point behind this whole ritual of swirling and sniffing is that what you smell should be pleasurable to you, maybe even fascinating, and that you should have fun in the process. But what if you notice a smell that you don't like?

Hang around wine geeks for a while, and you'll start to hear words like *petrol, manure, sweaty saddle, burnt match,* and *asparagus* used to describe the aromas of some wines. "Yuck!" you say? Of course you do! Fortunately, the wines which exhibit such smells are not the wines you'll be drinking for the most part — at least not unless you get really catch the wine bug. And when you do catch the wine bug, you might discover that those aromas, in the right wine, can really be a kick. Even if you don't learn to enjoy those smells (some of us do, honest!), you'll appreciate them as typical characteristics of certain regions or grapes.

Then there are the bad smells that nobody will try to defend. It doesn't happen often, but it does happen, because wine is a natural, agricultural product with a will of its own. Often when a wine is seriously flawed, it shows immediately in the nose of the wine. Wine judges have a term for such wines. They call them *DNPIM* — Do Not Put In Mouth. Not that you'll get ill, but why subject your taste buds to the same abuse that your nose just took? Sometimes it's a bad cork that is to blame, and sometimes it's some other sort of problem in the winemaking or even the storage of the wine. Just rack it up to experience and open a different bottle.

While you're choosing the next bottle, make up your own acronyms. *SOTYWE* (Serve Only To Your Worst Enemies) for example, or *ETMYG* (Enough To Make You Gag) or our own favorite, *SLADDR* (Smells Like a Dirty Dish Rag).

When it comes to smelling wine, many people are concerned that they aren't able to detect as many aromas as they think they should. Smelling wine is really just a matter of practice and attention. If you start to pay more attention to smells in your normal activities, you'll get better at smelling wine.

Tasting the wine

After you've looked at the wine and smelled it, you're finally allowed to taste it. This is when grown men and women sit around and make strange faces, gurgling the wine, and sloshing it around in their mouths with looks of intense concentration in their eyes. You can make an enemy for life if you distract a wine taster just at the moment when he is focusing all his energy on the last few drops of a special wine.

Before we explain the ritual, we want to assure you that; a) you don't have to apply this procedure to every single wine you drink; b) you won't look foolish doing it, at least in the eyes of other wine lovers (we can't speak for the other 90 percent of the human population), and; c) it's a great trick at parties to avoid talking with someone you don't like.

Take a medium-sized sip of wine. Hold it in your mouth, purse your lips, and draw in some air across your tongue, over the wine. (Be utterly careful not to choke or dribble, or everyone will strongly suspect that you're not a wine expert.) Then swish the wine around in your mouth as if you are chewing it. Then swallow it. The whole process should take several seconds, depending on how much you are concentrating on the wine.

What's really happening

Here's what is happening in your mouth when you taste wine the slow way. Different parts of the tongue specialize in registering different sensations; sweetness is perceived most keenly on the front of the tongue, sourness is triggered principally on the sides, and bitterness is detected across the rear of the tongue. By moving the wine around in your mouth, you give it a chance to hit all of these places so that you don't miss anything in the wine (even if sourness and bitterness sound like things you wouldn't mind missing).

As you swish the wine around in your mouth, you are also buying time. Your brain needs a few seconds to figure out what the tongue is tasting and make some sense of it. Any sweetness in the wine registers in your brain first because it corresponds to the first place the wine hits in your mouth; the *acidity* registers next (acidity, by the way, is what normal people call sourness), and then the bitterness. While your brain is working out the relative impressions of sweetness, bitterness, and acidity, you can be thinking about how the wine feels in your mouth — whether it's heavy, light, smooth, rough, and so on.

Tasting the smells

Until you cut your nose in on the action, that's all you can taste in the wine — those three sensations of sweetness, acidity, and bitterness and a general impression of weight and texture. Where have all the boysenberries gone?

They're still there in the wine, right next to the chocolate and plums. But — to be perfectly correct about it — these flavors are actually *aromas* that you taste, not through tongue contact, but by inhaling them up an interior nasal passage in the back of your mouth called the *retronasal passage* (see Figure 2-1). When you draw in air across the wine in your mouth, you are vaporizing the aromas just as you did when you swirled the wine in your glass. (There's a method to this madness.)

Nasal cavities

Figure 2-1:
Most wine flavors are actually aromas that are vaporized in the mouth and perceived through the rear nasal passage.

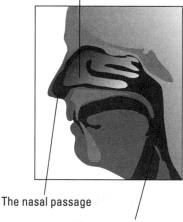

The nasal passage

The retronasal passage

After you go through all this rigamarole, it's time to reach a conclusion: Do you like what you tasted? The possible answers are yes, no, an indifferent shrug of the shoulders, or "I'm not sure, let me take another taste," which means that you have serious wine-nerd potential.

Just as a wine taster might use the term *nose* for the smell of a wine, he might use the word *palate* in referring to the taste of a wine. A wine's palate is the overall impression the wine gives in your mouth or any isolated aspect of the wine's taste — as in, "This wine has a harmonious palate," or "The palate of this wine is a bit acidic." When a wine taster says that he finds raspberries *on the palate*, he means that the wine tastes like raspberries to him.

The Pleasure Principle: Discovering What You Like

All this wine tasting stuff is so automatic to us by now that we probably practice it on every wine we taste and on every sip of every wine, without even realizing it. Sometimes we catch ourselves doing it with beer or orange juice — much to our embarrassment if we're out in public.

Ten aromas (or flavors) associated with wine

1. Fruits
2. Herbs
3. Vegetables
4. Earth
5. Flowers

6. Grass
7. Tobacco
8. Toast
9. Smoke
10. Coffee, mocha, or chocolate

Ten odors not associated with wine

1. Paint
2. Vinyl
3. Fax paper
4. Glue
5. Gorgonzola

6. Cannabis
7. Magic Marker
8. Elephant dung
9. Chanel No. 5
10. Fabric softener

We've discovered that there are drawbacks to tasting like this — besides the risk of looking foolish. When you taste wine the fancy way, you bring out all the characteristics of the wine, good *or* bad. Most wines are up to the challenge, but some wines are better left unscrutinized.

This brings us to the fundamental issue behind wine tasting: pleasure. If you're drinking mediocre wine, ignorance can be bliss. But when you can pick and choose the wine you drink, the exercise of tasting wine thoughtfully can help you find the wines that give you the most pleasure. And unless you discover what you like, how can you ask for it?

You get what you ask for

Now we have to confess that there is one more step between knowing how to taste wine and always drinking wine that you like. And it's a doozy. That step is putting taste into words.

We wouldn't have to bother with this detail if only we could choose our wines the way that customers choose cheese in a gourmet shop. (Can I try that one? No, I don't like it; let me taste the one next to it. Good. I'll take half a pound.)

"Like/Don't Like" is a no-brainer once you have the wine in your mouth. But most of the time you have to buy the stuff without tasting it first. So unless you want to drink the same wine for the rest of your life, you're going to have to decide what it is that you like or don't like in a wine and communicate that to another person who can steer you in the right direction.

Parlez-vous Winespeak?

There are two hurdles here: Finding the words to describe what you like or don't like, and then getting the other person to understand what you mean. Naturally, it helps if we all speak the same language.

Unfortunately, Winespeak is a dialect with an undisciplined and sometimes poetic vocabulary whose definitions change all the time, depending on who is speaking. In case you really want to get into this wine thing, we'll treat you to some sophisticated wine language in Chapters 3 and 18. For now, a few basic words and concepts should do the trick.

Describing Taste

Appearance and aroma are not critical in getting a wine you like. If you prefer white, red, or pink, it's because of the way the wine tastes, not because of the color itself (unless you're seriously into color coordinating your food). And the aromas of the wine are more or less similar to its flavors.

Describing the *taste* of a wine in your mouth is the whole trick. When we first began to taste wine, we noticed that we usually faced one of two opposite dilemmas: Either the wine was so simple that we really couldn't find anything to say about it, or the flavors of the wine came so fast and furious that we couldn't sort them out. We eventually learned to taste wine one step at a time.

The tastes of a wine actually reveal themselves sequentially according to where they are detected on the tongue. We recommend that you follow this natural sequence when you try to put words to what you're tasting.

Sweetness: Right there, on the tip of your tongue, as soon as you put the wine into your mouth, you can notice sweetness or the lack of it. In Winespeak, *dry* is the opposite of *sweet*. Classify the wine you're tasting as either *dry, medium-dry* (in other words, slightly sweet), or *sweet*.

Acidity: All wine contains acid (mainly *tartaric acid*, which exists in grapes), but some wines are more acidic than others. Acidity is more of a taste factor in white wines than in reds. For white wines, acidity is the backbone of the wine (it gives the wine firmness and definition in your mouth). White wines with a good amount of acidity taste *crisp;* and those without enough acidity, taste *fat* and *flabby*. The sides of the tongue trigger your perception of acidity. You can also sense the consequences of acidity (or the lack of it) in the style of the wine — whether it's a tart little number or a soft and generous sort, for example. Classify the wine you're tasting as *tart, crisp, soft,* or "couch potato."

Is it sweetness or fruitiness?

Beginning wine tasters sometimes describe dry wines as *sweet* because they confuse fruitiness with sweetness. A wine is *fruity* when it has distinct aromas and flavors of fruit. You smell the fruitiness with your nose; and in your mouth, you "smell" it through your retronasal passage.

Sweetness, on the other hand, is perceived on your tongue. When in doubt, try holding your nose when you taste the wine; if the wine really is sweet, you'll be able to taste the sweetness despite the fact that you can't smell the fruitiness.

Is it acid or tannin?

Red wines have acid as well as tannin, and distinguishing between the two as you taste a wine can be a real challenge. When you're not sure whether it's tannin or acid you're perceiving, pay attention to how your mouth feels *after* you've swallowed the wine. Both tannin and acid will make your mouth feel dry, but acid makes you salivate in response to the dry feeling (saliva is a base, so it neutralizes the acid). Tannin just leaves your mouth dry.

Tannin: Tannin is a substance that exists naturally in grapeskins and elsewhere in the grape (see Chapter 1). Because red wines are fermented with their grapeskins, tannin levels are far higher in red wines than in white wines. Have you ever taken a sip of a dark red wine and thought that you suddenly tasted ink or rapidly experienced a drying-out feeling in your mouth, as if someone had shoved a blotter in there? That's tannin.

To generalize a bit, *tannin* is to a red wine what acidity is to a white: a backbone. Because tannin often tastes bitter, you sense tannin near the back of your tongue, but you can detect it elsewhere, too — on the inside of your cheeks and between your cheeks and gums — if the amount of tannin in a wine is high. Depending on the amount of tannin, a red wine can be called *bitter*, *firm*, or *soft*.

Softness and firmness are actually *textural impressions* a wine gives you as you taste it. Just as your mouth feels temperature in a liquid, it feels texture in a liquid. Some wines literally *feel* soft and smooth in your mouth, while others feel hard or rough. In white wines, acid is usually responsible for impressions of hardness or firmness (or crispness); in red wines, tannin is usually responsible. Low levels of either substance can make a wine feel pleasantly soft — or too soft, depending on the wine. Alcohol and unfermented sugar also contribute to an impression of softness.

Body: A wine's body is an impression you get from the whole of the wine — not at any one place on your tongue. It's the impression of the weight and size of the wine in your mouth. We say "impression" because, obviously, one ounce of any wine will occupy exactly the same space in your mouth and weigh the same as one ounce of any other wine. But some wines *seem* fuller, bigger, or heavier in the mouth than others. Think about the wine's fullness and weight as you taste it. Don't tell your friends that you're doing this, but imagine that your tongue is a postal scale and judge how much the wine is weighing it down. Classify the wine as *light-bodied, medium-bodied,* or *full-bodied.*

Flavors: Wines have flavors (er, we mean *mouth aromas*), but wines don't come in a specific flavor. While you might enjoy the suggestion of chocolate in a red wine that you're tasting, you wouldn't want to go to a wine store and ask for a chocolatey wine, unless you don't mind the idea of people holding their hands over their mouths and trying not to laugh aloud at you.

Instead, you should refer to *families of flavors* in wine. There are your *fruity wines* (the ones that make you think of all sorts of fruit when you hold the wine in your mouth), your *earthy wines* (these make you think of mushrooms, walks in the forest, turning the earth in your garden, dry leaves, and so on), your *spicy wines* (cinnamon, cloves, black pepper or Indian spices, for example), your *herbal wines* (mint, grass, hay, rosemary, and so on), and so on, and so on. There are so many flavors in wine that we could go on and on (and we often do!), but you get the picture, don't you?

If you like a wine and want to try another wine that's similar but different (and it will always be different, we guarantee you), try to decide what flavors in the wine you like and mention that to the person selling you your next bottle. In Part II, you'll find wines that fit these specific flavors.

Now you have 13 words — and a whole community of families — that allow you to explain what kind of wine you like. (If you're superstitious, consider *couch* and *potato* as separate words, and you've got 14.) In Chapter 18, we'll elaborate on Winespeak and show you how to describe a wine as *round and supple, regal yet without pretension, gutsy yet not overbearing.*

The Quality Issue: What's a Good Wine?

Did you notice, by any chance, that nowhere on the list of terms we just used to describe wines were the words *great, very good,* or *good?* Instead of worrying about crisp wines, fruity wines, and earthy wines, wouldn't it just be easier to walk into a wine shop and say, "Give me a very good wine for dinner tonight"? Isn't *quality* the ultimate issue — or at least, quality within your price range, also known as *value?*

Well, quality is so important that, our cats will tell you with some embarrassment, we sometimes argue at the dinner table about the quality of the wine we're drinking. It's not that we don't know a great wine when we find one; in fact, we usually agree on whether the wine we are drinking is good. What we debate is *how* good the wine is or isn't — because it's a matter of personal taste.

One man's meat . . .

The instrument that measures the quality of a wine is a human being's *palate,* and because we're all different, we all have different opinions on how good a wine is. The combined opinion of a group of trained, experienced palates (also known as wine experts) is usually considered a definitive judgment of a wine's quality. But there's no guarantee that you will like the wine that the experts agree is very good. We have bought highly rated wines and emptied them down the sink because we didn't think they were very good at all.

We know it sounds like we're describing some kind of anarchy here, with everyone deciding for himself what's good and what isn't. But that's the way it is. When the primary purpose of a wine is to taste good, the person tasting the wine is the only one who can decide whether a particular wine works or not.

Of course, there are degrees of good and bad. Our old clunker works if it gets us where we're going, but it's probably not considered a good car because we feel every bump in the road. Somewhere along the way, someone established quality standards for cars that say that the best cars are quiet, ride smoothly, and are easy to steer — and ours isn't.

Quality standards exist for wine, too. What's frustrating is that there's no Detroit testing ground where scientific instruments can measure each wine against these quality standards. The measurement rests with your own palate.

So, what's a good wine? It is, above all, a wine that you like enough to drink. After that, how good a wine is depends on how it measures up to a set of (more or less) agreed-upon standards of performance established by experienced, trained experts. These standards involve mysterious concepts like *balance, length, depth, complexity,* and *trueness to type* (*typicity* in Winespeak, *typicité* in Snobwinespeak). None of these concepts are objectively measurable, by the way.

Balance: Those words you learned earlier — sweetness, acidity, tannin — represent three of the major *components* (parts) of wine. The fourth is alcohol. Besides being one of the reasons we usually want to drink a glass of wine in the first place, alcohol is an important element of wine quality.

Balance is the relationship of these four components to one another. A wine is balanced when nothing sticks out as you taste it, like harsh tannin or too much sweetness. Most wines are balanced to most people. But if you have any pet peeves about food — if you really hate anything tart, for example, or if you

Balance in action

For firsthand experience of how the principle of taste balance works, try this. Make a very strong cup of tea. When you sip it, the tea will taste bitter, because it's very tannic. Now add lemon juice; the tea will taste astringent, because the acid of the lemon and the tannin of the tea are accentuating each other. Now add lots of sugar to the tea. The sweetness should counter-balance the acid-tannin impact, and the tea will taste softer than it did before.

never eat sweets — you might perceive some wines to be unbalanced. If you perceive them to be unbalanced, then they are unbalanced for *you*. (Professional tasters know their own idiosyncrasies and adjust for them when they judge wine.)

As we described earlier, tannin and acidity are *hardening elements* in a wine (they make a wine taste firmer in the mouth), while alcohol and sugar (if any) are *softening elements*. The balance of a wine is therefore the interrelationship of the hard and the soft aspects of a wine.

Length: When we call wines *long* or *short,* we're not referring to the size of the bottle or how quickly we empty it. *Length* is a word used to describe a wine that goes all the way on the palate — you can taste it across the full length of your tongue — and doesn't stop short halfway through your tasting of it. A wine with good length hits all the taste centers on your tongue and lingers after you swallow it, too. Many wines today are very up front on the palate — they make a big impression as soon as you taste them — but they are short. Length is a sure sign of quality.

Depth: This is another subjective, unmeasurable attribute of a high-quality wine. We say a wine has *depth* when it does not taste flat and one-dimensional on the palate but instead seems to have underground layers of taste. A flat wine can never be great.

Complexity: There's nothing wrong with a simple, straightforward wine any more than there's something wrong with Al Bundy — they are what they are. But a wine that keeps revealing different things about itself, always showing you a new flavor or impression — a wine that has *complexity* — is considered better quality.

Typicity: In order to judge whether a wine is true to its type, you have to know how that type is supposed to be. So you have to know the textbook characteristics of wines made from the major grape varieties and the classic wine regions of the world. (For example, the Cabernet Sauvignon grape typically has an aroma and flavor of blackcurrants, and the French white wine called Pouilly-Fumé typically has a slight gunflint aroma.) Turn to Chapters 9 through 12 for all those details.

What's a Bad Wine?

Strangely enough, the right to declare a wine "good" just because you like it does not carry with it the right to call a wine a "bad" just because you don't. In this game, you get to make your own rules, but you don't get to force other people to live by them.

The fact is, there are very few bad wines in the world today compared to even 20 years ago. And many of the wines we could call bad are actually just bad *bottles* of wine — bottles that were handled badly, so that the good wine inside them got ruined. (Poor boy; he had everything going for him until he fell in with those wild kids. . . .)

Here are some characteristics that everyone agrees indicate a bad wine. Let's hope you never meet one. You might not.

- **Moldy fruit:** Have you ever eaten a raspberry from the bottom of the container that had a dusty, cardboardy taste to it? That same taste of rot can be in a wine if the wine was made from grapes that were not completely fresh and healthy when they were harvested. Bad wine.

- **Vinegar:** In the natural evolution of things, wine is just a pit stop between grape juice and vinegar. Most wines today remain forever in the wine stage because of technology or careful winemaking. If you find a wine that has crossed the line towards vinegar, it's bad wine.

- **Chemical or bacterial smells:** The most common are acetone (nail polish remover) and sulfur flaws (rotten eggs, burnt rubber, bad garlic). Bad wines.

- **Oxidized wine:** Smells flat, weak, or maybe cooked, and tastes the same. It might have been a good wine once, but air — oxygen — got in somehow and killed the wine. Bad bottle.

- ✔ **Cooked aromas and taste:** When a wine has been stored or shipped in heat, it can actually taste cooked or baked as a result. Often there's telltale leakage from the cork, or the cork is pushed up a little. Bad bottle. (Unfortunately, every other bottle of that wine that experienced the same shipping or storage will also be bad.)

- ✔ **Corky wine:** The most common flaw, a smell of damp cardboard that gets worse with air. It's caused by a bad cork, and even the best wines in the world are not immune to it. Bad bottle.

The Final Analysis: Do You Like It?

Let's not dwell too long on what can go wrong with a wine. If you find a bad wine or a bad bottle — or even a wine that is considered a good wine, but you don't like it — just move on to something you like better. Drinking a so-called great wine that you don't enjoy is as stupid as watching foreign films that bore you. Change the channel. Explore.

The ten most useful words in wine tasting (and what they mean)

1. **Aroma or bouquet:** The smell of the wine. Aroma generally applies to younger wines, and bouquet applies to older wines.

2. **Dry:** Not sweet.

3. **Crisp:** A wine with refreshing acidity.

4. **Soft:** A wine that is smooth and not crisp.

5. **Body:** The apparent weight of a wine in your mouth (light, medium, or full).

6. **Flavor intensity:** How strong or weak the flavors of a wine are.

7. **Oaky:** A wine that has oak flavors from being in contact with oak. (Not to be confused with *okay,* a wine that's not good and not bad.)

8. **Tannic:** A red wine that is firm and leaves the mouth feeling dry.

9. **Fruity:** A wine that has aromas and flavors of fruit.

10. **Finish:** The impression a wine leaves as you swallow it.

Five of the oddest expressions in wine

1. **Skin contact:** Association between legally consenting grapeskins and grape juice, for the purpose of creating more flavor in the wine.

2. **Blush wines:** Pink wines that call themselves white, whose popularity is enough to make the accountants blush.

3. **Friendly wines:** A wine that smiles at you and doesn't bite your nose off. In other words, a wine that is easy to drink and lots of people like.

4. **Generous wines:** Wines that are full and rich and give freely of their flavors. The opposite of stingy wines, which make you work to see their attributes.

5. **Fat wines:** Wines that are soft in the mouth without any firmness. If you don't like them, you can call them flabby; if you like them, call them voluptuous.

"WE CAN EITHER GET THE QUAKER STATE® CHARDONNAY OR THE BLACK AND DECKER® BORDEAUX. ONE HAS THE POWER TO CUT THROUGH A HEAVY SAUCE, BUT THE OTHER HOLDS ITS VISCOSITY AT OVEN TEMPERATURES REACHING 500 DEGREES FAHRENHEIT."

Chapter 3
Making Wine Taste Good

The most frustrating thing about wine has got to be the technical lingo. All you want is a crisp, fruity white wine to serve with tonight's fried chicken. But you have to fight your way through a jungle of jargon that confronts you on the back labels of the wine bottles, in the words the sales clerk uses to explain his recommendations, and on the signs all around the wine shop. Why on earth is everyone making wine so complicated?

Here's the problem: Wine is two products. On the one hand, it's a beverage, and it should taste good — period. On the other hand, it's an art form — something lots of people like to talk about, study, and collect. The people who enjoy wine as an art form (a *delicious* art form) are so engaged by the subject that they sometimes forget that other people aren't. They end up telling you information about winemaking techniques that you didn't ask for.

How much of this information (if any) is important, and how much is pretentious blabber? In other words, which techniques make wine taste good?

A Reality-Check for Wine Jargon

Winemakers use a number of procedures to make wine, which vary according to the grapes they have and the type of wine they intend to make. (If they're making large quantities of a wine that should sell for $5.99 retail, for example, they probably won't ferment the wine in new barrels of French oak because the cost of the oak alone could add $2 to the price of every bottle.)

None of these winemaking procedures is inherently good or inherently bad; it all depends on the grapes and the type of wine being made. Every winemaking technique affects the taste of the wine — in one way or another. And how the wine tastes is the final measure of the wine's quality: The procedures themselves are meaningless if they don't create a wine that is appealing to wine drinkers.

The *taste* of the wine involves the wine's aroma, body, texture, length, and so on (see Chapter 2) and not just its flavors. And the taste of a wine is a subjective experience.

Most of the technical words that are bandied about in wine circles represent procedures that *are* relevant to the taste of a wine. (Of course, if you dig deep enough, even dinosaur droppings can be relevant to the taste of a wine.) But these technical words each represent isolated elements in the making of the wine, *parts* of the total picture that hold limited significance individually.

The importance of these techniques has been blown out of proportion by the wine industry in response to a worldwide trend in wine consumption: People are drinking less wine, but better wine.

In competitive markets such as the U.S., wine producers are bending over backward to convince you that their wine is better than the next guy's wine — so that you'll buy it. To accomplish this goal, they talk technically. *"Our wine is 70% barrel-fermented in medium-toast Nevers oak that we replace on a five-year rotation; half of the wine was fermented with Epernay yeast and the rest of it with Montrachet; the wine sat on the lees for 11 months, and we stirred the lees twice a day; all of the wine underwent malolactic."*

The implied meaning behind most of the wine jargon you hear or read is simply, "This is a good wine" — as if words could make wine good.

Operation: Delicious

Everything that a winemaker does in producing his wine has just one purpose: to make the best-tasting wine possible. Some winemakers make wines that are intended to taste good right away, while others make wines that are intended to taste good down the road, after the wine has matured (see Chapter 20).

Producing wine actually involves two separate steps: the growing of the grapes, called *viticulture*, and the making of the wine, called *vinification*.

Sometimes both steps are performed by the same company, as with *estate-bottled* wines (see Chapter 8), and sometimes the two steps are completely separate. Some large wineries, for example, contract with hundreds of private grape growers. These growers don't make wine; they just grow grapes and sell their grapes to whatever wine company offers them the highest price per ton.

Vine-growing vernacular

Here are the key words related to grape growing that you're likely to find on wine labels or hear in conversation:

- ✔ **Low yields.** Example: "Our fruit comes from low-yielding vineyards." The operative concept is that the more grapes a grapevine produces (the higher its *yield*), the less intense the flavors of those grapes will be, and the lower in quality they — and their wine — will be.

  In most European vineyards, maximum yields are set by law, but in American vineyards there are no limits. Just about any wine producer anywhere can *claim* that his yields are low, because it's too complicated to prove otherwise. If the wine tastes thin or watery, we'd be suspicious.

- ✔ **Ripeness.** Example: "Our grapes were perfectly ripe at harvest." Harvesting the grapes when they are perfectly ripe — a brief stage between under-ripe and over-ripe — is one of the crucial points in wine production. But ripeness is a subjective issue. In cooler climates, full ripeness is an extraordinary thing that doesn't happen every year, and the wine should be unusually good as a result.

  In warmer climates, ripeness is almost automatic; the trick becomes not letting the grapes get too ripe too fast, which causes them to be physiologically mature but undeveloped in their flavors (like a physically precocious but immature teenager). And in some places, winemakers purposely pick their grapes a little early because they want higher acids in their wine. (See Chapter 9 for a discussion of how grapes ripen.) There's no fixed definition of perfect ripeness.

- ✔ **Canopy.** Example: "We use an open canopy to get perfect ripeness in our grapes." Left untended, grapevines would grow along the ground, up trees, wherever they could take hold (they're *vines*, after all!). But commercial viticulture involves attaching the shoots of vines to wires or trellises in a systematic pattern. The purpose of *training* the vine — as this activity is called — is to position the grape bunches so that they'll get enough sun and ripen well and so that the fruit will be easy to harvest.

An *open canopy* is a trellising method that maximizes the sunlight exposure of the grapes. *Canopy management,* the practice of maneuvering the grape leaves and fruit into the best position for a given vineyard, is a popular buzzword. Winemakers want you to know that they are doing everything possible to get their grapes ripe. But the proof is in the wine, not the words.

✔ **Microclimate.** Example: "Our vineyards benefit from a microclimate that assures perfect ripeness every year." Every wine region has climatic conditions (the amount and timing of sun, rain, wind, humidity, and so on) that are considered the norm for that area. But individual locations within a region — the side of a particular hill, for example — can have a climatic reality that is different from neighboring vineyards. The unique climatic reality of a specific location is called its *microclimate*. Naturally, every wine producer thinks his microclimate is ideal — or wants to convince you that it is.

The jargon of grape growing concerns issues that are really important to the people who earn a living from growing grapes or making wine. But none of these issues alone proves anything about the quality or taste of a wine. Every issue is just one element of the total picture — how the wine tastes.

Winemaking wonder words

The vinification end of wine producing is usually divided into two parts: *fermentation*, the period when the grape juice turns into wine, and *maturation* (or *finishing*) the period following fermentation when the wine settles down, loses its rough edges, goes to prep school, and gets ready to meet the world. Depending on the type of wine being made, the whole process could take three months or five years — or even longer if the bank isn't breathing down the winery's neck.

When wood becomes magic

Oak barrels, 60 gallons in size (about as big as a large garbage can) are often used as containers for wine either during fermentation or for maturation. The barrels are expensive — about $600 per barrel if they're made from French oak. (Most people consider French oak to be the finest.) We suppose the expense is one good reason to boast about using the barrels.

But not all oak is the same. Oak barrels vary in the origin of their oak, the amount of *toast* (a charring of the inside of the barrels) each barrel has, the age of the barrels (they lose their oakiness with time), and even the size of the barrels.

Even if all oak *were* the same, a wine could turn out differently depending on whether unfermented juice or actual wine went into the barrels, and how long it stayed there.

In fact, the whole issue of oak is so complicated that anyone who suggests that a wine is better simply because it has been oaked is guilty of gross oversimplification. *There is no automatic correlation between the use of oak and wine quality.*

The point of using oak barrels is twofold: They lend oaky flavor and aroma to the wine, which is generally very appealing; additionally, by allowing a slow exchange of oxygen with the wine, the oak acts as a catalyst for chemical changes in the wine. (The usual alternative to oak — stainless steel — is impermeable to air.) Most of the talk about oak these days, though, concerns only the first issue — the aroma and flavor of oak in the wine. To achieve oaky character in the wine without the expense of buying barrels, some winemakers actually immerse oak chips or oak shavings in their wine or add liquid essence of oak to the wine (less common than oak chips and illegal in some places) — a far cry from expensive, hand-made barrels. And just try getting any winemaker to admit to that practice.

Barrel-fermented versus barrel-aged

You don't have to venture very far into wine before you find someone explaining to you that a particular wine was barrel-fermented or barrel-aged — not that you asked. What in the world does he mean, and should you care?

The term *barrel-fermented* means that unfermented juice went into barrels (almost always oak) and changed into wine there. The term *barrel-aged* usually means that wine (already fermented) went into barrels and stayed there for a maturation period of a few months or a few years.

Because most wines that are fermented in barrels remain there for several months after the fermentation is finished, *barrel-fermented* and *barrel-aged* are sometimes used together. The term *barrel-aged* alone suggests that the fermentation happened somewhere other than the barrel — usually in stainless steel.

Is oaky okay?

So many wines are oaked these days that wine lovers use the word *oaky* all the time. But the magazine editor reviewing a wine column written by a friend of ours had never heard the term applied to wine, and he thought it was a typo. The editor changed the text to read: "Lovely okay nuances on the nose of this wine are followed by a strong okay flavor on the palate...."

Barrel-fermentation applies only to white wines, and the reason is very practical. As we mentioned in Chapter 2, the juice of red wines ferments together with the grape skins in order to become red, and that's a mighty messy mixture to have to clean out of a small barrel! Red wines are usually fermented in larger containers — stainless steel or even large wooden vats — and then *aged* in small oak barrels after the wine has been drained off the grape skins. (Some light, fruity styles of red wine might not be oaked at all.)

Here's why you might care whether a white wine is barrel-fermented or just barrel-aged. Wines that are fermented in barrels actually end up tasting *less* oaky than wines that were simply aged in barrels, even though they may have spent more time in oak. (A barrel-fermented and barrel-aged Chardonnay might have spent 11 months in oak, for example, and a barrel-aged Chardonnay may have spent only five months in oak.)

Lots of people who are supposed to know more about wine than you do — for example, the salesperson at your wine shop — get the effects of the two processes backward and tell you that the barrel-fermented wine tastes oakier. If you have a strong opinion about the flavor of oak in your wine, you'll end up buying the wrong wine on their advice.

Other winemaking terms

Become a wine expert overnight and dazzle your friends with this amazing array of wine jargon. (Just don't fool yourself into believing that any one of the procedures described necessarily creates a high quality wine. The merit of each procedure depends on the particular wine being made.)

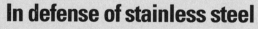

In defense of stainless steel

Because an aura of high quality surrounds the use of oak in winemaking, stainless steel often takes a bad rap among wine snobs. In reality, unless a winemaker specifically wants to make the style of wine that results from barrel-fermentation, stainless steel is the ideal material for fermentation tanks. It is easy to clean, it comes in all shapes and sizes, it enables easy regulation of the wine's temperature through the use of computerized controls, and it lasts forever. There are some very good wines that are made entirely in stainless steel, without seeing any oak.

✔ **Lees.** Example: "Our Chardonnay had 11 months of lees contact." *Lees* is the name for the various solids that precipitate to the bottom of a wine after fermentation. Lees include dead yeast cells that have finished their work of changing the grape juice into wine, as well as grape pulp and, in the case of red wines, pips and skins. When people talk about lees contact, it's the dead yeast cells that they are most concerned with. These cells can interact with elements of the wine and create more complex flavor in the wine. (Sometimes the winemaker stirs the lees in the wine periodically to accelerate this process.) A white wine with extended lees contact usually tastes richer and less overtly fruity than it would otherwise.

✔ **ML** or **malolactic.** Example: "We put our wine through a full malolactic." *Malolactic*, nicknamed *ML*, is a secondary fermentation that changes the nature of the acids in the wine. (During this fermentation process, *malic acid*, a harsh acid also found in apples, is converted into *lactic acid*, a milder acid that is also found in milk.) The net result is that the wine is softer and less acidic. ML usually happens naturally, but a winemaker can prevent it.

Red wines almost always undergo malolactic fermentation, but for white wines, it's a stylistic judgment call on the winemaker's part. A white wine that is meant to be crisp and tart with vivid fruit flavors — like a dry Riesling, for example — will achieve that style far better without ML. Sometimes, ML can contribute a buttery flavor to a white wine. Malolactic fermentation can be a key process in creating delicious white wines — if you like the style of wine it creates.

Many winemakers describe their wine as being "partially malolactic." That usually means that some of the barrels or tanks underwent ML and others didn't, and then the two were blended together for a middle-of-the-road effect. The winemaker prevents ML by using sulfur dioxide (which inhibits the bacteria that trigger ML) or by filtering the wine to remove the ML bacteria.

✔ **pH.** Example: "The pH of this wine is 3.4." The chemical term, pH, means exactly the same thing for wine as it does in other scientific fields. ("Our facial cream is pH-balanced for sensitive skin.") If you want a technical explanation, look up your former chemistry teacher. If you'll settle for the general concept, pH is a measurement of acidity; wines with low pH (approximately 3.4 or less) have higher acidity and wines with high pH have lower acidity.

✔ **fining** and **filtering.** Example: "*Our* wine is unfined and unfiltered." The processes of *fining* and *filtering* are carried out on most wines near the end of the maturation period when they are almost ready for bottling. The purpose of these procedures is to *clarify* the wine — that is, to remove any cloudiness or solid matter in the wine — and to *stabilize* it — to remove any yeast, bacteria, or other microscopic critters that might change the wine for the worse after it is bottled.

There's a popular belief among anti-tech wine lovers that fining and filtration strip a wine of its character — and that unfined, unfiltered wines are inherently better. But it's a complex issue. (For one thing, there are *degrees* of fining and filtration, like *light* fining and *gentle* filtration.)

✔ **Blending.** Example: "We blend the wines of five different grapes to create layers of complexity in our wine." This one is easy. *Blending* means the same thing in winemaking as it does in baking: mixing different ingredients together. In winemaking, the ingredients are usually the wines of different grape varieties that are fermented separately and then brought together afterward. But *blending* also applies to the mixing of various barrels (or *lots*) of wine from the same grape variety to create one homogeneous lot of wine before bottling. Blending is also the term for mixing liquid oak extract in a wine. Hold the confectioner's sugar, please.

Blending wines from different grape varieties together is more common than we realize. Many wines that carry the name of a single grape are really made from more than one grape but are named for the principal grape using the 75 percent (or 85 percent) rule. (See "Hello, my name is Chardonnay" in Chapter 7.)

The reasons for blending wines of different grapes together are either

✔ To reduce costs by diluting an expensive wine like Chardonnay with something else far less expensive

✔ To improve the quality of the wine by using complementary grapes whose characteristics enhance each other

Many of Europe's traditional wines — such as red Rioja, red Bordeaux, Châteauneuf-du-Pape and Champagne — are blended wines that owe their personality to several grapes.

No Winemaking Technique Is an Island

If you really get into wine, and if you're the kind of person who enjoys knowing how things work, some of the winemaking and grape growing terms described in this chapter are likely to become part of your vocabulary. If you're a hedonist who just wants to enjoy wine without all the technical talk, unfortunately you'll be exposed to the jargon anyway when you attend wine tastings, visit wine country, or read about wine.

Either way, a sense of perspective is paramount. Remember that winemaking is a complicated process in which every step depends on every other step. In the end, the quality and style of a wine exist in the glass, not in the words.

Chapter 4
Navigating a Wine Shop

. . . .

. . . .

*U*nless you enjoy a permanent, dependent relationship with an indulgent and knowledgeable wine lover, the day will come when you have to purchase a bottle of wine or order a wine in a restaurant yourself. If you're lucky, the shop owner or the restaurant manager will just happen to be some enlightened fellow whose life purpose is to make good wine easy and accessible to others. If you're lucky, you'll also be awarded an honorary doctorate from Harvard and receive a tax-free inheritance from a great aunt you've never met. The odds are about equal.

Buying Wine Can Intimidate Anyone

Common sense suggests that buying a few bottles of wine should be less stressful than, say, applying for a bank loan or interviewing for a new job. What's the big deal? It's only grape juice.

But memories tell *us* otherwise. There was the time the wine shop wouldn't take back one of the two bottles of inexpensive German wine that we bought the week before, even when we explained how awful the first bottle had been. (Were *we* wrong about the wine or were *they* arrogant? We wasted days wondering.) And the time we pretended we knew what we were doing and bought a full case — twelve bottles — of a French wine based on the brand's general reputation, not realizing that the particular vintage we purchased was a miserable aberration from the producer's usual quality. (Why didn't we just *ask* someone in the store?) Then there was all that time we spent staring at shelves lined with bottles whose labels might as well have been written in Greek, for all that we could understand from them.

Fortunately, our enthusiasm for wine caused us to persevere. We eventually discovered that wine shopping can be fun.

We also discovered a strange thing about bottles of fermented grape juice: The prospect of buying or selling them can turn normally kind and sensitive individuals into victimizers or victims, depending on whether they are trying to prove that they know more than they do or trying to hide what they don't know. But it doesn't have to be that way.

Too much information about wine is constantly changing — new vintages each year, hundreds of new wineries, new wines, advances in wine technology, and so on — for *anyone* to presume that he knows it all or for anyone to feel insecure about what he doesn't know.

Just think about this for a moment: If you could know everything there is to know about every wine in existence right now (which, anyway, is a completely impossible feat), at the point of the next grape harvest you would have to start all over again learning about the wines that were born at that harvest. In the meantime, the wines you already know are changing as they age. And in another year, there will be another grape harvest and more new wines. . . .

Wine is such a rich field that no one in the world knows everything there is to know about it. And that's just what makes wine so interesting. There's always something to learn.

Our experience has taught us that the single most effective way to assure yourself of more good experiences than bad ones in buying wine is to come to terms with your knowledge — or lack thereof — of the subject. If we'd all quit pretending that we know more than we do and give up our defensiveness about what we don't know, buying wine would become the simple exchange that it should be.

Where Wine Is Sold

There are three really great things about buying wine in a store to drink later at home. Stores usually have a much bigger selection of wines than restaurants. The wine is less expensive than in restaurants. And the guy who sold it to you can't watch you or listen to what you say when you're drinking it.

On the other hand, you have to provide your own wine glasses, and you have to open the bottle yourself (see Chapter 6 for the lowdown on all that). And that big selection can be downright daunting. But at least you can touch the bottles and compare the labels.

You can buy wine at all sorts of stores: from supermarkets to wine superstores, discount warehouses, or small specialty wine shops. Each comes with its own advantages and disadvantages in terms of selection, price, or service.

Because wine is a regulated beverage in most countries, governments get involved in deciding where and how wine may be sold (and sometimes even when). So you will have more or fewer choices of where to buy your wine depending on where you live.

Some states within the U.S. and some provinces in Canada have raised government control of alcoholic beverage sales to a fine art. They not only decide *where* you can buy wine, but they also decide *which wines* will be available for you to buy. If you love wine and you live in one of those areas (you know who you are), take comfort in the fact that a) you have a vote; b) freedom of choice lies just across the border; and c) if the Berlin Wall could fall, there's hope for your local government, too.

We'll assume a healthy, open-minded, free-market economy for wine in our discussion of retail wine sales. We hope that applies where you live because your enjoyment of wine will blossom all the more easily if it does.

Supermarkets

In truly *open* wine markets, wine is sold in supermarkets, like any other food product. Supermarkets make wine accessible to everyone. If you can buy what it takes to make a meal, you can buy a bottle of wine to drink with the meal.

When wine is sold in supermarkets, the mystique surrounding the product evaporates. (Who can waste time feeling insecure about a wine purchase when there are much more critical issues at hand, such as how much time is left before the kids turn into monsters and which is the shortest line at the checkout?) And the prices, especially in large stores, are usually quite reasonable.

We know for a fact that some people in the wine business disapprove of the straightforward attitude toward wine in supermarkets; to them, wine is sacrosanct and should always be treated like an elite beverage. At least you won't run into *them* as you browse the wine aisles in your supermarket.

Discount warehouses and superstores

Some stores sell wine on the scale of a supermarket, but they aren't supermarkets, strictly speaking. Most discount warehouse chains fall into this category. Along with your wine, you can pick up any spirits, carbonated beverages, snack foods, or party supplies that you need. The stores are large and their prices are usually quite good.

In some places, lucky wine buyers have access to wine superstores, which can have terrific prices — but often the wines are sold *by the case* only, which means you have to buy twelve bottles of the same wine. (Some special, expensive wines come in six-bottle cases.)

The downside of supermarkets and superstores

If you choose to buy your wine at a supermarket or discount warehouse, you'll usually enjoy a large selection, a no-nonsense attitude, and affordable prices — maybe even the best prices in town.

On the downside, you might feel shortchanged in terms of service. In large, self-service operations, it can be difficult to find someone who can guide you with knowledgeable advice. More likely than not, you are on your own.

To guide you on your solo journey, there will be plenty of *shelf-talkers* (small signs on the shelves that describe individual wines). But the shelf-talkers have probably been placed there by the company selling the wine, which is more interested in convincing you to grab a bottle than in offering you information to help you understand the wine. Flowery phrases, hyperbolic adjectives, and safe, common-denominator stuff like "delicious with chicken" (*any* chicken, cooked in *any* way?) are what you're most likely to find, and the information will be of limited value.

In supermarkets and discount warehouses, you also might discover that the seemingly limitless selection of wines is actually somewhat limited. Most of the wines in the store are wines produced in large enough quantities to support chain store sales. Nothing is wrong with that, unless you're looking for one of those special, limited production wines that wine lovers spend hours discussing in hushed tones. (Of course, those special wines just wouldn't taste as good anyway if they were purchased someplace that didn't shroud them with elitism!)

The bottom line is that supermarkets and discount warehouses can be great places to buy everyday wine for casual enjoyment. But if what you really want is to learn about wine as you buy it, or if you want an unusually interesting variety of wines to satisfy your rapacious curiosity, you will probably find yourself shopping elsewhere.

TIP

Supermarket survival tip

If you're shopping in a supermarket where there's no one to turn to for advice, do one of the following:

1. Try to remember the names of the recommended wines in the last wine article you read. Or better yet, bring the article or list with you.

2. Go to the telephone and call a wine-knowledgeable friend, or, better yet, bring her with you (assuming that her palate and yours get along).

3. Buy the wine with the prettiest label. What have you got to lose?

Wine specialty shops

Wine specialty shops are small to medium-sized stores that sell wine and liquor and sometimes wine books, *corkscrews* (see Chapter 6 for more on those), wine glasses, or a few specialty foods. The foods sold in wine shops tend to be *gourmet* items rather than just run-of-the-mill snack foods. Shops like these target upscale customers.

If you decide to pursue wine as a serious hobby, shops like these are where you'll probably end up buying your wine because they offer many advantages that larger operations cannot. For one thing, wine specialty shops almost always have some wine-knowledgeable staffer on the premises. Also, you can usually find an interesting, varied selection of wines at all price levels.

(We once met a specialty wine retailer who was located down the road from a discount warehouse. He lamented that his was a *13th bottle* store: Customers would consult him about new or unusual wines and would buy one bottle of whatever he recommended. If they liked his recommendations, they'd rarely come back for more of the same. Instead, they headed down the road and bought a case [twelve bottles of it] at a discounted price. Then they turned to him for advice on their next *13th bottle*.)

Inside the wine shop

Wine shops often organize their wines by country of origin and — in the case of classic wine countries, such as France — by region (for example, Bordeaux, Burgundy, Rhône, Champagne, and so on). Red wines and white wines are often in separate sections within these country areas. There might be a special section for sparkling wines and another section for dessert wines.

In some wine shops, there is a special area (or even a special *room*) for the *better* or more expensive wines. In some stores, it's a locked vault-like room. In other stores, it's the whole back area of the store. If the special-wine area is large, you can deduce something about the wines in the rest of the store — that they're mostly, let's say, under $10 a bottle. When you're looking for a very good to excellent wine, you can feel at home in the special section. Naturally, many customers will shop in both parts of the store.

Over in a corner somewhere, often right by the door to accommodate quick purchases, there's usually a *cold box*, a refrigerated cabinet with glass doors where bottles of best-selling white and sparkling wines sit. Unless you really *must* have an ice-cold bottle of wine *immediately* (the two of you have just decided to elope, the marriage minister is a mile down the road, and the wedding toast is only ten minutes away), avoid the cold box. The wines in there are usually too cold and might not be in good condition.

Near the front of the store you might also see boxes or bins of special *sale* wines. These sale displays are usually topped with *case cards* — large cardboard signs that stand above the open boxes of wine — or similar descriptive material. Our words of caution on the credibility of shelf-talkers apply to case cards, too; but because case cards are a lot bigger, there's more of a chance that some useful information may appear on them.

Choosing the Right Wine Merchant

It's as simple to size up a wine merchant as it is to size up any other specialty retailer. The main criteria are *selection, service, expertise,* and *price.* But the conditions in which a shop stores its wines are paramount.

Price

When you're a novice wine buyer, your best strategy is to shop around with an eye to service and reliable advice more than to price. After you've found a merchant who has suggested several wines that you've liked, stick with him, even if he doesn't have the best prices in town. It makes better sense to pay a dollar or so more for wines that are recommended by a reliable merchant (wines that you'll probably like) than to buy wines in a cut-rate or discount store and save a buck, especially if that store has no special wine adviser or if the advice you receive is suspect.

When you have more knowledge of wine, you'll have enough confidence to shop at stores with the best prices. But even then, price must take a backseat to the storage conditions of the wine (see "Wine storage," later in this chapter).

Selection

You won't necessarily know on your first visit whether a particular store's selection is adequate for you. If you notice many wines from many different countries at various prices, give the store's selection the benefit of the doubt. If you outgrow the selection as you learn more about wine, you can seek out a new merchant at that point.

Expertise

Don't be too ready to give a merchant the benefit of the doubt when it comes to expertise, though. Some retailers are not only extremely knowledgeable about the specific wines they sell, but they are extremely knowledgeable about wine in general. But some know less than their customers. Just as you expect a butcher to know his cuts of meat, you should expect a wine merchant to know a lot more about wine than most of his customers do! Be free with your questions and judge how willing and able he is to answer them.

Expect a wine merchant to have *personal* knowledge and experience of the wines he sells. These days, lots of retailers use the ratings of a few critics as a crutch to sell their wines. They plaster their shelves with the critics' scores (usually a number like 90 on a scale of 100) and advertise their wines by these numbers (see "Wine magazines" and "Wine newsletters" in Chapter 17). We agree that it's one quick way of communicating an approximate sense of the wine's quality (remember, that doesn't mean you'll *like* it!). But the retailer's knowledge and experience of the wines simply must go beyond the critic's numbers, or he's not doing his job properly.

Service

Most knowledgeable wine merchants pride themselves in their ability to guide you through the maze of wine selections and help you find a wine that you will like. Trust a merchant's advice at least once or twice and see if his choices are good ones. If he's not flexible enough — or knowledgeable enough — to suggest wine that suits your needs, obviously you need another merchant. All it will have cost you is the price of a bottle or two of wine. A bit less costly than choosing the wrong doctor or lawyer!

Speaking of service, any reputable wine merchant will accept a bottle back from you if he has made a poor recommendation or if the wine seems damaged. After all, he wants to keep you as a customer. But with the privilege comes responsibility: Be reasonable. You should only return an *open* bottle if you think it is defective (and then it should be mostly full!). And don't wait several months before returning an un-opened bottle of wine. By that time, the store might have a hard time getting its money back from the wholesaler. After a week or two, it's yours — whether you like it or not.

Wine storage

Here's a fact about wine that's worth learning early on: Wine is a perishable product. It doesn't go moldy like cheese, and it can't host e-coli bacteria, as meat can. In fact, some wines — usually the more expensive ones — can get better and better as they get older. But if wine is not stored properly, its flavor can suffer. (For advice on storing wine in your own home, see "Creating a Healthy Environment for Your Wines" in Chapter 15.)

In sizing up a wine shop, especially if you plan to buy a lot of wine or expensive wine, check out the store's wine storage conditions. What you don't want to see is an area that's warm — for example, wines stored near the boiler so that they *cook* all winter or wines stored on the top floor of the building where the sun can smile on them all summer. The very best shops will have climate-controlled storerooms for the wines — although frankly these shops are in the minority. If a shop does have a good storage system, the proprietor will be happy to show it off to you because he'll be rightfully proud of all the expense and effort he put into it.

Unfortunately, the problem of wine spoilage doesn't begin at the retail outlet. Quite frequently, the *wholesaler* or *distributor* — the company from whom the retailer purchases his wine — doesn't have proper storage conditions, either. And there have certainly been instances when wine has been damaged by extremes of weather even before it got to the distributor, for example, while sitting on the docks in the dead of winter (or the dead of summer) or while traveling through the Panama Canal. A good retailer will check out the quality of the wine before he buys it, or he will send it back if he discovers the problem after he has already bought the wine. He'll also take back your damaged merchandise. (For more information on ideal wine storage conditions, see Chapter 15.)

How to avoid encounters with poorly stored wine

If you don't know how a wine has been stored — and let's face it, most of the time you won't — you can do two things to minimize the risk of getting a bad bottle.

First, patronize retailers who seem to care about their products and provide their customers with good service. Second, be attentive to seasonal weather patterns when buying wine or when having it shipped to you. We're very cautious about buying wine at the end of, or during, a very hot summer, unless the store has a good climate-control system. And we never have wine shipped to us (other than short deliveries from our local shop) at the height of summer or the dead of winter.

Another way of knowing that the wine you are buying is sound is just to buy the best-selling, most popular wines — assuming you don't mind being a slave to taste trends. Wines that move through the distribution chain very quickly have less opportunity to be damaged along the way. Sometimes we wonder if the wines that sell the most just sell the most because they sell the most. . . .

Strategies for Wine Buying at Retail

When you get beyond all the ego-compromising innuendos associated with buying wine, you can really have fun in wine shops. We remember when we first caught the wine *bug*. We spent countless hours on Saturdays, visiting different wine stores near our home (to a passionate wine lover, 30 miles can be *near*). Trips to other cities offered new opportunities to explore. So many wines, so little time. . . .

We discovered good, reliable stores — and stores that we would Recommend Only To Our Worst Enemies (ROTYWE). Naturally, we made our share of mistakes along the way, but we learned a lot of good lessons.

See a chance, take it

When we first started buying wine, our repertoire was about as broad as a two-year-old child's vocabulary. We'd buy the same brands again and again because they were safe choices, we knew what to expect from them, and we liked them well enough — all good reasons to buy a particular wine. But in retrospect, we let ourselves get stuck in a rut because we were afraid to take a chance on anything new.

If wine was really going to be fun, we realized, we had to be a little more adventuresome.

If you want to experience the wonderful array of wines in the world, experimenting is a must. New wines can be interesting and exciting. Now and then you might get a lemon, but at least you'll learn not to buy *that* wine again!

Explain what you want

The following scene — or something very much like it — occurs in every wine shop every day (and ten times every Saturday):

Customer: I remember that it's got a beige label. I had it in this little restaurant last week.

Wine Merchant: Do you know what country it's from?

Customer: No, but I think it has a flower on the label.

Wine Merchant: Do you recall the vintage?

Customer: I think it's young, but I'm not sure. Maybe if I walk around, I can spot it.

Needless to say, most of the time that customer never finds the wine he is looking for.

When you come across a wine you like in a restaurant or friend's house, write down as much specific information about the wine from the label as you can. Don't trust your memory. By the time you arrive in your wine store, you may not recall many details about the wine if you haven't written them down. If your wine merchant can see the name, he can give you that wine or — if he doesn't have that exact wine — he might be able to give you something very similar to it.

It's clearly to your advantage to be able to tell your wine retailer anything you can about the types of wine that you have liked previously or that you want to try. Often, telling him about the food you are planning to have with the wine is helpful.

Name your price

Because the price of a bottle of wine can range from two or three dollars to — literally — hundreds of dollars, it's a good idea to decide approximately how much you want to spend and to tell the wine merchant. A good retailer with an adequate selection should be able to make several wine suggestions in your preferred price category.

A good wine merchant is more interested in the repeat business he'll get by making you happy than he is in trading you up to a bottle of wine that's beyond your limits. If all you want to spend is five dollars a bottle, just say so, and stand firm, without embarrassment. There are plenty of decent, enjoyable wines at that price.

Ten clues for identifying a store where you should NOT buy wine

1. The dust on the wine bottles is more than ⅛ inch thick.

2. Most of the white wines are light brown in color.

3. The youngest vintage in the store is 1984.

4. The colors on all the wine labels have faded from bright sunlight.

5. It's warmer than a sauna inside.

6. All the bottles are standing up.

7. A sign recommends, "Free bottle of wine with fill-up."

8. Three-quarters of the bottles have screw caps.

9. The July wine of the month has a picture of Santa Claus on the label.

10. The owner resembles Fred Flintstone.

Four easy steps to getting a wine you like

Step One

Decide how much you want to spend on a bottle:

a) for everyday purposes (this might change with time; the $5 to $6 range you started with often goes to $10 to $15 as you discover better wines)

b) for special occasions

Tell your wine merchant your price range; this will narrow the arena of wines to consider.

Step Two

Describe to your wine merchant the kind of wine you like in clear, simple terms. For example, for white wine, you might use such words as "crisp, dry," or "fruity, ripe, oaky, buttery, full-bodied." For red wines, you might say "big, rich, tannic," or "medium-bodied, soft." (Turn to Chapter 2 to learn other helpful descriptors.) After all, he can't decide what you'll like by reading your mind.

Step Three

Tell your wine merchant what kind of food you plan to have with the wine if you know. This will narrow down your choices even further. The wine you drink with your filet of sole is probably not the one you want with pot roast! A good wine merchant should prove invaluable in helping you match your wine with food.

Step Four

If available in your store, ask for tasting samples. (Stores often have wine samples available for tasting every Saturday, where legal.) Of course, the sample will probably come to you in a plastic cup and the temperature might not be the best for that particular wine; therefore, the sample might not be truly indicative of the quality or taste of that wine. But at least you'll get a general idea of whether or not it's your cup of tea.

The Bottom Line of Wine Buying

The best wine merchant provides you with the wine you want and the wine you like at a reasonable price. And, if he or she is educating you about wine in the process, that is a definite plus. You have found a good wine merchant!

No such species in your neighborhood? In Chapter 16, we talk about the advantages and disadvantages of buying wine by catalog, telephone, mail, or the Internet (which can be good alternatives if you don't have access to a decent wine shop where you live).

Five questions you should ask in a wine shop

1. If it's a wine over $10: What kind of storage has this wine received? Hemming and hawing on the part of the wine merchant should be taken to mean, "Poor."

2. How long has this wine been in your store? (This is especially important if the store does not have a climate-control system.)

3. What are some particularly good buys this month? (Provided you trust the wine merchant, and you don't think he's dumping some overstocked, close-out wine on you.)

4. If applicable: Why is this wine selling at such a low price? (The merchant may know that the wine is too old, or otherwise defective; unless he comes up with a believable explanation, assume that's the case.)

5. Will this wine go well with the food I'm planning to serve?

Five questions you should *not* ask in a wine shop

1. Do you have a nice, fruity wine? (Too vague.)

2. Is this wine oaky? (If the retailer thinks you want an oaky wine, he'll very likely give you an over-oaked monster of a wine, which might be *too* oaky for you.)

3. Can you give me a wine without any sulfites? (*All* wines contain a tiny amount of sulfites— a preservative that does far more good to the wine than it does harm to the great majority of drinkers, especially in the tiny amounts used in wine; it is said that only one-quarter of one percent of the population, usually those with severe asthma, has justifiable concern over sulfites in wine.)

4. Can you give me a cold bottle from the fridge? (In some stores, the wine may have been in that fridge for months. It could be *numb* — without expression, just like a numb limb—or if it's supposed to be bubbly, it could be flat. You're better off chilling the wine yourself.)

5. What's your best wine? I'm not worried about the price. (The merchant will probably sell you his most expensive wine, which isn't necessarily his best.)

Chapter 5

Navigating a Restaurant Wine List

● ●

● ●

*W*hen you buy a bottle of wine in a restaurant, you get to taste it right then and there: instant gratification. If you've chosen well, you can bask in the compliments of your family and friends during the whole meal and go home three feet taller. If you haven't chosen well . . . well, we all know *that* feeling: self-defensive statements marching through your head, over-tipping to compensate for your vague feelings of inadequacy. At least you can take comfort in the thought that next time it will be someone else's turn to order the wine.

Buying Wine in a Restaurant

Here and there, you might come across a restaurant with a retail wine shop on the premises, a useful hybrid of a place where you can look all the bottles over, read the labels, browse through wine books and magazines, and then carry your chosen bottle to your table. Unfortunately, such establishments are rarer than four-leaf clovers. In most restaurants, you have to choose your wine from a piece of paper that tells you only the name of the wines and the price per bottle — and manages to make even that little bit of information utterly incomprehensible. Welcome to the *restaurant wine list*.

Restaurant wine lists can be infuriating: They don't tell you enough about the wines, or they tell you nonsense. Either there's nothing worth drinking, or the choice is so huge that you're immobilized. Often, the lists are simply not accurate; you spend ten good minutes of your life deciding which wine to order, only to discover that it's "not available tonight" (and probably hasn't been for months).

When you pick up a restaurant wine list, chances are you'll find that you haven't heard of most of the wines on the list. You might not feel like wading through it at all, knowing that it can be an ego-deflating experience. But don't give up without a fight. With a little guidance and a few tips, you can navigate the choppy waters of the wine list.

How Wine Is Sold in Restaurants

Believe it or not, restaurateurs really do want you to buy their wine. They make a profit on every sale, their servers earn bigger tips and become happier employees, and you enjoy your meal more, going home a happier customer.

Traditionally, however, restaurants have done more to hinder wine sales than to encourage them. Fortunately, the old ways are changing. (*Un*fortunately, they're changing slowly.)

Wines availabie for sale in a restaurant these days can be divided into as many as four categories (not all restaurants offer wines in all four categories, though):

- The *house wines*: usually one white and one red, sometimes also a sparkling wine; can be purchased *by the glass* or in a *carafe*
- *Premium* wines available by the glass: a wider selection than the house wines, and usually better quality
- The restaurant's *regular*, or standard, *wine list*
- A special wine list of older and rarer wines, sometimes called a *reserve wine list*

The choice of the house

The wine list looks so imposing that you finally give up laboring over it. You hand it back to the server and say (either a bit sheepishly, because you're acknowledging that you can't handle the list, or with defiant bravado, signifying that you're not going to waste your time on this nonsense), "I'll just have a glass of white wine." Smart move, or big mistake?

You'll probably know the answer to this question as soon as the house wine hits your lips. It could be just what you wanted — and with less than half the effort of plowing through that list. But in theory, we'd say, "Mistake."

Usually, a restaurant's *house wines* are some inferior stuff that the restaurant owner is making an enormous profit on. (Cost-per-ounce is a restaurant owner's main criterion in choosing a house wine.) House wines can range in price from $3 to $4 up to $7.50 a glass (with an average of $5 to $6). Often, the entire bottle costs the proprietor the price of one glass, or less! No wonder the "obliging" server fills your glass to the brim.

We've found that only a small percentage of better restaurants — and most wine-conscious restaurants located in enlightened places like Napa or Sonoma — offer a house wine worth drinking. And it's practically never a good value. Under most circumstances, avoid the house wine.

If circumstances are such that a glass of white wine makes the most sense to you (if you're the only one in your group who's having wine with dinner, for example), ask the server what the house wine is. Don't be satisfied with the response, "It's Chardonnay"; ask for specifics. Chardonnay from where? What brand? Ask to see the bottle. Either your worst fears will be confirmed (you've never heard of the wine, or it has a reputation for being inferior), or you'll be pleasantly surprised (you *have* heard of the wine, and it has a good reputation). And at least you'll know what you're drinking, for future reference.

Premium pours

The word *premium* is used very loosely by the wine industry. You might think that it refers to a rather high-quality wine, but when annual industry sales statistics are compiled for the U.S., *premium* indicates any wine that sells for more than three dollars a bottle in stores!

As used in the phrase, *premium wines by the glass,* however, *premium* usually does connote good quality. These are red and white wines that a restaurant offers at a higher price than its house wines. (Oh, we get it: You pay a premium for them!) Premium wines are usually in the $6 to $12 price range per glass.

A restaurant might offer just one premium white and one red, or it might offer several choices. These premium wines are not anonymous beverages, like the house red and white, but are identified for you somehow — on the wine list, on a separate card, verbally, or sometimes even by a display of bottles. (Why would you ever pay a premium for them if you didn't know what they were?) In some informal restaurants, wines by the glass are listed on a chalkboard.

Ordering premium wines by the glass is a fine idea, especially if you want to have only a glass or two or if you and your guests want to experiment by trying several wines. Sometimes we order a glass of a premium white wine as a starter and then go on to a bottle of red wine.

Why aren't there more wines by the glass?

You might be wondering why more restaurants don't offer a larger selection of wines by the glass; a larger selection could enhance your pleasure so much ("Let's see, we'll have one of these, and a glass of that one, and . . ."). The problem for the restaurateur is preserving the wine in all of those open bottles. The more wines a restaurant manager offers by the glass, the greater the odds that there will be wine left over in each bottle at the end of the evening, and that wine won't be fresh enough to serve the next day.

Unless he has an expensive wine preservation system — often an attractive console that injects inert gas into the open bottles to displace oxygen — or unless he's lucky enough to finish every bottle every night, the restaurateur will waste an enormous amount of wine. His wine profits will go right down the drain!

Of course, there's a catch. Only a small percentage of wine-conscious restaurants offer premium wines by the glass. Also, you'll end up paying more for the wine if you order a bottle's worth of individual glasses than you would if you ordered a whole bottle to begin with.

If two or three of you are ordering the same wine by the glass — and especially if you might want refills — ask how many ounces are poured into each glass (usually five or six ounces) and compare the price with that of a 25.6-ounce (750 ml) bottle of the same wine. Sometimes, for the cost of only three glasses you can have the whole bottle.

Special, or reserve, wine lists

Some restaurants — only a few, and usually the fanciest — offer a special wine list of rare wines to supplement their regular wine list. These special lists appeal to two types of customers: very serious wine connoisseurs and "high rollers." If you're not in either category, don't even bother asking if the restaurant has such a list. Then again, if you're not paying for the meal or if you seriously want to impress a client or a date, you might want to look at it! Try to get help with the list from some knowledgeable person on the restaurant staff, though: Any mistake you make could be a costly one.

The (anything but) standard wine list

Most of the time, you'll probably end up turning to the restaurant's wine list to choose your wine. Lucky you.

We use the term *standard wine list* to distinguish a restaurant's basic wine list from its special, or reserve, wine list. Unfortunately, there's nothing standard about wine lists at all. They come in all sizes, shapes, degrees of detail, degrees of accuracy, and degrees of user-friendliness (the latter usually ranging from low to nil).

If you're still hung up on the emotional-vulnerability potential of buying wine, don't even pick up a wine list. (Instead, turn to Chapter 4 and reread our pep talk about wine buying in the section, "Buying Wine Can Intimidate Anyone.") When you're ready, follow these steps to get a wine you'll like with minimum angst.

How to Scope Out a Wine List

Your first step in the dark encounter between you and the wine list is to size up the opposition. Note how the wine list is organized.

Read the headings on the wine list the way you'd read the chapter titles in a book that you were considering buying. Figure out how the wines are categorized and how they are arranged within each category. Notice how much or how little information is given about each wine. Check out the style of the list. Estimate the number of wines on it — there could be 12 or 200. (An indirect benefit of this procedure is that the purposeful look in your eyes as you peruse the list will convince your guests that you know what you're doing.)

When the restaurant doesn't have a license—BYOB

In most places, establishments that sell alcohol beverages—both retail stores and restaurants—must be licensed by the government to assure that all appropriate taxes are paid and to aid in the enforcement of local laws. Sometimes a restaurant doesn't have a liquor license due to circumstance or choice, and it therefore cannot sell wine. In those restaurants, you can BYOB (bring your own bottle of wine) to enjoy with your meal.

Many Chinese restaurants fall into this category, for example. (Although it can be difficult to match Asian cuisine with wine, we have found that Champagne and sparkling wine generally go well, as does German or Alsace Gewurztraminer.) Other examples include restaurants that have recently opened and have not yet received their liquor licenses, or restaurants that for some reason do not qualify for a license (they may be located too close to a school or a church, for instance).

Sizing up the organization of the list

There's no way of predicting exactly what you'll find on the list, other than prices. Generally speaking, though, you may discover the wines arranged in the following categories:

- ✔ Champagne and sparkling wines
- ✔ (Dry) white wines
- ✔ (Dry) red wines
- ✔ Dessert wines

After-dinner drinks like Cognac, Armagnac, single-malt Scotches or liqueurs usually will not appear on the list, or if they do, they'll have their own section near the back of the list.

Some restaurants further subdivide the wines on their list according to country, especially in the white and red wine categories: French red wines, Italian red wines, North American reds, and so on. These country segments might then be subdivided by wine region. France, for example, might have listings of Bordeaux, Burgundy, and possibly Rhône all under *French red wines. USA reds* may be divided into California wines, Oregon wines, and Washington wines.

SNOB ALERT

Wine list power struggles

In many restaurants, the servers don't give you enough time to study the wine list. (Really good restaurants recognize that choosing a bottle of wine can take some time and, therefore, don't put you in this position.) If your waiter asks, somewhat impatiently, "Have you selected your wine yet?", simply tell him (firmly) that you need more time. Don't let him bully you into making a hasty choice.

Usually, your table will receive only one wine list. An outmoded convention dictates that only the host (the masculine is intentional) needs to see the list. (It's part of the same, outmoded thinking that dictates that females should receive menus with no prices on them.) At our table of two, there are *two* thinking, curious, decision-making customers. We ask for a second wine list.

Invariably, the wine list is handed to the oldest or most important-looking male at the table. If you are a female entertaining business clients, this can be insulting and infuriating. Speak up and ask for a copy of the wine list for yourself. If it's important enough to you, slip away from the table and inform the server that you are the host of the table.

Or you may find that the categories under white wines and red wines are the names of grape varieties — for example, a Chardonnay section, a Sauvignon Blanc section, and a miscellaneous *other dry whites* section, all under the general heading of white wines. If the restaurant features a particular country's cuisine, the wines of that country might be listed first (and given certain prominence), followed by a cursory listing of wines from other areas.

No two lists are exactly alike, unless both restaurants are part of the same chain or unless they've both surrendered control of their wine list to their favorite wine distributor, who has loaded the list with his own wines presented his own way.

Sometimes, you'll discover that the list is very small, with hardly any wines on it. It's tough to look purposeful for very long when you're studying a list like that.

Getting a handle on the pricing setup

Often you'll find that within each category, the wines are arranged in ascending order of price with the least expensive wine first. The restaurateur is betting that you won't order that first wine out of fear of looking cheap. He figures you'll go for the second, third, or fourth wine down the price column or even deeper if you're feeling insecure and need the reassurance that your choice is a good one. (Meanwhile, nothing is wrong with that least expensive wine.)

The lowdown on high prices

Most restaurateurs count on wine and liquor sales to provide a disproportionate percentage of their business profit. The typical restaurant, therefore, charges two to two-and-a-half (sometimes three!) times the retail store price for a bottle of wine. That means that the restaurant is earning *three to four times* the price it paid for the bottle.

Admittedly, restaurateurs incur costs for wine storage, glasses, breakage, service, and so on. But those costs don't justify such extraordinary markups in the eyes of most wine drinkers.

Some savvy restaurateurs have discovered that by marking up their wines less, they actually sell *more* wine and make *more money* in the end. We try to patronize *those* restaurants.

If you frequent restaurants in Canada, you should know that restaurateurs there have a serious disadvantage (except in the province of Alberta): They must purchase their wines from the provincial liquor control authorities *at the same price as you would purchase the wines* for drinking in your own home. There's no such thing as wholesale for them.

Determining what the list doesn't tell you

The more serious a restaurant is about its wine selection, the more information it gives you about each wine.

Here is some information that's likely to be on the wine list:

✔ An *item number* for each wine. These are sometimes called *bin numbers*, referring to the specific location of each wine in the restaurant's cellar or wine storage room.

Item numbers make it easier for the server to locate and pull the wine quickly for you, after you order it. They're also a crutch to help the server bring you the right wine in case he doesn't have a clue about wine. They're also a crutch for *you* in ordering the wine in case you don't have a clue how to pronounce what you've decided to drink. (And you can always pretend that you're using the number for the waiter's benefit.)

✔ The name of each wine. These names might be grape names or place-names (see Chapter 7), but they had better also include the name of each producer (Château this or that, or such-and-such Winery), or you'll have no way of knowing exactly which wine any listing is meant to represent.

✔ A vintage indication for each wine — the year that the grapes were harvested. If the wine is a blend of wines from different years, it will say *NV*, for *non-vintage*. (Chapter 7 discusses why this might happen.) Some-times, you'll see *VV*, which means that the wine is a vintage-dated wine, but you're not allowed to know *which* vintage it is unless you ask. We're often tempted to walk out when we see lists with an attitude like that.

✔ Sometimes, a brief description of the wines — but this is unlikely if dozens of wines are on the list.

✔ There will *always* be a price for each wine.

The world's most complicated wine list

We've heard that there's a restaurant in Colorado whose wine list is like this:

"1. White wine

2. Red wine

3. Rosé wine

To avoid confusing the waiter, please order your wine by number."

Rating the list's style

Once upon a time, the best wine lists consisted of hand-lettered pages inside heavy leather covers embossed with the words *Carte des Vins* in gold. Today, the best wine lists are more likely to be laser-printed pages or cards that more than make up in functionality what they sacrifice in romance.

The more permanent and immutable a wine list seems, the less accurate its listings are likely to be — and the less specific. Such lists suggest that no one is really looking after wine in that restaurant. Chances are that many of the wines listed will be out of stock.

Sometimes, the list of wines is actually included on the restaurant's menu, especially if the menu is a computer-printed page or two that changes from week to week or from month to month. Restaurants featuring immediate, up-to-date wine listings like this can be a good bet for wine.

How to Ask for Advice

If after sizing up the wine list, you decide that you are not familiar with most of the wines on it, ask for help with your selection.

If the restaurant is a fancy one, ask if there's a *sommelier* (pronounced *sum-mel-yay*) — a specially trained, high-level wine specialist who is responsible for putting the wine list together and for making sure that the wines offered on the list complement the cuisine of the restaurant. (Unfortunately, only a few restaurants employ one — usually the most wine-conscious.)

If the restaurant is not particularly fancy, ask to speak with the wine specialist. Often someone on the staff, frequently the proprietor, knows the wine list well.

If someone on the restaurant staff knows the wine list well, this person is your best bet to help you select a wine. He or she will usually know what wines go best with the food you are ordering. He will also be extremely appreciative of your interest in the list. For these reasons, even though we are familiar with wine, we often consult the sommelier, proprietor, or wine specialist for suggestions from the wine list.

Timing counts

As soon as your server comes to the table, ask to see the wine list. Besides communicating to the server that you feel comfortable with wine (whether it's true or not), your asking for the list quickly gives you more time to examine the list.

Order the wine at the same time that you order the food — if not sooner; otherwise, you might be sipping water with your first course.

Here are some face-saving methods of getting help:

- ✓ If you are not sure how to pronounce the wine's name, point to it on the list, or use the wine's bin number (if there is one).

- ✓ Point out two or three wines on the list to the sommelier or server and say, "I'm considering these wines. Which one do you recommend?" This is also a subtle way of communicating your price range.

- ✓ Ask to *see* one or two bottles; the labels might help you make up your mind.

- ✓ Ask if there are any half-bottles (375 ml) or 500 ml bottles available (sometimes, they're not listed). Smaller bottles give you wider possibilities in ordering: For example, a party of four might drink one half-bottle of white wine and a half or full (750 ml) bottle of red wine.

- ✓ Mention the food you plan to order and ask for suggestions of wines that would complement the meal.

How to Bluff Your Way Through the Wine Presentation Ritual

In many restaurants, the wine presentation occurs with such ceremony that you'd think it were a solemn experience. The hushed tones of the waiter, the ritualized performance, the seriousness of it all can make you want to laugh (but that seems wrong — like laughing in church). At the very least, you might be tempted to tell your waiter, "Lighten up! It's just a bottle of fermented fruit juice!"

Actually, though, there's some logic behind the Wine Presentation Ritual.

Step by step, the Ritual (and the logic) goes like this:

1. **The waiter or sommelier presents the bottle to you (assuming that you are the person who ordered the wine) for inspection.**

   The point of this procedure is to make sure that it *is* the bottle you ordered. Check the label carefully. In our experience, 15 to 20 percent of the time it's the wrong bottle. (This is also a good time for you to pretend to recognize something about the label, as if the wine is an old friend, even if you've never seen it before.)

2. **The server then pulls the cork and either hands it to you or places it in front of you.**

   The purpose of this step is for you to determine, by smelling and visually inspecting the cork, whether the cork is in good condition.

   In rare instances, a wine may be so corky (see Chapter 2) that the cork itself will have an unpleasant odor. On even rarer occasions, the cork might be totally wet and shriveled or very dry and crumbly — either situation suggesting that air may have gotten into the wine and spoiled it.

   Once in your life, you might discover a vintage year or winery name on your cork that is different from the label. (Quick! Call the wine fraud police!) If the cork does cause you to suspect a problematic bottle, you should still wait to smell or taste the wine itself before rejecting it. But most of the time, the presentation of the cork is inconsequential.

   Once, when one of our wise-guy friends was presented the cork by the server, he proceeded to put it into his mouth and chew it, and then he pronounced to the waiter that it was fine!

3. **If your wine needs decanting, the server will decant it at this point.**

   (For more information on decanting, see "How to Aerate Your Wine" in Chapter 6.)

4. **The server pours a small amount of wine into your glass and waits.**

   At this point, you're *not* supposed to say, "Is that all you're giving me?!" You're expected to take a sniff of the wine, perhaps a little sip, and then either nod your approval to the waiter or murmur, "It's fine." Actually, this is an important step of the Wine Presentation Ritual because if something *is wrong* with the wine, *now* is the time to return it (not after you've finished half of the bottle!).

   If you're not really sure whether the condition of the wine is acceptable, ask for someone else's opinion at your table and then make a group decision; otherwise, you risk feeling foolish by either returning the bottle later when it's been declared defective by one of your guests, or by drinking the stuff when you know there's something wrong with it. Either way, you suffer. Take as long as you need to on this step.

If you do decide that the bottle is out of condition, describe to the server what you find wrong with the wine, using the best language you can. (*Musty* or *dank* are descriptors that are easily understood.) Be sympathetic to the fact that you're causing more work for him but don't be overly apologetic (why should you be; you didn't make the wine!). Let him smell or taste the wine himself if he would like. But don't let him make you feel guilty.

Depending on whether the sommelier or captain agrees that it's a bad bottle or whether he believes that you just don't understand the wine, he might bring you another bottle of the same, or he might bring you the wine list so that you can select a different wine. Either way, the Ritual begins again from the top.

5. **If you do accept the wine, the waiter will pour the wine into your guests' glasses and then finally into yours. Now you're allowed to relax.**

If You Are Truly on Your Own

If no one is available in the restaurant who knows any more than you do about the wine list, follow a few simple guidelines in deciding which wine will go best with your meal:

- ✔ Choose a wine that won't overpower the food — or be overpowered by it. For example, choose a relatively light red wine, such as a Pinot Noir or French Burgundy, with light meat dishes, poultry, or full-flavored fish, such as salmon. A light-bodied white wine, such as a Soave or a French Chablis, would be fine with lighter fish or shellfish dishes. A full-bodied Chardonnay would be good with lobster and richer fish dishes. (See Chapters 10 through 12 for a discussion of these wines.)

Twice the price

Some profit-minded restaurateurs train their servers to maximize wine sales in every way possible — even at the customers' expense. For example, some servers are trained to refill wine glasses liberally so that the bottle is emptied before the main course arrives (this can happen all the more easily when the glasses are large). Upon emptying the bottle, the server asks, "Shall I bring another bottle of the same wine?" Depending on how much wine is in everyone's glass and how much wine your guests tend to drink, you might not *need* another bottle, but your tendency will be to say yes to avoid looking stingy.

An even trickier practice is to refill the glasses starting with the host, so that the bottle runs dry before each of the guests has had a refill. How can you refuse a second bottle at the expense of your guest's enjoyment?! You'll have to order that second bottle — and you should let the manager know how you feel about it when you leave.

✔ Some foods, like chicken or pasta, are equally at home with white or red wines. Look to see what sauce accompanies the dish to give you a clue about the appropriate wine. The texture and weight of the sauce will be determining factors. For example, a pasta with a meaty tomato sauce probably would be better with a red wine, whereas a pasta with vegetables or a cream sauce would go well with a white or sparkling wine.

✔ Full-flavored dishes, such as stews, roasts, game, duck, and so on usually go best with full-bodied red wines.

✔ Spicy dishes, such as the ones you find in Chinese, Indian, or Mexican cuisine, are great with Champagne or other sparkling wines (or beer).

✔ All of the preceding "rules" are guidelines. Follow your instincts and maintain a spirit of adventure.

(See Chapter 19 for more on wine and food match-ups.)

Restaurant Wining Tips

There are so many decisions to make about wine in restaurants that you really do need a guidebook. Should you leave the wine in an ice bucket? What should you do if the wine is bad? And can you bring your own wine?

Safe wine choices in a restaurant

White Wine:

Soave, Pinot Grigio, or Sancerre (if you like crisp, dry wines)

Sauvignon Blanc from California, South Africa, New Zealand (dry, light but assertive flavors)

Mâcon-Villages or Pouilly-Fuissé (dry, lively, medium-bodied wines)

Californian or Australian Chardonnay (if you want a full-bodied white wine)

Meursault (a dry wine, but with a honeyed, nutty character)

Chenin Blanc or Vouvray (medium-dry wines, if you don't like a wine to be too dry)

Red Wine:

Beaujolais (especially from a reputable producer, like Louis Jadot or Georges Duboeuf)

California red Zinfandel (relatively inexpensive; goes with many dishes)

Oregon or California Pinot Noir (lighter red; can be appreciated when young)

Bourgogne Rouge (the basic French version of Pinot Noir)

Barbera or Dolcetto (in Italian restaurants; dry, light, relatively inexpensive)

Chianti Classico (in Italian restaurants; very dry; usually reliable)

(See Chapters 10 through 12 for more information on these wines.)

When is an ice bucket necessary? Usually, an ice bucket is assumed to be necessary to chill white wines and sparkling wines. But sometimes the bottle is already so cold when it comes to you that the wine would be better off warming up a bit on the table. If your white wine goes into an ice bucket but you think it's getting *too* cold, remove it from the bucket or have the waiter remove it. Just because that ice bucket is sitting there on your table (or next to your table) doesn't mean that your bottle has to be in it!

Sometimes, a red wine that is a bit too warm can benefit from five or ten minutes in an ice bucket. (But be careful! It can get too cold very quickly. And if the server acts as if you're nuts to chill a red wine, ignore him.)

Do I have to use these tiny glasses? When there are various glasses available, you can exercise your right to choose a different glass from the one you were given. If the restaurant's red wine glass is quite small, the water glass might be more appropriate for the red wine.

Should the wine "breathe"? If a red wine you ordered seems to need aeration to soften its harsh tannins (see Chapter 6), pulling the cork will do practically nothing to help (the air space at the neck of the bottle is too small). Decanting or pouring the wine into glasses is the best tactic.

Where's my bottle? We prefer to have our bottle of wine on or near our table, not out of our reach. We can look at the label that way, and we don't have to wait for the server to remember to refill our glasses, either. Okay, call us controlling.

If you don't have access to the bottle, you might discover that the servers can be so busy that they forget to refill your glasses. Get their attention, or you'll be eating your dinner with an empty wine glass.

What if the bottle is bad? Refuse any bottle that tastes or smells unpleasant (unless you brought it yourself!). A good restaurant will always replace the wine, even if it thinks there's nothing wrong.

May I bring my own wine? Some restaurants allow you to bring your own wine — especially if you express the desire to bring a special wine, or an older wine. Restaurants will usually charge a *corkage* fee (a fee for wine service, use of the glasses, and so on) that can vary from $5 to even $25 a bottle, depending on the attitude of the restaurant. You should never bring a wine that is already on the restaurant's wine list; it's cheap and it's insulting. (Call and ask the restaurant when you're not sure whether the wine is on its list.) Anyway, you certainly should call ahead to determine whether or not it's possible to bring wine (in some places, the restaurant's license prohibits it) and to ask what the corkage fee is.

When Traveling Abroad

If you journey to countries where wine is made, such as France, Italy, Germany, Switzerland, Austria, Spain, or Portugal, by all means try the local wines. They will be fresher than the imports, in good condition, and the best values on the wine list. It would not be a very good idea to order French wines, such as Bordeaux or Burgundy, in Italy, for example. Or California Cabernets in Paris. Among other reasons, you'll have to pay the built-in charge of importing the wines into that country.

Top ten ways to recognize a restaurant where you're better off drinking beer

1. The bottles of wine are standing up all around the restaurant (some on top of the radiator) and look like they've been there for years.

2. The red wine you ordered comes out of the fridge, ice-cold.

3. When you ask the server for the wine list, he snarls, "We got red or white."

4. The wine list is old and heavy, and some of the decrepit wine labels pasted inside have fallen loose.

5. The only wines available are *house wines* (white or red) poured from carafes.

6. The server can't pronounce "Chardonnay."

7. The only wine expert on the premises is the bouncer.

8. The wine glasses are barely bigger than shot glasses.

9. The server doesn't know how to use a cork-screw.

10. The most expensive wine on the list is White Zinfandel.

Wine Bars

Wine bars are somewhat popular in London, Italy, and Paris. They are establishments that offer an extensive choice of wines by the glass — from 12 to 100 — as well as simple food to accompany the wines. The wine bottles are usually either hooked up to an inert-gas injection system, which keeps the wine fresh, or are topped up with inert gas from a free-standing dispenser after each serving. The former system often makes a dramatic centerpiece behind the bar.

In wine bars, you are sometimes offered a choice of two different *sizes* of wines by the glass. You can have a *taste* of a wine (about two-and-a-half ounces) for one price, or a *glass* of a wine (often five ounces) for another price.

Wine bars haven't yet caught on in much of the United States, but there are a few in major cities such as New York and San Francisco. Wine bars are the ideal way to try lots of different wines by the glass — an educational as well as a satisfying experience. Hopefully, their numbers will increase with the years.

The 5th Wave By Rich Tennant

"I'M PRETTY SURE YOU'RE SUPPOSED TO JUST <u>SMELL</u> THE CORK."

Chapter 6

How to Open a Bottle — and What to Do Next

*H*ave you ever broken a cork or taken an unusually long time to remove a stubborn cork, while your guests smiled at you uneasily? This has certainly happened to us from time to time and probably to just about everyone else who has ever pulled a cork out of a bottle of wine.

In wine shops, we've noticed some people opting for either screw-top bottles of wine or for bag-in-a-box wines (large boxes that hold the equivalent of four or five bottles of wine in a collapsible plastic sack; you pour the wine through a nozzle near the bottom of the box). Wines packaged like this are inexpensive, and that's one good reason to buy them. But we strongly suspect that many people buy screw-top bottles or bag-in-a-box wines not just for value but because, lurking in their minds, there is an actual fear of opening a bottle of wine that has a cork in it.

Maybe an unsuccessful encounter with an unyielding cork during their forma-tive wine-drinking years has traumatized the screw-top and bag-in-a-box drinkers, causing them to develop *corkophobia.* If so, they have our sympathy. Besides the emotional trauma they've experienced, corkophobics have de-prived themselves of most of the world's best wines — because just about all of those wines come with a cork in the bottle. The solution? Be armed with the right tools.

The First Step: Getting the Lead Out

The bigger the winery, the more time and money it spends creating attractive bottles that grab your eye as you walk down the aisle of the wine shop or supermarket. Part of the fetching package is the capsule, the colorful covering over the cork end of the bottle. The good news is that it's pretty; the bad news is that some capsules are made of lead.

Lately, many wineries are using colored foil or plastic capsules rather than lead. But when we open wine bottles ourselves, we usually play it safe and remove the entire capsule from the bottle, just in case it contains lead. (That's one moment when we actually appreciate the lead capsules — they're easier to remove than the plastic ones!)

After removing the capsule, wipe clean the top of the bottle with a damp cloth because sometimes the cork is dark with mold that developed under the capsule. (That's actually a good sign; it means that the wine has been stored in humid conditions. See Chapter 15 for information on humidity and other aspects of wine storage.)

Sometimes wine lovers just can't bring themselves to remove the whole capsule out of respect for the bottle of wine that they are about to drink. (In fact, traditional wine etiquette dictates that you do not remove the entire capsule.) Some wine drinkers use a handy gizmo called a foil cutter that sells for about six or seven dollars in wine shops, kitchen stores, or specialty catalogs. The problem is that the foil cutter does not cut the foil (or the lead capsule) low enough, in our opinion, to prevent wine from dripping over the edge of the foil into your glass. If you want to leave the capsule on, sacrifice convenience for safety and cut the foil with a knife under the second lip of the bottle, which is approximately three-fourths of an inch below the top of the bottle.

Getting the Cork Out

Corkophobia or not, anyone can conquer most corks with a good corkscrew.

We suspect it's probably wise not to mention that we actually use three different corkscrews, each for certain situations, or that there are some cork-screws we would use only in desperation, as a last resort before drinking screw-top or bag-in-a-box wine. We don't want to sound like snobs or fanatics. After all, who cares what kind of corkscrew you use as long as you can extract the cork and drink the wine?

We agree that getting to the wine is the important thing. But the voyage to the wine is much smoother sailing with a good corkscrew. And struggling over a puny piece of cork with a second-rate corkscrew will surely put you in a miserable mood before you even get to the wine.

The corkscrew not to use

The one corkscrew we absolutely avoid happens to be the most common type of corkscrew around. We don't like it for one very simple reason: It mangles the corks, almost guaranteeing that brown flakes will be floating in your glass of wine. (We also don't like it because it offends our sense of righteousness that an inferior product should be so popular.)

The corkscrew is the infamous Wing Type Corkscrew, a bright silver-colored, metal device that looks something like a pair of pliers. Its major shortcoming is its very short worm, or auger (the curly prong that bores into the cork), which is too short for many corks and overly aggressive on all of them. Unfortunately, the Wing Type is the most commonly found corkscrew in most stores. No wonder people have trouble with corks!

Rather than finding out the hard way that this corkscrew just doesn't cut it, as we did, invest a few dollars in a decent corkscrew right off the bat. The time and hassle you'll save will be more than worth the investment.

The corkscrew to buy

The one indispensable corkscrew for every household is the Screwpull. It was invented in the early 1980s by a Houston engineer, who was apparently tired of having a ten-cent piece of cork get the better of him.

The Screwpull is about six inches long. It consists of a six-inch piece of plastic (looks like a clothespin on steroids) straddling an inordinately long, five-inch worm, coated with Teflon® (see Figure 6-1). To use it, you simply place the plastic over the bottle top (having removed the capsule), until a lip on the upper end of the plastic is resting on the top of the bottle. Hold on to the plastic firmly while turning the lever atop the worm clockwise. The worm descends into the cork. Then you simply keep turning the lever in the same clockwise direction, and the cork magically emerges from the bottle. To remove the cork from the Screwpull, simply turn the lever counterclockwise while holding on to the cork.

Figure 6-1:
The
Screwpull
corkscrew.

The Screwpull comes in many colors — burgundy, black, and China red being the most common — and costs about $15 in wine shops, kitchen stores, and specialty catalogs. It's very simple to use, does not require a lot of muscle, and is our corkscrew of choice for over 95 percent of the corks that we encounter.

Other corkscrews worth owning

Did we say 95 percent? Well, you see, that's why we have two other corkscrews for the remaining 5 percent of the corks that the Screwpull can't remove (or threatens to break itself on; after all, it is mostly plastic, and $15 is $15).

Our two alternative corkscrews are smaller devices that — besides working better now and then — can conveniently fit into your pocket or apron. Their size is one reason that they are favored by servers in restaurants.

The two-pronged type that they use in California

One is called, unofficially, the Ah-So because (according to legend, anyway) when people finally figure out how it works, they say, "Ah, so that's how it works!" (Some people also refer to it as the Butler's Friend, but who has a butler these days?)

It's a simple device made up of two thin, flat metal prongs, one slightly longer than the other (see Figure 6-2). To use it, you slide the prongs down into the tight space between the cork and the bottle (inserting the longer prong first), using a back-and-forth seesaw motion until the top of the Ah-So is resting on the top of the cork. Then you twist the cork while you gently pull it up.

Figure 6-2:
The Ah-So
corkscrew.

One advantage of the Ah-So is that it delivers an intact cork, without a hole in it, that can be reused to close bottles of homemade vinegar, to make cutesy bulletin boards, or to retile your swimming pool.

Although more difficult to operate than the Screwpull, the Ah-So really comes into its own with very tight-fitting corks when no other corkscrews, including the Screwpull, seem to be able to budge the cork. Also, the Ah-So can be effective with old, crumbly corks when other corkscrews cannot get a proper grip.

The Ah-So is useless with loose corks that move around in the bottle neck when you try to remove them. The Ah-So just pushes such corks down into the wine. At that point, you'll need another tool called a cork retriever (which we describe in the "Waiter, there's cork in my wine!" section, later in this chapter).

The Ah-So sells for around five to eight dollars. It seems to be especially favored in California for no particular reason that we have ever been able to figure out.

The most professional corkscrew of them all

Our final recommended corkscrew, probably the most commonly used corkscrew in restaurants all over the world, is simply called the Waiter's Corkscrew. A straight metal base holds three other pieces of metal that fold into it, like a Swiss Army knife: a lever, a small, two-inch worm, and a little knife (see Figure 6-3). The latter is especially handy for removing the capsule from the bottle.

Figure 6-3:
The Waiter's
Corkscrew.

Using the Waiter's Corkscrew requires some practice. (Could that be another reason for corkophobia?) First, wrap a fist around the top of the bottle. The trick then is to guide the worm down through the center of the cork through an opening in your fist so that the worm goes right through the middle of the cork. After the worm is fully descended into the cork, place the lever on the lip of the bottle and push against the lever while lifting the cork up. Give a firm pull at the very end or wiggle the bottom of the cork out with your hand.

If your cork ever breaks and part of it gets stuck in the neck of the bottle, the Waiter's Corkscrew is indispensable for removing the remaining piece. Use the method we just described, but insert the worm at a 45-degree angle instead. In most cases, you will successfully remove the broken cork.

If the darn cork still doesn't come out, just shove the remaining piece into the bottle. Then, if you have a cork retriever, described in the next section, use that; otherwise, pour the wine through a paper coffee filter into a decanter or pitcher to catch the remaining pieces of cork.

The Waiter's Corkscrew sells for about five to six dollars.

Waiter, there's cork in my wine!

Every now and then, even if you've used the right corkscrew and used it properly, you can still have pieces of cork floating in your wine. They can be tiny dry flakes that crumbled into the bottle, actual chunks of cork, or even the entire cork.

What genius thought of using corks in the first place?

We confess to not knowing the name of the first genius to close a bottle of wine with a piece of cork, but we know that the French monk, Dom Perignon, was the genius who popularized the cork as a closure for Champagne.

It was a stroke of genius that endures to this day. The bark of the cork tree has enviable properties — such as compressibility (which enables the cork to be squeezed into the tiny neck of a bottle) and elasticity (which enables it to expand again and hug that tiny neck) — that make it almost ideal for keeping the air out of wine bottles and keeping the wine in for long periods of time.

Remember to store wine bottles horizontally rather than upright to keep the cork moist. If a bottle of wine is kept upright (especially in a dry environment) for a few months, the cork will dry out, lose its resilience, and permit oxygen to pass into the bottle and spoil the wine. Standing a bottle upright for a month or so probably won't affect the wine.

Corks aren't perfect for two reasons: They can sometimes develop a moldiness that spoils the wine, no matter which way the bottle is lying, and they are a frustrating barrier between us and the wine. For wines that are intended to be consumed young — like most white wines — a screw cap would be less risky, simpler to remove, and just as effective in keeping out the air. But traditions die hard, and the cork will probably be the closure of choice even on young wines for some time to come.

Because a certain percentage of corks do develop moldiness, however, plastic and composition (cork pieces pressed together) corks are being used experimentally by some wineries. The composition corks look especially promising.

Before you start berating yourself for being a klutz, you should know that the Floating Cork Syndrome has happened to all of us at one time or another, no matter how experienced we are. Cork won't harm the wine. And besides, there's a wonderful instrument called a cork retriever (no, it's not a small dog from the south of Ireland!) available in specialty stores and in catalogs, although it's considerably more difficult to find than a corkscrew.

The cork retriever consists of three 10-inch pieces of stiff metal wire with hooks on the ends. This device is remarkably effective in removing floating pieces of cork from the bottle. We have even removed a whole cork from the neck with a cork retriever (fearing the whole time that the bottle neck would explode when we tried to force the cork with the retriever back up through that tiny neck).

Alternatively, you can just pick out the offending piece(s) of cork with a spoon after you pour the wine into your glass. (That's one occasion when it's rude to serve your guest first, because the first glass has more cork pieces in it.)

A Special Case: Opening Champagne

Opening a bottle of sparkling wine is often an exciting occasion. Who doesn't enjoy the ceremony of a cold glass of bubbly? Is there a more festive beverage in the world? If there is, we haven't found it.

Forget how the winners do it in locker rooms

Part of the fun of sparkling wine for us is in the opening. If the bottle has just traveled, though, let it rest for a while, preferably a day. Controlling the cork is difficult when the carbonation has been stirred up. (Hey, you wouldn't open a large bottle of soda that's warm and shaken up, either, would you? Sparkling wine has much more carbonated pressure than soda, so it needs more time to settle down.)

If you're in the midst of a sparkling wine emergency and need to open the bottle anyway, one quick solution is to calm down the carbonation by submerging the bottle in an ice bucket for 20 to 30 minutes. (Fill the bucket with one-half ice cubes and one-half ice-cold water.)

In any case, be careful when you remove the wire cage, which is twisted around the top of the bottle, helping to hold the cork in place. We have a hole in our kitchen ceiling from one encounter with a flying cork. As a precaution, keep one hand on top of the cork while removing the wire and be sure to point the bottle away from people and other fragile objects.

Never, ever use a corkscrew on a bottle of sparkling wine. The pressure of the trapped carbonation, when suddenly released, could send the cork and corkscrew flying right into your eye.

To pop or not to pop

If you like to hear the champagne pop, just yank the cork out. When you do that, however, you'll lose some of the precious wine, which will froth out of the bottle top as foam. Also, the noise could interfere with your guests' conversation. Besides, it ain't too classy!

We'll never forget a party that a doctor friend of ours threw to celebrate his baby girl's birth. At an appropriate moment with all the guests watching, he anchored the champagne bottle between his legs to remove the cork. The cork popped out with more gusto than he anticipated, propelling the bottle backward through his legs and across the floor in a zig-zag motion, spilling champagne everywhere. We were all on the verge of laughter until his disapproving stepmother proclaimed chillingly, "You don't know how to do anything right, do you?" Our friend stood there with a frozen grin on his face.

A sigh is better than a pop

Removing the cork from sparkling wine with just a gentle sigh rather than a loud pop is fairly easy. Simply hold the bottle at a 45-degree angle with a towel wrapped around it if it's wet. (Try anchoring the base of the bottle on your hipbone.) Twist the bottle while holding on to the cork so that you can control the cork as it emerges. When you feel the cork starting to come out of the bottle, push back against the cork with some pressure as if you don't want to let it out of the bottle. In this way, the cork will emerge slowly with a hissing or sighing sound rather than a pop.

Every once in a while, you'll come across a really tight cork that doesn't want to budge. Try running the top of the bottle under warm water for a minute or two. That usually loosens the cork up enough for you to remove it.

Or you could purchase some fancy gadget resembling a pair of pliers (there are actually three gadgets: Champagne Pliers, a Champagne Star, and a Champagne Key) that you place around the part of the cork that's outside the bottle. (Sparkling wine corks have a mushroom-shaped head that sticks out of the bottle.) Or you could probably try using regular pliers, although lugging in the toolbox will break the mood of the occasion.

Does Wine Really Breathe?

Most wine is alive in the sense that it changes chemically as it slowly grows older. Wine absorbs oxygen and, like our own cells, it oxidizes. When the grapes turn into wine in the first place, they give off carbon dioxide, just like us. So we suppose you could say that wine breathes, in a sense.

But that's not what the server means when he asks, "Shall I pull the cork and let the wine breathe, sir (or madam)?" The term *breathing* usually refers to the process of aerating the wine, exposing it to air. Sometimes a wine that is very young will improve a little if it is aerated. But just pulling the cork out of the bottle and letting the bottle sit there is a truly ineffective way to aerate the wine. The little space at the neck of the bottle is way too small to allow your wine to breathe very much.

How to aerate your wine

If you really want to aerate your wine, do one or both of the following:

1. Pour the wine into a *decanter* (a fancy word for a container — usually glass — that is big enough to hold the contents of an entire bottle of wine).

2. Pour the wine into large glasses at least ten minutes before you plan to drink it.

It doesn't matter what your decanter looks like or how much it costs. In fact, the very inexpensive, wide-mouthed carafes are fine. Low-priced Paul Masson-brand wines come in such decanters.

Two reasons to decant your wine

There are two basic reasons to decant a bottle of wine — that is, to pour the wine from the bottle into a decanter before serving:

1. To let the wine "breathe." When the oxygen in the air combines with the wine, it opens up the wine's flavors; remember, the wine has been trapped in the bottle — sometimes for many years — in a retarded state of development. Also, any off-odors (sometimes referred to as "bottle stink") will have a chance to dissipate in the air.

2. To separate the sediment from the wine; sediment usually begins to develop in red wines around eight years after the vintage.

Which wines need decanting?

Many red wines but only a few white wines — and some dessert wines — can benefit from aeration. Most white wines can be consumed upon pouring, unless they're too cold, but that's a discussion for later.

Young, tannic red wines

Young red wines, especially those that are high in tannin (see Chapter 2 for more on tannin) — such as Cabernet Sauvignons, most Red Zinfandels, Bordeaux, many wines from the Rhône Valley, and many Italian wines — actually taste better with aeration because their tannins soften and the wine becomes less harsh. The younger and more tannic the wine is, the more time it needs to breathe.

As a general rule of thumb, one hour of aeration seems to be sufficient time for most tannic, young red wines to soften up. A glaring exception to the one-hour rule would be many young Barolos or Barbarescos (red wines from Piedmont, Italy); these wines are frequently so tannic that they can practically stand up by themselves without a decanter. They often can benefit from three or four hours of aeration.

Older red wines with sediment

Many red wines develop *sediment* (tannin and other particles in the wine that solidify over time and drop to the bottom of the bottle) usually after eight or ten years of age. The sediment can taste a bit bitter (remember, it's tannin). Also, the dark particles floating in your wine, usually near the bottom of your glass, don't look very appetizing.

To remove sediment, keep the bottle of wine standing upright at least a day or two before you plan to drink it so that the sediment settles at the bottom of the bottle. Then decant the wine into a decanter: Pour the wine out of the bottle slowly while watching the wine inside the bottle as it approaches the neck. You watch the wine so that you can stop pouring when you see cloudy wine from the bottom of the bottle making its way to the neck. To actually see the wine inside the bottle as you pour, you need to have a bright light shining up through the bottle.

Candles are commonly used for this purpose, and they are romantic, but a flashlight standing on end works even better. (It's brighter, and it doesn't flicker.) Stop pouring the wine into the decanter when you reach the sediment, which should be toward the bottom of the bottle.

The older the wine, the more delicate it may be. Don't give old, fragile-looking wines excessive aeration. (Look at the color of the wine through the bottle before you decant; if it looks pale, the wine could be pretty far along on its maturity curve.) The flavors of really old wines will start fading rapidly after

10 or 15 minutes of being exposed to air. Remember what happened to the people who left the Hidden Valley of Shangri-La in *Lost Horizon?* They withered into wizened ancients in a matter of minutes!

If the wine needs more aeration after decanting, let it breathe. If the wine has a dark color, chances are that it is still quite youthful and will need to breathe further. Conversely, if the wine has a brick red or garnet color, it probably has matured and might not need much more aeration.

A few white wines

Some very good, dry white wines — such as full-bodied white Burgundies and white Bordeaux, as well as the best Alsace whites — also get better with aeration. For example, if you open up a young Corton-Charlemagne (a great white Burgundy), and it doesn't seem to be showing much aroma or flavor, chances are that it needs aeration. Decant it and try it again in a half hour. In most cases, your wine will dramatically improve.

Vintage Ports

One of the most famous fortified wines is vintage Port. We'll discuss this wine and others like it in more detail in Chapter 14.

For now, we'll just say that, yes, vintage Port needs breathing lessons, very much so indeed! Young vintage Ports are so brutally tannic that they demand many hours of aeration (eight would not be too much). Even older Ports will improve with four hours or more of aeration. Older vintage Ports require decanting, also, because they are chock-full of sediment (often, the bottom 10 percent of the bottle). Keep vintage Ports standing for several days before you open them.

Exceptions to the "decant your red wines and Ports" rule

The exceptions prove the rule. The majority of red wines you drink do not require decanting, aeration, or any other special preparation other than pulling the cork out and having a glass handy.

The following red wines *do not* need decanting:

- Lighter-bodied red wines, such as Pinot Noirs, Burgundies, Beaujolais, Côtes du Rhônes; lighter Red Zinfandels; and lighter-bodied Italian reds, such as Dolcettos, Barberas, and lighter Chiantis. These wines don't have much tannin and, therefore, don't need much aeration.

- Inexpensive (less than $6) red wines. Same reason as preceding.

- Tawny ports — in fact, any other Ports except vintage Ports. These wines should be free from sediment (which stayed behind in the barrels when the wine was aging) and are ready to drink when you pour them.

Does It Really Matter Which Glass You Use?

If you are just drinking wine as refreshment with your meal and you are not thinking about the wine much as it goes down, the glass you use probably doesn't matter in the least. A jelly glass? Why not? Plastic glasses? We've used them dozens of times on picnics, not to mention in airplanes.

But if you have a good wine, a special occasion, friends who want to talk about the wine with you, or the boss for dinner, *stemware* (glasses with stems) is called for. And it's not just a question of etiquette and status: Good wine will taste better out of good glasses. Really.

Compare wine glasses to stereo speakers. Any old speaker brings the music to your ears, just like any old glass brings the wine to your lips. But (assuming that you can tell the difference and that you care to notice it) can't you appreciate the sound so much more, aesthetically and emotionally, from good speakers? The same principle holds true with wine and wine glasses. You can appreciate wine's aroma and flavor complexities so much more out of a fine wine glass. The medium is the message.

First, the right color

Unless you're playing some kind of perverse game on your wine expert friends, your wine glasses should be clear. (Jelly glasses may have pictures of the Flintstones on them, as long as the background is clear.) Those pretty pink or green glasses may look nice in Aunt Betty's china cabinet, but they mess up your ability to distinguish the true colors of the wine. Those opaque black glasses that were popular a while ago may be appropriate for a devil-worshipping ceremony, but certainly not for wine appreciation.

Now the size, breadth, and shape

Believe it or not (we didn't always), the flavor of a wine changes when you drink it out of different types of glasses. A riot almost broke out at one wine event we organized because the tasters thought we served them different wines in each glass and just pretended that it was the same wine, to fool them — so different did the wine taste in different glasses. We learned that three aspects of a glass are important: its size, its shape, and the thickness of the glass.

Size

For dry red and white wine, small glasses are anathema — besides that, they're a pain in the neck. You just can't swirl the wine around in those little glasses without spilling it, which makes it almost impossible for you to really appreciate the nose of the wine. And furthermore, who wants to bother continually refilling them? Small glasses can work adequately only for sherries or dessert wines, which have strong aromas to begin with and are generally drunk in smaller quantities than table wines.

- ✔ For red wines, your glass should hold a minimum of 12 ounces; many of the best glasses have capacities ranging from 16 to 24 ounces, or more.

- ✔ For white wines, 10 to 12 ounces should be the minimum capacity.

- ✔ For sparkling wines, a capacity ranging from 8 to 12 ounces is fine; with wine glasses, larger is usually better.

Breadth (thickness) and shape

Very thin, fine crystal costs a lot more than normal, thick glass. That's one reason why many people don't use it (and one reason why some people do).

The better reason for using fine crystal is that the wine tastes better out of it. We're not sure whether the elegant crystal simply heightens the aesthetic experience of the wine drinking or whether there's some more scientific reason.

Tulips, flutes, balloons, and other picturesque wine-glass names

You thought that a tulip was a flower and a flute was a musical instrument? Well, the tulip also happens to be the name of the ideally shaped glass for sparkling wine (see Figure 6-4). It is tall, elongated, and more narrow at the rim than in the middle of the bowl. This shape helps hold the bubbles in the wine longer, not allowing them to escape freely (the way the wide-mouthed, sherbet cuplike, so-called champagne glasses do).

The flute is also a good sparkling wine glass because of its narrow, elongated shape (see Figure 6-5); but it is less ideal than the tulip because it does not narrow at the mouth. The trumpet actually widens at the mouth, making it less suitable for sparkling wine but very elegant looking (see Figure 6-6).

The balloon glass is ideal for aerating many red wines, such as Burgundies, Barolos, and so on, because of its ample shape.

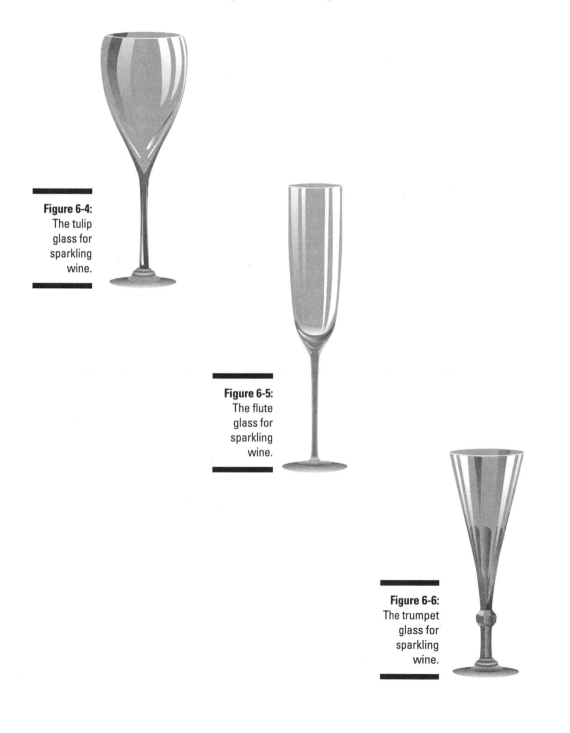

Figure 6-4:
The tulip glass for sparkling wine.

Figure 6-5:
The flute glass for sparkling wine.

Figure 6-6:
The trumpet glass for sparkling wine.

Half empty or half full?

"Fill 'er up" might be fine for your service station attendant, but not for the person pouring the wine. It always annoys us when servers fill our glasses to the top. We guess they don't want to bother repouring the wine too often. Or maybe they want to give us our money's worth. But how can we stick our nose into a full glass without looking like an idiot? Once a kid at a nearby table blurted out, "Look, Mom, that man is drinking with his nose!"

To leave some margin of safety for swirling and smelling the wine, fill the glass only partially. One-third capacity, at the most, is the best fill-level for serious red wines. (This goes back to that idea of aerating the wine.) White wine glasses can be half full, while sparkling wines can be three-quarters full. On the other hand, if you're using paper cups or jelly glasses, you might as well "Fill 'er up."

Certain shapes of glasses seem to enhance the flavors of particular wines. For example, an oval-shaped bowl that is narrow at its mouth (see Figure 6-7) is ideal for many red wines, such as Bordeaux, Cabernet Sauvignons, Merlots, Chiantis, and Zinfandels. On the other hand, some red wines, such as Burgundies, Pinot Noirs, and Barolos, are best appreciated in wider-bowled, apple-shaped glasses (see Figure 6-8). Champagne is best in long, thin tulip- or flute-shaped glasses, which hold the bubbles in the wine longer.

Figure 6-7:
The
Bordeaux
glass.

Figure 6-8:
The
Burgundy
glass.

How many glasses do I need, anyway?

So what's a wine lover to do: Buy different glasses for each kind of wine? Fortunately, there are some all-purpose red and white wine glasses that combine the best features of all the above types. And you don't have to pay a fortune for decent wine glasses. A company called St. George Crystal makes crystal glasses in all sizes and shapes that sell for three to four dollars a glass. They are available in most wine stores.

If you want something finer, try Riedel Crystal. Riedel is an Austrian glass manufacturer that specializes in making the right wine glass for each kind of wine. Riedel has done a good deal of research to discover which glass shapes are best suited for major types of wine, for example, Bordeaux, Burgundy, Chardonnay, Champagne, and so on.

Riedel produces three lines of wine glasses: the relatively inexpensive ($7.25 per glass) Overture series, the medium-priced ($15 to $20 per glass) Vinum series, and its state-of-the-art, hand-blown Sommelier glasses for serious connoisseurs (at $50 to $70 a glass, you'd better be serious!). Riedel is widely available in catalogs and in wine stores.

The more you care to pay attention to the flavor of the wine, the more you really and truly appreciate and enjoy wine from a good wine glass. If you just don't have an ear for music, that's okay, too.

Washing your crystal glasses

Detergents often leave a filmy residue in glasses, which can affect the aroma and flavor of your wine. We strongly advise that you clean your good crystal glasses by hand, using washing soda or baking soda (washing soda is the better of the two; it doesn't cake up, like baking soda). Neither product leaves any soapy, filmy residue in your glass. Washing soda can be found in the soap/detergent section of all supermarkets. Buy the least expensive store brand. It won't have any added, perfumey aromas.

Serving Wine: Not Too Warm, Not Too Cold

Just as the right glass will enhance your wine experience, serving wine at the ideal temperature is a vital factor in your enjoyment of wine. Frequently, we have tasted the same wine at different temperatures (and, believe it or not, at different barometric pressures) and have loved the wine on one occasion but disliked it the other time!

Most red wines are at their best at cool room temperature, 62° to 65°F (16 to 18°C). Once upon a time, in drafty old English and Scottish castles, that was simply room temperature (actually it was probably warm room temperature!). Today when you hear room temperature, you think of a room that's about 70°F (21°C), don't you? Red wine served at this temperature can taste flat, flabby, lifeless, and often too hot — a burning sensation from the alcohol.

Fifteen minutes in the fridge will do wonders to revive red wines that have been suffering from heat prostration. But don't let the wine get too cold. Red wines served too cold taste overly tannic and acidic, decidedly unpleasant. Light, fruity, red wines, such as Beaujolais, are most delightful when served slightly chilled at about 58° to 60°F (14° to 15.5°C).

Are you wondering how to know when your bottle is 58° to 60°F? You could buy a nifty digital thermometer that wraps around the outside of the bottle and gives you a color-coded reading. Or you could buy something that looks like a real thermometer that you place into the opened bottle (in the wine's mouth, you might say). We have both of those, and we never use them. Just feel the bottle with your hand and take a guess. Practice makes perfect.

Just as many red wines are served too warm, most white wines are definitely served too cold, judging by the service that we have received in many restaurants. The higher the quality of a white wine, the warmer it should be so that you can properly appreciate its flavor.

- ✔ Fine white wines are best between 58° and 62°F (14° and 16.5°C).
- ✔ Simpler, inexpensive, quaffing-type white wines are best served colder, between 50° and 55°F (10° and 12.8°C).
- ✔ Rosés and blush wines can be treated in the same manner as inexpensive white wines.
- ✔ Inexpensive sweet wines should be served cold, similar to inexpensive dry white wines.
- ✔ Finer dessert wines, such as a good Sauternes or Port, taste their best at the same temperature as better white wines (for Sauternes, 58° to 62°F, 14° to 16.5°C) and better red wines (for Port, 62° to 65°F, 16° to 18°C).
- ✔ Champagnes are at their best when cold, about 45°F (7°C).

To avoid the problem of warm champagne, keep an ice bucket handy. Or put the bottle back in the refrigerator between pourings. By the way, a sparkling-wine stopper, a device that fits over the opened bottle and keeps it closed, is really effective in keeping any remaining champagne or sparkling wine fresh (often for several days) in the refrigerator.

CAUTION!

An aside about atmospheric pressure

File this under FYI ("For Your Information") — or maybe under "Believe It or Not."

A few years ago, we were enjoying one of our favorite red wines, an Italian Barbera, in the Alps. It was a perfect, high-pressure day — crisp, clear, and cool. The wine was also perfect — absolutely delicious with our salami, bread, and cheese. A couple of days later, we had the very same wine at the seashore, on a humid, low-pressure day. The wine was heavy, flat, and lifeless. What had happened to our wonderful mountain wine? We made inquiries among some of our wine-drinking friends and discovered that they had had similar experiences. For red wines, at least, atmospheric pressure apparently influences the taste of the wine: high pressure, for the better; low pressure, for the worse. So the next time one of your favorite red wines doesn't seem quite right, check the air pressure! Believe it or not.

Storing Leftover Wine

We've already mentioned the sparkling-wine stopper for leftover Champagne. But what do you do when you have red or white wine left in the bottle?

You can put the cork back in the bottle if it still fits and put the bottle into the refrigerator. (Even red wines will stay fresher there; just take the bottle out to warm up about one hour before serving it.) But there are three other ways that will probably be surer methods of keeping your remaining wine from oxidizing:

- ✔ If you have about half a bottle of wine left, you can simply pour the wine into a clean, empty half-sized wine bottle and recork it. We sometimes buy wines in half-bottles, just to make sure that we have the empty half-bottles around.

- ✔ There is a handy, inexpensive, miniature pump that you can buy in any wine store, called a Vac-U-Vin. This pump removes the oxygen from the bottle, and the rubber stoppers that come with it keep more oxygen from entering the bottle. It should keep your wine fresh for up to a week.

- ✔ You can buy small cans of inert gas in some wine stores. Just squirt a few shots of the gas into the bottle through a skinny straw, which comes with the can. The gas acts as a layer between the wine and the oxygen in the bottle, thus protecting the wine from oxidizing without itself combining with the wine. Simple and effective.

To avoid all this, just drink the wine! Or, if you're not too fussy, just place the leftover wine in the refrigerator and drink it in the next day or two — before it goes into a coma.

Part II
If You Are an Occasional Imbiber

The 5th Wave   By Rich Tennant

"The problem with wine tastings is you're not supposed to swallow, and Clifford refuses to spit. Fortunately, he studied trumpet with Dizzy Gillespie."

In this part...

We're flattered if you got to this point by reading every word we've written so far. But we know that you might have landed here by skipping over lots of stuff earlier in the book. That's okay — the meat and potatoes of the book are right here.

Five of the chapters in this part are chock-full of information about the major wines of the world, including our recommendations on specific wines to buy. This part also contains everything you ever needed to know (and some details you didn't know you needed) about wine labels, the names of wines, and grape varieties — just as a side dish.

Chapter 7

Is It a Grape? Is It a Place?

*W*e remember a cartoon in *The New Yorker* in 1980 that depicted the students of a private New York nursery school lined up for their class picture. The caption identified the children by their first names. Every girl was named Jennifer, and every boy was named Scott.

When you walk into a wine shop these days, you'd think that the people who name wines have the same fixation as the parents of those nursery school children. More than half the white wines are named *Chardonnay,* and the majority of the red wines are named *Cabernet Sauvignon*.

Actually, one Chardonnay is no more identical to the next one than one little Jennifer is identical to the next Jennifer. But to distinguish one Chardonnay from the other (without opening the bottles, that is), you need more information. You need to read the rest of the label.

What's in a Name

All sorts of names can appear on wine labels: the name of the *grape* from which the wine was made; a *brand name*; the name of the company or person that made the wine (called the *producer*); sometimes a special name for that particular wine (called a *proprietary name*); and the name of the *place* where the grapes were grown (sometimes *two* places, such as the wine region and the name of the specific vineyard property). Then there's the *vintage* year (the year the grapes were harvested), which is part of the wine's name; and sometimes you see a descriptor like *reserve*, which either has specific legal meaning or means nothing at all, depending on where the wine came from.

Beware of the simple wine label

Think twice when you encounter a wine label that tells you next to nothing about the wine. Chances are, the producer is trying to fool you into thinking that the wine is something it's not. There's a best-selling brand of wines from Chile, for example, whose labels state the brand (a very Yankee-sounding name), the name of the grape variety (such as Merlot), and — in tiny print — the place where the wine comes from (Rapel, an area in Chile that most people have never heard of). We bet that 98 to 99 percent of the people who buy that wine think they're buying a California Merlot and don't realize that the wine is from Chile. No harm done, necessarily. If you like the wine, who cares where it comes from? Hats off to the marketers who have been able to build a successful brand. But somehow we feel deceived.

 In this age of full disclosure, the more enlightened the producer, the more information he will give you on the wine label. Good winemakers want you to know that they have nothing to hide.

Veteran wine lovers appreciate all that information because they know what it all means. But to those who are just discovering wine, the information contained in wine names and on wine labels is far more confusing than enlightening. Although we'd all agree that little Jennifer needs more than just the name *Jennifer* to identify herself in the world (unless she plans to become a rock star or comedienne), does she really need the equivalent of: Jennifer Smith, "Jenny," Caucasian female, produced by Don and Louise Smith, New York City, Upper West Side, 1980?

Of course she doesn't. But — we know you don't want to hear this — for bottles of wine the answer, frankly, is yes.

The Wine Name Game

Most of the wines that you find in your wine shop or on restaurant wine lists are named in one of two basic ways: either for their *grape variety* or for their *place of production*. That information, plus the name of the producer, becomes the shorthand name we use in talking about the wine.

Robert Mondavi Cabernet Sauvignon, for example, is a wine made by Robert Mondavi Winery and named after the Cabernet Sauvignon grape. Ruffino Chianti is a wine made by the Ruffino winery and named after the place called Chianti.

You might recognize some names as grape names and other names as place-names right off the bat; but if you don't, don't panic. That information is the kind of thing you can look up (Chapters 9 through 14 will help), and it's also the kind of thing you learn quickly because it's very fundamental.

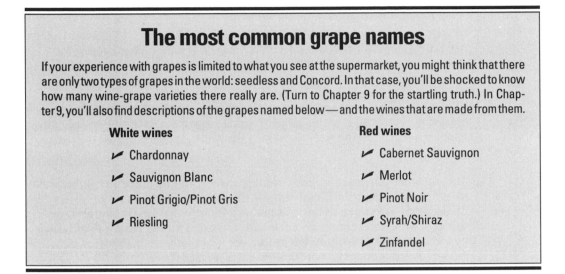

The most common grape names

If your experience with grapes is limited to what you see at the supermarket, you might think that there are only two types of grapes in the world: seedless and Concord. In that case, you'll be shocked to know how many wine-grape varieties there really are. (Turn to Chapter 9 for the startling truth.) In Chapter 9, you'll also find descriptions of the grapes named below—and the wines that are made from them.

White wines
- Chardonnay
- Sauvignon Blanc
- Pinot Grigio/Pinot Gris
- Riesling

Red wines
- Cabernet Sauvignon
- Merlot
- Pinot Noir
- Syrah/Shiraz
- Zinfandel

Hello, my name is Chardonnay

A *varietal* wine is a wine that is named after either the *principal* or the *sole* grape variety that makes the wine.

Not just any wine can be a varietal. Each country (and in the U.S., some individual states) has laws that dictate the minimum percentage of the named grape that must be in the wine if that wine wants to call itself by the grape name. The issue is truth in advertising.

In California, the minimum percentage of the named grape required by law in a wine is 75 percent (which means that your favorite California Chardonnay could have as much as 25 percent of some *other* grape in it). In Oregon, the minimum is 90 percent (except for Cabernet, which can be 75 percent). In Washington, it's 75 percent. In Australia, it's 85 percent. And in the countries that form the European Union (EU), the minimum is 85 percent.

Some varietal wines are made *entirely* from the grape variety for which the wine is named. There's no law against that anywhere. The minimum percentage is what the laws concern themselves with.

Not every wine that is eligible to be a varietal *wants* to be a varietal. Much of the point of naming a wine after its grape variety is that wine lovers will recognize the name, have some notion of what the wine is, believe that it's a good wine, and buy it. If the grape variety is an unknown or unappreciated one (like Chenin Blanc or Riesling), a varietal name could actually be a deterrent to sales. The marketers often think up a better (that is, more effective) name for those wines. That's one reason why *proprietary names* were invented. (See the section, "Wines with proprietary names," later in this chapter.)

Why name a wine after a grape variety

Grapes are the raw material of a wine. Except for whatever a wine absorbs from oak barrels (certain aromas and flavors, as well as tannin), the juice of the grapes is what any wine *is*. So to name a wine after the grape it came from is very logical.

Naming a wine after its grape variety is also very satisfying to exacting consumers. What type of oil is in this salad dressing; how many grams of fat are in this soup; is any MSG in the egg roll; what is this wine made from? Just the facts, ma'am.

And, on some unconscious level, naming a wine after its grape variety appeals to our sense of fairness. Chardonnay is Chardonnay, and one nation's Chardonnay is as good as the next nation's Chardonnay. In the hierarchical world of wine, where some countries are accorded more prestige than others by virtue of their history, varietal wines are inherently egalitarian and classless (as in "classless society," not "this wine has no class").

Varietal wines are not an American invention — but they might as well be, considering how prevalent such names are in the U.S. and how well varietal wines do at the cash register. Most California (and New York and Washington and Oregon) wines carry varietal names. Likewise, most Australian, South American, and South African wines are named using the *principal* principle. Even some countries that don't normally name their wines after grapes, like France, are jumping on the varietal-name bandwagon for certain wines that they especially want to sell to Americans.

A common perception among most wine lovers is that a varietal wine is somehow *better* than a non-varietal. Although we understand how that perception came to be, we believe it has gotten entirely out of hand. The fact that a wine is named after its principal grape variety is absolutely *no indication of quality*.

The varietal name game

For several decades after Prohibition was repealed in 1933, most American wines were named after types of European wines, such as Chianti, Burgundy, Champagne, and Chablis. (Some still are, but their numbers are fading fast.) The wines didn't necessarily resemble *real* Chianti, Burgundy, Champagne or Chablis — that is, the wines that really come from those *places* — but the names were familiar and understandable to the people who bought the wine. There were no American controls over names like these. Anyone could use any name for the wine he made. Today, we call such names *generic*.

Rumor has it that some wineries used to bottle the same wine under a couple of different labels. A customer would buy either Chianti or Burgundy according to personal preference, but they were both the same wine! We're too young to have any personal knowledge of all this, but we wouldn't be surprised if it were true.

About 25 years ago, when California wineries began naming their wines after grape varieties, intelligent wine drinkers all over America began to feel more comfortable with the wines. Even if, in those days, the law said the wine had to contain only 51 percent of the named grape, we felt that we were drinking Known Entities rather than some labeling gimmick.

The wineries that used varietal names in those days were the most avant-garde wineries around, which usually meant that they produced the best wines. Varietal wines were, almost by definition, better, more genuine, and more interesting than generic wines.

Now, varietal wines are commonplace. When you buy a wine named after a grape variety today, you are *not* necessarily getting a wine on the cutting edge of the quality wine movement. You definitely *are* getting a wine made by someone who knows the selling power of a varietal name. And you are still getting the same cozy feeling from knowing exactly what you are drinking.

Hello, my name is Bordeaux

Unlike American wines, most European wines are named for the *region* (place) where they are made rather than for their grape variety. Many of the European wines are made from precisely the same grape varieties as American wines (like Chardonnay, Cabernet Sauvignon, Sauvignon Blanc, and so on), but they don't say so on the label. Instead, the labels say Burgundy, Bordeaux, Sancerre, and so on: the *place* where those grapes grow.

The most common place-names

Bardolino	Chianti	Rioja
Beaujolais	Côtes du Rhône	Sancerre
Bordeaux	Mosel	Sauternes
Burgundy (Bourgogne)	Port (Porto)	Sherry
Chablis	Pouilly-Fuissé	Soave
Champagne	Rhine (Rheingau, Rheinhessen)	Valpolicella

Is this some nefarious plot to make wine incomprehensible to English-only wine lovers who have never visited Europe and flunked geography in grade school?

Au contraire! The European system of naming wines is actually intended to provide more information about each wine and more understanding of what's in the bottle than varietal naming provides. The only catch is that you have to learn something about the different regions from which the wines come. (Turn to Chapters 10 through 14 for more information.)

Why name a wine after a place?

Grapes, the raw material of wine, have to grow somewhere. Depending on the type of soil, the amount of sunshine, the amount of rain, the slope of the hill, and the many other characteristics that each *somewhere* has, the grapes can be different. If the grapes are different, the wine is different. Each wine, therefore, reflects the place where the grapes are grown.

When we say *the grapes can be different* according to where they're grown, we mean two things. First, the same grape variety, such as Chardonnay, can turn out differently when it is planted in two different places. The same variety can get riper in one place than the other, for example (the riper grapes make a wine higher in alcohol with riper fruit flavors), or the grapes (and wine) can have some subtle, unusual flavors — such as mineral flavors — attributable to a particular place. In one way or another, the place will *always* affect the character of the grapes.

Second, in two different places you might very well have different grape varieties planted. Even if business sense dictates that you always plant Chardonnay because it makes the easiest wine to sell, Chardonnay might not be the grape best suited to a particular piece of land with the climate and soil that land has (and had and always will have). So you'd have to plant a different grape, which, naturally, makes a different wine.

In Europe, where grape growers/winemakers had centuries to figure out which grape grows best where, they have systematized most of their grape/location match-ups and codified them into law. Therefore, the name of a *place* where they grow grapes and make wine in Europe automatically connotes the grape (or grapes) used to make the wine of that place. The label on the bottle usually doesn't tell you the grape (or grapes), though. Which brings us back to our original question: Is this some kind of nefarious plot to make wine incomprehensible to non-Europeans?

Decoding common European place-names

Wine Name	Country	Grape Varieties
Bardolino	Italy	Corvina, Molinara, Rondinella*
Beaujolais	France	Gamay
Bordeaux (red)	France	Cabernet Sauvignon, Merlot, Cabernet Franc, and others*
Bordeaux (white)	France	Sauvignon Blanc, Sémillon, Muscadelle*
Burgundy (red)	France	Pinot Noir
Burgundy (white)	France	Chardonnay
Chablis	France	Chardonnay
Champagne	France	Chardonnay, Pinot Noir, Pinot Meunier*
Châteauneuf-du-Pape	France	Grenache, Mourvédre, Syrah, and others*
Chianti	Italy	Sangiovese, Canaiolo, and others*
Côtes du Rhône	France	Grenache, Mourvèdre, Carignan, and others*
Mosel	Germany	Riesling or others (named on label)
Port (Porto)	Portugal	Touriga Nacional, Tinta Barroca, Touriga Francesa, Tinta Roriz, Tinto Cão, and others*
Pouilly-Fuissé	France	Chardonnay
Rhine (Rheingau, Rheinhessen)	Germany	Riesling or others (named on label)
Rioja (red)	Spain	Tempranillo, Grenache, and others*
Sancerre	France	Sauvignon Blanc
Sauternes	France	Sémillon, Sauvignon Blanc*
Sherry	Spain	Palomino
Soave	Italy	Garganega and others*
Valpolicella	Italy	Corvina, Molinara, Rondinella*

*Indicates that a blend of grapes is used to make these wines.

The terroir name game

Now seems as good a time as any to hit you with the current hot fifty-cent word in wine: *terroir*.

Terroir (pronounced *ter wahr*) is a French word that has no direct translation in English, so wine people just use it in French. Using the word in French is not a sign of snobbery, it's a sign of expediency.

There's no fixed definition of *terroir;* it's a concept, and people tend to define it more broadly or more narrowly to suit their own needs. The word itself is based on the French word *terre*, which means soil; so some people define *terroir* as, simply, dirt (as in "Our American dirt is every bit as good as their French dirt").

But *terroir* is really much more complex (or complicated) than just dirt. *Terroir* is the combination of immutable natural factors — such as soil, underlying rock, climate (sun, rain, wind, and so on), slope of the hill, and altitude — that a particular vineyard site has. Chances are, no two vineyards in the entire world have precisely the same combination of these factors. So we consider *terroir* to be the unique combination of natural factors that a particular vineyard site has.

Terroir is the guiding principle behind the European concept that wines should be named after the place they come from (thought we'd gotten off the track, didn't you?). The name of the place connotes which grapes were used to make the wine of that place (because the grapes are dictated by law) — the thinking goes — and the place influences the character of those grapes in its own unique way. Therefore, the most accurate name that a wine can have is the name of the place where its grapes were grown, not the name of its grapes.

It's not some nefarious plot; it's just a whole different way of looking at things.

Place-names on American wine labels

France might have invented the concept that wines should be named after their place of origin, but neither France nor even greater Europe has a monopoly on the idea. Wine labels from countries outside of Europe can also tell you where a wine is made — usually by featuring a place-name (called an *appellation of origin* in Winespeak) somewhere on the label. But there are a few differences.

First of all, on an American wine label (or an Australian or Chilean or South African label, for that matter) you have to go to some effort to find the place-name on the label. The place of origin is not the fundamental name of the wine (as it is for most European wines); the grape usually is.

Bigger than a bread basket

When we travel to other countries, we realize that people in different places have different ways of perceiving space and distance. If someone tells us that we'll find a certain restaurant "just up ahead," for example, we figure it's the equivalent of about three blocks away — but they might mean two kilometers.

Discussing place names for European wines can be just as problematic. Some of the *places* are as small as several acres, some are 100-square miles big, and others are the size of New Jersey. Certain words used to describe wine zones suggest the relative size of the place. In descending order of size and ascending order of specificity:

- Country
- Region
- District
- Subdistrict
- Commune
- Vineyard

Second, place-names in the U.S. mean far less than they do in Europe. Okay, if the label says Napa Valley, and you've visited that area — and you loved eating at Mustards, and you'd like to spend the rest of your life in one of those houses atop a hill off the Silverado Trail — Napa Valley will mean something to you. But *legally*, the name Napa Valley only means that at least 85 percent of the grapes came from an area defined by law as the Napa Valley wine zone. The name Napa Valley does not define the type of wine that can be made, nor does it imply specific grape varieties, the way a European place-name does. (Good thing the grape name is there, as big as day, on the label.)

Place names on labels of non-European wines, for the most part, merely pay lip service to the concept of *terroir*. For example, some non-European appellations are ridiculously broad. We have to laugh when we think how the typical European winemaker must react to all those wine labels that announce a wine's place of origin simply as *California*.

Great. This label says that this wine comes from a specific area that is 30 percent larger than the entire country of Italy! Some specific area! (Italy has more than 220 specific wine areas.)

 When the place on the label is merely *California,* in fact, it tells you next to nothing about the wine. California's a big place, and those grapes could come from just about anywhere. Same thing for all those Australian wines labeled *South Eastern Australia* — an area only slightly smaller than France and Spain *combined.*

Grape names on European wines

Although most European wines are named after their place of production, grape names do sometimes appear on labels of European wines.

In Italy, for example, several place-names routinely have grape-names appended to them — the name Trentino (place) Pinot Grigio (grape) is an example. Or the official name of a wine could be a combination of place and grape — like the name Barbera d'Alba, which translates as Barbera (grape) of Alba (place).

In France, some producers are deliberately adding the grape name to their labels even though the grape is already implicit in the wine name. For example, a white Bourgogne (place-name) might also have the word Chardonnay (grape) on the label, for those wine drinkers who don't know that white Bourgogne is always 100 percent Chardonnay.

And German wines often carry grape names along with their official place-names.

But even if a European wine does carry a grape name, the most important part of the wine's name, in the eyes of the people who make it, is the place.

Wines named in other ways

Now and then, you might come across a wine that is neither named for its grape variety nor for its region of origin. Such wines usually fall into three categories: *branded wines, wines with proprietary names,* or *generic wines.*

Branded wines

Most wines have brand names, including those wines that are named after their grape variety — like Simi (brand name) Sauvignon Blanc (grape) — and those that are named after their region of origin — like Bolla (brand name) Soave (place). These brand names are usually the name of the company that made the wine, called a *winery.* Because most wineries make several different wines, the brand name itself is not specific enough to be the actual name of the wine.

But sometimes a wine has *only* a brand name. For example, the label says *Salamandre* and *red French wine* but provides little other identification. And sometimes the brand name is *not* the actual name of the company that made the wine but is simply a brand. For example, a wine might be called Rocky Road Chardonnay, and there's not really a winery named Rocky Road. This second situation is somewhat common for California wines; anyone can purchase wines in bulk, rent the services of a winery to blend and bottle the wines, and sell the wine with his own brand name on it.

Wines that have *only* a brand name on them, with no indication of grape or of place — other than the country of production — are generally the most inexpensive, ordinary wines you can get. If they're from a European Union country, they won't even be *vintage dated* (that is, there won't be any indication of what year the grapes were harvested) because EU law does not allow such wines the privilege of carrying a vintage date. Just remember what somebody's mother once said: No matter how cheap it is, it's no bargain unless you really like it.

On the other hand, wines that have a brand name that is not the winery's name can be decent enough wines and very good values. Such wines usually name the grape variety or place of origin on their labels, and they carry the name of the winery somewhere in the fine print at the bottom of the label. The only thing missing in these wines (compared to wines whose brand is the winery name) is the warm feeling you get from knowing that you are drinking a wine that someone was proud enough to put his own name on.

Branded wines of this type usually fall into two categories:

- ✔ *Second-label wines* from established wineries (wine that wasn't quite up to a producer's personal quality standard and, therefore, was bottled under a secondary name)
- ✔ Wines invented by the forces of marketing (quality, style, label, and all)

In the first case, the wine will be relatively inexpensive because the producer must price the wine below his regular line; in the second case, the wine will be relatively inexpensive because affordability is a cornerstone of wine marketing these days. Mouton-Cadet is a prime example of a branded wine from Bordeaux; Liberty School is a branded wine from California.

Wines with proprietary names

You can find some pretty creative names on wine bottles these days: Tapestry, Conundrum, Insignia, Cardinale, Isosceles, Mythology, Trilogy. Is this stuff to drink, to drive, or to dab behind your ears?

Names like these are *proprietary names* (often trademarked) that producers create for special wines. In the case of American wines, the bottles with proprietary names usually contain wines made from a *blend* of grapes; therefore, no one grape name can be used as the name of the wine. (Remember California's 75 percent rule?) In the case of European wines, the grapes used to make the wine were probably not the approved grapes for that region, and the regional name could, therefore, not be used on the label.

A brand name can apply to several different wines. You can find Zinfandel, Cabernet Sauvignon, Chardonnay, and numerous other wines under the Fetzer brand from California, for example, and you can find Beaujolais, Pouilly-Fuissé, Macon-Villages and numerous other wines under the Louis Jadot brand from France. But a proprietary name applies to one specific wine.

A producer who creates a wine with a proprietary name has high-minded motives. He is driven by artistic impulse, intellectual curiosity, or sheer ego to form a wine that exceeds the norm for his part of the world. He develops the wine personally, nurses it to maturity, and then dresses it up in the best possible package so that all the world can see how fine the expression of his art, intellect, or ego is. The price tag on the bottle confirms the magnitude of his endeavor.

Wines with proprietary names are usually made in small quantities, are quite expensive ($20 to $75 a bottle), and are, in fact, at a high level of quality. They particularly satisfy wine lovers who must be the first in their crowd to taste the newest, most unusual wines. Sometimes they draw rave reviews from the critics and end up as established successes that endure in the marketplace. Sometimes they take the route of old soldiers.

Generic wines

A generic name is a wine name that has been used inappropriately for so long that it has lost its original meaning in the eyes of the government (exactly what Xerox, Kleenex, and Band-Aid are afraid of becoming).

Burgundy, Chianti, Chablis, Champagne, Rhine wine, Sherry, Port, and Sauterne are all names that rightfully should apply only to wines made in the specific places that those names imply. But these names have been usurped by very large and powerful wine companies. So now both the U.S. and Canadian governments recognize these names as broad *types* of wine rather than as wines from specific regions.

Most California wines were generically named until the late sixties or early seventies when varietals came into vogue. Generics are still around, but they are less popular in the marketplace with every passing year.

When you buy a generic wine, you have absolutely no idea what you are getting except that it is a piece of history.

Chapter 8
Judging a Wine by Its Label

*W*e're standing at the Immigration Desk in some foreign airport, and a distrustful officer is studying our passports. We're disheveled after six hours of trying to sleep in seats too small to sit in. He needs to make a judgment about us, and all he has to go on is the sketchy information in our passport and our tired faces.

Do you sometimes feel like that Immigration officer when you stand in front of an array of wine bottles and attempt to make a judgment about which to buy? With an occasional exception, the labels hardly say more than a passport, and the pretty pictures on the labels are even less relevant to what's inside the bottles than passport photos are to a traveler's true appearance.

The Wine Label and What It Tells You

Every bottle of wine must have a label, and that label must provide certain minimal information about the wine. Some of the information on a wine label is stipulated and defined by the country where the wine is *made*. Other items of information are stipulated and defined by the country where the wine is being *sold*. When the requirements are different in the two places, life can get very, very complicated for label writers!

The forward and backward of wine labels

Many wine bottles have two labels. The *front label* names the wine and grabs your eye as you walk down the aisle, and the *back label* gives you a little more information, ranging from really helpful suggestions like "this wine tastes delicious with food" to really useful data such as "this wine has a total acidity of 6.02 and a pH of 3.34."

Now, if you're on your toes, you might be thinking: How can you tell the difference between front and back on a round bottle?

The government authorities in the U.S. apparently haven't thought that one through yet. They (and other governments) require certain information to appear on the front label of all wine bottles — basic stuff, such as the alcohol percentage, the type of wine (usually *red table wine* or *white table wine*), and the country of origin — but they don't define *front label.* So sometimes producers put all that information on the smaller of two labels and call that one the front label. Then the producers place another larger, colorful, dramatically eye-catching label — with little more than the name of the wine on it — on the *back* of the bottle. Guess which way the front label ends up facing when the bottle is placed on the shelf?

We don't feel at all outraged about this situation. We'd rather look at colorful labels on the shelf than boring information-laden ones any day. And we're not so lazy that we can't just pick up the bottle and turn it around to find out what we need to know. Besides, we enjoy the idea that wine producers and importers — whose every word and image on the label is scrutinized by the authorities to make sure that there are no sexual connotations or even the slightest suggestion that wine is healthful (regardless of medical findings) — have found one small way of getting even with the government.

Contains sulfites? Whose government warning?

Ironically, two items of label information (that are dear to politicians' hearts) required for wines sold in the U.S. — the words "Contains Sulfites" and the *government warning* regarding alcohol consumption during pregnancy or while using heavy machinery — *cannot* appear on U.S. wine labels when the wine is exported to any country in the European Union (EU). The way the European labeling laws work, anything that is not explicitly permitted to appear on the label is forbidden. Sorry, surgeon general.

The mandatory information

The federal government mandates that certain items of information appear on labels of wines sold in the U.S. (See Figure 8-1). Such items are generally referred to as *the mandatory*. These include

- ✓ A brand name
- ✓ Indication of class or type (*table wine, dessert wine,* or *sparkling wine*)
- ✓ The percentage of alcohol by volume
- ✓ Name and address of the bottler
- ✓ Net contents (expressed in milliliters; the standard wine bottle is 750 ml, which is 25.6 ounces)
- ✓ The phrase *Contains Sulfites* (with very, very few exceptions)
- ✓ The *government warning* (that we won't dignify by repeating here; just pick up any bottle of wine and you'll see it)

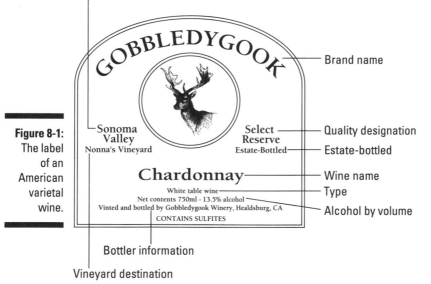

American Viticultural Area (AVA)

GOBBLEDYGOOK

Brand name

Sonoma Valley
Nonna's Vineyard

Select Reserve
Estate-Bottled

Quality designation

Estate-bottled

Chardonnay

Wine name

White table wine

Type

Net contents 750ml - 13.5% alcohol

Alcohol by volume

Vinted and bottled by Gobbledygook Winery, Healdsburg, CA

CONTAINS SULFITES

Bottler information

Vineyard destination

Figure 8-1: The label of an American varietal wine.

Will the real producer please stand up?

Although U.S. and Canadian labeling laws require wine labels to carry the name and address of the *bottler* or *dealer,* respectively, this information does not necessarily tell you who made the wine.

Of the various phrases that may be used to identify the bottler on labels of wine sold in the U.S., only the words *produced by* or *made by* indicate the name of the company that actually fermented 75 percent or more of the wine (that

is, who really *made* the wine); words such as *cellared by* or *vinted by* mean only that the company subjected the wine to cellar treatment (holding it for a while, for example).

On labels of wine sold in Canada, the dealer whose name and address must be indicated is the person for whom or by whom the wine is produced for sale. The person might or might not be the actual producer of the wine, however.

Labels on wines that are made outside the U.S. but sold within the U.S. must also carry the phrase *imported by* as well as the name and business location of the importer.

Canadian regulations are similar. Those regulations require wine labels to indicate the *common name* of the product (that is, *wine*), the net contents, the percentage of alcohol by volume, the name and address of the producer, the wine's country of origin (although only 75 percent of the grapes or wine must come from that country), and the container size. Many of these items must be indicated in both English and French.

The European mandate

Some of the mandatory information on American and Canadian wine labels is also required by the European Union's wine authorities to appear on labels of wines produced or sold in the EU. But additional label items are prescribed by the EU for wines produced in its member countries.

The most important of these additional items is an indication of a wine's so-called quality level — which really means the wine's status in the EU's hierarchy of place-names. In short, every wine made in an EU member country *must* carry one of the following items on the label:

- A registered place-name, along with an official phrase that confirms that the name is in fact a registered place-name
- A phrase indicating that the wine is a *table wine,* a status lower than a registered place-name

Remember, for U.S. wines, the *table wine* category encompasses all non-sparkling wines that contain up to 14 percent alcohol. This is a distinctly different use of the term *table wine.*

Appellations of origin

A registered place-name is called an *appellation of origin.* In fact, each EU place-name defines far more than just the name of the place that the grapes come from: The place-name connotes the wine's grape varieties, grape-growing methods, and winemaking methods. Each appellation is, therefore, a definition of the wine as well as the wine's name. European governments regulate their wine appellations in various ways to determine that wines carrying registered place-names conform to the legal definitions of those names.

The phrases on certain European labels that confirm that a wine has a registered place-name include the following:

- ✔ **France:** *Appellation Contrôlée or Appellation d'Origine Contrôlée* (AC or AOC, in short), translated as *regulated name* or *regulated place-name.* Also, on labels of wines from places of slightly lower status, the initials AO VDQS, standing for *Appellation d'Origine — Vins Délimités de Qualité Supérieure*; translated as *place-name, demarcated wine of superior quality.*

- ✔ **Italy:** *Denominazione d'Origine Controllata* (DOC), translated as *regulated place-name;* or for certain wines of an even higher status, *Denominazione d'Origine Controllata e Garantita* (DOCG), translated as *regulated and guaranteed place-name.*

- ✔ **Spain:** *Denominación de Origen* (DO), translated as *place-name*; and *Denominación de Origen Calificada* (DOCa), translated as *qualified-origin place-name* for regions with the highest status (of which there is only one, Rioja).

- ✔ **Portugal:** *Denominação de Origem Controlada* (DOC), translated as *regulated place-name* for the major place-names; and *Indicação de Proveniencia Regulamentada* (IPR), translated as *regulated place indication* for other registered place-names.

- ✔ **Germany:** *Qualitätswein bestimmter Anbaugebiete* (QbA), translated as *quality wine from a specific region;* or *Qualitätswein mit Prädikat* (QmP), translated as *quality wine with special attributes,* for the best wines. (Read more about Germany's complex appellation system in Chapter 11.)

Table 8-1 lists the European wine designations for easy reference.

Table 8-1	European Wine Designations at a Glance		
Country	*QWPSR Designation(s)*	*Table Wine Designation with Geographic Indication*	*Table Wine Designation without Geographic Indication*
France	AOC	Vin de pays	Vin de table
	VDQS		
Italy	DOCG	Vino da tavola	Vino da tavola
	DOC	(and geographic name)	
Spain	DOCa	Vino de la tierra	Vino de mesa
	DO		
Portugal	DO	Vinho de mesa regional	Vinho de mesa
	IPR		
Germany	QmP	Landwein	Deutscher tafelwein
	QbA		

Phrases on European labels that indicate that a wine is a table wine include

- **France:** *Vin de pays (country wine)*

- **Spain:** *Vino de la tierra (country wine)*

- **Italy:** *Vino da tavola (table wine),* usually followed by a region name as in Vino da tavola di Toscana

- **Germany**: *Landwein (country wine)*

- **Portugal**: *Vinho de mesa regional (country wine)*

Figure 8-2 shows a European wine label, as it would appear in the U.S..

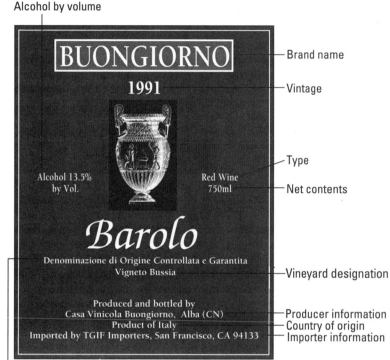

Alcohol by volume

BUONGIORNO —— Brand name

1991 —— Vintage

Type

Alcohol 13.5%
by Vol.

Red Wine
750ml

Net contents

Barolo

Denominazione di Origine Controllata e Garantita
Vigneto Bussia

—— Vineyard designation

Produced and bottled by
Casa Vinicola Buongiorno, Alba (CN) —— Producer information
Product of Italy —— Country of origin
Imported by TGIF Importers, San Francisco, CA 94133 —— Importer information

QWPSR category

Figure 8-2:
The label of
a European
wine.

There is no U.S. counterpart to all of these foreign place-name phrases. Registered place-names in America are called *American Viticultural Areas* (AVAs). But the phrase does *not* appear on wine labels. Nor does any such phrase appear on labels of Australian or South American wines.

The optional information

All sorts of other words can appear on wine labels. These words can be meaningless phrases designed to make you think that you're getting a special quality wine, or words that provide useful information about what's in the bottle. Sometimes the same word can fall into either category, depending on the label. This ambiguity occurs because some words that are strictly regulated in some producing countries are not at all regulated in others.

TECHNICAL STUFF

The EU hierarchy of wine

Although each country within the European Union makes its own laws regarding the naming of wine, these laws must fit within the framework of the larger European Union law. This framework provides two levels into which all EU-produced wines must fit:

✔ **Quality wine:** Wines with appellations of origin that are defined and regulated by the European country where the wine is produced. (Each appellation law defines the geographic area, the grapes that may be used, grape-growing practices, winemaking and aging techniques, and so on.) This category is abbreviated as **QWPSR** in English (Quality Wine Produced in a Specific Region) or VQPRD in several other European languages. All AOC, DOC, DO, and QbA wines — to use the abbreviations men-

tioned previously in this chapter — fall into this category.

✔ **Table wine:** All other wines produced within the EU. If a table wine carries a precise geographic indication on its label, such as French *vin de pays* or Spanish *vino de la tierra* wines do, it enjoys a higher privilege than table wines with no geographic indication except the country of origin (for example, it may carry a vintage or a grape name).

All other wines sold in the EU fall into a third category:

✔ **Wine:** Wines produced by countries outside the EU, such as the U.S., Canada, or Australia. If a wine has a geographic indication smaller than the country of origin, it enjoys higher status than otherwise.

Vintage

The word *vintage* followed by a year, or the year listed alone without the word *vintage,* is the most common optional item on a wine label (refer to Figure 8-2). Sometimes the vintage appears on the front label, and sometimes it has its own small label above the front label.

TIP

The *vintage year* is nothing more than the year in which the grapes for a particular wine were harvested. But there is an aura surrounding vintage-dated wine that causes many people to believe that any wine with a vintage date is by definition better than a wine without a vintage date. *In fact, there is no correlation between the presence of a vintage date and the wine's quality.* (Because a vintage date is *perceived* as an indication of quality by consumers, however, the EU denies simple table wines the privilege of listing a vintage date.)

Most of the wines you'll find in wine shops, supermarkets, and restaurants are *vintage wines* in the sense that 95 percent or more of that wine came from grapes harvested in a single year — the official U.S. definition for a vintage wine. (*Non-vintage* wines are blends of wines whose grapes were harvested in different years.) Most wines are also *vintage-dated wines* — they state the year on the bottle — because vintage-dated wines sell better (thanks to that aura).

Vintage wines can vary in style and quality from one vintage to the next because the weather (which affects the grapes) is different every year (naturally). But generally speaking, *what* vintage a wine is — that is, whether the grapes grew in a year with perfect weather or whether the grapes were meteorologically challenged — is an issue you need to consider a) only when you buy top quality wines, and b) mainly when those wines come from parts of the world that experience significant variations in weather from year to year — in a nutshell, Europe. Vintage variation does exist in California and Australia, but the swing in quality from year to year is less dramatic than for most European wines. In the case of less expensive wines — those that sell for up to about $10 a bottle retail — differences from year to year are usually insignificant.

Reserve

Reserve is our favorite meaningless word on American wine labels. The term is used to convince you that the wine inside the bottle is something special. This trick usually works because the word *does* have specific meaning and *does* carry a certain amount of prestige on labels of wines from many other countries. So *reserve* carries positive connotations when it appears on U.S. wines, even when it means nothing.

In Italy and Spain, for example, the word *reserve* (or its foreign language equivalent, which always looks something like *reserve*) indicates a wine that has received extra aging at the winery before release. Implicit in the extra aging is the idea that the wine was better than normal and, therefore, worthy of the extra aging. So a Chianti Classico Riserva is considered a better and more expensive wine than the same producer's basic Chianti Classico. A Rioja Gran Reserva (Spain even has *degrees* of reserve) is better than the same producer's Rioja Reserva, which is better than that producer's regular Rioja. You get the picture.

Why not vintage?

There are really just two situations in which producers might be inclined to blend wines from two or more years and create a non-vintage wine. If a winery is situated in a climatic zone where full ripeness of the grapes is a best-case scenario rather than the norm (parts of Germany, for example, or Champagne, which are both cool, northerly areas), the producer might choose to hold back wine from one year to blend in with the next year's wine in case he has a poor crop the next year. The decision is as much financial as qualitative: He needs to guarantee that he will have a product to sell the next year.

The second reason for creating a non-vintage blend is price. When a winery purchases wine on the bulk market (as large wineries do, to supplement their own production), it has more opportunity to lower its costs if it does not limit its bulk purchases to wine from a specific vintage.

In some other countries, like France, the use of *reserve* is not regulated. However, its use is generally consistent with the notion that the wine is better in quality than a given producer's norm.

Historically, the word *reserve* has been used in that sense in the U.S., too — as in Beaulieu Vineyards Georges de Latour Private Reserve, the best Cabernet that Beaulieu Vineyards makes. But in the past ten years or so, the word has been bandied about until it no longer has meaning. There are California wines labeled *Proprietor's Reserve* that sell for about $4 a bottle. Those wines are not only the *least* expensive wines in a particular producer's lineup, but also some of the least expensive wines, period. There are Special Reserve wines, Vintage Reserve wines, Vintner's Reserve wines, and Reserve Selection wines — all utterly meaningless phrases.

Estate-bottled

Estate is a genteel word for a wine farm, a combined grape-growing and wine-making operation. The words *estate-bottled* on a wine label indicate that the company that bottled the wine also grew the grapes and made the wine. In other words, *estate-bottled* suggests accountability from the vineyard to the winemaking through to the bottling. The winery does not necessarily have to own the vineyards, but it has to control the vineyards and perform the vineyard operations.

Estate-bottling is an important concept to those of us who believe that you can't make good wine unless the grapes are as good as they can possibly be. If *we* made wine, we'd sure want to control our own vineyards.

We wouldn't go so far as to say that great wines *must* be estate-bottled, though. Ravenswood Winery — to name just one example — makes some terrific wines from the grapes of small vineyards owned and operated by private landowners. And there are some large California landowners, such as the Sangiacomo brothers, who are quite serious about their vineyards but do not make wine themselves (they sell their grapes to various wineries). None of those wines would be considered estate-bottled.

Sometimes French wine labels carry the words *domaine-bottled* or *château-bottled* (or the phrase *mis en bouteille au château/au domaine*). The concept is the same as estate-bottled, with *domaine* and *château* being equivalent to the American term *estate*.

There's only one loophole in the use of the phrase *estate-bottled*. *Cooperative wineries* (large operations in which hundreds of grape growers turn their grapes over to a central winery that vinifies the juice) can claim that their wines are estate-bottled because the grape growers are members of the cooperative — that is, owners of the winery. In Europe, where some huge co-op wineries turn out millions of cases of wine a year, this interpretation seems to stretch the concept of estate-bottled a bit too far.

Vineyard name

Wines in the medium-to-expensive price category — those that cost about $12 or more — might carry on the label the name of the specific *vineyard* that grew the grapes for that wine. Sometimes one winery will make two or three different wines that are distinguishable only by the vineyard name on the label. Each wine is unique because the *terroir* of each vineyard is unique. (For an explanation of *terroir*, see Chapter 7.)

These single vineyards may or may not be identified by the word *vineyard* next to the name of the vineyard.

Italian wines, which are really into the single-vineyard game, will have *vigneto* or *vigna* or sometimes the French word *cru* on their labels next to the name of the single vineyard. Or they won't. It's optional.

Just reading the pictures

A young American friend of ours lived in France for many years, and upon his return to the States, he developed one of the most unusual systems for decoding French wine labels that we've ever heard of.

Although his budget in France had unfortunately precluded tasting and learning much of anything about fine wine, he found himself beseiged by friends and acquaintances demanding a full explanation ("at last!") of French wine labels. Not wanting to disappoint them, he realized that as long as he said something in the proper tone people would believe anything he said — at least for a while. After all, this was always in a fun context, and wine was nearby. So he made up the following theory:

✔ First and foremost, note the presence or absence of colored ink: Red ink indicates better wine than just black ink; gold ink means it's a top quality wine. Red and gold together, embossed, well, that wine is beyond tops.

✔ Next, examine the illustration (lack of illustration means lack of quality, no doubt!). An image of just the gates to a chateau indicates only moderate wine, whereas an etching showing a full-blown chateau indicates the best wine. Overwrought gates with a chateau in the background indicate an overly proud winemaker, and that wine is to be avoided.

✔ Finally, a delicate, frilly typeface and not one but two or even three borders are a sign of the best wines.

Of course, by the middle of this labored and fantastic theory, presented with elaborate gestures and emphasis, his tablemates had usually caught on and started grinning. After a good chuckle at the revelation of his joke, serious drinking would begin and taste alone would rule. Any worry about interpreting labels was forgotten by the second glass.

Other optional words on the label

You'll be pleased to know that we have just about exhausted our list of terms that you might find on a wine label (not to mention exhausting ourselves — and probably you — in the process).

One additional expression on some French labels is *Vieilles Vignes,* which translates as *old vines.* Because old vines produce a very small quantity of fruit compared to younger vines, the quality of their grapes and of the resulting wine is considered to be very good. The problem is, the phrase is unregulated. Anyone can claim that his vines are old.

The word *superior* can appear in French *(Supérieure)* or Italian *(Superiore)* as part of an AOC or DOC place-name (refer to the section, "The mandatory information," earlier in this chapter for a refresher on these acronyms). It means the wine attained a higher alcohol level than the nonsuperior version of the same wine. Frankly, it's a distinction not worth losing sleep over.

The word *Classico* appears on the labels of some Italian DOC and DOCG wines when the grapes come from the heartland of the named place.

Foreign-Language Label Terms

The following words or phrases could appear on bottles of French, German, Italian, Spanish, or Portuguese wines. (For wines sold in the U.S., much of this information is actually translated into English.)

> ✔ **French Labels**
>
> *Clos* — walled vineyard
>
> *Cru* — growth, usually a good vineyard
>
> *Grand vin de* — unregulated phrase meaning *great wine of*
>
> *Mis en bouteille au château* — estate-bottled
>
> *Mis en bouteille au domaine* — estate-bottled
>
> *Négociant* — company that makes wine by purchasing grapes or wine, blending, and bottling
>
> *Propriétaire* — owner
>
> *Récolte* — vintage or harvest
>
> *Vendange* — vintage or harvest

Vieilles Vignes — old vines (an unregulated phrase suggesting quality)

Vignoble — vineyard

Vin — wine

> ✔ **German Labels**

Amtliche Prüfungsnummer (abbreviated as AP number, or similarly) — refers to a mandatory quality-control test

Erzeugerabfüllung — estate-bottled

Halbtrocken — medium-dry

Trocken — dry

Wein — wine

Winzergenossenschaft — co-operative winery

(See "Germany's wine laws: Ripeness is king" in Chapter 11 for an explanation of the words *Kabinett, Spätlese, Auslese, Beerenauslese,* and *Trockenbeerenauslese.*)

> ✔ **Italian Labels**

Annata — vintage

Azienda agricola/vinicola/vitivinicola — refers to the producer

Casa vinicola/vitivinicola — refers to the producer

Cantina sociale — co-operative winery

Consorzio — trade association of producers

Fattoria — estate

Imbottigliato all'origine — estate-bottled

Produttore — producer

Tenuta — estate

Vendemmia — vintage

Vigna or *Vigneto* — vineyard

Vino — wine

Vitigno — grape variety

✔ **Spanish Labels**

    Bodega — winery

    Elaborado — produced by

    Embotellado — bottled by

    Tinto — red

    Vendimia — vintage

    Viña — vineyard

    Vino — wine

✔ **Portuguese Labels**

    Adega — winery

    Adega cooperativa — co-operative winery

    Colheita — vintage

    Quinta — estate or vineyard

    Tinto — red

    Vinho — wine

Chapter 9

Pinot Envy and Other Secrets about Grapes

● ●

In This Chapter

▶ Genus, species, variety, clone

▶ Soils that grapes love

▶ Endangered species and mixed marriages

▶ Major grape varieties and their styles

● ●

*W*ouldn't it be a pity if a mad scientist were to invent a way to make wine without using actual grapes? We'd hate to see grapes eliminated from the process, because grapes are one of the most fascinating things about wine.

Land covered with row upon row of grapevines is a stirring sight to wine drinkers. The tending of the vines and the harvesting of the grapes hold ritualistic meaning for farmers all over the world who grow grapes and for the winemakers who transform those grapes into wine. Grapes are the link — literally and emotionally — between the land and the wine.

Grapes also give us one of the easiest ways of classifying wine and making sense of the hundreds of different types of wine that exist.

It's the Grape Whodunit

If anyone were to invent a mystery game about wine, it would probably be a big flop because there's no real mystery in knowing what makes most wines taste the way they do. The grapes done it. With Mother Nature and a winemaker as accomplices, the grapes are responsible for the style and personality and, sometimes, the quality of every wine, because they are the starting point of the wine. (Sure, a winemaker can do things to make the grapes unrecognizable in the final wine — like over-oaking the wine or letting it oxidize — but the grapes dictate the genetic structure of the wine and how it will respond to everything that is done to it.)

Think back to the last wine you drank. What color was it? If it was white, the odds are that's because it came from white grapes; if it was pink or red, that's because the wine came from red grapes.

Did it smell herbal or earthy or fruity? Whichever; those aromas came from the grapes. Was it firm and tannic or soft and voluptuous? Thank the grapes (with a nod to their two co-conspirators, Mother Nature and the winemaker).

The specific grape variety (or varieties) that makes any given wine is largely responsible for the sensory characteristics the wine offers — from its appearance to its aromas, its flavors, and its alcohol-tannin-acid profile.

Of genus and species

By *grape variety,* we mean the fruit of a specific type of grapevine: the fruit of the Cabernet Sauvignon vine, for example, or the fruit of the Chardonnay vine.

The term *variety* actually has specific meaning in scientific circles. A variety is a subdivision of a species. Most of the world's wines are made from grape varieties that belong to the species *vinifera* — a subdivision of the genus *Vitis*. This species originated in Europe and western Asia; other distinct species of *Vitis* are native to North America.

Some wine *is* made from grapes of other species; for example, the Concord grape, which makes Concord wine as well as grape juice and jelly, belongs to the native American species *Vitis labrusca.* But the grapes of this species have a markedly different flavor from vinifera grapes — *foxy* is the word used to describe that taste. The number of non-vinifera wines is small because their flavor is unpopular in wine. In juice or jelly, the grapes do fine; just ask Welch's!

If endangered species lists had existed at the end of the 19th century, *Vitis vinifera* would certainly have been on them. The entire species was nearly eradicated by a tiny louse called *phylloxera* that emigrated to Europe from America and proceeded to feast on the roots of vinifera grapevines, wiping out vineyards across the continent.

To this day, no remedy has been found to protect vinifera roots from phylloxera. What saved the species was grafting vinifera vines onto rootstocks of native American species that are resistant to the bug. The practice of grafting the fruit-bearing part of *Vitis vinifera* onto the rooting part of other, phylloxera-resistant species continues today everywhere in the world where phylloxera is present and fine wine is made. (The fruit-bearing part is called a *scion*, and the rooting plant is called a *rootstock*.) Somehow, each grape variety maintains its own character despite the fact that its roots are alien.

Mixed marriages

A few grape varieties that are used to make wine are not really *Vitis vinifera* but are *hybrids* — grape varieties that have been bred by man from parent plants of two different species, usually a vinifera and an American species. (They are bred by cross-pollinating two different varieties and planting the seeds that result — a process distinctly different from grafting.)

When the phylloxera devastation hit Europe, one of the earlier solutions the French tried was cross-breeding their vines with American vines in order to develop totally new grape varieties that (they hoped) would have flavors similar to vinifera grapes but would be (they hoped) phylloxera-resistant. These came to be called *French-American* hybrids.

The most successful of these hybrids is Seyval Blanc, which grows in England, Canada, and the eastern U.S. As it turns out, Seyval Blanc is one of the few French-American hybrids whose flavors show no trace of foxiness, and it also endures well in cool climates. Some other hybrids that are used for wine production include Vidal, Vignoles and Aurore, Baco Noir, Maréchal Foch, and De Chaunac.

Hybrid grapes are considered ignoble by the wine establishment, and they cannot be used to make wine in European Union member countries. (England has been an exception because of the "experimental" status of her wine industry, but this is subject to change.)

Vine varieties that have been cross-bred between *two vinifera parents* are usually referred to as *crossings*, not hybrids. The Pinotage grape — grown in South Africa — is a famous example. It is a crossing of the Pinot Noir and the Cinsault grapes, both *Vitis vinifera*.

A variety of varieties

Snowflakes and fingerprints aren't the only examples of Nature's infinite variety. Within the genus Vitis and the species vinifera, there are as many as 10,000 varieties of wine grapes. If wine from every one of these varieties were commercially available and you drank the wine of a different variety every single day, it would take you more than 27 years to experience them all!

Not that you would want to. Within those 10,000 varieties there are grapes that have the ability to make extraordinary wine, grapes that tend to make very ordinary wine, and grapes that only a parent could love. Most of the 10,000 varieties are obscure grapes whose wines rarely enter into international commerce.

An *extremely* adventuresome wine nut who has plenty of free time to explore the back roads of Spain, Portugal, Italy, and Greece might be able to encounter 1,500 different grape varieties (only four years' worth of drinking) in his lifetime. The grape varieties you might encounter in the course of your normal wine enjoyment would number fewer than 50.

How the Grape Done It

All sorts of attributes distinguish each of those 50 grape varieties from the next. These attributes fall into two categories: personality traits and performance factors. *Personality traits* are the characteristics of the fruit itself — its flavor, for example. *Performance factors* refer to how the grapevine grows, how its fruit ripens, and how quickly it can get from 0 to 60 miles per hour.

Both the personality traits of a specific grape variety and its performance factors affect the ultimate taste and style of the wines that are made from that grape.

Personality traits of grape varieties

Skin color is the most fundamental distinction among grape varieties. Every grape variety is considered either a white variety or a red (black) one, according to the color of its skins when the grapes are ripe. (A handful of red-skinned varieties are further distinguished by having red pulp rather than white pulp.)

Individual grape varieties can also be distinguished by their aromatic compounds. Some grapes (like Muscat) contribute floral aromas and flavors to their wine, for example, while other grapes contribute herbaceous aromas and flavors (like Sauvignon Blanc). Some grapes have very neutral aromas and flavors and, therefore, make fairly neutral wines. (The Trebbiano grape that is used for lots of Italian white wines is an example.)

Acidity levels differ from variety to variety: Some grapes are naturally disposed to higher acid levels at harvest time than others, which naturally influences the wine made from those grapes.

Thickness of the grapeskins and the size of the individual ripe grapes (called *berries*) are other important distinguishing traits. Grapes with thick skins naturally have more tannin than grapes with thin skins; ditto for small-berried varieties compared to large-berried varieties.

The skins of the grapes, the grape *pips* (or seeds), and the stems all contain *tannin*, that somewhat-bitter-tasting substance that is important to the style of red wines. Generally, the stems are eliminated before fermentation, so their tannin doesn't count. White wines are usually made only from the juice, without the skins or seeds, so tannin is less of an issue. But during red wine fermentation, the skins and the seeds both soak in the grape juice and contribute their tannins to the wine. Tannins are a mixed bag: some of them are beneficial to the wine, giving the wine firmness and character, and some of them are not, loading the wine with pungent and overly bitter flavors. It's up to the winemaker to figure out how to get the good tannins into the wine without the bad ones. Assuming that the winemaking is equal, grape varieties that have thick skins or small berries (and therefore a greater skin-to-juice ratio) will make a more tannic wine.

The composite personality traits of each grape variety are fairly evident in the wines that are made from that grape. A Cabernet Sauvignon wine is almost always more tannic and slightly lower in alcohol than a Merlot wine, for example, because that's the nature of those two grapes.

Performance factors of grape varieties

The performance factors that distinguish grape varieties are vitally important to the grape grower because those factors determine how easy — or how challenging — it will be for him to cultivate a specific grape variety in his vineyard. But performance factors also affect the flavor and style of the wines made from each grape variety, according to the specific location where the grape variety grows.

Every grape variety has a predictable length-of-ripening period, for example. If a grape variety with a long ripening period is grown in a region where summers are short and cool, the grapes won't ripen sufficiently, and the wine made from them could taste tart and *vegetal* (like green vegetables). If a grape variety that ripens quickly is grown in a very warm climate, it could ripen so fast that the wine made from it tastes overly ripe (like mushy fruit) and is very high in alcohol.

Worst-case ripening scenarios

Just like any other fruit, grapes are hard when they first form and are very high in acid. As they ripen, they gradually lose acidity and take on sugar, through photosynthesis and other normal vine metabolism processes. They also gain color and swell to their proper size, and their aromatic (and flavor) elements develop.

If grapes do not ripen sufficiently for some reason — a particular variety was planted in the wrong climate, or the weather was very cool in a particular year, or a greedy grape grower tried to grow more fruit than his land could bear — the berries will be higher in acid and lower in sugar than they should be, and their flavors will be underdeveloped. The wine made from such grapes will be low in alcohol (due to insufficient sugar in the grapes) and very high in acid (due to high acidity levels in the grapes), with under-ripe flavors. (Ever bite into a pear you pulled from the tree before it was ripe?)

If circumstances are such that the grapes get too ripe, the reverse occurs: high-alcohol, low-acid wines that feel flabby in your mouth and taste like fruit that you wish you had eaten a week sooner.

Some grape varieties have very dense, compact bunches of fruit. Grow a variety like that in a warm, damp climate, and you'd better be prepared to spend the whole summer fighting off the mildew that wants to grow within the grape clusters. If the grapes manage to get slightly moldy despite your best efforts, they'll give a dusty, moldy taste to the wine.

Some grape varieties have a natural tendency to grow more leaves and shoots than others. This vegetation can shade the fruit and prevent the grapes from ripening completely, giving under-ripe flavors to the wine. If that grape variety is naturally high in acid, the wine will taste doubly tart.

The reasons some grape varieties perform brilliantly in certain places are so complex that winemakers haven't figured them all out yet. The amount of heat and cold, the amount of wind and rain (or lack of it), and the slant of the sun's rays on the hillside of vines are among the factors affecting the vine's performance. But remember that no two vineyards in the world have precisely the same combination of these factors — precisely the same *terroir* (see Chapter 7). The issue simply defies simple generalizations.

"Chardonnay, do you take this limestone soil?"

One of the elements of terroir that certainly is a factor in how well a grape variety performs is the soil in which the grapevine grows. Some classic grape/soil compatibilities have become evident over the centuries: Chardonnay in limestone or chalk, Cabernet Sauvignon in gravelly soil, Pinot Noir in limestone, and Riesling in slatey soil. At any rate, these are the soils of the regions where these grape varieties perform at their legendary best.

Soil affects a grapevine in several ways (besides simply anchoring the vine): it is a nutrition-carrying medium for the grapevine; it can influence the temperature of the vineyard to the extent that the soil may or may not retain heat;

and it provides a water-management system for the plant. Of these three tasks, providing a water-management system is considered the most important, and influencing the temperature of the vineyard is considered the least important.

A safe generalization is that the best soils are those that have good drainage and are not particularly fertile. (An extreme example is the soil — if we can call it that — of the Châteauneuf-du-Pape district in France's Rhône Valley: it's just stones.) The wisdom of the ages decrees that the grapevine must struggle to produce the best grapes — and well-drained, less fertile soils challenge the vine to struggle, regardless of what specific variety the grapevine is.

Like grape, like wine

There are things a winemaker can do to correct deficiencies or excesses in his grapes — to an extent.

He can add acid to the juice if the grapes are too ripe, for example, or add sugar to the juice to simulate a level of ripeness that Mother Nature denied that year. (That added sugar will be fermented into alcohol.) If he decides to put his juice or his wine into oak barrels, he could create oaky aromas and flavors in the wine that are beyond what the grapes brought to the wine.

But for the most part, what the grapes give is what the wine is. The personality traits of each grape variety, tempered by its performance wherever it's grown, more or less define the nature of each wine.

An embarrassment of riches

If you consider the number of *Vitis vinifera* grape varieties there are — even limiting the discussion to those varieties whose wines are commercially available — and then you factor in all the different places where each grape is grown, it becomes clear why there are so many different wines in the world.

It also becomes clear that — although wines made from the same grape variety share certain family resemblances — *the grape variety alone* is not a completely reliable indication of what a wine will taste like. The wine will also reflect the grape's performance according to where it grew — and anything the winemaker might have done to change what the grapes brought to the wine. But the grape variety is the fundamental unit.

Royalty and Commoners in the Grape Kingdom

Bees have their queens, wolves have their alpha males, gorillas have their silverbacks, and humans have their royal families. In the grape kingdom, there are nobles, too — at least as interpreted by the human beings who drink the wine made from those grapes.

Noble grape varieties (as they are referred to colloquially by wine people) have the potential to make great — not just good — wine. Every noble grape variety can claim at least one wine region where it is the undisputed king. The wines made from noble grapes on their home turf can be so great that winemakers in far-flung regions are inspired to grow the same grape in their own vineyards. The noble grape might prove itself noble there, too — but frequently the grape does not. Adaptability is not necessarily a prerequisite of nobility.

The classic examples of noble grape varieties at their best are

- The Chardonnay grape and the Pinot Noir grape in Burgundy, France
- The Cabernet Sauvignon grape in Bordeaux, France
- The Syrah grape in France's Northern Rhône Valley
- The Chenin Blanc grape in France's Loire Valley
- The Nebbiolo grape in Piedmont, Italy
- The Sangiovese grape in Tuscany, Italy
- The Riesling grape in the Mosel and Rheingau regions of Germany

Cloning the perfect grapevine

If you hang around wine people long enough, you're sure to hear them talk about *clones* or *clonal selection* of grape varieties. Has the Brave New World of grape growing arrived?

In botanical terms, a *clone* is a subdivision of a variety. Remember all those things we said about how every grape variety is different from the next? Well, the individuality doesn't end with the grape variety. Even within a single variety, such as Chardonnay, there can be differences from one plant to the next. Some vines may ripen their fruit slightly more quickly or produce grapes with slightly different aromas and flavors than the next vine.

Grapevines are usually propagated asexually by taking cuttings from a *mother plant* and allowing those cuttings to root (until the plant is mature enough to be grafted onto phylloxera-resistant roots). Of course, the new plants are genetically identical to the mother plant. Naturally, grape growers usually choose the most ideal plants (in terms of ripening, fruit flavor, disease resistance, heartiness — or whatever it is they're looking for) to use as the mother plants. Voilá! They have made a clonal selection.

Actually, much of the clonal selection these days takes place in universities and other research institutions where the mother vines are checked for viruses before they are propagated. Commercial nurseries obtain mother plants from these institutions, and grape growers purchase their grapevines from the nurseries, specifying which particular clones they want.

Fortunately for most of us, human parents don't have the same options!

A Primer on the Major Grape Varieties

Once upon a time, putting grape names on wine labels was not as common as today — and only real wine nerds cared about the specific characteristics of various grape varieties. But today there are so many varietal wines that the grapes and the wines have become synonymous — and the difference between Cabernet Sauvignon and Merlot has become meaningful to wine drinkers.

 European wines are generally named for their place of production rather than for their grape — but knowing something about the grape variety (such as Chardonnay) can still help you understand the wine (such as white Burgundy). See Chapter 7 for a chart of European wines and their respective grapes.

Here are descriptions of the most important vinifera varieties today — 12 white and 12 red grapes. In describing the grapes, naturally we describe the type(s) of wine that are made from each grape. You'll encounter these wines in various guises: as varietal wines, or as place-name wines that don't mention the grape variety anywhere on the label. You'll also encounter these grapes as blending partners for other grapes — sometimes public partners, sometimes secret cohorts.

White grape varieties

The differences among white grape varieties are mainly in their acidity levels and aromas, or flavors. Turn back to Chapter 2 for a quick review of some of the descriptors we use in this section.

Chardonnay

Today's darling white grape, Chardonnay is a shoo-in for Miss Congeniality. But despite its populist appeal, Chardonnay is actually quite a regal grape — producing the greatest dry white wines in the world, white Burgundies. Chardonnay is also one of the main grapes of champagne.

The Chardonnay grape is planted in practically every wine-producing country of the world. This white grape is universal for two reasons: the variety is relatively adaptable to a wide range of climates, and the name *Chardonnay* on a wine label is, these days, a sure-fire sales tool.

Because Chardonnay juice and Chardonnay wine are very compatible with oak barrels — and because white Burgundy (the great prototype) is generally an oaked wine, and because wine drinkers generally love the flavor of oak — most Chardonnay wine has received some oak treatment either during or after fermentation. (For the best Chardonnays, oak treatment means expensive barrels of French oak; but for lower-priced Chardonnays it could mean soaking oak chips in the wine or even adding liquid essence of oak. See Chapter 3 for more on oak.) In fact, outside of northern Italy and France's Chablis and Mâconnais districts, it's hard to find a Chardonnay wine today whose flavor has not been influenced by oak.

Oaked Chardonnay is so common that some wine drinkers confuse the flavor of oak with the flavor of Chardonnay. If your glass of Chardonnay smells or tastes toasty, smoky, nutty, spicy, or vanilla-like, that's the oak you're perceiving, not the Chardonnay!

Chardonnay itself has fruity aromas and flavors that range from apple — in cooler wine regions — to tropical fruits, especially pineapple, in warmer regions. Chardonnay also can display earthy aromas, such as mushroom or mineral accents. Chardonnay wine has medium to high acidity. It can be fairly rich or medium-bodied, depending on where the grapes were grown and how the wine was made.

Classically, Chardonnay wines are dry. But there are a lot of Chardonnays coming out of California these days that are off-dry — especially, but not exclusively, at the lower-price end.

Chardonnay is a grape that can stand on its own in a wine, and the top Chardonnay-based wines (except for Champagne and similar bubblies) are 100 percent Chardonnay. But less expensive wines that are labeled *Chardonnay* — those selling for less than six dollars a bottle in the U.S., for example — are likely to have some other, far less distinguished grape blended in. That's because blending in wine from an ordinary grape like Colombard helps reduce the cost of making the wine. Anyway, it's perfectly legal. And who can even tell if it's all Chardonnay or not, behind all that oak?

Sauvignon Blanc

While just about everybody likes Chardonnay, Sauvignon Blanc is controversial with wine drinkers. That's because it has such distinctive character.

For one thing, Sauvignon Blanc is high in acidity — great if you like crisp wines, but not so great otherwise. For another thing, its aromas and flavors can be *herbaceous* (suggestive of herbs or grass) — delicious and intriguing to some wine lovers, but too pronounced for others.

Sauvignon Blanc wines are light-bodied to medium-bodied and usually dry. European examples are unoaked more often than oaked, but in California they are often oaky and not fully dry — in the Chardonnay-wanna-be style.

Besides herbaceous character (sometimes referred to as *grassy*), Sauvignon Blanc displays mineral aromas and flavors, vegetal character, or — in warmer climates — fruity character, such as ripe melon.

There are two classic wine regions for the Sauvignon Blanc grape in France: Bordeaux and the Loire Valley; the Bordeaux wine is called Bordeaux Blanc, and the Loire wines are called Sancerre or Pouilly-Fumé (both described in Chapter 10). In Bordeaux, Sauvignon Blanc is sometimes blended with a grape called Sémillon (described in Table 9-1); some of the wines that are blended 50-50 from the two grapes are so great that we include them among our Investment Wine candidates listed in Chapter 15. Sauvignon Blanc is also important in regions like California, northeastern Italy, and New Zealand.

Riesling

The great Riesling wines of Germany have put this grape on the map as an undisputedly noble variety. But Riesling shows its real class only in a few places outside of Germany. The Alsace region of France, the Finger Lakes district of New York, and Washington are among the few.

Riesling wines are as unpopular today as Chardonnay is popular. Maybe that's because Riesling is the antithesis of Chardonnay. While Chardonnay is usually gussied up with oak, Riesling never is; while Chardonnay may be full-bodied and rich, Riesling is more often light-bodied and refreshing. Riesling's fresh, vivid personality can make many Chardonnays taste clumsy in comparison.

The common perception of Riesling wines is that they are sweet, and many of them are — but plenty of them aren't. Alsace Rieslings are normally dry, many German Rieslings are dry, and there are quite a few dry Rieslings from America. (Riesling can be vinified either way, according to the style of wine a producer wants to make.) Look for the word *trocken* (meaning dry) on German Riesling labels and the word *dry* on American labels if you prefer the dry style of Riesling.

High acidity, low to medium alcohol levels, and aromas/flavors that range from ebulliently fruity to flowery to minerally are the trademarks of Riesling wines.

From Germany alone, you can find several different styles of Riesling wines, each varying in dryness level and in its aromas and flavors. Some of the greatest dessert wines of all are Rieslings (mainly from Germany) made with overripe grapes that have shriveled on the vine (read "What's noble about rot?" in Chapter 11) — rich, thick wines with flavors of apricots.

Riesling wines are sometimes labeled as *White Riesling* or *Johannisberg Riesling* — both synonyms for the noble Riesling grape. With wines from Eastern European countries, though, read the fine print: Olazrizling, Laskirizling, and Welschriesling are from another grape altogether.

If you consider yourself a maverick who hates to follow trends, check out the Riesling section of your wine shop instead of the Chardonnay aisle.

Going organic

Although just about everyone wants to support the health of the planet, buying organic is easier said than done when it comes to wine. Wine can be considered organic in various ways: It could be made from organically grown grapes, for example, or the winemaking itself could be organic in the sense that chemicals are not used. But is sulfur dioxide — a derivative of elemental sulfur and oxygen — a chemical? Some organizations that accredit organic products permit the use of SO_2 in winemaking (see Chapter 1 for more on sulfur dioxide), while others do not. Until everyone agrees on a definition, *organic wine* is a moving target.

Pinot Gris/Pinot Grigio

The Pinot Gris grape is one of several grape varieties called *Pinot:* there's Pinot Blanc (white Pinot), Pinot Noir (black Pinot), Pinot Meunier (we don't know how that one translates), and Pinot Gris (gray Pinot). Until about ten years ago, some people included Chardonnay in this group, calling it Pinot Chardonnay, but now we know that Chardonnay is no relation to the others.

Pinot Gris is believed to have mutated from the black Pinot Noir grape. Although it's considered a white grape, its skin color is unusually dark for a white variety.

Wines made from Pinot Gris can be deeper in color than most white wines — although Italy's Pinot Grigio wines are quite pale. Pinot Gris wines are medium- to full-bodied, with rather low acidity and fairly neutral aromas. Sometimes the flavor and aroma can suggest the skins of fruit, such as peach skins or orange rind.

Pinot Gris is an important grape throughout northeastern Italy and is also present in Germany, where it is called Ruländer. The only region in France where Pinot Gris is important is in Alsace, where it really shows its stuff. Oregon has had good success with Pinot Gris, and some winemakers in California are taking a shot at it.

Gewürztraminer

That's *ga-VERZ-tra-mee-ner.* It's German for "spicy grape from Tramin," a town that's actually located in the German-speaking part of northern Italy. The Italians call their town Terlano, but all the world calls the grape Gewürztraminer.

Gewürztraminer is a wonderfully exotic grape. It makes fairly deep-colored, aromatic white wines. Roses and lychee fruit are the classic descriptors for the aroma of Gewürztraminer wines. To experience Gewurztraminer, try a bottle from Alsace, France. Although the wine smells floral and fruity and has pronounced, exotic fruit and floral flavors, it is actually dry — fascinating and delicious.

As a grape, Gewürztraminer tends to be high in sugar but low in acid. Its wines are therefore high in alcohol and soft. (Because their acidity is low, these wines age quickly.) Gewürztraminer wines also have high *extract,* which counterbalances all that softness on the palate. (*Extract* is a particularly difficult wine term to translate; it's the solid matter of the wine left if you were to boil off all the water and anything else that evaporates. On the palate, high extract comes across as an impression of substance and character.)

A best-selling style of Gewürztraminer in the U.S. is light and sweetish, with the grape's flowery aroma and flavor toned down several decibels from the Alsace versions. *Dry* Gewürztraminer is also made in California and Oregon.

Other white grapes

We don't have room to describe more than a few grapes in any sort of detail. Table 9-1 describes some other grapes whose names you will see on wine labels, or whose wine you could drink in place-name wines without realizing it.

Table 9-1	Other White Grapes and Their Characteristics
Grape Type	**Characteristics**
Chenin Blanc	A noble grape in the Loire Valley of France, for Vouvray and other wines. The best wines have high acidity and a fascinating "oily" texture (they feel slightly thick or viscous in your mouth). Some good dry Chenin Blanc comes from California, but so does a ton of very ordinary off-dry wine. In South Africa, Chenin Blanc is called *Steen.*
Muller-Thurgau	Germany's most-planted grape variety, reportedly a crossing between Riesling and Silvaner. Because its fruit ripens very early, this grape is useful in cool climate regions such as England, New Zealand, northern Italy, and Austria, but its wines can lack character.
Muscat	An aromatic grape that makes Italy's sparkling Asti (which, incidentally, tastes *exactly* like ripe Muscat grapes). Extremely pretty floral aromas. In Alsace, makes a dry wine, and in lots of places (southern France, southern Italy, Australia) makes a delicious sweet dessert wine through the addition of alcohol.

(continued)

Table 9-1 (continued)

Grape Type	Characteristics
Pinot Blanc	Fairly neutral in aroma and flavors, but with far more character than, say, Trebbiano. High acidity and low sugar levels translate into dry, crisp, medium-bodied wines. Alsace, Austria, northern Italy, and Germany (where it is called Weissburgunder) are the main production zones, with California in the wings.
Sémillon	Sauvignon Blanc's blending partner and a good grape in its own right. Sémillon is relatively low in acid (compared to Sauvignon Blanc, anyway) and has attractive but subtle aromas — lanolin sometimes, although it can be slightly herbaceous when it is young. A major grape in Australia, South Africa, and southwestern France, including Bordeaux (where it is the major player in Sauternes), and an emerging grape for Washington state.
Trebbiano	Called *Ugni Blanc* in France. A thoroughly unremarkable grape except that so much Italian white wine is based on it. High acid, light body, neutral aromas, low sugar. Makes wines that provide a useful, neutral background for all sorts of foods.
Viognier	A grape from France's Rhone Valley that is becoming popular in California, although quantities are minuscule. Floral aroma, delicately apricot-like, medium- to full-bodied with low acidity.

Aliases and a.k.a.'s

The same grape variety will often go by different names in different countries or even in different districts within the same country. Often it's just a case of traditional local synonyms. But sometimes grape growers call one variety by the name of another because they think that's what they're growing (until a specialized botanist called an *ampelographer* examines their vines and tells them otherwise). In California, for example, some of the so-called Pinot Blanc is really another grape entirely: the Melon de Bourgogne, also know as Muscadet. Is this sort of like the lawyers telling you that your darling three-year-old was switched with another child at birth?

For more tales of viticultural intrigue, read Jancis Robinson's classic book on grape varieties, *Vines, Grapes and Wines* (Alfred A. Knopf), an indispensable and fascinating reference.

Red grape varieties

Red grapes differ in their tannin levels, as well as their aromas/ flavors and the amount of alcohol they tend to deliver to wines made from them.

The grape varieties described below are used in wines that carry the grape name, as well as in place-name wines that do not carry a designation of their grape varieties. See Chapter 7 for a chart listing the grape varieties of the major place-name wines.

Cabernet Sauvignon

Cabernet Sauvignon is not only a noble grape variety but also an adaptable one, growing well in just about any climate that isn't very cool. It became famous through the age-worthy red wines of the Médoc district of Bordeaux (that usually also contain Merlot and Cabernet Franc, a related grape, in varying proportions; see Chapter 10). But today California is an equally important region for Cabernet Sauvignon — not to mention the rest of the U.S. and vineyards in southern France, Italy, Australia, South Africa, Chile, and so on.

The Cabernet Sauvignon grape makes wines that are high in tannin and are medium- to full-bodied. The textbook descriptor for Cabernet Sauvignon's aroma and flavor is *blackcurrants* or *cassis*; the grape can also contribute vegetal tones to a wine if the grapes' ripeness in a given location or year is not ideal.

Cabernet Sauvignon is like Chardonnay in that the name alone is a powerful sales device. As a result, there are Cabernet Sauvignons at all price and quality levels. The least-expensive versions are usually quite soft — belying the grape's characterization as tannic — and vaguely fruity (not specifically blackcurrants), with medium body at best. The best wines are rich and firm with great depth and classic Cabernet flavor. *Serious* Cabernet Sauvignons can age for 15 years or more.

Because Cabernet Sauvignon is fairly tannic (and because of the blending precedent in Bordeaux), the wine is often blended with other grapes; usually Merlot — being less tannic — is considered an ideal partner. In Australia, there is an unusual practice of blending Cabernet Sauvignon with Syrah.

Cabernet Sauvignon often goes by just its first name, Cabernet (although there are other Cabernets) or even by its nickname, *Cab.*

Merlot

Deep color, full body, high alcohol, and low tannin are the characteristics of wines made from the Merlot grape. The aromas and flavors can be plummy or sometimes chocolatey.

Merlot — not Cabernet Sauvignon — is actually the most-planted grape variety in Bordeaux. But Merlot's history in that region is shorter. The legendary Bordeaux wines of the 19th century were Cabernet-dominant blends. Not until after World War II did the Merlot-dominant wines of Bordeaux's *Right Bank* (the eastern part of Bordeaux) gain prominence — and Merlot with them (more on Bordeaux in Chapter 10).

Merlot is much easier to like than Cabernet Sauvignon because it is less tannic. (But some winemakers feel that Merlot is not satisfactory in its own right, and it is thus often blended with Cabernet Sauvignon, Cabernet Franc, or both.)

Besides Bordeaux, Merlot is important in Washington state, California, the Long Island district of New York, northeastern Italy, and, increasingly, Chile.

Pinot Noir

The late Andre Tchelitscheff, the legendary winemaker of some of California's finest Cabernets, once told us that if he could do it all over again, he'd make Pinot Noir instead of Cab. He's probably not alone. While Cabernet is the sensible wine to make — a good, steady, reliable wine that doesn't give too much trouble and can achieve excellent quality — Pinot Noir is finicky, trouble-some, enigmatic, and challenging. But a great Pinot Noir can be one of the greatest wines ever.

The prototype for Pinot Noir wine is red Burgundy, from France, where tiny vineyard plots yield rare treasures of wine from 100 percent Pinot Noir. Oregon and California also produce good Pinot Noir. But Pinot Noir's production is rather limited, because the variety is very particular regarding climate and soil.

Pinot Noir wine is lighter in color than Cabernet or Merlot wine. It has relatively high alcohol, medium-to-high acidity, and medium-to-low tannin (although oak barrels can contribute additional tannin to the wine). Its flavors and aromas can be very fruity — often like a melange of red berries — or earthy and woodsy depending on how it is grown and/or vinified.

Syrah/Shiraz

The northern part of France's Rhône Valley is the classic site of greatness for the Syrah grape, and Rhône wines like Hermitage and Côte-Rôtie are the inspiration for its dissemination to Australia, California, South Africa, and Italy.

Syrah produces deeply colored wines with full body, firm tannin, and aromas/flavors that can suggest smoked meat, roasted peppers, tar, or even burnt rubber (believe it or not). In Australia, though, Syrah (called *Shiraz*) is made in a broad range of styles — some of them soft, medium-bodied wines with strawberry-like flavor that are quite the opposite of the northern Rhone's majestic Syrahs. Turn to "Winemaking, grapes, and terroir," in Chapter 12 for more on Shiraz.

Syrah does not require any other grape to complement its flavors, although in Australia it is commonly blended with Cabernet.

Zinfandel

White Zinfandel is such a popular wine — and so much better known than the red version of Zinfandel — that its fans might argue that Zinfandel is not a red grape. But — it is so!

Zinfandel is one of the oldest grapes in California; therefore, Zinfandel has a certain stature there. Its aura is enhanced by its mysterious history: Although Zinfandel is clearly a *vinifera* grape and not a native American variety, authorities are uncertain where it really came from. The current theory suggests that Zinfandel came from the Dalmatian region of the former Yugoslavia.

Zin — as devotees of Red Zinfandel call it — is a rich, deeply colored wine that is high in alcohol and medium to high in tannin. It can have a blackberry or raspberry aroma and flavor, a spicy character, or even a jammy flavor. There are Zins that are meant to be enjoyed young and serious Zins that are built for aging. (You can tell which is which by the price.)

Nebbiolo

This noble grape is short on adaptability. Outside of scattered sites in northwestern Italy — mainly the Piedmont region — Nebbiolo just doesn't make remarkable wine. But the extraordinary quality of Barolo and Barbaresco, two Piedmont wines, prove what greatness it can achieve under the right conditions.

The Nebbiolo grape is high in both tannin and acid, which can make a wine tough. Fortunately, it also gives enough alcohol to soften the package. Its color can be deep when the wine is young, but can develop orangy accents within a few years. Its aroma is fruity (strawberry), earthy and woodsy (tar, truffles), and herbal (mint, eucalyptus).

Lighter versions of Nebbiolo are meant to be drunk when young (the wine, not you) — wines labeled Nebbiolo d'Alba, Roero, or Nebbiolo delle Langhe, for example — while Barolo and Barbaresco are wines that really deserve a *minimum* of six years' age before drinking (see Chapter 20 on how wines age).

Sangiovese

This Italian grape has proven itself in the Tuscany region of Italy, especially in the Brunello di Montalcino and Chianti districts.

Sangiovese makes wines that are medium to high in acidity and medium in tannin; the wines can be light-bodied to full-bodied, depending on exactly where the grapes grew and how the wine was made. The aromas and flavors of the wines are fruity — especially cherry — with floral nuances of violets and sometimes a slightly nutty character.

Tempranillo

Tempranillo is Spain's candidate for greatness. It gives wines deep color, low acidity, and only moderate alcohol. However, much of the color can be lost to extended wood aging and blending with varieties that lack color, such as Grenache, as is the practice in Spain's Rioja district.

Other red grapes

Table 9-2 describes additional red grape varieties that you could encounter, either as varietal wines or as the basis of wines that are named for their place of production.

Table 9-2	Other Red Grapes and Their Characteristics
Grape Type	**Characteristics**
Aglianico	Little known outside of southern Italy, where it makes Taurasi and other age-worthy, powerful red wines.
Barbera	Italian grape that, oddly, has little tannin but very high acidity. When fully ripe it can give big, fruity wines with refreshing crispness. Lately, producers are aging the wine in new oak to increase the tannin level of their wine.
Gamay	Excels in the Beaujolais district of France. It makes grapey wines that are deep in color and relatively low in tannin. Neither the grape called *Gamay Beaujolais* in California nor the grape called *Napa Gamay* is true Gamay.
Grenache	A Spanish grape by origin, called Garnacha, Grenache is identified with France's southern Rhône Valley (more than with Spain) by most wine drinkers. Sometimes Grenache makes light-colored wines that are high in alcohol but not much else. Under the right circumstances, Grenache can make deeply colored wines with velvety texture and fruity aromas and flavors suggestive of raspberries.

Chapter 10

If It's Tuesday, This Must Be France

. . . .

In This Chapter

▶ *Crus*, classified growths, *chateaux,* and *domaines*

▶ Why Bordeaux wines are legendary

▶ The scarcity issue in fine Burgundy

▶ Robust red Rhônes

▶ White gems of the Loire and Alsace

. . . .

France. What comes to mind when you hear that word? Strolling down Paris' famous boulevard, the Champs Elysées? Love? The beautiful, blue water and golden sun on the French Riviera?

When we think of France, we think of wine. Bordeaux, Burgundy, Beaujolais, Chablis, Champagne, and Sauternes are not only famous wines — they are also places in France where people live, work, eat, and drink (wine, of course!). France has the highest per capita wine consumption of any country in the world. And the island of Guadeloupe in the French West Indies has an even higher per capita consumption than the rest of France!

France: Standard Setter of the Wine World

Why has France become the most famous place in the world for wine? For one thing, the French have been doing it for a long time — making wine, that is. Centuries before the Romans conquered Gaul and planted vineyards, the Greeks had arrived with their vines.

Equally important is French *terroir*, that magical combination of climate and soil that, when it clicks, can yield grapes that give us breathtaking wines. And what grapes! France is the home of almost all the renowned varieties in the world — Cabernet Sauvignon, Chardonnay, Merlot, Pinot Noir, Syrah, and Sauvignon Blanc, just to name a few.

France is the model, the standard setter, for all the world's wines: Most countries that produce wine now make their own versions of Cabernet Sauvignon, Chardonnay, Merlot, Pinot Noir, and so on thanks to the success of these grapes in France. If imitation is the sincerest form of flattery, French winemakers have had good reason to blush for a long time now.

Understanding French wine law

French lawmakers have reason to blush, too. France's system of defining and regulating wine regions — the *Appellation Controlée*, or AOC (translated as *regulated place name*) system, established in 1935 — has been the legislative model for most of the other European countries. The European Union's (EU) framework of wine laws, within which the AOC system now operates, is also modeled on the French system.

To understand French wines, you need to know three things:

- ✔ Most French wines are named after places. (These are not arbitrary places; they are places registered and defined under French wine law.) When we talk about French wines and the regions they come from, most of the time the region and the wine have the same name (as in Burgundy, from Burgundy).

- ✔ The French wine system is hierarchical. Some wines (that is, the wines of some places) officially have higher rank than other wines.

- ✔ Just because a wine carries a high rank doesn't necessarily mean that it's better than the next wine; it just means that it should be better. The laws are not infallible.

There are four possible ranks a French wine can carry, according to French wine law. You can determine the rank of a French wine at a glance by seeing which of the following French phrases appears on the label. (Wines of higher rank generally cost more.) From highest to lowest, the ranks are

- ✔ **Appellation Controlée,** or AOC (or AC), the highest rank. On the label, the place-name of the wine usually appears between the two French words, as in Appellation Bordeaux Controlée.

- ✔ **Vins Délimités de Qualité Supérieure,** or VDQS wines (translated as *demarcated wine of superior quality*)

- ✔ **Vins de pays,** meaning *country wines*. On the label, the phrase is always followed by a place name, such as Jardin de France; the places are generally much larger than the places referred to in the two higher rankings.

- ✔ **Vins de table,** ordinary French table wines that carry no geographic indication other than France. (By law, they also have no grape variety nor vintage indicated.)

Here's how these four ranks of French wines fit within the European Union's two-tier system described in Chapter 8:

- ✔ All AOC and VDQS wines fall into the EU's higher tier, QWPSR (Quality Wine Produced in a Specific Region, or simply *quality wine*).
- ✔ All *vins de pays* and *vins de table* fall into the EU's lower tier, table wines.

Fine distinctions in the ranks

France's system of place-naming its wines is actually a bit more complex than the four neat ranks might imply, however. Although all AOC wines/places hold exactly the same legal status — they're all generals in the French wine army, let's say — the market accords some AOCs higher regard (and higher prices) than others, based on the specificity of their terroir. Some of the generals have silver stars.

Imagine three concentric circles. Any wines produced from grapes grown within entire the area of the three circles may carry a particular AOC place-name, such as Bordeaux (assuming that the proper grape varieties are used and the wine conforms to the law in all other aspects); but wines whose grapes come from the territory of the two smaller circles are entitled to a different, more specific AOC name, such as Haut-Médoc. And wines whose area of production is limited to the smallest circle can use yet another AOC name, such as Pauillac. (They're all generals, but some have better credentials than others.)

The more specific the place described in the wine name, the finer the wine is generally considered to be in the eyes of the market and the higher the price the winemaker can ask. Naturally, every winemaker will use the most specific name to which his wine is entitled.

In increasing order of specificity, an AOC name can be the name of

- ✔ A region (Bordeaux, Burgundy)
- ✔ A district (Haut-Médoc, Côte de Beaune)
- ✔ A subdistrict (Côte de Beaune Villages)
- ✔ A village or commune (Pauillac, Meursault)
- ✔ A specific vineyard (Le Montrachet)

Unfortunately, you won't always know one from the other by looking at the label. You can sometimes gauge how specific an appellation is by knowing the wine's price, and some names you just have to memorize.

France's wine regions

We'll single out five of France's ten wine regions for discussion here: Bordeaux, Burgundy, the Rhône, the Loire, and Alsace. Each of these regions specializes in certain grape varieties for its wines, based on climate, soil, and local tradition. Table 10-1 provides a quick reference to the grapes and wines of these five regions.

Two other major wine regions of France are Provence and Languedoc-Roussillon. Sunny Provence, in southeastern France, is the home of many rosé, red, and white wines, most of which are uncomplicated, easy-drinking wines that are delightful accompaniments to the grilled fish and seafood of the region. Provence is especially known for its dry rosé wines, which are excellent for warm weather or casual enjoyment (other dry, French rosés can be found in the Rhône and the Loire regions).

Equally sunny Languedoc-Roussillon in southern France is the country's largest region by far, in terms of quantity of wine produced. Many varietally named wines — such as Cabernet Sauvignon, Chardonnay, Syrah, and Merlot — come from here, usually wearing the table wine appellation, *Vin de Pays d'Oc*. The wines are of decent quality and, at $6 to $10 a bottle, quite good value. Two well-known brands are Réserve St. Martin and Fortant de France.

Bordeaux: The Incomparable

You must know French wine to know wine — French wines are that important in the wine world. Likewise, you must know Bordeaux to know French wine.

Bordeaux, a wine region in western France named after the fourth-largest French city (see Figure 10-1), produces 10 percent of all French wine and 26 percent of all AOC wine. Most Bordeaux wines are dry reds; fifteen percent of the region's production is dry white, however, and two percent is sweet white wine, such as Sauternes.

Bordeaux produces wines at many levels of price and quality. Prices, for example, range from $5 a bottle for simple Bordeaux to over $300 a bottle for Château Pétrus, the most expensive red Bordeaux wine (*old* vintages of Pétrus cost even *more!*). Most of the finer Bordeaux wines, both red and white, begin selling at about $15 a bottle when they are young.

Table 10-1   The Wine Regions of France and Their Wines

Red Wines	White Wines	Grape Varieties
Bordeaux		
Bordeaux		Cabernet Sauvignon, Merlot, Cabernet Franc, Petite Verdot, Malbec*
	Bordeaux Blanc	Sauvignon Blanc, Sémillon, Muscadelle*
Burgundy		
Burgundy		Pinot Noir
	White Burgundy	Chardonnay
Beaujolais		Gamay
	Chablis	Chardonnay
Rhône		
Hermitage		Syrah
Côte Rôtie		Syrah, Viognier*
Châteauneuf-du-Pape		Grenache, Mourvèdre, Syrah, (many others)*
Côtes du Rhône		Grenache, Mourvèdre, Carignan, (many others)*
	Condrieu	Viognier
Loire		
	Sancerre;Pouilly Fumé	Sauvignon Blanc
	Vouvray	Chenin Blanc
	Muscadet	Muscadet
Alsace		
	Riesling	Riesling
	Gewurztraminer	Gewurztraminer
	Tokay-Pinot Gris	Pinot Gris
	Pinot Blanc	Pinot Blanc

* *wines blended from several grape varieties*

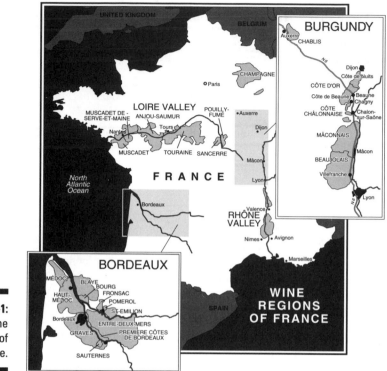

Figure 10-1:
The Wine
Regions of
France.

Bordeaux's reputation as one of the greatest wine regions in the world revolves around the legendary red wines of Bordeaux — *grands vins* (great wines) made by historic *châteaux* (wine estates) and capable of improving for many decades (see Chapter 20). These wines occupy the highest ranks of red Bordeaux, but quantitatively speaking, they are only a small facet of the region's reds. Many middle-rank Bordeaux reds are made to be consumed within 10 to 15 years of the harvest, and even more middle-rank Bordeaux reds are meant to be enjoyed young, within two to five years of the vintage date.

The taste of really great Bordeaux

When young, the finest red Bordeaux have a deep cranberry hue, with aromas of blackcurrants, spice, cedar, and cassis. For the first ten years or so, they can be very dry, almost austere, with tannin masking the fruit flavors. Eventually, these wines turn slightly garnet, develop an extraordinarily complex bouquet and flavor, and soften in tannin. The very finest red Bordeaux wines will frequently take 20 years or more before reaching their maturity; some have lasted well over 100 years (see Chapter 20).

The subregions for red Bordeaux

The Gironde River and its tributary, the Dordogne, divide the Bordeaux region in two, creating two distinct wine production zones. These two areas have come to be called the Left Bank and the Right Bank — just like Paris. While many of the least expensive Bordeaux reds are blended from grapes grown all through the Bordeaux region — and thus carry the region-wide AOC, Bordeaux — the better wines come from specific AOC *districts* or AOC *communes* in the Right Bank or the Left Bank.

Four districts are most important for red wine:

Left Bank (the western area)	Right Bank (the eastern area)
Médoc	St-Emilion
Graves/Pessac-Léognan	Pomerol

The Left Bank and the Right Bank differ mainly in soil composition: on the Left Bank, gravel predominates, whereas clay prevails on the Right Bank. As a result, Cabernet Sauvignon, which has an affinity for gravel, is the principal grape variety in the Médoc (*meh doc*) and the Graves (*grahv*), while Merlot, happier in clay, dominates the St-Emilion (*sant em eel yon*) and Pomerol (*pohm eh roll*) wines. (Both areas grow Cabernet Sauvignon *and* Merlot, as well as Cabernet Franc and two less significant grapes.)

You can therefore conclude correctly that Left Bank and Right Bank Bordeaux are markedly different from one another. But wines from the Médoc and the Graves or Pessac-Léognan (pronounced *pay sac lay oh nyahn;* Pessac-Léognan is the northern part of the Graves) are quite similar to each other; likewise, it can be difficult to tell the difference between a Pomerol and a St-Emilion.

Left Bank versus Right Bank

Each bank — in fact, each of the four districts — has its avid fans. The older, more established Left Bank generally produces more austere, tannic wines with a more pronounced blackcurrant flavor. Left Bank wines usually need many years to develop and will age for a long time, often for decades — typical of a Cabernet Sauvignon wine.

Right Bank Bordeaux are better introductory wines for the novice Bordeaux drinker. Because they are dominated by Merlot, they are more approachable; you can enjoy them well before their Left Bank cousins, often five to eight years after the vintage. They are less tannic, richer and more plummy in flavor and contain a bit more alcohol than Left Bank reds.

The Médoc mosaic

The subdivisions of Bordeaux don't stop there. The Médoc encompasses two subdistricts: the Médoc in the north and the Haut-Médoc (*oh may doc*), by far the more important district for wine, in the south. The Haut-Médoc itself encompasses four famous wine communes: St. Estèphe (*sant eh steff*), Pauillac (*poy yac*), St-Julien (*san jolee ehn*) and Margaux (*mahr go*). Table 10-2 gives a general description of each commune's wines.

Two other communes in the Haut-Médoc (whose wines are less well-known) are Listrac (*lee strahk*) and Moulis (*moo lees*). Any châteaux in the Haut-Médoc that are not located in the vicinity of these six communes have the district appellation, *Haut-Médoc*, rather than that of a specific commune.

The names of these districts and communes are part of the official name of wines made there and appear on the label.

Table 10-2 The Four Principal Communes in the Haut-Médoc

Commune	*Wine Characteristics*
St-Estèphe	Hard, tannic, full-bodied, earthy, acidic, chunky, slow to mature; typical wine — Château Montrose
Pauillac	Rich, powerful, firm, tannic, full-bodied; blackcurrants and cedar aromas; very long-lived; home of three of Bordeaux's most famous wines — Lafite-Rothschild, Mouton-Rothschild, and Latour
St-Julien	Rich, flavorful, medium/full-bodied; cedary bouquet; wines of elegance and finesse; typical wine — Château Beychevelle
Margaux	Perfumed, fragrant bouquet; medium-bodied, supple, complex; typical wine — Château Palmer

Classified information

Have you ever wondered what a wine expert was talking about when he smugly pronounced that a particular Bordeaux was a *second growth?* Wonder no more. He's talking about a château (as wine estates are called in Bordeaux) that got lucky 140 years ago.

Back in 1855, when an Exposition (akin to a World's Fair) took place in Paris, the organizers asked the Bordeaux Chamber of Commerce to develop a classification of Bordeaux wines for the Fair. The Chamber of Commerce delegated the task to the Bordeaux wine brokers, the people who bought and sold the wines of Bordeaux. These merchants named 61 top red wines, dividing them into five categories, known as *crus* (in Bordeaux, a *cru,* or growth, refers to a wine estate). The listing is known as the classification of 1855; to this day, these *classified growths* enjoy special prestige among wine lovers. The following list shows the five categories and lists the first growths (60 Médoc Growths; 1 Graves Growth); the entire 1855 classification is in Appendix A.

- **First Growths (5 Châteaux)**

  Château Lafite-Rothschild
  Château Latour
  Château Margaux
  Château Haut-Brion
  Château Mouton-Rothschild (elevated from a Second Growth in 1973)

- **Second Growths (14 Châteaux)**
- **Third Growths (14 Châteaux)**
- **Fourth Growths (10 Châteaux)**
- **Fifth Growths (18 Châteaux)**

The 61 ranked wines are sometimes referred to as Great Growths or *Grands Crus Classés.* To appreciate the honor attached to being one of the Great Growths, bear in mind that there are about 8,000 châteaux (and over 13,000 wine producers) in Bordeaux!

The only two districts of Bordeaux that were classified in 1855 were the Médoc and Sauternes (a sweet wine area in the southern Graves; see Chapter 14). The classification was based on the prices of the wines at the time and the prestige of each château over the previous 100 years — and in 1855, Médoc and Sauternes wines enjoyed the greatest reputation. The only non-Médoc red Bordeaux in the classification was Château Haut-Brion, a wine from the Graves district, whose prestige in 1855 compelled the brokers to include it in the Médoc classification — and, in fact, to make it a first growth.

The 1855 classification has held up remarkably well over the last 140 years. Certainly, a few of the 61 properties are not performing up to their classification ranking today, while other unclassified châteaux possibly deserve to be included today. But because of the politics involved, no changes in classification ranking have been made, with one dramatic exception (see "The Mouton exception") nor are any foreseen in the near future.

Top wines to try when you're feeling flush

If you're curious to try a prestigious red Bordeaux, let this list guide you. In addition to the five first growths listed in the section, "Classified information," we recommend the following classified growths from the Médoc (second through fifth growths), as well as some wines from the three other principal subregions. Consult the "Practical-advice on drinking red Bordeaux" section just ahead before you drink the wine.

Médoc wines

Château Léoville-Las-Cases
Château Léoville-Barton
Château Rausan-Ségla
Château Palmer
Château Cos D'Estournel

Château Clerc-Milon
Château Gruaud-Larose
Château Pichon-Lalande
Château Lagrange
Château Pichon-Baron
Château Lascombes

Château Lynch-Bages
Château Montrose
Château Ducru-Beaucaillou
Château Grand-Puy-Lacoste
Château La Lagune

Pessac-Léognan wines

Château La Mission Haut-Brion
Château Pape-Clément

Château Haut-Bailly
Domaine de Chevalier

Château de Fieuzal
Château La Louvière

Pomerol wines

Château Pétrus*
Château Lafleur*
Château La Conseillante

Château Trotanoy
Château Clinet
Château Latour à Pomerol
Château Certan de May

Château L'Evangile
Château La Fleur de Gay
Vieux-Château-Certan

* very expensive

St-Emilion wines

Château Cheval Blanc
Château Figeac
Château Troplong Mondot

Château La Dominique
Château Grand Mayne
Château Ausone
Château Canon

Château Pavie
Château L'Arrosée
Château Pavie-Macquin

The Mouton exception

The one dramatic exception to the "no changes in the 1855 classification" rule occurred in 1973 when the late Baron Philippe de Rothschild, having waged a 50 year battle with the French government to have his beloved Château Mouton-Rothschild upgraded from a second growth to a first growth, finally (and rightfully) triumphed. The Minister of Agriculture decreed that Château Mouton-Rothschild was indeed a first growth (which Bordeaux wine lovers considered it to be all along, in quality if not in status). The Baron's motto, written in French on his family crest, had to change. Before 1973, it read

> First, I cannot be; second, I do not deign to be; Mouton, I am.

The Baron changed the motto on his 1973 Château Mouton-Rothschild to read:

> First, I am; second, I was; Mouton does not change.

A postscript to this wonderful story: We acquired an adorable little kitten, a Blue Point Siamese, in 1973. Since Mouton-Rothschild was one of our favorite wines, and since our little kitten demonstrated the same firm, tenacious qualities as the wine, we named him Mouton. He was with us for 20 years, proving that he had the same quality of longevity as the wine for which he was named. He is buried in our backyard, in an empty wooden crate of 1973 Mouton-Rothschild.

The value end of the Bordeaux spectrum

As you might have expected, the best buys in Bordeaux wines are not found among classified growths. For really good values (and for Bordeaux that you can drink within a few years of the vintage), look for wines that were not included in the 1855 classification. In the Médoc, about 400 red wines are now grouped under the classification, *cru bourgeois*. These wines generally sell in the $8 to $18 price category; some of them are even as good as the lesser-quality classified growths. We recommend the following cru bourgeois wines:

Château Monbrison	Château Phélan-Ségur	Château d'Angludet
Château Sociando Mallet	Château Meyney	Château Coufran
Château Poujeaux	Château Chasse-Spleen	Château Fourcas-Hosten
Château de Pez	Château Gloria	Château Lanessan
Château Les Ormes-de-Pez	Château Haut-Marbuzet	

Even less expensive is the vast group of Bordeaux, both red and white, that has never received any classification; these wines are informally referred to as *petits châteaux*. Such wines retail for $6 to $10, are usually light-bodied, and are ready to drink when they are released. *Petits châteaux* are the Bordeaux wines of choice when you are looking for a young, inexpensive, approachable Bordeaux with dinner. Of course, these wines don't say *petits châteaux* on their labels. (We never said Bordeaux would be easy.) You'll know them by their price.

Practical advice on drinking red Bordeaux

Because the finest red Bordeaux wines take many years to develop, they are usually not good choices in restaurants where young vintages predominate. And when mature Bordeaux wines do appear on restaurant wine lists, they are usually extremely expensive. Order a lesser Bordeaux when you're dining out, and save the best ones for drinking at home.

Red Bordeaux wines go well with lamb, venison, simple cuts of meat, and hard cheeses, such as cheddar. If you plan to serve a fine red Bordeaux from a good but recent vintage (see Appendix B), you should decant it at least an hour before dinner and let it aerate (see Chapter 6); serve it at about 66°F (18 to 19°C). Better yet, if you have good storage conditions (see Chapter 15), save your young Bordeaux for a few years — it will only get better.

Great recent Bordeaux vintages have been 1982, 1985, 1986, 1988, 1989, and 1990. And 1994 looks promising, judging by our preliminary tastings.

Bordeaux also comes in white

The Graves district of Bordeaux is home to the finest white wines of Bordeaux, both dry and sweet, including the great dessert wine, Sauternes (which we'll cover in Chapter 14), from the southern Graves. Across the Garonne River (another tributary of the Gironde) lies Entre-Deux-Mers (*ahn treh-douh-mare*), another district known for its dry and sweet white Bordeaux wines. But it is in the northern Graves, specifically the district of Pessac-Léognan, where you can find some of the greatest *dry* white wines of the world.

Sauvignon Blanc and Sémillon, in various combinations, are the two grape varieties that dominate the production of white Bordeaux. It is a fortunate blend, because the Sauvignon Blanc grape offers immediate charm, while the slower-developing Sémillon adds a viscous quality and depth to the wine.

The best dry white Graves are crisp and lively when they are young, but they develop a full-bodied richness and a honeyed bouquet with age. In good vintages (see Appendix B), the best white Graves need at least ten years to develop and can live many years more. (See Chapter 20 on older Bordeaux.)

Table 10-3 lists the Graves district's top ten white Bordeaux and their grape blend. We've separated the wines into an A and B group because the three wines in the first group literally are in a class by themselves, quality-wise. Their prices reflect the fact — the A-group wines range from $50 to $75 per bottle, whereas the B group wines are priced between $18 and $30.

Table 10-3	Top Ten White Bordeaux
Wine	**Grape Varieties**
Group A	
Château Haut-Brion Blanc	Sémillon, 50 to 55%; Sauvignon Blanc, 45 to 50%
Château Laville-Haut-Brion	Sémillon, 60%; Sauvignon Blanc, 40%
Domaine de Chevalier	Sauvignon Blanc, 70%; Sémillon, 30%
Group B	
Château de Fieuzal	Sauvignon Blanc, 50 to 60%; Sémillon, 40 to 50%
Château Pape-Clément	Sémillon, 45%; Muscadelle, 10%; Sauvignon Blanc, 45%
Château La Louviere	Sauvignon Blanc, 70%; Sémillon, 30%
Château Couhins-Lurton	Sauvignon Blanc, 100%
Clos Floridene	Sémillon, 70%; Sauvignon Blanc, 30%
Château La Tour-Martillac	Sémillon, 60%; Sauvignon Blanc, 30%; other, 10%
Château Smith-Haut-Lafitte	Sauvignon Blanc, 100%

Burgundy: The Other Great French Wine

Burgundy, a wine region in eastern France, southeast of Paris (refer to Figure 10-1), ranks side-by-side with Bordeaux as one of France's two greatest regions for light (table) wines. Unlike Bordeaux, however, Burgundy's fame is shared nearly equally by its white and red wines — and the best white Burgundies are even more expensive than their red counterparts.

Also unlike Bordeaux, good Burgundy is often scarce. The reason is simple: Not counting Beaujolais (technically Burgundy, but really a separate type of wine) Burgundy produces only 25 percent as much wine as Bordeaux!

Burgundy's vineyards are smaller and more fragmented than Bordeaux's. The French Revolution in 1789 is partly to blame. Prior to the Revolution, French nobility and the Catholic Church were the major vineyard owners in Burgundy, but after the Revolution, vineyards were distributed among the populace. (Bordeaux, once owned by the English, was considered to be a British wine, and was not really affected by the Revolution.) France's Napoleonic Code, which requires all land to be equally divided among one's heirs, further fragmented each family's small vineyard holdings.

Today, Burgundy is a region of small vineyard plots. Large vineyards have multiple owners, with some families owning only two or three rows of vines in a particular vineyard. (One famous Burgundy vineyard, Clos de Vougeot, has about 82 owners!) The typical Burgundy winemaker's production varies from 50 cases to 1,000 cases of wine a year — far from enough to satisfy wine lovers all over the world. Compare that to Bordeaux, where the average Château owner makes 15,000 to 20,000 cases of wine annually.

In Burgundy, the winemaker calls his property a *domaine,* certainly a more modest name than *château*, and a proper reflection of the size of his winery.

Chardonnay, Pinot Noir, Gamay

Burgundy has a *continental* climate (hot summers, cold winters) subject to localized hailstorms in the summer, which can damage the grapes and cause rot. The soil is mainly limestone and clay.

Burgundy's *terroir* is particularly suited to the two main grape varieties of the region, Pinot Noir (for red Burgundy) and Chardonnay (for white Burgundy). In fact, nowhere else in the entire world does the very fickle, difficult Pinot Noir grape perform better than in Burgundy.

As you go farther south, into the Beaujolais district of Burgundy, the soil becomes primarily granitic, which is very suitable for the Gamay grape of this area.

Five Burgundies and an impostor

Burgundy has five districts, all of which make quite different wines. The districts include Chablis (*shah blee*), the Côte d'Or (*coat dore*), the Côte Châlonnaise (*coat shal oh naze*), the Mâconnais (*mack coh nay*), and Beaujolais (*boh jhoe lay*). The heart of Burgundy, the *Côte d'Or* (which literally means *golden slope*), is further divided into two parts: Côte de Nuits (*coat deh nwee*) and the Côte de Beaune (*coat deh bone*).

Table 10-4 lists the districts geographically from north to south, along with the grape varieties used in each region. A quick glance at Table 10-4 immediately shows that, even though Beaujolais is part of Burgundy, Beaujolais is an entirely different wine. The same is true of Mâcon Rouge — even the small amount made from Pinot Noir does not resemble true red Burgundy. (Actually, very little red Mâcon is exported; the world sees mainly white Mâcon).

Table 10-4	The Districts of Burgundy	
Red Wine	*White Wine*	*Grape Variety*
Chablis		
	Chablis	Chardonnay
Côte d'Or: Côte de Nuits		
Red Burgundy		Pinot Noir
Côte d'Or: Côte de Beaune		
Red Burgundy		Pinot Noir
	White Burgundy	Chardonnay
Côte Chalonnaise		
Red Burgundy		Pinot Noir
	White Burgundy	Chardonnay
Mâconnais		
Mâcon Rouge		Gamay; Pinot Noir
	Mâcon Blanc	Chardonnay
Beaujolais		
Beaujolais		Gamay

Thus, the term *red Burgundy* refers primarily to the red wines of the Côte d'Or and also to the less well-known — and less expensive — red wines of the Côte Chalonnaise. Likewise, when wine lovers talk about *white Burgundy,* they are usually referring just to the white wines of the Côte d'Or and the Côte Chalonnaise. They'll use the more precise names, Chablis and Macon, to refer to the white wines of those parts of Burgundy. On the other hand, when wine lovers talk about the region, Burgundy, they could very well be referring to the whole shebang, including Beaujolais, or all of Burgundy *except* Beaujolais. It's an imprecise language.

Don't ever mistake the inexpensive red California wine that calls itself *burgundy* — or the inexpensive California wine that calls itself *chablis* — for the real McCoys from France. The imposter Burgundy and Chablis are the product of various ordinary grapes grown in large, industrial vineyards 6,000 miles away from the Côte d'Or. We'd be surprised if either one had even a drop of the true grapes of Burgundy — Pinot Noir or Chardonnay — in them. They're both medium-dry wines blended for mass appeal, and they sell fairly well. But you should know that they bear absolutely no resemblance to true (100 percent Pinot Noir) red Burgundy from Burgundy, France — or true (100 percent Chardonnay) Chablis from Chablis, France.

From the regional to the sublime

Because of the nature of Burgundy's origins, the soils of the region vary from hillside to hillside and even from the middle of each hill to the bottom. You can find two different vineyards growing the same grape but making distinctly different wines, only two meters apart from each other across a dirt road!

In a region with such varied *terroir*, specificity of site becomes extremely relevant. A wine made from a tiny vineyard with its own particular characteristics is more unique, precious, and rare than a wine blended from several vineyards or a wine from a less-favored site.

The AOC structure for Burgundy wines recognizes the importance of site. While there are region-wide AOCs and district-wide AOCs and commune AOCs — just as in Bordeaux — *there are also AOC names that refer to individual vineyard sites.* In fact, some of these vineyards are recognized as better than others: Some of them are *premier cru (prem yay crew)*, meaning first growth, while the very best are *grand cru*, meaning great growth.

The terms *premier cru* and *grand cru* are used in Bordeaux, too, but in Bordeaux the terms generally represent status bestowed on a property by a classification outside the AOC law. In Burgundy, *premier cru* and *grand cru* are official distinctions of the AOC law. Their meaning is extremely precise.

Table 10-5 gives examples of AOC names in Burgundy, listed in increasing order of specificity. The two broadest categories — regional and district place-names — account for 65 percent of all Burgundy wines. Such wines retail for $10 to $15 a bottle. (You *can* buy affordable Burgundies at this level.) Commune (also referred to as *Village*) wines, such as Nuits-St. Georges, make up 23 percent of Burgundy and are in the $20 to $30 per bottle price range. Fifty-three communes in Burgundy have their own appellations.

Premier crus, such as Meursault Les Perrières, account for 11 percent of Burgundy wines; there are 561 vineyards entitled to the *premier cru* appellation. The wines can range from $30 to $75 per bottle. The 32 *grand crus*, such as Chambertin, represent only *one percent* of Burgundy's wines. Prices for *grand cru* Burgundies — both red and white — start in the $60 to $70 price range and can go up to well over $500 a bottle for Romanée-Conti, normally Burgundy's most expensive wine.

Table 10-5	The Structure of Burgundy AOC Names
Specificity of Site	*Examples*
Region-wide	Bourgogne Rouge
District-wide	Côte de Beaune-Villages; Mâcon-Villages
Village or Commune	Pommard; Gevrey-Chambertin; Volnay
(The following two classifications refer to specific vineyard sites.)	
Premier Cru	Nuits-St. Georges Les Vaucrains; Beaune Grèves; Vosne-Romanée Les Suchots
Grand Cru	Musigny; La Tâche; Montrachet

Thankfully, you can actually tell the difference between a *premier cru* and a *grand cru* Burgundy by looking at the label. *Premier cru* wines carry the name of their commune plus the vineyard name — in *the same-sized lettering* — on the label. If the vineyard name is in smaller lettering than the commune name, the wine is not a *premier cru* but a wine from a single-vineyard site in that commune. *Grand cru* Burgundies carry only the name of the vineyard on the label.

If a wine is made by blending the grapes of two or more *premier crus* in the same commune, it can be called a *premier cru* but it won't carry the name of a specific *premier cru* vineyard. The label will carry a commune name and the words *premier cru*, sometimes written as *1er cru*.

Burgundy AOCs (once again, with feeling)

Burgundies with regional, or region-wide, AOCs are easy to recognize — they always start with the word *Bourgogne* (*boor guh nyeh*). In the list below, read the AOC names down each column to see how the names change, becoming more specific from district to *grand cru.*

	Red Burgundy	**White Burgundy**
District:	Côte de Nuits-Villages	Côte de Beaune (also red)
Commune:	Chambolle-Musigny	Puligny-Montrachet
Premier Cru:	Chambolle-Musigny Les Amoureuses	Puligny-Montrachet Les Pucelles
Grand Cru:	Musigny	Bâtard-Montrachet; Montrachet

The taste of fine red Burgundy

The Pinot Noir grape does not have nearly as much color as the Cabernet Sauvignon or Merlot grapes. Red Burgundy, therefore, is paler than Bordeaux, ranging in color from garnet to cherry or ruby. It's medium-bodied to full-bodied in terms of its alcohol and is relatively low in tannin. The characteristic aroma is small red fruits — cherries and berries — and woodsy or damp-earth scents. When a red Burgundy ages, it often develops a silky texture, richness, and a natural sweetness of fruit flavors; sometimes a bouquet of leather and well-hung game or aged beef evolves.

With some exceptions (for example, a powerful wine from a great vintage, such as 1990), red Burgundy should be consumed within ten years of the vintage — and even sooner in a weaker vintage (see Appendix B).

Practical advice on buying and drinking Burgundy

Nice of the Burgundians to make everything so stratified and clear, isn't it? *Premier cru* Burgundies are always better than commune wines, and *grand crus* are the best of all, right? *Well, it ain't necessarily so!* In order of importance, these are the criteria to follow when you are buying Burgundy:

- ✔ **The producer's reputation:** Based on wines he has made in recent years
- ✔ **The vintage year:** There are great fluctuations in quality from year to year
- ✔ **The appellation:** The name of the commune or vineyard and its specificity

The producer and the vintage are *considerably* more important than the appellation in Burgundy. 1990, 1989, and 1988 were good vintages for red Burgundy (especially the 1990). For white Burgundy, 1992 and 1989 are quite good.

The taste of fine white Burgundy

White Burgundy combines a fullness of flavor — peaches, hazelnuts, and honey in Meursault; floweriness and butterscotch in a Puligny or Chassagne-Montrachet — with lively acidity and a touch of oak. With age, even more flavor complexity develops. The wine finishes on the palate with a lingering reminder of all its flavors. Chardonnay wines from other regions and countries can be good, but there's nothing else quite like a great white Burgundy.

Red Burgundy is a particularly good wine to choose in restaurants. Unlike Bordeaux and other Cabernet Sauvignon-based wines, it is usually approachable when young because of its softness, along with its enticing, developed aromas and flavors of red fruits.

Moreover, red Burgundy, like all Pinot Noirs, is a versatile companion to food. It is the one red wine that can complement fish or seafood; it is ideal with salmon, for example. Chicken, turkey, or ham would also be good matchups for Burgundy. For fuller-styled red Burgundies, beef and game birds (such as duck, pheasant, rabbit, or venison) all go well.

Red Burgundy is at its best when served at cool temperatures — about 60° to 62°F (17°C). It should *not* be decanted (even older Burgundies seldom develop much sediment), but poured straight from the bottle. Too much aeration would cause you to lose the wonderful Burgundy aroma, which is one of the greatest aspects of this wine.

The Côte d'Or

The heart of Burgundy is the Côte d'Or, a narrow 40-mile stretch of land with some of the most expensive real estate in the world. This is the region where all the famous red and white Burgundies originate.

The northern part of the Côte d'Or is named the Côte de Nuits, after its most important (commercial) city, Nuits-Saint-Georges. Red Burgundies almost exclusively are made here (although one superb white Burgundy, Musigny Blanc, does exist). The following wine communes, from north to south, are in the Côte de Nuits:

- **Marsannay** *(mahr sah nay)*: Known mainly for rosés

- **Fixin** *(fee san)*: Sturdy, earthy, rustic red wines

- **Gevrey-Chambertin** *(jehv ray sham ber tan)*: Full-bodied, rich, red wines; eight *grand crus*, such as Chambertin, Chambertin Clos de Bèze

- **Morey-Saint Denis** *(maw ree san d'nee)*: Full, sturdy red wines; *grand crus* include Bonnes Mares (part), Clos de la Roche, Clos Saint-Denis, Clos de Tart, Clos des Lambrays

- **Chambolle-Musigny** *(shom bowl moo sih nyee)*: Soft, elegant red wines; *grand crus* include Musigny and Bonnes Mares (part)

- **Vougeot** *(voo joe)*: Medium-bodied red wines; *grand cru* is Clos de Vougeot

- **Vosne-Romanée** *(vone roh mah nay)*: Elegant, rich, velvety red wines; *grand crus* include Romanée-Conti, La Tache, Richebourg, Romanée-Saint-Vivant, La Romanée, and La Grand Rue

- **Flagey-Échezeaux** *(flah gee eh sheh zoe)*: Hamlet of Vosne-Romanée; *grand crus* are Grands-Échezeaux and Échezeaux

- **Nuits-Saint-Georges** *(nwee san johrjes)*: Sturdy, earthy, red wines; no *grand crus*; fine *premier crus*

All these red wines are made entirely with the Pinot Noir grape. The different characteristics of the wines are due to their individual *terroirs*.

The southern part of the Côte d'Or, the Côte de Beaune, is named after its most important city, Beaune (the commercial and tourist center of the Côte d'Or). Both white and red Burgundies are made in the Côte de Beaune, but the white Burgundies are more renowned. The following communes, from north to south, make up the Côte de Beaune:

- **Pernand-Vergelesses** *(per nahn ver jeh less)*: Little-known red and white wines; good buys

- **Aloxe-Corton** *(ah luss cor ton)*: Full, sturdy wines; one red *grand cru* (Corton) and one magnificent white *grand cru* (Corton-Charlemagne)

- **Chorey-lès-Beaune** *(shor ay lay bone)*: Some good-value red wines here

- **Savigny-lès-Beaune** *(sah vee nyee lay bone)*: Mostly red wines; good values here, too

- **Beaune** *(bone)*: Soft, medium-bodied reds; some whites; fine *premier crus* here

- **Pommard** *(pohm mahr)*: Sturdy, full red wines; some good *premier crus* (Rugiens and Epenots)

- **Volnay** *(vohl nay)*: Soft, elegant red wines; good *premier crus* (Caillerets and Clos des Ducs)

- **Auxey-Duresses** *(awe see duh ress)*, **Monthélie** *(mon tel lee)*, **Saint-Romain** *(san roh man)*, **Saint-Aubin** *(sant oh ban)*: Four little-known villages producing mainly red, but some white wines; good values

- **Meursault** *(muhr so)*: First important white Burgundy commune; full-bodied, nutty wines; some excellent *premier crus* (Les Perrières and Les Genevrières)

- **Puligny-Montrachet** *(poo lee nyee mon rah shay)*: Home of elegant white Burgundies; *grand crus* include Montrachet (part), Chevalier-Montrachet, Bâtard-Montrachet (part)

✔ **Chassagne-Montrachet** *(shah sahn nyah mon rah shay)*: A bit sturdier than Puligny; the rest of the Montrachet and Bâtard-Montrachet *grand crus*; also, some earthy, rustic reds

✔ **Santenay** *(sant nay)*: Light-bodied, inexpensive red wines here.

Tables 10-6 and 10-7 list the best Burgundy producers and their greatest wines.

Table 10-6	Best Red Burgundy Producers and Their Greatest Wines
Producer	*Recommended Wines*
Domaine Leroy*	Musigny, Richebourg, Chambertin (*all* of Leroy's *grand crus* and *premier crus* recommended)
Domaine de la Romanée-Conti*	Romanée-Conti; La Tâche; Richebourg; Grands Echézeaux
Georges Roumier	Musigny; Bonnes Mares; Chambolle-Musigny Les Amoureuses
Ponsot	Clos de la Roche (Vieilles Vignes); Chambertin; Clos St-Denis (Vieilles Vignes)
Armand Rousseau	Chambertin (*all* of his *grand crus*); Gevrey-Chambertin Clos St-Jacques
Méo-Camuzet	Vosne-Romanée *premier crus* (any of his three); Clos de Vougeot; Richebourg; Corton
Hubert Lignier	Clos de la Roche; Charmes-Chambertin
Jean Gros	Richebourg; Vosne-Romanée Clos des Réas
Joseph Roty	Any of his *grand cru* Chambertins
Domaine Comte de Vogüé	Musigny (Vieilles Vignes); Bonnes Mares
Mongeard-Mugneret	Richebourg; Grands Échézeaux
Louis Jadot	Romanée-St-Vivant; Chambertin Clos de Beze
Chopin-Groffier	Clos de Vougeot
Domaine Maume	Mazis-Chambertin
Michel Lafarge	Any of his Volnay *premier crus*
Domaine Comte Armand	Pommard Clos des Epeneaux

* *these wines are* very *expensive*

Table 10-7	Best White Burgundy Producers and Their Greatest Wines
Producer	*Recommended Wines*
Domaine Ramonet*	Montrachet; Bâtard-Montrachet; Bienvenue-Bâtard-Montrachet; any of his Chassagne-Montrachet *premier crus*
Coche-Dury*	Corton-Charlemagne; Meursault *premier cru* (any)
Domaine des Comtes Lafon	Meursault *premier crus* (any)
Domaine Leflaive	Chevalier-Montrachet; Bâtard-Montrachet; Puligny-Montrachet *premier crus* (any)
Michel Niellon	Bâtard-Montrachet; Chevalier-Montrachet; Chassagne-Montrachet Les Vergers
Louis Latour	Corton-Charlemagne
Domaine Étienne Sauzet	Bâtard-Montrachet; Bienvenue-Bâtard-Montrachet; Puligny-Montrachet Les Combettes
Verget	Bâtard-Montrachet; Chevalier-Montrachet; Meursault *premier crus* (any)

* these wines are very expensive

Bargain Burgundies: The Côte Chalonnaise

The sad fact about Burgundy is that most of the good wines are costly. But one of Burgundy's best-kept secrets is the wines of the Côte Chalonnaise (the district which lies directly south of the Côte d'Or). Five villages here are home to some very decent Burgundies. True, the Côte Chalonnaise Burgundies are not so fine as the Côte d'Or Burgundies (they're a bit earthier and coarser), but we're talking $10 to $20 retail per bottle here. The five appellations to look for are the following:

- **Mercurey** *(mer cure ay)*: Mostly red; a small amount of white; the best wines of the Châlonnaise come from here, also the most expensive ($15 to $20)

- **Rully** *(rue yee)*: About half red and half white wines; the whites, although a bit earthy, are significantly better than the reds; look for the wines of the producer Antonin Rodet

- **Givry** *(gee vree)*: Mostly red; a small amount of white; reds are better than the whites (but quite earthy)

> ✔ **Montagny *(mon tah nyee)*:** All white wines (Chardonnay); look for
>   Antonin Rodet's and Louis Latour's Montagny
>
> ✔ **Bouzeron *(boo zer ohn)*:** Aubert de Villaine is the quality producer here;
>   try his Bourgogne Rouge, Bourgogne Blanc, or Bourgogne Aligoté (a
>   second white grape permitted in Burgundy that does well here)

Chablis: A unique white wine

The village of Chablis, northwest of the Côte d'Or, is the closest Burgundian
commune to Paris (about a two-hour drive). Although Chablis's wines are 100
percent Chardonnay — just like the white Burgundies of the Côte d'Or — they
are quite a different style from Côte d'Or whites. Whereas almost all of the Côte
d'Or white Burgundies use oak barrels both in fermentation and aging, most
Chablis producers now use only stainless steel. Also, Chablis's climate is cooler
than that of the Côte d'Or, producing wines that are intrinsically lighter-bodied,
austere, and more acidic. Chablis is very dry and sometimes flinty, without the
rich, ripe flavors of Côte d'Or white Burgundies.

Chablis is an ideal companion to seafood, especially oysters. Like all other
white Burgundies, it should be served cool (58 to 60°F, or 15°C), not cold.

The Chablis worth trying

Chablis is at its best on the *grand cru* and *premier cru* level. Simple village
Chablis is priced in the $10 to $18 price range, but, frankly, at that price better
white wines can be found in Mâcon, in the Chalonnaise, or in the Côte d'Or
(Bourgogne Blanc).

The seven *grand cru* Chablis are

Les Clos	Valmur	Les Preuses
Vaudésir	Grenouilles	Bougros
	Blanchot	

Another, La Moutonne, is actually a part of Vaudésir and Grenouilles but is
entitled to its own appellation. *Grand cru* Chablis range in price from $25 to $65,
depending on the producer. Chablis from good vintages (see Appendix B) can
age and improve for 15 years.

There are 22 *grand cru* Chablis appellations, but the seven most well-known
(and probably the best) are

Fourchaume	Montée de Tonnerre	Vaillons
Mont de Milieu	Montmains	Butteaux
	Les Forêts	

Premier cru Chablis ranges in price from $18 to $45, depending on the producer, and can age up to ten years in good vintages.

Three outstanding producers of Chablis

Three producers really stand out in Chablis. You should try to buy their *grand* or *premier cru* Chablis for a true understanding of this underrated wine. *Try* is the operative word here: These are small producers whose wines are available only in better stores. The first two producers listed still use oak for fermenting and aging their wine (which is unusual for Chablis); the third uses stainless steel:

Francois Raveneau
René et Vincent Dauvissat
Louis Michel

Mâcon: Affordable whites

If you're thinking that $20 or more sounds like too much to spend for a bottle of white Burgundy or Chablis for everyday occasions, we have an alternative white wine for you: the white wines of Mâcon. Many of the best white wine buys — not only in France, but in the world, as well — come from the Mâconnais district, which lies directly south of the Châlonnaise and north of Beaujolais.

The Mâconnais has a mild, sunny climate. Wine production is centered around the beautiful city of Mâcon, a gateway city to Provence and the Riviera. In northern Mâcon, you can find a village called Chardonnay, for which the famous grape was perhaps named. The hills in the Mâconnais contain the same chalky limestone beloved by Chardonnay that can be found in Burgundy districts to the north.

Mâcon's white wines, in fact, are 100 percent Chardonnay. Most of them are simply called *Mâcon* or *Mâcon-Villages* (slightly better than Mâcon, because it comes from specific villages); the wines retail for $6 to $10 a bottle. Better yet are Mâcons that come from just one village. The name of the village is added to their appellation (such as Mâcon-Lugny or Mâcon-Viré).

Mâcon whites are a good value. They are medium-bodied, crisp, unoaked, fresh, and lively. They should be consumed while they are young, generally within three years of the vintage.

The best Mâcon whites come from the southernmost part of the district and carry their own appellations — Pouilly-Fuissé *(pwee fwee say)* and Saint-Véran *(san ver ahn)*. Pouilly-Fuissé is a richer, fuller-bodied wine than a simple Mâcon, is often oaked, and is a bit more expensive (around $15 to $17). To try an outstanding example of Pouilly-Fuissé, buy Château Fuissé, which, in good vintages, compares favorably with more expensive Cote d'Or white Burgundies. Saint-Véran is very possibly the best-value wine in all of Màcon ($10 to $14). Especially fine is the Saint-Véran of Verget, who is one of the best producers of Màconnais wines.

Beaujolais: As delightful as it is affordable

Are you surprised that Beaujolais is in the Burgundy region? Beaujolais is so famous that it stands on its own. It even has its own red grape: the Gamay.

Beaujolais and *Beaujolais Supérieur* (one percent higher in alcohol) are district-wide AOCs, but actually they come from the southern part of Beaujolais where the soil is mainly clay. They are fresh, fruity, uncomplicated, light-bodied wines that sell for $6 to $8 and are at their best a year or two after the vintage. They are excellent wines for warm weather, when a heavier, more tannic red wine would be inappropriate.

If you're a white wine, white Zinfandel, or rosé wine drinker (or even a non-wine drinker!), Beaujolais is the *ideal* first red wine to drink — a bridge, so to speak, to more serious red wines. It's delicious, and doesn't require serious contemplation. Beaujolais is truly a fun wine.

Beaujolais has its serious side, too. The best Beaujolais are made in the northern part of the Beaujolais district where the soil is granite-based. *Beaujolais-Villages* is a wine blended from (some of) 39 designated villages that produce fuller, more substantial wine than simple Beaujolais. It costs a dollar or so more but is well worth the difference.

Even higher quality Beaujolais comes from ten specific villages in the north. The wines of these villages are known as *cru* Beaujolais, and only the name of the cru appears in large letters on the label. *Cru* Beaujolais have more depth, and, in fact, need a little time to develop; some of the *crus* can age and improve for four or five years or more. They range in price from about $8 to $14. Table 10-8 lists the ten *cru* Beaujolais as they are geographically situated, from south to north, along with a brief description of each *cru*.

Almost all of Beaujolais is sold by large *négociants* — firms that buy grapes and wine from growers and blend, bottle, and sell the wine under their own labels. Two of the best and most reliable Beaujolais négociants are Georges Duboeuf and Louis Jadot.

SNOB ALERT

Celebration time: Beaujolais Nouveau

Each year on the third Thursday in November, the new vintage of Beaujolais — Beaujolais Nouveau — is released all over the world with great fanfare. This youngster — only six weeks old! — is a very grapey, easy-to-drink wine with practically no tannin but lots of fruit. Beaujolais Nouveau is particularly popular in the U.S., where it is served with many Thanksgiving dinners because of the timing of its annual debut. It sells for five to seven dollars and is at its best within six months of the vintage.

Table 10-8	The Ten *Cru* Beaujolais
Cru	*Description*
Brouilly *(broo yee)*	The largest *cru* in terms of production and the most variable in quality; light and fruity; drink within three years
Côte de Brouilly	Distinctly better than Brouilly, fuller and more concentrated; vineyards are higher in altitude; drink within three years
Regnie *(ray nyay)*	The newest village to be recognized as a *cru;* very similar to Brouilly; not nearly as good as Côte de Brouilly
Morgon *(mor gohn)*	At its best, full and earthy; can age for five to seven years; look for Duboeuf's Morgon (*Domaine Jean Descombes*)
Chiroubles *(sheh roob leh)*	One of our favorites; the quintessential, delicate, delicious perfumed Beaujolais; tastes of young red fruits; very pretty; drink it within two years of the vintage
Fleurie *(flehr ee)*	Medium-bodied, rich, with a velvety fruitiness; the most popular cru (and, along with Moulin-á-Vent, the most expensive, at $12 to $14); quite reliable; can age for four years
Moulin-á-Vent *(moo lahn ah vahn)*	Clearly the most powerful, concentrated cru, and the one that can age the longest (ten years or more); this is one Beaujolais that really needs three or four years to develop
Chénas *(shay nahs)*	Bordering Moulin-á-Vent (in fact, much of it can be legally sold as the more famous Moulin-á-Vent); what is sold as Chénas is usually well-priced; drink within 4 years
Juliénas *(jool yay nahs)*	The insider's Beaujolais; often the most consistent and the best of the *crus;* full-bodied and rich, can last five years or more; seldom disappoints
Saint-Amour *(sant ah more)*	The most northerly *cru* in Beaujolais; perfectly named for lovers on Valentine's Day (or any other day); soft, light to medium-bodied, delicious berry fruit; drink within two or three years

Beaujolais in action

Beaujolais is located in the heart of one of the greatest gastronomic centers of the world; good restaurants abound in the area, as well as in the nearby city of Lyon. To really get a feeling for being in France, visit a bistro in Paris or Lyon and order a carafe of young Beaujolais with your charcuterie, pâte, or cold chicken. No wine slides down the throat as easily!

Young, uncomplicated Beaujolais should *definitely* be served chilled, at about 55°F (13°C), to capture its fruity exuberance. The fuller *cru* Beaujolais, on the other hand, are best at about the same temperature as red Burgundy (60°F to 62°F; 17°C).

The Hearty Rhônes of the Valley

For a good, reliable dry red wine that costs about $6 to $18, look no farther than the Rhône *(rone)* Valley and its everyday red wine, Côtes du Rhône. The Rhône Valley makes more serious wines — mostly red, and some white and dry rosé as well — but Côtes du Rhône is one of the best inexpensive red wines in the world.

The Rhône Valley is in southeastern France, south of Beaujolais, between the city of Lyon and the region of Provence, where the growing season is sunny and hot. The wines reflect the weather: the red wines are full, robust, and high in alcohol. Even some of the white wines tend to be full, earthy, and long-lived. But the wines from the southern part of the Rhône are distinctly different from those in the northern Rhône Valley.

Generous wines of the south

Most (in fact, 95 percent of) Rhône wines come from the southern Rhône. They are generally inexpensive and uncomplicated. The dominant grape variety in the southern Rhône is the prolific Grenache, which makes wines that are high in alcohol.

Besides Côtes du Rhône, other southern Rhône appellations to look for are

- Côtes du Ventoux *(vahn too)*, which is similar, but a bit lighter than Côtes du Rhône
- Côtes du Rhône-Villages (17 villages making fuller and a bit more expensive wines than Côtes du Rhône)
- The single-village wines, Gigondas *(jhee gon dahs)* and Vacqueyras *(vah keh rahs)*

The last two wines are former Côtes du Rhône-Villages wines that graduated and are now entitled to their own appellations. Gigondas, which sells in the $12 to $15 range, is particularly rich and robust and can live for ten years or more in good vintages. 1989 and 1990 were both excellent vintages in the southern Rhône.

Two dry rosé wines of interest in the southern Rhône are Tavel *(tah vel)* and Lirac *(lee rahk)*; the latter is less well-known and therefore less expensive. Both are made mainly from the Grenache and Cinsault grapes; they can be delightful on hot, summer days or at picnics. As with most rosé wines, they are best when they are young.

But Châteauneuf-du-Pape *(shah toe nuf doo pahp)* is the king in the southern Rhône. Its name recalls the 14th century, when nearby Avignon (not Rome) was the home of the Popes. Almost all Châteauneuf-du-Pape is a blended red wine: As many as 13 grape varieties can be used, but Grenache, Mourvèdre, and Syrah predominate. At its best, Châteauneuf-du-Pape is full-bodied, rich, round, and rather high in alcohol. In good vintages, it will age well for 15 to 20 years. The two finest Châteauneuf-du-Papes are clearly *Château Rayas* (100 percent Grenache, very old vines) and *Château Beaucastel* (can age 20 years or more).

Noble wines of the north

The two best red wines of the entire Rhône, Côte Rôtie *(coat roe tee)* and Hermitage *(er mee tahj)*, are produced in the northern Rhône Valley. Both are made from the noble Syrah grape (a bit of white Viognier wine is sometimes used in Côte Rôtie).

Although both are rich, full-bodied wines, Côte Rôtie is the more subtle of the two. It has a wonderfully fragrant nose, which always reminds us of green olives and soft, fruity flavors. In good vintages, Côte Rôtie can age for 20 years or more (1991 was particularly fine for Côte Rôtie). The most famous producer is Guigal; his single-vineyard Côte Rôties — *La Mouline*, *La Landonne*, and *La Turque* — are great, but particularly expensive. Most Côte Rôties are in the $20 to $45 price range.

Red Hermitage is clearly the most full-bodied, longest-lived Rhône wine. It is a complex, rich, tannic wine that needs several years before it begins to develop, and it will age easily for 30 years or more in good vintages (1988, 1989, 1990, and 1991 were all excellent vintages in the northern Rhone; 1989 was especially great for Hermitage). The three best producers of Hermitage are Jean Louis Chave, Chapoutier, and Paul Jaboulet Aîné (for his better Hermitage, *La Chapelle*). The best Hermitages sell today for $35 to $60, although lesser Hermitages are as low as $20 to $25 a bottle.

Jaboulet also makes a less expensive little brother this Hermitage, a *Crozes-Hermitage* (a separate appellation) called *Domaine de Thalabert*. It's as good as — if not better than — many Hermitages, can age and improve for 10 to 15 years in good vintages, and is reasonably priced at $17 to $18: A wine to buy.

A small amount of white Hermitage is produced from the Marsanne and Rousanne grape varieties. White Hermitage is traditionally a full, heavy, earthy wine that needs eight to ten years to really develop. Chapoutier's fine Hermitage Blanc, *Chante-Alouette*, however, is made in a more approachable style. The other great white Hermitage is Chave's. It is complex and almost as long-lived as his red Hermitage.

Condrieu *(con drew)*, made from 100 percent Viognier, is the other white wine to try in the northern Rhône. It's one of the most fragrant, floral wines in existence. Its flavors are delicate but rich, with delicious fresh apricot and peach undertones; it makes a wonderful accompaniment to fresh fish. Condrieu (which sells for about $20 to $25) must be consumed young, however.

The Loire Valley: White Wine Heaven

Have you been Chardonnay-ed out yet? If you're looking for white-wine alternatives to Chardonnay, discover the Loire *(lwahr)* Valley wine region. Lots of white wines come from there, but none of them are Chardonnay! For the record, you can find red wines and some dry rosés, too, in the Loire, but the region is really known for its white wines.

The Loire Valley stretches across northwest France, following the path of the Loire River from central France in the east to the Atlantic Ocean in the west. The cool climate, especially in the west, produces relatively light-bodied white wines.

In the eastern end of the Valley, just south of Paris, are the towns of Sancerre and Pouilly-sur-Loire, located on opposite banks of the Loire River. Here, the Sauvignon Blanc grape thrives, making lively, dry wines that have spicy, green-grass flavors.

Of the two principal wines in this area, Sancerre *(sahn sehr)* is the lighter, drier, more lively one. It is perfect for summer drinking, especially when accompanied by shellfish or light, fresh water fish, such as trout. The wine made around the town of Pouilly-sur-Loire is called Pouilly-Fumé *(pwee foo may)*. It is slightly fuller and less spicy than Sancerre and can have attractive gun-flint and mineral flavors. Pouilly-Fumé can be quite a fine wine when made by a good producer such as Ladoucette. Because it is fuller, Pouilly-Fumé goes well with rich fish, such as salmon, or with chicken or veal. Both wines sell in the $10 to $15 price range. They are at their best when they're young and fresh; drink them within three or four years after the vintage.

You might get the two *Pouilly* wines, Pouilly-Fuissé and Pouilly-Fumé, confused — but they are very different wines. The Chardonnay-based Pouilly-Fuissé, from the Mâcon in Burgundy, is a more full-bodied wine. The Pouilly-Fumé, made from Sauvignon Blanc, is lighter and more acidic.

In the central Loire Valley near the city of Tours (where beautiful châteaux of former French royalty can be found), lies the town of Vouvray *(voo vray)*. The Chenin Blanc grape makes better wine here than it does anywhere else in the world. The wines of Vouvray comes in three styles: dry, medium-dry, or sweet (called *moelleux*), but the sweet wines can only be made in vintages of unusual ripeness, which occur infrequently. There is also a sparkling Vouvray.

The best wines of Vouvray need several years to develop and can last almost forever, thanks to their remarkable acidity. The better Vouvrays begin in the $15 to $17 range. The two most respected producers are Gaston Huet and Philippe Foreau of Clos Naudain.

Less expensive Vouvrays, priced at $6 to $10, are pleasant to drink young. Even the drier versions are not really bone dry and are a good choice for you if you cannot tolerate very dry wines. They go well with chicken or veal in a cream sauce or with fruit and cheese after dinner.

The third wine district of the Loire Valley is called the Pays Nantais *(pay ee nahn tay),* after the city of Nantes, right where the Loire River empties into the Atlantic Ocean. The vineyard area around Nantes is home of the Muscadet grape (also known as the Melon). The wine, also called Muscadet *(moos cah day)*, is light and very dry — a perfect accompaniment to clams, oysters, and river fish (and, naturally, ideal for summer drinking).

The best Muscadet comes from the Sèvre-et-Maine region, and those words appear on the label. Frequently you will also see the term *sur lie*, which means that the wine was aged on its *lees* (fermentation yeasts) and bottled straight from the barrel. This procedure gives the wine liveliness, freshness, and sometimes a slight prickle of carbon dioxide on the tongue.

The best news about Muscadet is the price. You can buy a really fine Muscadet in the $6 to $8 range. Buy the youngest one you can find because Muscadet is at its best within one two years of the vintage. It is not an ager.

Alsace Wines: French, Not German

It's understandable that much of the wine-drinking populace confuses the wines of Alsace *(ahl zas)* with German wines. Alsace, in northeastern France, is just across the Rhine River from Germany. Originally a part of Germany, Alsace became part of France in the 17th century. Germany took the region back in 1871 only to lose it to France again as a result of World War I (1919). To complicate things further, both Alsace and Germany grow some of the same grapes (Riesling and Gewurztraminer). But there is where the similarity ends: Alsace wines are *dry*, whereas many German wines are medium-dry or sweet.

Alsace's identity crisis has hurt her wines in the international marketplace. As a result, the wines of Alsace are a very good value.

Alsace wines are unique among French wines in two ways. All Alsace wines come in a tall, thin bottle called a *flûte*. And almost all Alsace wines carry a grape variety name *and* a place-name, which is simply Alsace.

Considering Alsace's northerly latitude (refer to Figure 10-1), you'd expect the region's climate to be cool. But thanks to the protection of the Vosges Mountains to her west, Alsace's climate is quite sunny and temperate and one of the driest in France — in short, perfect weather for grape growing.

Although some light-bodied Pinot Noir is made, 93 percent of Alsace's wines are white. Four are particularly important: Pinot Blanc, Riesling, Pinot Gris, and Gewurztraminer. Although each reflects the characteristics of the grape from which it is made, they all share a certain aroma and flavor, sometimes called a spiciness, that can only be described as the flavor of Alsace.

Alsace Pinot Blanc is the lightest of the four wines. In a slight re-interpretation of traditional Alsace style, some producers make their Pinot Blanc medium dry to appeal to wine drinkers who are unfamiliar with the region's wines. Other producers make it bone dry. Either way, it's at its best in its youth. Pinot Blanc is quite inexpensive, selling in the $6 to $10 range.

Riesling is the king of Alsace wines (remember: it's a *dry* wine here). Alsace Riesling has a flowery nose, but firm, dry, almost steely, flavors. Although it can be consumed young, like most Alsace wines, a Riesling from a good vintage is easily capable of aging and improving for ten years or more. Rieslings are in the $12 to $20 price range.

Tokay-Pinot Gris is an Alsace wine whose name recalls a famous Hungarian dessert wine, Tokaji — but there is no relationship. Tokay-Pinot Gris is made from Pinot Gris, the same variety that you find in Italy as Pinot Grigio. Here in Alsace, it is a rich, spicy, full-bodied wine with a lot of character. It is relatively low in acidity and high in alcohol. Alsace's Pinot Gris retails in the $10 to $15 range; it goes well with spicy meat dishes.

The Gewurztraminer grape has such an intense, pungent, spicy aroma and flavor that it's a *love it or leave it* wine (one of us loves it — the other leaves it!). But it certainly has its followers. And it is clearly at its best in Alsace. If you haven't tried an Alsace Gewurztraminer yet, you haven't tasted one of the most unique wines in the world. It's quite low in acidity and high in alcohol, a combination which gives an impression of fullness and softness. It goes best with *foie gras* and strong cheeses, and some people like it with spicy Asian cuisine. Gewurztraminer sells for about the same price as Riesling but doesn't age quite as well.

Chapter 11

Doing Europe

● ●

In This Chapter

▶ Old World, New World

▶ Italy's big B's

▶ New finds in Portugal

▶ Germany's secret recipe: frozen grapes and noble rot

▶ Unusual wines from Alpine climes

● ●

*T*en years ago, we never used the phrase *European wine* in talking generally about the wines of France, Italy, Spain, Portugal, and Germany. The wines had nothing in common.

But today, two factors have changed the way we look at the wines of these countries. First, Europe has unified, and the wines of the European Union member countries now exist under a common legislative umbrella. Second, non-European wines — wines from California, Australia, and to some extent South America — have inundated the U. S. market, popularizing a nomenclature (varietal names, such as Chardonnay) and flavors (fruity, fruitier, fruitiest) foreign to the European, or *Old World*, model.

Compared to non-European, or *New World,* wines, Europe's wines have many things in common after all. European wines are usually named for their place of production instead of their grape (see Chapter 7); European winemaking is tethered to tradition; the wines reflect local tastes more than international trends; and the wines are relatively low in fruitiness. European wines embody the traditions of the people who make them and the flavors of the earth from which they grow, compared to New World wines, which embody a grape variety.

Despite these similarities among European wines, the countries of Europe each make distinctly different wines. France's importance has earned her a whole chapter, while the rest of Europe shares the spotlight here.

Italy: The Vineyard of Europe

Tiny Italy — 60 percent the size of France, three-quarters the size of California — makes more wine than any other country in the world in most years. Wine is the lifeblood of the Italian people. Vines grow everywhere, and no meal could possibly occur without a bottle of wine on the table.

The downside of wine's omnipresence in Italy is that it's taken for granted. Italy took 28 years longer than France to develop a wine classification system, for example; and still today, more than 30 years after creating that system, Italy has yet to incorporate any official recognition of vineyard sites *(crus)* for her best wines. Italy's casual attitude toward wine has slowed the acceptance of top-quality Italian wines on international markets.

Another reason top-quality Italian wines have not been quickly accepted on international markets is that most Italian wines are made from native grape varieties, such as Nebbiolo, Sangiovese, Aglianico, Barbera, and so on. These grapes can be outstanding, but because they don't exist in other countries (and when transplanted, they don't perform nearly as well as in Italy), their names are unfamiliar to wine lovers.

On the upside, Italy is blessed with such a variety of soils and climates — from Alpine foothills in the north to Mediterranean coastlines in the south — that the range of her wines is almost endless. (A curious wine lover could keep busy for a lifetime exploring the hundreds of wines in Italy!) Italy's hilly landscape provides plenty of high-altitude relief for grapevines even in the warm south, and many craggy slopes with poor soil challenge vines to perform small miracles.

Italy's wines, as we outside of Italy know them, fall into two distinct groups: 1) inexpensive red and white wines often sold in large value-priced bottles for everyday drinking with meals in the casual Italian fashion and 2) the better wines, which range from good to great in quality.

One of the best-known Italian wines in the first category is Lambrusco, a frothy, slightly sweet (and delicious) red wine that has been a first wine for many wine drinkers outside Italy. In the second category are the drier version of Lambrusco that is drunk in the home market, the Italian wines we describe in this chapter, and many other wines that space does not permit us to mention.

Italy is said to have 20 wine regions, which correspond exactly to her political regions (see Figure 11-1). What would be called a wine region in France, such as Burgundy or Alsace, is usually referred to as a wine *zone* in Italy to avoid confusion with the political region. We'll continue that practice.

Figure 11-1:
The Wine
Regions of
Italy.

Although wine is produced throughout Italy, many of the finest wines come
from the north: the Piedmont region in the northwest, Tuscany in north-central
Italy, and the three regions (sometimes informally called the *Tre Venezie*) of
northeastern Italy. Table 11-1 lists the major wines of these five regions and
their grape varieties.

Table 11-1	The Wines of Italy's Main Regions	
Red Wine	*White Wine*	*Grape Variety*
Piedmont		
Barolo		Nebbiolo
Barbaresco		Nebbiolo
Gattinara		Nebbiolo, Bonarda*
Barbera d'Alba and similar DOCs		Barbera
Dolcetto d'Alba and similar DOCs		Dolcetto
	Gavi (Cortese di Gavi)	Cortese
	Roero Arneis	Arneis
Tuscany		
Chianti, Chianti Classico		Sangiovese, Canaiolo and others*
Brunello di Montalcino		Sangiovese Grosso
	Vernaccia di San Gimignano	Vernaccia
Vino Nobile di Montepulciano		Sangiovese, Canaiolo, and others*
Carmignano		Sangiovese, Cabernet Sauvignon*
Super-Tuscans**		Cabernet Sauvignon, Sangiovese
Veneto		
	Soave	Gargenaga, Trebbiano, and others*
Valpolicella		Corvina, Rondinella, Molinara*
Amarone della Valpolicella		(same grapes; semi-dried)
Bardolino		Corvina, Rondinella, Molinara*
	Bianco di Custoza	Trebbiano, Gargenaga, Tocai*
	Lugana***	Trebbiano

Trentino-Alto Adige		
	Pinot Grigio (various DOCs)	Pinot Gris
	Pinot Bianco (various DOCs)	Pinot Blanc
	Chardonnay (various DOCs)	Chardonnay
	Sauvignon (various DOCs)	Sauvignon Blanc
Friuli-Venezia Giulia		
	Tocai Friulano (various DOCs)	Tocai Friulano
	Pinot Grigio (various DOCs)	Pinot Gris
	Chardonnay (various DOCs)	Chardonnay
	Pinot Bianco (various DOCs)	Pinot Blanc
	Sauvignon (various DOCs)	Sauvignon Blanc

*   *Blended wines, made from two or more grapes.*

**   *Untraditional wines produced mainly in the Chianti district; see the discussion under* Tuscany.

*** *Much of the Lugana wine zone is actually in Lombardy.*

Because Italy is a member of the EU, her wine appellation system must conform to the two-tier EU categorization of wines: QWPSR wines (Quality Wines Produced in a Specific Region) on the top tier; and table wines (see Chapter 8).

At the QWPSR level are

✔ DOCG wines *(Denominazione di Origine Controllata e Garantita)*, a small group of elite wines, currently 13. The phrase corresponding to DOCG appears on the labels of these wines.

✔ DOC wines *(Denominazione di Origine Controllata)*, Italy's basic QWPSR wines. More than 250 place-named wines have been recognized by the Italian government to date. The phrase *Denominazione di Origine Controllata* appears on the labels of these wines.

At the table wine level are

✔ Table wines with geographic designation; these are called merely *vino da tavola* (followed by the geographic designation).

✔ Ordinary table wines that carry no geographical indication except "Italy."

The terms *DOC* and *DOCG* refer to both wine zones and the wines of those zones. The DOC Soave, for example, is both a place (a specific production zone defined and regulated by Italian law, named after a town called Soave) and the wine of that place.

Barolo and the reds reign in Piedmont

Piedmont, bordering France and Switzerland, is a region that is part agricultural (producing rice, kiwis, hazelnuts, and white truffles, among other crops), part industrial (Turin, home of Fiat, is situated here), and part Alpine (see Figure 11-1). Wine is made throughout much of the region, but the most important wine zones are around the towns of Asti, especially known for sparkling wine (see Chapter 13), and Alba, known for red wines.

Piedmont's claim to wine fame is the Nebbiolo grape, a noble red variety that produces great wine only in northwestern Italy. The proof of Nebbiolo's nobility is twofold: Barolo *(bah RO lo)* and Barbaresco *(bar bah RES co)* are two of the world's great red wines; both are DOCG wines made entirely from Nebbiolo in the Langhe hills around Alba, and each is named after a village in its production zone.

Both Barolo and Barbaresco are robust reds — very dry, full-bodied, and high in tannin, acidity, and alcohol. Their aromas suggest tar, violets, roses, ripe strawberries, and (sometimes) truffles — the kind that grow in the ground, not the chocolate! Barolo is more full-bodied than Barbaresco and usually requires a bit more aging; otherwise, the two wines are very similar. Like most Italian wines, they show their best with food. Good Barolo and Barbaresco wines usually retail for $25 to $45 per bottle .

When traditionally made, Barolo and Barbaresco require several years of aging before they are ready to drink — sometimes ten years or more — and they definitely benefit from a few hours of aeration before drinking (see Chapter 6). However, some avant-garde producers are making these wines so that they are enjoyable sooner and are even using French *barriques* (oak barrels) for aging, giving Barolo and Barbaresco a more international flavor.

Both Barbaresco and, especially, Barolo have something in common with Burgundy in France: *You must find a good producer to really experience the wine at its best.* On the next page, we list the best producers of each wine in our rough order of preference, grouped according to style — traditional or modern. (We prefer the traditionally made wines, but excellent producers can be found in both camps.) Piedmont recently enjoyed three excellent vintages in a row (just like Bordeaux): 1988, 1989, and 1990.

Another good Nebbiolo-based wine, the DOCG Gattinara *(gah tee NAH rah)*, comes from northern Piedmont, where the Nebbiolo grape is called *Spanna*. Although Gattinara seldom gets the praise that the two Big B's (Barolo and Barbaresco) enjoy, it offers the same enticing Nebbiolo aromas and flavors in a slightly less full-bodied style. Attractively priced at $15 to $18 a bottle, Gattinara from a good producer has to be one of the world's most underrated wines. Look for Antoniolo's and Travaglini's Gattinaras.

Traditional Producer	*Modern Producer*

Barolo

Giacomo Conterno	Luciano Sandrone
Giuseppe Mascarello	Ceretto
Vietti	Renato Ratti
Bartolo Mascarello	Gaja
Giuseppe Rinaldi	Roberto Voerzio
Bruno Giacosa	Paolo Scavino
Aldo Conterno	Manzone
Caretta	Elio Altare
Francesco Rinaldi	Clerico
Marcarini	Parusso
Prunotto	Corino
Pio Cesare (heading toward modern-style)	Conterno-Fantino
Fontanafredda	
Marchesi di Barolo	

Barbaresco

Bruno Giacosa	Gaja
Marchesi di Gresy	Moccagatta
Cigliuti	Ceretto
Produttori del Barbaresco	
Castello di Neive	

Weekday reds

The Piedmontese reserve serious wines like Barolo and Barbaresco for Sunday dinner or special occasions. What they drink on an everyday basis are the red wines Dolcetto *(dohl CHET to)* and Barbera *(bar BEAR rah)*. Of the two, Dolcetto is the lighter-bodied and is usually the first red wine served in a Piedmontese meal.

If you know enough Italian to translate the phrase *la dolce vita,* you might think that the name *Dolcetto* indicates a sweet wine. Actually, the Dolcetto *grape* tastes sweet but the *wine* is distinctly dry, somewhat grapey with low acidity but ample tannins. Dolcetto is often compared to Beaujolais (France's light-bodied red wine; see Chapter 10) but it is drier and goes better with food. Dolcetto sells in the $10 to $12 price range. The best Dolcetto wines are from the Alba wine zone (Dolcetto d'Alba). Just about all of our recommended Barolo producers make a Dolcetto d'Alba.

Barbera (along with Sangiovese) is the most widely planted grape variety in Italy. But it is in Piedmont, specifically the Alba and Asti wine zones, that Barbera excels. It's a rich, black-cherry red wine with high acidity and generous fruit character. Barbera d'Alba is a bit fuller, riper, and richer than the leaner Barbera d'Asti. (Link the *d'* with the word following it when pronouncing these names: *DAL ba, DAHS tee.*) Barbera happens to be our favorite everyday wine, especially with pasta or pizza — or anything tomatoey.

Barbera is more popular in the United States than it has ever been, and we couldn't be more delighted, as it's now more widely available. Two different types of Barbera are available: the traditional style, aged in oak casks (large oak containers that impart little, if any, oak flavor to the wine), which sells in the $10 to $15 range and the newer, oak-influenced barrique-aged Barbera which sells in the $20 to $40 range (somebody has to pay for those expensive oak barrels!). Although both types of Barbera are very good, we prefer the simpler, less expensive, traditional style. (Frankly, we're getting a bit tired of all the oak flavor in wines these days.)

Three excellent producers of Barbera d'Alba are Vietti, Giacomo Conterno, and Giuseppe Mascarello. One especially fine Barbera d'Alba is Vietti's Scarrone Vigna Vecchia from 50-year-old vines in Vietti's Scarrone vineyard. At $19 to $20 a bottle, it's a bit more expensive than Vietti's other Barberas, but it's worth the difference.

A third weekday red from Piedmont is Nebbiolo d'Alba, from vineyards outside the Barolo or Barbaresco zones. The wine is lighter in body and easier to drink than either Barolo or Barbaresco, and it sells for about $10 to $15 a bottle.

Whites in a supporting role

Almost all of Piedmont's wines are red, but two interesting whites are made here. Gavi is a very dry wine with pronounced acidity, named for a town in southern Piedmont. Most Gavis sell for $10 to $15 (rather expensive for what it is, perhaps because Gavi has become a chic wine), while a premium Gavi, La Scolca's Black Label, costs around $35. Arneis *(ahr NASE)* is produced in the Roero zone near Alba from a long-forgotten grape called Arneis, which was resurrected by Vietti several years ago. Arneis is a dry to medium-dry wine with a rich texture. It's best when it is consumed the year following the vintage; a bottle sells for $15 to $18.

Tuscany the beautiful

Florence, Siena, Michelangelo's David, the leaning tower of Pisa . . . the beautiful region of Tuscany has more than her share of attractions. Only one wine could possible compare in fame — and that, too, comes from Tuscany: Chianti.

Here a Chianti, there a Chianti

Chianti is a large wine zone extending through much of Tuscany. The zone — all of it DOCG status, deservedly or not — is divided into seven districts. Chianti wines may use the name of their district or the simpler appellation, Chianti, if their production does not qualify for a district name (if grapes from two districts are blended, for example). The district known as *Chianti Classico* is the heartland of the zone, the best area, and — lucky for us — the one district whose wines are widely available. The only other Chianti district that can rival Chianti Classico in quality is Chianti Rufina *(ROO fee nah)*.

Besides varying according to their district of production, Chianti wines vary in style according to their aging: *Riserva* wines are often aged in French oak, are released only after three years or more at the winery, and have potential for longer life. Chianti wines can also vary according to their grape blend — although, in practice, most Chiantis are made almost entirely from the Sangiovese grape.

Chianti is a very dry red wine (there's no such animal as *white* Chianti) that, like most Italian wines, tastes best with food. It often has an aroma of cherries and sometimes violets, and its taste is reminiscent of tart cherries. The best Chiantis contain quite a bit of acidity and usually taste best from five to eight years after the vintage — although in good vintages they have no problem aging for ten or more years. The best recent years for Chianti have been the 1985, 1988, and especially the 1990 vintage.

These days, Chianti is better than ever. From simple $6 Chianti to the more substantial Chianti Classico (generally priced between $10 and $15), Chianti remains one of the wine world's great values. Even Chianti Classico Riservas are priced only about $2 more than regular Chianti Classico.

Chianti is more consistent in quality than Barolo, especially in the classico district, but it's still smart to know the good producers. Here is a list of some of our favorites. (If 28 favorite producers seems excessive, remember that Chianti is a fairly large area with many thousands of growers and winemakers.)

Badia a Coltibuono	Dievole	Renzo Masi
Brolio (recent vintages)	Fattoria di Felsina	Ruffino
Castell'in Villa	Fontodi	San Felice
Castellare	Frescobaldi	San Giusto a Rentennano
Castello dei Rampolla	Isole e Olena	Selvapiana
Castello di Ama	Melini	Villa Antinori
Castello di Cacchiano	Monsanto	Villa Cafaggio
Castello di Fonterutoli	Monte Vertine	Villa Cerna
Castello di Gabbiano	Podere Il Palazzino	Viticcio
Castello di Volpaia		

Brunello di Montalcino, overnight celebrity

While Chianti has been famous for centuries, another great Tuscan wine, Brunello di Montalcino, exploded on the scene only recently — and became an overnight success with staying power.

South of the Chianti zone sits the fortress town of Montalcino. The local wine, Brunello di Montalcino *(brew NEL lo dee mon tahl CHEE no)*, originated in the last century but was pretty much unheard of outside Tuscany until 1970 when the Biondi-Santi family, the leading producer in Montalcino, presented some of its oldest wines to writers. The 1888 and 1891 vintages were still showing well! The rest is history, as they say. Today, Brunello di Montalcino, a DOCG wine, is considered one of the greatest, long-lived red wines in existence, with a price-tag to match ($25 to $40 and up).

This stalwart cousin to Chianti is an intense, concentrated, tannic wine that demands aging (up to 20 years) when traditionally made and benefits from several hours of aeration before serving. Lately, some producers in Montalcino have been making a more approachable version of Brunello.

Rosso di Montalcino is a less expensive ($10 to $15), ready-to-drink wine made from the same grapes, and the same production area, as Brunello di Montalcino. Rosso di Montalcino from a good Brunello producer is a great value, offering you a glimpse of Brunello without breaking the bank.

To really appreciate Brunello di Montalcino, seek out one of the producers recommended in the following list (in rough order of preference). Brunellos from traditional winemakers need at least 15 to 20 years of aging in good vintages (1975, 1985, 1988, and 1990 are recent great vintages for Brunello). Brunellos from modern-style producers can be enjoyed within ten years. Younger than ten years — drink Rosso di Montalcino.

Traditional producers	*Modern producers*
Soldera (very expensive)	Il Poggione
Biondi-Santi (very expensive)	Poggio Antico
Costanti	Altesino
Pertimali	Argiano
Fattoria dei Barbi	Caparzo (especially, their La Casa)
Lisini	Col d'Orcia
Camigliano	Castelgiocondo
Campogiovanni	Villa Banfi

Two reds and a white

Three more Tuscan wines of note include two reds, Vino Nobile di Montepulciano *(mon tay pul chee AH no)* and Carmignano *(car mee NYAH no)*, and Tuscany's best white wine, Vernaccia di San Gimignano *(ver NAH cha dee san gee mee NYAH no)* — all three DOCG wines.

Montepulciano is located southeast of the Chianti zone. Vino Nobile's principal grape is the Prugnolo Gentile (also known as *Sangiovese*). From a good producer, Vino Nobile di Montepulciano can rival the better Chianti Classicos. Three producers we recommend are Avignonesi, Poliziano, and Poderi Boscarelli. Vino Nobile producers now make a lighter, readier-to-drink wine than Vino Nobile, Rosso di Montepulciano.

The Carmignano wine region is directly west of Florence. What distinguishes Carmignano from Chianti is that up to ten percent Cabernet Sauvignon can be used in the wine. As a result, Carmignano's taste can be described as "a Chianti with the finesseful touch of a Bordeaux." The one outstanding producer of Carmignano is Villa di Capezzana.

Vernaccia di San Gimignano is named for the medieval walled town of San Gimignano, west of the Chianti Classico zone. Vernaccia is generally a fresh white wine with a slightly oily texture and an almondy flavor, and it is meant to be drunk young. For an unusual interpretation, try Teruzzi & Puthod's oak-aged riserva, Terre di Tufo, a pricey but very good Vernaccia ($18 to $20). Most other Vernaccias are in the $6 to $8 range. Producers to look for are Falchini and Montenidoli.

Super-Tuscans

When Chianti fell into an economic slump in the 1970s, producers like Piero Antinori caught the attention of the world by creating new wines (like Solaia and Tignanello) that are today collectively known as *super-Tuscans*. These wines could not be called Chianti because their grape blend (generally Sangiovese and Cabernet Sauvignon) did not conform to DOC requirements for Chianti.

The actual grape blend of super-Tuscan wines varies from wine to wine, some producers using Merlot or even Syrah with their Sangiovese, others using only native Tuscan grapes. What these wines have in common is that they are expensive, ranging from $30 or $40 on up to $75 to $100 per bottle. The most famous super-Tuscan wines, Sassicaia and Solaia, prized by wine collectors, can cost $200 in good vintages such as 1985.

Now that Chianti has reestablished itself in the world market, these expensive new wines have become less prominent — but most major Chianti producers still make a super-Tuscan wine. Two of our favorites are Le Pergole Torte, made by Monte Vertine, and San Giusto a Rentennano's Percarlo. Both are made from 100 percent Sangiovese and are in the $30 to $40 price range. For us, these two are among Italy's finest wines. Vintages to look for: 1985, 1988, and especially 1990. Decant young (less than ten years old) super-Tuscan wines several hours before serving.

Doing Romeo and Juliet proud

Chances are that if your first Italian wine wasn't Chianti, it was one of Verona's big three: the white Soave *(so AH vay)* or the reds, Valpolicella *(val po lee CHEL lah)* and Bardolino *(bar do LEE noh)*. These enormously popular wines hail from northeast Italy around the picturesque city of Verona — Romeo and Juliet's hometown — and the beautiful Lake Garda.

Sangiovese at the table

Lighter Chiantis go well with pasta, prosciutto, and roast chicken or sqaub. With Chianti Classicos and riservas, lamb, roast turkey, veal, steak, and roast beef are fine accompaniments. For the robust Brunello di Montalcino and super-Tuscan wines, try pheasant, steak, game, or chunks of fresh Parmesan cheese. Serve these wines at cool room temperature, 65° to 67°F (19°C).

Of the two Veronese reds, Valpolicella is the fuller; the lighter Bardolino is a pleasant summer wine when served slightly cool. (Bolla and Masi are two of the largest producers of both.) Valpolicella, Bardolino, and Soave are attractively priced in the $6 to $8 range, as are two other white wines of the region, Bianco di Custoza and Lugana (Santi is one of the leading producers of these two). Recommended producers of the Veronese wines mentioned include

- **Soave:** Pieropan, Anselmi, Santa Sofia
- **Valpolicella:** Allegrini, Le Ragose, Guerrieri-Rizzardi, Alighieri, Tommasi, Masi
- **Bardolino:** Guerrieri-Rizzardi

Amarone della Valpolicella, one of Italy's most popular full-bodied red wines, is made from the same grapes as Valpolicella (see Table 11-1), but the ripe grapes are dried on straw mats for several months before fermentation, concentrating their sugars and flavors. The resulting wine is a rich, potent (14 to 16 percent alcohol), velvety, long-lasting wine, perfect for a cold winter night and a plate of mature, hard cheeses. Some of the best producers of Amarone are Quintarelli, Bertani, Masi, Tommasi, Le Ragose, Allegrini, and Bolla.

The Austrian-Italian alliance

If you have traveled much in Italy, you probably realize that in spirit Italy is not one unified country but 20 or more different countries linked together politically. Consider Trentino-Alto Adige, for example. Not only is this mountainous region (the northernmost in Italy; see Figure 11-1) dramatically different from the rest of Italy, but also the mainly German-speaking Alto Adige (or South Tyrol) in the north is completely different from the Italian-speaking Trentino in the south. (Before World War I, the South Tyrol was part of the Austro-Hungarian Empire.) The wines of the two areas are different, too — yet it is one region!

Although red wine is made here, most of it goes to Austria. The rest of the world sees Alto Adige's white wines: Pinot Grigio, Chardonnay, and Pinot Bianco priced in the $8 to $15 range. Along with nearby Friuli, this region produces Italy's best white wines. One producer to look for is Alois Lageder. His 1993 Pinot Bianco, Haberlehof vineyard, is simply sensational — the best Pinot Blanc we've tasted since the 1961 Pinot Bianco made by Alto Adige's legendary winemaker, Giorgio Grai. If you can find any of Grai's wines, try them (but not much is exported).

Some excellent Chardonnays comes from Trentino, and one of the best is made by Pojer & Sandri (in fact, we recommend any of the wines under this label). Another Trentino producer who specializes in red wines made from the local variety, Teroldego Rotaliano, is Elisabetta Foradori. Try her Teroldego-based red wine, Granato.

The northeast corner: Friuli-Venezia Giulia

Italy has been justifiably known in the wine world for its red wines. But in the last 20 years, the northeastern region of Friuli-Venezia Giulia (see Figure 11-1), led by the pioneering winemaker, Mario Schiopetto, has made the world conscious of Italy's white wines as well.

Near the region's eastern border with Slovenia, the districts of Collio and Colli Orientali del Friuli produce Friuli's best wine. Red wines exist here, but it is the white wines that have given the region its renown. In addition to Pinot Grigio, Pinot Bianco, Chardonnay, and Sauvignon, two local favorites are Tocai Friulano and Ribolla Gialla (both fairly rich, full, and viscous).

An admirable white wine made here is Silvio Jermann's Vintage Tunina, a blend of five varieties, including Pinot Bianco, Sauvignon, and Chardonnay. Vintage Tunina is a rich, full-bodied, long-lived white of world-class status. It sells for about $35 and, frankly, is worth the money. Give the wine eight to ten years to age and then try it with rich poultry dishes or pasta. In addition to Jermann, other recommended producers in Friuli are

- Livio Felluga
- Puiatti
- Gravner
- Doro Princic
- Borgo Conventi
- Franco Furlan

- Mario Schiopetto
- Walter Filiputti
- Pighin
- Mario Felluga

Cameo appearances from the rest of Italy

Italy's wines are not confined to the five regions that we've just highlighted. A quick tour of some of Italy's other regions will prove the point. Refer to Figure 11-1 for the location of each region.

- **Lombardy:** In the northern part of this region, near the Swiss border, the Valtellina wine district produces four light-bodied red wines from the Nebbiolo grape: Sassella, Inferno, Grumello, and Valgella. All of these wines are inexpensive (under $10) and, unlike Barolo or Barbaresco, can be enjoyed young.

- **Emilia-Romagna:** The home of Lambrusco, one of Italy's most successful wines on the export market. For a different Lambrusco experience, try one *without* the screw cap if you can find it. (You might have to go to Emilia-Romagna for that — but, hey, that's not so bad. Bologna and Parma, two gastronomic meccas, are in this region.)

- **Marche:** Verdicchio, a dry, inexpensive white wine that goes well with fish, is widely available, and quality increases with every vintage.

- **Umbria:** The region of Perugia and Assisi, Umbria makes some good red and white wines. Orvieto, a white wine, is widely available for under $10 from Tuscan producers such as Antinori and Ruffino. Two interesting red wines are Torgiano, a Chianti-like blend (try Lungarotti's Rubesco Riserva DOCG), and Sagrantino di Montefalco DOCG, a medium-bodied, elegant wine made from a local grape variety (Sagrantino) that has been a well-kept secret outside of Umbria.

- **Latium:** This region of Rome makes the ubiquitous, inexpensive Frascati, a light, neutral wine from the Trebbiano grape; Fontana Candida is a popular brand.

- **Abruzzo:** Montepulciano d'Abruzzo, a very inexpensive, easy-drinking, low tannin, low-acid red wine, comes from here; it's a terrific everyday red if you like the style.

- **Campania:** Here, near Naples, the most serious wines in southern Italy are produced. The full-bodied, tannic Taurasi, a DOCG wine from the Aglianico grape, is one of the great, long-lived red wines in Italy. The outstanding producer is Mastroberardino; his single-vineyard Taurasi,

Radici, is especially worth trying. Mastroberardino also produces two unique white wines, Greco di Tufo and Fiano di Avellino. The Greco is a full-flavored, viscous wine with a great aging capacity. It sells in the $15 to $18 range. The Fiano has a flowery, delicate nose with a flavor of hazelnuts. It needs a few years to develop, but can age for 15 years or more. It sells for about $35.

✔ **Basilicata:** The instep of the Italian boot, Basilicata has one important red wine, Aglianico del Vulture. It's similar to Taurasi, but not quite so intense and concentrated. D'Angelo is the leading producer.

✔ **Apulia:** More wine is made here than in any other region in Italy. An important wine is Salice Salentino, an inexpensive, full-bodied red. Cosimo Taurino is a leading producer.

✔ **Sicily:** Two producers of note in Sicily are Corvo and Regaleali. The latter makes wines from grapes grown at high altitudes to counteract Sicily's warm climate. Regaleali's best red wine is called Rosso del Conte; Regaleali also makes a dry *rosato* (rosé) that sells for about $8. Corvo is the brand name for wines made by the Duca di Salaparuta winery. The everyday white and red wines sell for under $10 and are particularly popular in Italian restaurants. But the Duca Enrico — a rich, velvety, full-bodied, concentrated red wine with an intense bouquet (made from the local Nero d'Avola grape) — is the star performer of Duca di Salaparuta. Introduced in 1989, Duca Enrico has already established itself internationally as one of the great red wines of Italy. It sells for $32 – $34.

Spain: Flamenco, Paella, and Rioja

Spain is a hot, dry mountainous country with more land under vines than any other country in the world. It ranks third in the world in wine production, after Italy and France.

Spain's wine image has been one of inexpensive, pedestrian, oaky wines — mainly red. And this is still partly true. However, Spanish wines have improved tremendously in recent years and can now compete comfortably on the world market.

The evolution in quality began in the late 1950s in Spain's most famous table wine region, Rioja *(ree OH ha)*. The recently discovered (by the rest of the world, at least) Ribera del Duero *(ree BEAR ah dell DWAIR oh)* region has also helped to renew world interest in Spanish wines other than Sherry (for Sherry, see Chapter 14). And an exciting, new white wine, Albariño, is now being made in the Rías Baixas *(REE ahse BYCE ahse)* region of Galicia *(gah LEETH ee ah)*. See Figure 11-2.

Like Italy, Spain's wine laws provide for a bi-level QWPSR category: *Denominaciónes de Origen* (DO) and a higher classification, *Denominaciónes de Origen Calificada* (DOCa), the latter created in 1991. So far the only DOCa is Rioja, Spain's classic red wine from the region of the same name. Wines that do not qualify as DO fall into the table wine category *Vino de la Tierra* (equivalent to the French *Vins de Pays*).

Where the viñas grow

Two regions in Spain are renowned for their red wines (Rioja and Ribera del Duero regions), one for red and white wines (Penedés region), and two are becoming well-known for their white wine (Rías Baixas and Rueda regions).

Rioja

Rioja, in north-central Spain (see Figure 11-2), has historically been the most important red wine region in the country (Ribera del Duero is catching up). The principal grape is Tempranillo, clearly Spain's greatest red variety; but another three varieties are permitted for red Rioja, and the wine is usually a blend. The Rioja region has three districts, the cooler Rioja Alavesa and Rioja Alta and the warmer Rioja Baja. Most of the best Riojas are made from grapes in the two cooler districts, but some Riojas have grapes blended from all three.

Traditional production for red Rioja involved many years of aging in small barrels of American oak before release, which created pale, gentle, sometimes tired and heavily oaked wines that lacked fruitiness. The trend has been to replace some of the cask aging with bottle aging, and the wines are now much fresher and better than ever. American oak, which gives Rioja its characteristic vanilla aroma, is sometimes now joined by French oak in the cellars of the more progressive winemakers.

Red Riojas have several faces. Sometimes the wine receives no oak aging at all and is released young; sometimes the wine is aged (in oak and in the bottle) for two years at the winery and is labeled *crianza*; some wines are aged for three years and carry the designation *reserva*; and the finest wines age for five years or even longer, earning the status of *gran reserva*.

Three-quarters of Rioja's wine is red, 15 percent *rosado* (rosé), and 10 percent white. Prices start at around $10 for *crianza* reds and go up to $25 for some of the *gran reservas*. 1982 and 1989, followed by the 1981 and 1990, are the best recent vintages for Rioja.

Figure 11-2:
The Wine
Regions of
Spain.

The following producers have been particularly consistent in quality for their red wines:

- ✔ CVNE (Compañía Vincola del Norte de España)
- ✔ La Rioja Alta
- ✔ Muga
- ✔ Marqués de Murrieta
- ✔ Lopez de Heredia

Most white Riojas these days are merely fresh, neutral, inoffensive wines, but Marqués de Murrieta still makes a traditional white Rioja, golden-colored and oak-aged, from a blend of local white grape varieties, predominantly Viura. We find the Murrieta white fascinating: lots of flavor, voluptuous, capable of aging, with attractive traces of oxidation. It's not everybody's cup of tea, true, but the wine sure has character! It has so much body that it can go with foods normally associated with red wine, as well as traditional Spanish food, such as paella or seafood. The Murrieta white sells for $14 to $16.

Penedés

The Penedés wine region is in Catalonia, south of Barcelona (refer to Figure 11-2). It is home to most of Spain's sparkling wines, which are discussed in Chapter 13.

One producer dominates the light wine (table wine) business: Torres. The Torres line includes many wines made from French grape varieties (Cabernet Sauvignon, Chardonnay, and so on) as well as local grapes, such as Tempranillo. All of the Torres wines are clean, well-made, reasonably priced, and widely available. Wines start in the $6 to $8 range (for the red Sangre de Toro and Coronas and the white Viña Sol) while the top-of-the-line Gran Coronas Black Label, a Cabernet Sauvignon, sells for $25 to $30.

Jean León, owner of La Scala restaurant in Los Angeles, also makes good, long-lived Cabernet Sauvignon and Chardonnay in Penedés; both sell for $12 to $14. (Jean León's winery was recently purchased by Torres.)

Ribera del Duero

Ribera del Duero, north of Madrid, is Spain's fastest growing wine region. For many years, it was dominated by one producer, the legendary Vega Sicilia. In fact, Spain's single most famous wine is Vega Sicilia's Unico (mainly Tempranillo, with 20 percent Cabernet Sauvignon) — an intense, concentrated, tannic red wine with enormous longevity; it is aged for ten years in casks and then sometimes further aged in the bottle.

The 1970 Unico was not released by the winery until 1995 (yes, it was aged for 25 years)! It sells for a whopping $150 per bottle, but it will be snapped up by collectors even at that price. This dark, spicy, complex wine still needs some time to develop. Two simpler, more approachable, less expensive wines from Vega Sicilia are the Tinto Valbuena (aged for three years) and the Valbuena (aged for five years).

Alejandro Fernández's Pesquera, made from 100 percent Tempranillo, has been gaining high praise in wine circles. Pesquera is a big, rich, oaky, tannic wine with intense fruit character. The Reserva sells for about $25, and the younger Pesquera is less than $20. Another producer to watch in Ribera del Duero is Bodegas Mauro, which is making a red wine that rivals Pesquera.

The Verdejo from Rueda

The Rueda region, west of Ribera del Duero, has been producing one of Spain's best white wines from the Verdejo grape. The wine is clean, elegant, has good fruit character, and sells for an affordable $6 to $8. The Rioja producer Marqués de Riscal makes one of the leading and most available examples.

The white wine from Galicia

Galicia, in northwest Spain, next to the Atlantic Ocean and Portugal (refer to Figure 11-2) was not a province known for its wine. But from a region with the unlikely name of Rías Baixas, an exciting new, white wine has emerged — Albariño. It is a wine of very high acidity (and therefore will not be to everyone's taste), a floral nose and an apricoty, delicate flavor that is not unlike Condrieu (from the Rhone Valley; see Chapter 10). A fine example of Albariño is made by Bodegas Morgadío; it sells for about $17. There are inexpensive Albariños, but they cannot compare to the Morgadío.

Portugal: More Than Just Port

Portugal is justifiably famous for its great dessert wine, Port (see Chapter 14). And millions of wine drinkers have enjoyed the medium-dry, slightly effervescent Portuguese rosés, Mateus and Lancer's. But lately, Portugal has been seriously modernizing her winemaking; and better table wines, especially red wines, are beginning to appear. We can look forward to Portugal's well-priced wines playing a larger role in world wine markets as we enter the 21st Century.

Some Spanish wine terms

You will see some of the following terms on a Spanish wine label:

Crianza: For red wines, this means that the wine has been aged for at least two years, including a period in oak; for white and rosé wines, Crianza means that the wines are at least one year old.

Reserva: Wines produced in the better vintages; red *reservas* must be aged in oak and bottle a minimum of three years; white and rosé *reservas* must be aged for two years, including six months in oak.

Gran Reserva: Wines produced only in exceptional vintages; red wines must be aged for at least five years in wood and bottle; white and rosé *gran reservas* must be aged at least four years before release, including six months in oak.

Cosecha or **Vendimia:** The vintage year

Bodega: Winery

Tinto: Red

Blanco: White

Viejo: Old

Viña: Vineyard

Portugal's highest rank for wines is the *Denominação de Origen Controlada* (DOC), which has been awarded to only eleven wine regions. The next-highest rank, similar to France's VDQS (a secondary level within the QWPSR category), the *Indicação de Proveniência Regulamentada* (IPR), has been awarded to 32 regions (DOCs-in-waiting). The table wine category includes *Vinho de Mesa Regional*, equivalent to France's *Vin de Pays*. All other wines are classified simply as *Vinho de Mesa*.

Portugal's "green" white

On many warm summer evenings, the only appropriate wine is a cold, slightly effervescent bottle of white Vinho Verde *(VEEN yo VAIRD)*. The high acidity of Vinho Verde has a bracing, cleansing effect on the palate. It is an especially good wine to accompany grilled fish or seafood.

The Minho region, where Vinho Verde is made, is in the northwest corner of Portugal, directly across from the Rías Baixas wine region of Spain. (The region is particularly verdant because of the rain from the Atlantic Ocean — one theory behind the wine's name.)

Two quality levels of white Vinho Verde exist on the market place. The most-commonly found brands (Aveleda and Casal Garcia) sell for $6 to $7. These brands are medium-dry wines of average quality and are best served cold. The more expensive Vinho Verdes ($15 to $20) are made from the Alvarinho grape (same grape as Rías Baixas's Albariño). They are a more complex, longer-lasting version of Vinho Verde and are Portugal's best white wines. Unfortunately, the more expensive Vinho Verdes are more difficult to find than the inexpensive ones; look for them in finer wine shops or in Portuguese neighborhoods (or on your next trip to Portugal!).

There is also a red Vinho Verde — in fact, the majority of wines from this DOC region are red. It is a *highly* acidic wine — you definitely need to acquire a taste for it (which we haven't acquired yet!).

Noteworthy Portuguese red wines

The best red wine in Portugal, *Barca Velha,* comes from the Douro region, where Port is made. The Ferreira Port House makes this wine from the same local grapes used to make Port and only in good vintage years. Barca Velha is a full-bodied, intense, concentrated wine that needs years to age — Portugal's version of Vega Sicilia's Unico, but at a much lower price (the 1985 costs about $35). Like Vega Sicilia, not much is made, and consequently, Barca Velha is hard to find.

The good news is that the Port house of Ramos Pinto (recently acquired by Roederer Champagne) is now also making some fine, inexpensive, top-quality red wines that will be more readily available. The 1992 *Duas Quintas* has ripe, plummy, velvety fruit; it is a surprisingly rich but supple wine, drinkable now and selling at $8 to $10. The more full-bodied, intense 1991 *Duas Quintas Reserva* needs a few years to age; it is an outstanding wine at any price — at $18 to $19, this Douro red is an amazing value.

Other good red Portuguese wines to look for include:

✔ **Quinta do Carmo:** This estate in the Alentejo in southern Portugal was recently purchased by Château Lafite-Rothschild's owners. A rich, full-bodied wine, the 1987 sells for $15 to $18.

✔ **Quinta de Pancas:** Made with Cabernet Sauvignon and local grapes, in the Alenquer region, north of Lisbon, this well-made wine is a steal at $6 to $7.

✔ **Quinta da Bacalhôa:** An estate-bottled Cabernet Sauvignon made by the esteemed Portuguese winemaker, Joào Pires, in Azeitão (south of Lisbon); the Bacalhôa has the elegance of a Bordeaux; the 1990 sells for $12 – $13.

✔ **Tapada do Chaves:** This impressive, rich, full-bodied wine from the Portalegre region in eastern Portugal (near the border of Spain) does not have an importer in the U.S. yet, but look for it when it does arrive; one of the most impressive wines that we've tried in Portugal.

✔ **The red wines of J.M. da Fonseca** (no relation to the Port house of the same name): This firm is producing some of the best red wines in Portugal. Look for *Quinta da Camarate, Morgado do Reguengo, Garrafeira TE*, and *Tinto Velho Rosado Fernandes*.

Portuguese wine terms

The following terms might appear on Portuguese wine labels:

Reserva: A wine of superior quality from one vintage

Garrafeira: A reserva that has been aged at least two years in a cask and one in a bottle for a red wine; six months in a cask, six months in a bottle for a white wine

Quinta: Estate or vineyard

Colheita: Vintage year

Seco: Dry

Adega: Winery

Tinto: Red

Vinho: Wine

Germany: Europe's Individualist

German wines march to the beat of a different drum. They come mainly in one color: white. They are fruity in style, often medium-dry or sweet, low in alcohol, and they are rarely oaked — the antithesis of current taste trends. Their labels carry grape names, which is an anomaly in Europe. And their classification system is not based on the French AOC system, as most other European wines are.

Germany is one of the northernmost wine-producing countries in Europe — which means that its climate is cool. Except in pockets of warmer weather in southern Germany, red grapes don't ripen adequately (by the standards of the rest of the wine world) in Germany; about 85 percent of Germany's wine production is therefore white wine. The climate is also erratic from year to year, meaning that vintages do matter for fine German wines.

Germany's finest vineyard sites are situated by rivers like the Rhine and the Mosel, which temper the extremes of the weather and aid the grapes in ripening fully.

Riesling and its cohorts

In Germany's cool climate, the noble Riesling grape finds true happiness. But Riesling ripens successfully and predictably year after year only in Germany's best vineyards. Thus, Riesling represents only 21 percent of Germany's vineyard plantings.

The grape variety most planted throughout Germany is Müller-Thurgau (pronounced *MOO ler TER gow*), a crossing purportedly between the Riesling and Silvaner grapes. Müller-Thurgau ripens early, thus taking much of the anxiety out of harvest season for its growers. Its wines are softer than Riesling with less character and little potential for greatness.

After Müller-Thurgau and Riesling, a number of grapes make up the balance of Germany's white vineyard plantings: Silvaner, Kerner, Scheurebe *(SHOY reb beh)* and Ruländer (Pinot Gris) being the most important. Among Germany's red grapes, Spätburgunder (Pinot Noir) is the most widely planted, mainly in the warmer parts of the country.

Germany's wine laws: Ripeness is king

Like most European wines, German wines are named after the places they come from — usually a combination of a village name and a vineyard name, such as Piesporter (town) Goldtröpfchen (vineyard). Unlike most European wines, however, the grape name is also usually part of German wine names (as in Piesporter Goldtröpfchen *Riesling*). And the finest German wines have yet another element in their name — a *prädikat (PRAY di cat)*, an indication of the ripeness of the grapes (as in Piesporter Goldtröpfchen Riesling *Spätlese*). Wines with a *prädikat* hold the highest rank in the German wine system.

Germany's system of assigning the highest rank to the ripest grapes is completely different from the concept behind most other European appellation systems, which is to bestow the highest status on the best vineyards or districts. Germany's system underscores the country's grape growing priorities: Ripeness — never guaranteed in a cool climate — is the highest goal.

There are six *prädikat* levels. From the least ripe to the ripest (that is, from the lowest to the highest), they are:

- ✔ Kabinett *(KAB ee net)*
- ✔ Spätlese *(SHPATE lay seh)*
- ✔ Auslese *(OUSE lay seh)*
- ✔ Beerenauslese *(BEER en OUSE lay seh)*
- ✔ Eiswein *(ICE vine)*
- ✔ Trockenbeerenauslese *(TROH ken BEER en OUSE lay seh)*

At the three highest *prädikat* levels, the amount of sugar in the very ripe grapes is so high that the wines are inevitably sweet. Many people, therefore, mistakenly believe that the *prädikat* level of a German wine is an indication of the wine's sweetness. In fact the *prädikat* is an indication of the amount of sugar in the *grapes at harvest,* not the amount of sugar in the resulting wine. At lower *prädikat* levels, the sugar in the grapes can be fermented fully, to dryness; and for those wines there is *no direct correlation between prädikat level and sweetness of the wine.*

Wines whose (grape) ripeness earns them a *prädikat* are categorized as QmP wines (*Qualitätswein mit Prädikat*), translated as *quality wines with special attributes* (their ripeness). They are QWPSR wines in the eyes of the EU (see Chapter 8). When the ripeness of the grapes in a particular vineyard is insufficient to earn the wine a *prädikat* name, the wine can still qualify as a "quality wine" in Germany's second QWPSR tier, called QbA (*Qualitätswein bestimmter Anbaugebiet*), translated as *quality wine from a special region.* Often the term *Qualitätswein* alone will appear on labels of QbA wines.

Less than ten percent of Germany's wine production falls into the table wine categories *Landwein* (table wines with geographic indication) or *Deutscher Tafelwein.*

Fooling Mother Nature

Unfortunately for Germany, codifying ripeness levels into wine law does nothing to change the reality of Mother Nature's cool climate. In reality, even grapes that are ripe enough to qualify as *kabinett* can still have such high acid levels and low sugar levels that the wine made from them is destined to be very light-bodied and tart — not necessarily well-balanced or pleasurable in the eyes of many wine drinkers.

Somewhere along the way, however, German wine producers found a way to mimic the ripeness that Mother Nature denies them. By making many of their wines in a medium-dry to sweet style, they change the balance in their wines, creating wines that most wine drinkers consider delicious and pleasurable.

In the mouth, acidity counterbalances — and is counterbalanced by — sweetness and alcohol. If a white wine has high alcohol or has sweetness, its acidity is perceived as lower than it actually is, and even a wine with very high acidity can then taste relatively soft.

The way that the Germans devised to keep some sweetness in their wines is called the *süssreserve* method. In this method, a winemaker ferments his wine fully dry, ending up with a low alcohol, high acid dry wine. Before fermentation, however, he holds back a small quantity of his grape juice and does not ferment it. Later, he blends this grape juice with his dry wine. The unfermented grape juice (the *süssreserve*) contributes its natural, juicy sweetness to the wine.

Germany's most famous wine

The light, fresh style of German wines makes them particularly appropriate for people just beginning to enjoy wine. One German wine, in fact, has single-handedly introduced millions of people to the pleasures of wine. That wine is Liebfraumilch *(LEEB frow milsh)*. Liebfraumilch, translated as *milk of the virgin,* takes its name from a vineyard in Worms, in the Rheinhessen region, which surrounds a majestic church named for Our Lady. Liebfraumilch today is a wine blended from several grape varieties, mainly Müller-Thurgau with some Riesling, Silvaner and/or Kerner. It can be produced in four of Germany's wine regions: the Rheinhessen, the Pfalz (these two accounting for the great majority of its production), the Nahe, and the Rheingau. Liebfraumilch is, by definition, a medium-dry, QbA-level wine; it is usually low in alcohol and should be enjoyed as young as possible.

Dry, half-dry, or gentle?

Most inexpensive German wines, such as Liebfraumilch, are produced with *süssreserve*. They are light-bodied, fruity wines with pleasant sweetness — wines that are easy to enjoy without food. The German term for this style of wine is *lieblich*, which translates as gentle — a poetic but apt descriptor.

While *lieblich*-style German wines are popular all over the world, German consumers themselves have begun to favor dryer wines in recent years, especially for drinking with meals. The very driest German wines are called *trocken* (dry). Wines that are sweeter than *trocken* but dryer than *lieblich* are called *halbtrocken* (half-dry). These words usually appear on the label, but not always.

What's noble about rot?

No matter how much of a dry tooth German consumers develop, they will undoubtedly admit that the greatest wines of their country are the sweet wines. Wine connoisseurs all over the world, in fact, recognize Germany's sweetest wines as among the greatest wines on the face of the earth.

Oddly enough, Germany's great sweet wines do not owe their sweetness to *süssreserve* but rather to the same Mother Nature who so often denies the rest of Germany's wines adequate ripeness. Although Germany has a cool climate with short summers, German autumns are long and often warm. When grapes from the best vineyard sites are allowed to hang on the vine longer than usual, they can become infected by the ugly but magical fungus known as *botrytis cinerea*, commonly called *noble rot*.

Noble rot dehydrates the berries, concentrating their sugar and their flavors in the process. When these infected berries are used for the production of wine, the wine they give is sweet, amazingly rich, and complex beyond description. It can also be expensive: $100 a bottle or more!

Wines of the *prädikat* levels *beerenauslese* (abbreviated as BA) and *trockenbeerenauslese* (abbreviated as TBA) are usually made entirely from grapes infected with noble rot (called *botrytised* grapes) and are generally richly textured and sweet. *Auslese* level wines often are made with some partially botrytised grapes, and when they are, they are likely to be sweet although never to the extent of a BA or TBA.

Another way that Nature can contribute unusual sweetness to German wines is by freezing the grapes on the vine late in the autumn or in early winter. When the grape grower harvests the frozen grapes and crushes them, much of the water in the berries separates out as ice. The juice that is left to ferment is concentrated in sugar and flavor and makes a lush sweet wine that carries the *prädikat eiswein* (literally, *ice wine*). *Eisweins* differ from BAs and TBAs because they lack a certain flavor that derives from botrytis, sometimes described as a honeyed character.

Both botrytised wines and *eisweins* are referred to as *late-harvest wines*, not only in Germany but all over the world, because the special character of these wines comes from conditions that normally occur only when the grapes are left on the vine beyond the usual point of harvest.

Germany's wine regions

With the reunification of Germany, Germany has 13 wine regions — 11 in the west and another 2 in the eastern part of the country (see Figure 11-3).

The most famous of these 13 are the Mosel-Saar-Ruwer region, named for the Mosel River and two of its tributaries, along which the region's vineyards lie; and the Rheingau region along the Rhine River.

The Mosel-Saar-Ruwer is a dramatically beautiful region, its vineyards rising steeply along the slopes of the twisting and turning Mosel River. The wines of the region are among the lightest in Germany; they are generally delicate and charming, often containing a slight amount of carbon dioxide, which accentuates their freshness and their liveliness. Riesling dominates the Mosel-Saar-Ruwer with 55 percent of the plantings, while the Müller-Thurgau grape occupies half as much vineyard land as Riesling. Place-names from the Mosel-Saar-Ruwer most commonly found on wine labels include: *Zell, Piesport,* and *Bernkastel.* Wines from this region are instantly recognizable because they come in green bottles rather than the brown bottles that other German wines use.

A secret code of German place-names

If you don't speak German and you don't know German geography intimately, you'll surely find deciphering German wine names tricky. But here's a bit of information that can help. In German, the possessive is formed by adding the suffix *er* to a noun. When you see names like Zeller or Hochheimer — names that end in *er* — on a wine label, the next word is usually a vineyard area that "belongs" to the commune or district with the *er* on its name (Zell's Swartze Katz, Hochheim's Kirchenstück). You still have to learn what the *prädikats* mean, though.

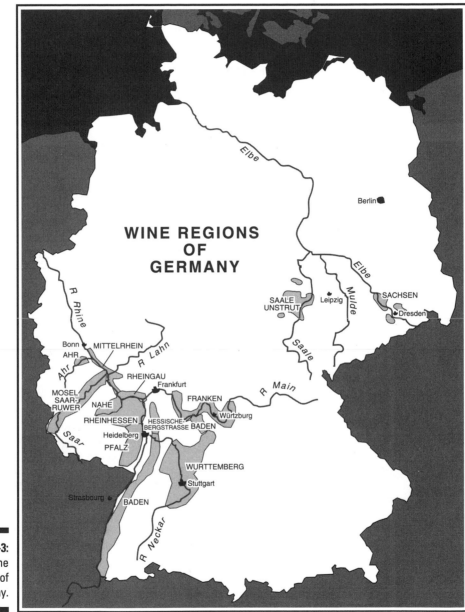

The Rheingau is among Germany's smaller wine regions. It, too, has dramatically steep vineyards bordering a river, but here the river is Germany's greatest wine river, the Rhine. The Riesling grape occupies more than 80 percent of the Rheingau's vineyards, and the Rheingau is, in fact, the origin of some of Germany's very best Rieslings — thanks at least partially to the region's south-facing slopes that give the Riesling an extra edge of ripeness. Rheingau wine styles tend toward two extremes, *trocken* wines on the one hand and sweet late-harvest and *eisweins* on the other.

Carrying the banner for dry Rheingau Rieslings is an impassioned group of winery owners called the Charta Association, whose *trocken* or *halbtrocken* wines carry the Charta symbol (a double arch) on their capsules and back labels. Some Rheingau place-names likely to be seen on wine labels include *Hochheim, Rüdesheim, Hattenheim,* and *Erbach.*

The Rhine River lends its name to three other German wine regions, Rheinhessen, the Pfalz (until recently called the Rheinpfalz), and the Mittelrhein. The Rheinhessen is Germany's largest wine region, producing large quantities of simple wines for everyday enjoyment. Liebfraumilch originated here, and it is one of the most important wines of the region today — although now it can by law be produced in three other regions, as well. Numerous grape varieties grow in the Rheinhessen, with Müller-Thurgau and Silvaner at the top of the list. Many of the region's vineyards extend far away from the Rhine River, but the Rhinehessen's highest quality wines come from the Rheinterrasse, a vineyard area along the river. District or commune names from the Rheinhessen include *Nierstein, Nackenheim,* and *Oppenheim.*

Almost as big as the Rheinhessen, the Pfalz has earned somewhat more respect from wine lovers for its fairly rich and full-bodied white wines and its very good red wines — all of which owe their style to the region's relatively warm climate. Müller-Thurgau, Riesling, Silvaner, and Kerner are among the most planted grape varieties of the Pfalz, but qualitatively Scheurebe and Blauburgunder (Pinot Noir) are important. Village names from the Pfalz that are seen in export markets include *Wachenheim, Forst,* and *Deidesheim.*

The Mittelrhein is one of Germany's tiniest wine regions, producing mainly Riesling wines along the banks of the northern Rhine.

Two other German regions of importance are the Nahe (named for the Nahe River and situated west of the Rheinhessen) and Baden, Germany's southern-most region, which enjoys a warmer climate than any other region in Germany and produces fairly full-bodied German wines as a result.

Pronunciation guide to Germany's wine regions

Ahr	*AHRE*	Nahe	*NAH heh*
Baden	*BAH den*	Pfalz	*FALLZ*
Franken	*FRAHN ken*	Rheingau	*RYNE gow*
Hessische	*HESS ish sheh*	Rheinhessen	*RYNE hess ehn*
Bergstrasse	*BERG strahs seh*	Saale-Unstrut	*SAHL-UN strutt*
Mittelrhein	*MIT tel ryne*	Sachsen	*SAHCK sen*
Mosel-Saar-Ruwer	*MOH zel-zar-ROO ver*	Württemberg	*VERT tem berg*

Switzerland: Stay-at-Home Wines

Nestled between Germany, France, and Italy, Switzerland is in a perfectly logical location for growing grapes and making fine wine. In fact, Switzerland has a small but proud wine industry: Vineyards grace the country's three faces — French-speaking, German-speaking and Italian-speaking. But few wine lovers outside of Switzerland have much opportunity to taste Swiss wines because the production is small and because the wines are so popular within Switzerland itself.

About two-thirds of Switzerland's wines are white; most are made from Chasselas — a grape cultivated with much less distinction in Germany, eastern France, and the Loire Valley. In Switzerland, Chasselas wines tend to be dry, fairly full-bodied, and unoaked, with mineral and earthy flavors. Other white grapes include Pinot Gris, Sylvaner, Marsanne, Petit Arvine, and Amigne — the latter two indigenous to Switzerland. Merlot is an important red grape (especially in the Italian-speaking Ticino region) along with Pinot Noir and Gamay.

As befits a country with varied terrain (hills of varying altitudes, large lakes, sheltered valleys), numerous microclimates contribute to many wine styles, from relatively full-bodied red and white wines to more delicate, crisp white wines.

Switzerland's major wine regions include the Vaud, along Lake Geneva; Valais, to the east, along the Rhone River; Neuchatel, in western Switzerland north of the Vaud; Ticino, in the south, bordering Italy; and Thurgau in the north, bordering Germany.

When you do find a bottle of Swiss wine, you might be surprised to discover how costly it is — $15 and up in the U.S., reflecting high production costs. If you buy a bottle of white Swiss wine in Switzerland, you might also be surprised to find a screw cap closure — one of Switzerland's more courageous contributions to the art of wine enjoyment, considering the poor image of screw cap wines.

Austria: A New Quality Direction

Austria makes three times as much wine as Switzerland, but none of it comes from the parts of the country that border Switzerland, Germany, or Italy. Only in eastern Austria, where the Alps recede into hills, do vineyards decorate the landscape.

Once a supplier of inexpensive bulk wines to other countries, Austria's wine industry has transformed itself in the past ten years and now shows a fresh face: dedicated young winemakers, private estates bottling their own production, and quality dry wines appropriate for a quality-conscious world market. The relatively small presence of Austrian wines in North America is bound to increase as a result.

The ratio of white to red wines in Austria is 80/20, the red wines being produced mainly in the region of Burgenland bordering Hungary, one of the warmest parts of the country. The red wines are medium- to full-bodied, often engagingly spicy with moderate tannin and vivid fruit. Many of the red wines are based on unusual grape varieties such as Blauer Zweigelt, rarely found elsewhere.

Austria's white wines occupy two camps: dry, firm whites ranging from light- to full-bodied, and lush late-harvest whites, made from botrytised grapes or extremely ripe grapes. While the excellence of Austria's sweet whites has long been recognized, her dry whites and reds are just beginning to gain recognition.

The country's single most important grape variety is the white Gruner Veltliner, which Austria can claim as her very own. Its wines are full-bodied yet crisp, with herbal and sometimes spicy-vegetal flavors (especially green pepper). Müller-Thurgau and Welschriesling are tied for second in plantings. Welschriesling, a grape popular in Eastern Europe for inexpensive commercial wines, reaches its finest quality in Austria.

Of Austria's four wine regions, Lower Austria, in the north, produces the largest quantity, mainly along the plain of the Danube River. Burgenland, in the east, ranks second; Styria, a southern region bordering Slovenia, and the tiny region of Vienna are the other two.

Austria's wine laws are based on the German system, with QWPSR wine divided into *Qualitätswein* and *Prädikatswein* categories. The *prädikat* levels are the same as in Germany, except that *Prädikatswein* begins at *spätlese* (*kabinett* wine falls into the *Qualitätswein* group). The minimum ripeness requirements for each level are also higher in Austria than in Germany, and the wines are higher in alcohol.

In some parts of Austria, for example in the Wachau district of Lower Austria, wines are named in the German system — a town name ending in *er* followed by a vineyard name and a grape variety — while in other parts, such as Burgenland, the wine names are generally a grape name followed by the name of the region.

Ten white wines you should try at least once

Wine	*Grape Varieties*	*Country of Origin*	*Approximate Price*
1. Chablis '92/'93 (R. & V. Dauvissat)	Chardonnay	France (Chablis)	$15 to $16 Premier Cru, $20 to $25
2. Domaine de Pouy (R. Kacher, Importer) (most recent vintage)	Ugni Blanc (Gascony)	France	$4 to $5
3. Chardonnay, '92/'93 (Kistler Vineyards)	Chardonnay	U.S. – California (Sonoma)	$25 to $35 (Dutton, McCrea, or Kistler)
Chardonnay, '92/'93 (Long Vineyards)	Chardonnay	U.S. – California (Napa)	$25 to $30
4. Sauvignon Blanc, '93 (Peter Michael)	Sauvignon Blanc	U.S. – California (Napa – Howell Mt.)	$16 to $18
Fumé Blanc Reserve, '93 (Robert Mondavi)	Sauvignon Blanc Semillon	U.S.– California (Napa)	$16 to $18
5. Pinot Gris, '91/'92 (Eyrie Vineyards)	Pinot Gris	U.S. – Oregon	$14 to $15
Pinot Gris, '94 (Rex Hill Winery)	Pinot Gris	U.S. – Oregon (Willamette Valley)	$12 to $14
6. Tocai Friulano, '93 (Livio Felluga)	Tocai Friulano	Italy (Friuli – Collio)	$15 to $16
7. Sauvignon Blanc (Cloudy Bay)	Sauvignon Blanc	New Zealand (Marlborough)	$16 to $18

(continued)

(continued from preceding page)

Wine	Grape Varieties	Country of Origin	Approximate Price
8. **Albariño, '94 (Bodegas Morgadío)**	Albariño	Spain (Galicia – Rías Baixas)	$17 to $18
9. **Chassagne-Montrachet, '92 (Niellon)**	Chardonnay	France (Burgundy)	$25 to $27 Premier Cru $32 to $33
10. **Meursault, '92 (Verget)**	Chardonnay	France (Burgundy)	$25 to $35 various Premier Crus
Saint Véran, '92/'93 (Verget)	Chardonnay	France (Burgundy)	$12 to $14
Up and Coming Wines to Look For:			
Viognier, '92/'93 (Calera)	Viognier	U.S. – California (San Benito – Mt. Harlan)	$23 to $24
Viognier, '92/'93 (Alban Vineyards)	Viognier	U.S. – California San Luis Obispo – Edna Valley	$16 to 18

Chapter 12

The Brave New World of Wine

*W*hat do the wines of North America, South America, Africa, and Australia have in common? None of them are produced in Europe. In fact, you could say that they are the wines of "Not Europe."

The name most often used in wine circles for Not Europe is the *New World*. Undoubtedly this phrase, with its ring of colonialism, was coined by a European. Europe, home of all the classic wine regions of the world, producer of more than half the wine in the world, is the Old World. Everything else is nouveau riche.

When we first heard the expression *New World* applied to wines, we thought it was absurd. How can you lump together wine regions as remote as Napa Valley, the Finger Lakes, Coonawarra, and Santiago? (It's a bit like saying that Thailand, the U.S., and Liechtenstein are all the same because they're countries.)

But then we started thinking about it. In Europe, they've been making wines for hundreds of years. Which hillsides to plant, which grapes should grow where, how dry or sweet a particular wine should be — these decisions were all made long ago, by the grandfathers and great-great-grandfathers of today's winemakers. In Not Europe, the grape growing and winemaking game is wide open; every winery owner gets to decide for himself where to grow his grapes, what grape variety to plant, and what style of wine to make. The wines of the New World do have that in common.

The more we thought about it, the more similarities we found among New World wine regions as compared to Europe. Finally, we concluded that the New World is an actual winemaking entity whose legislative reality, spirit, and winemaking style are unique from those of the Old World — as generalizations go.

We could easily fill 400 pages on the wines of the U.S., Canada, South America, Australia, New Zealand, and South Africa alone, if only we had the space. Fortunately, New World wines are easy for you to explore without a detailed road map: In the New World, there's very little encoded tradition to decipher and very little historical backdrop against which the wines need to be appreciated. Think of New World wines as modern art; you can approach them and enjoy them at face value without ever having studied art history. They come at you loud and clear.

America, America

Even though some wine was made commercially in the last century, the United States wine industry arrived big time only in the past generation. Prohibition from 1920 to 1933, the Great Depression, and WW II were serious blows to the wine business — and recovery was slow.

From the 1930s through the 1960s, American wine consisted mainly of sweet, fortified wines and *jug wines* (inexpensive generic wines; see Chapter 7), many from California's hot Central Valley and the gigantic Gallo winery. Jug wines and their younger sibling, bag-in-the-box wines, are still a sizable part of U.S. wine sales, but major change has occurred during the last 25 to 30 years. And once you graduate from jug wines, there's no going back.

The 1970s began the Wine Rush Era in California. Before 1970, only a few operating wineries existed in the state; today, California has more than 800 bonded wineries (mainly small, family-owned operations) — and the numbers are growing.

California's growth has stimulated interest in wine all across the country. Today, wineries exist in 43 of the 50 United States. But wine production is an important industry only in four states: California (the largest wine producing state, by far), Washington, Oregon, and New York. The U.S. now ranks fourth in world wine production — although well behind Italy, France, and Spain.

The old and the new

In wine terms, the New World is not just geography but also an attitude. Some winemakers in Europe approach wine the liberated New World way, and some winemakers in California are certainly dedicated Old World traditionalists. Keep that in mind as you look over the following comparison between the Old and the New. And remember, we're talking generalizations here — and generalizations are never always true.

New World	*Old World*
Innovation	Tradition
Wines named after grape varieties	Wines named after region of production
Winemaking goal is expression of the fruit	Winemaking goal is expression of *terroir*
Technology is revered	Old-fashioned methods are favored
Flavorful, fruity wines	Subtle, less-fruity wines
Grape-growing regions are broad and flexible	Grape-growing regions are small and fixed
Winemaking as science	Winemaking as art
If a winemaking process can be controlled, control it	Intervene as little as possible
The winemaker gets credit for the wine	The vineyard gets the credit

Home-grown ways

The wines of the U.S. — especially California — are the essence of New World wine think. Winemakers operate freely, planting whatever grape variety they wish wherever they wish to plant it. They blend wines from different regions together as they wish. (Blending among states is trickier, because of federal rules.)

U.S. wines have elevated grape varieties to star status. Until California began naming wines after grapes, Chardonnay and Cabernet were just behind-the-scenes ingredients of great wines — but now they *are* the wine. Lest anyone thinks that all wines from a particular grape are the same, however, winemakers have emerged as celebrities who put their personal spin on the best wines. In the California scenario especially, the land — the *terroir* — is secondary.

American winemakers have made technology their ally in their efforts to create wines that taste like fruit. California's two important universities for wine-making — the University of California (U.C.) Fresno and, especially, the U.C. Davis — have become world leaders in the scientific study of wine. Even European winemakers now make pilgrimages to California to study at the U.C. Davis.

Playing by their own rules

An appellation system for wines does exist in the U.S., and like the classic French model, it defines the regions where wine is made. But the U.S. system of American Viticultural Areas (AVAs) establishes only the geographical boundaries of wine zones; it does not stipulate which grape varieties can be planted, the maximum yield of grapes per acre (see "Vine growing vernacular" Chapter 3), or anything else that would link the geography to a wine style. AVA names, the name of the region of production, therefore have secondary importance on wine labels after the name of the grape.

Wines labeled with the name of a grape variety in the U.S. must be made at least 75 percent from that grape variety, according to federal law. Wines with an AVA indication must derive 85 percent of their grapes from that AVA. Wines with vintage years must derive at least 95 percent from the named vintage.

A smorgasbord of AVAs

Winemakers often forego using a smaller, more specific AVA designation in order to widen their options in buying grapes and wine. A winery in Alexander Valley, within Sonoma County, for example, might use the broader *Sonoma County* AVA instead, if he buys grapes from (or owns vineyards in) other areas of the county; he could use the larger *North Coast* AVA if he blends in wine from neighboring counties, like Napa; and if low price is a goal, the winery will use the even broader *California* AVA in order to buy less expensive grapes from the industrial vineyards of the Central Valley (the San Joaquin Valley) or other parts of the state where grapes and wine are less

expensive. (This practice doesn't occur in smaller viticultural areas, such as southern Pennsylvania, where there are few alternative sources of grapes.) While specificity of place is admired, on the one hand, making a good wine at a good price through geographical blending is also admired. The relative merits depend on who's doing the admiring.

Traditional or not, America's way of making wine and naming wine sits just right with wine drinkers in the U.S.: American wines now account for approximately 75 percent of all wine sales in the United States.

California, USA

When you think about American wine, you think of California. That's not surprising — California accounts for 96 percent of U.S. wine production.

California's Gallo winery is the largest winery by far — producing one out of every four bottles of wine sold in the U.S. If Gallo were a separate country, it would rank about 13th or 14th in the world for wine production, with an output roughly equivalent to Chile's — if not higher (but without a national debt).

It was the Robert Mondavi Winery, however, that provided the stimulus to produce fine wine in the U.S. When Robert Mondavi left his family's winery (Charles Krug Winery) in 1966 to begin his own operation dedicated to premium wines, his move symbolized the beginning of an age of awareness of better-quality wines in the U.S. These finer wines would be varietally named Cabernet Sauvignon, Chardonnay, and so on — a reaction to the nondescript jug wines labeled with names borrowed from Europe's wine regions, such as Burgundy and Chablis. Today, even Gallo is very much in the varietal wine business.

California's fine wine regions

In sunny California, there's no lack of warm areas for growing grapes. For fine wine production, the challenge is to find those areas that are cool enough, with poor enough soil, so that grapes don't ripen too quickly, too easily, without full flavor development (see "Vine growing vernacular" in Chapter 3). Nearness to the Pacific coast and/or altitude are important determinants of climate in California — more so than latitude. Premium wines are, therefore, made up and down almost the whole length of the state.

The most important fine wine regions and districts include the following (see Figure 12-1):

✔ **North Coast Region (North Coast AVA):**

> Napa Valley
> Sonoma Valley
> Mendocino and Lake Counties

✔ **North-Central Coast Region:**

> Livermore and Santa Clara Valleys (San Francisco Bay area)
> Santa Cruz Mountains
> Monterey County

- **Sierra Foothills Region**
- **South-Central Coast Region:**

    San Luis Obispo County
    Santa Barbara County

Weather variations from year to year are far less dramatic in California than they are in most European wine regions. One important reason is that it doesn't rain during the growing season in much of California (rain at the wrong time is the usual cause of Europe's poorer vintages). Using irrigation, winemakers in effect control the rain themselves. Ironically, one factor that can cause vintage variation in California is lack of water for irrigation: drought.

Figure 12-1: The Wine Regions of California.

Wine lovers who are interested in making fine distinctions of quality will be happy to know that California has enjoyed an amazing streak of five excellent vintages, from 1990 to 1994 (1990 and 1991 being the best for red wines, 1990, 1992, and 1993 for whites). Among older vintages, 1984, 1985 and 1987 were good red wine vintages, while 1986 was a fine year for white wines.

Napa Valley: America's most famous wine region

Napa Valley is about a ninety minute drive northeast of the beautiful bay city of San Francisco. Many of California's most prestigious wineries — and certainly its most expensive vineyard land — are in the small Napa Valley, where more than 200 wineries have managed to find space. (In 1960, there were only ten wineries.) The region's size is much tinier than its reputation: Napa produces only five percent of California's grapes.

The southern part of the Valley, affected by ocean breezes and mists from the San Pablo Bay, is the coolest area, especially the Carneros district. Carneros — which extends westward into Sonoma County — has become the vineyard area of choice for grapes that enjoy a cool climate: Chardonnays, Pinot Noirs, and grapes for sparkling wines. North towards Calistoga— away from the bay influence— the climate gets quite hot (but always with cool nights).

From $4 to $40

You can find Chardonnays and Cabernets from California at prices as low as $4 a bottle. Better wines are in the $12 to $20 range, however. The *reserves, single-vineyard wines,* and *special selection wines* generally cost from $20 to $40 and up.

Most good Pinot Noirs and Merlots start at about $15 and can go as high as $30 (a few even higher).

Sauvignon Blancs—somewhat less in demand— are the best values among California's premium wines. You can find many good ones for under $10 although a few are priced as high as $15. Red Zinfandels are still a bargain, but their prices are climbing as they become more popular: You can still find many Red Zins from $10 to $15 although a few premium Zinfandels are as high as $20. If you like White Zinfandels, you can save yourself a bundle; they're in the $4 to $6 range.

The words *reserve, special selection, private reserve, barrel select, vintners reserve, classic,* and so on have no legal definition in the U.S. Although many premium wineries use one of these terms to indicate their special or better wines, most of the larger wineries use the same terms on their inexpensive bottlings as marketing tools (see the "Reserve" section in Chapter 8).

Wineries and vineyards are located throughout Napa Valley, many on the valley floor, some in the hills and mountains to the west (Mayacamas Mountains), and some in the mountains to the east (Howell Mountain). Napa winemakers and grape growers have established eight AVAs besides the broad Napa Valley AVA itself and the Carneros AVA, which Napa and Sonoma share. These other eight are

- Spring Mountain and Mt. Veeder (both in the western mountains)
- Howell Mountain, Stags Leap District, Atlas Peak (all hilly or mountainous areas), and Wild Horse Valley, all in the eastern part of Napa
- Rutherford and Oakville, on the valley floor

The grapes of Napa

Almost everyone in Napa who makes table wine makes a Cabernet Sauvignon and a Chardonnay, and many Napa producers are now also making Merlot. Softer, less tannic, and more approachable than Cabernet Sauvignon, Merlot has become the hot, new red wine in the U.S., especially with consumers who are just getting into red wine.

The six most important wines in Napa are the two whites, Chardonnay and Sauvignon Blanc (often labeled Fumé Blanc), and the four red wines, Cabernet Sauvignon, Merlot, Pinot Noir (mainly from cool Carneros), and Zinfandel. But blended wines have become increasingly important in the last ten years. If red, these blends are usually made from red Bordeaux varieties (Cabernet Sauvignon, Cabernet Franc, Merlot, and sometimes even Malbec and Petit Verdot). If white, they're usually made from the white Bordeaux grapes (Sauvignon Blanc and Sémillon). Some of these blends are referred to as Meritage wines — not just in Napa but across the U.S. — although few carry the word *Meritage* on their labels.

Who's who in Napa (and for what)

If just about every winery in Napa makes a Chardonnay and a Cabernet, how can you distinguish the various wineries from one another? Good question — and there's no easy answer. The following list indicates some of the better table wine producers in Napa Valley, as well as their best wines, and could help steer you in the right direction. We know the list looks overwhelming, but . . . that's Napa!

Our list includes Napa classics as well as some personal favorites. Sparkling wine producers are covered under "California" in Chapter 13.

- **Atlas Peak Vineyards:** Sangiovese
- **Beaulieu Vineyards:** Cabernet Sauvignon Private Reserve (Georges de Latour)
- **Beringer Vineyards:** Cabernet Sauvignon Private Reserve, Chardonnay Reserves
- **Burgess Cellars:** Zinfandel
- **Cain Cellars:** Cain Five (a blend of five Bordeaux varieties)
- **Cakebread Cellars:** Cabernet Sauvignon, Sauvignon Blanc
- **Carneros Creek:** Pinot Noir (especially Signature Reserve)
- **Caymus Vineyard:** Cabernet Sauvignon (especially *Special Selection*)
- **Chappellet:** Chenin Blanc, Cabernet Sauvignon
- **Chateau Montelena:** Cabernet Sauvignon, Chardonnay, Zinfandel
- **Chateau Woltner:** Chardonnay
- **Clos du Val:** Cabernet Sauvignon, Merlot, Sémillon
- **Dalla Valle:** Cabernet Sauvignon, Maya (blend of Cabernet Franc/ Cab Sauvignon)
- **Dominus:** Dominus (mainly Cabernet Sauvignon)
- **Duckhorn:** Merlot (especially Three Palms Vineyard), Cabernet Sauvignon, Sauvignon Blanc
- **Dunn Vineyards:** Cabernet Sauvignon (especially Howell Mountain)
- **Étude:** Pinot Noir, Cabernet Sauvignon
- **Far Niente:** Chardonnay, Cabernet Sauvignon
- **Flora Springs:** Soliloquy (Sauvignon Blanc), Trilogy (Cab Sauvignon, Merlot, Cab Franc)
- **Forman Vineyards:** Chardonnay, Cabernet Sauvignon
- **Franciscan Vineyards:** Chardonnay, Merlot, Cabernet Sauvignon
- **Freemark Abbey:** Cabernet Sauvignon (Bosché and Sycamore Vineyards), Chardonnay
- **Frog's Leap Winery:** Zinfandel, Sauvignon Blanc, Cabernet Sauvignon, Chardonnay
- **Grace Family Vineyards:** Cabernet Sauvignon (small production; mailing list only; see Chapter 16)
- **Green and Red Vineyard:** Zinfandel

- **Grgich Hills Cellar:** Chardonnay, Cabernet Sauvignon, Zinfandel, Fumé Blanc

- **Groth Vineyards:** Cabernet Sauvignon, Chardonnay

- **Harrison Vineyards:** Cabernet Sauvignon, Chardonnay

- **Heitz Wine Cellars:** Cabernet Sauvignon (Martha's/Bella Oaks vineyards), Grignolino

- **Hess Collection Winery:** Cabernet Sauvignon, Chardonnay

- **La Jota Vineyard:** Cabernet Sauvignon, Viognier

- **Lamborn Family Vineyards:** Zinfandel

- **Long Vineyards:** Chardonnay

- **Markham Vineyards:** Chardonnay, Cabernet Sauvignon, Merlot

- **Mayacamas Vineyards:** Cabernet Sauvignon, Chardonnay

- **Merryvale Vineyards:** Chardonnay, Merlot

- **Robert Mondavi:** Cabernet Sauvignon, Pinot Noir, Fumé Blanc (especially the Reserves)

- **Monticello Cellars:** Cabernet Sauvignon (Corley Reserve, Jefferson Cuvée)

- **Newton Vineyard:** Cabernet Sauvignon, Merlot

- **Niebaum-Coppola Estate:** Rubicon (mainly Cabernet Sauvignon), Zinfandel

- **Opus One:** Opus One (mainly Cabernet Sauvignon)

- **Pahlmeyer Winery:** Caldwell Vineyard (mainly Cabernet Sauvignon)

- **Joseph Phelps Vineyards:** Cabernet Sauvignon Backus, (also Cab-based Insignia)

- **Pine Ridge Winery:** Cabernet Sauvignon

- **Kent Rasmussen Winery:** Pinot Noir

- **Raymond Vineyard:** Cabernet Sauvignon

- **St. Clement Vineyards:** Chardonnay, Cabernet Sauvignon, Sauvignon Blanc

- **Saintsbury:** Pinot Noir (especially Carneros and Reserve), Chardonnay Reserve

- **Shafer Vineyards:** Cabernet Sauvignon (especially Hillside Select), Merlot

- **Silver Oak Cellars:** Cabernet Sauvignon

- **Silverado Vineyards:** Cabernet Sauvignon, Merlot

- ✔ **Robert Sinskey Vineyards:** Merlot, Carneros Claret (mainly Merlot)
- ✔ **Smith-Madrone:** Riesling, Chardonnay
- ✔ **Spottswoode Winery:** Cabernet Sauvignon
- ✔ **Stag's Leap Wine Cellars:** Cask 23 (Cab blend), Cabernet Sauvignon (SLV), Chardonnay, Riesling
- ✔ **Sterling Vineyards:** Cabernet Sauvignon (Diamond Mt.), Chardonnay (Winery Lake)
- ✔ **Stony Hill Vineyard:** Chardonnay, Riesling
- ✔ **Storybook Mountain:** Zinfandel
- ✔ **Swanson Vineyards:** Cabernet Sauvignon, Chardonnay
- ✔ **Philip Togni Vineyard:** Cabernet Sauvignon, Sauvignon Blanc
- ✔ **Trefethen Vineyards:** Cabernet Sauvignon, Chardonnay, dry Riesling
- ✔ **Turnbull Vineyards** (formerly Johnson Turnbull): Cabernet Sauvignon
- ✔ **Whitehall Lane Winery:** Cabernet Sauvignon (especially Single-Vineyard Reserve), Merlot
- ✔ **Z D Winery:** Chardonnay, Cabernet Sauvignon (estate)

The diverse terroir of Sonoma

If you leave San Francisco over the beautiful Golden Gate Bridge, you'll be in Sonoma in an hour. The differences between Napa and Sonoma are remarkable. Whereas many of Napa's wineries are showy (and downright luxurious), most of Sonoma's are rustic, country-like, and laid back. The millionaires bought into Napa; Sonoma is just folks.

On the other hand, Sonoma *is* the home of the famously successful Sebastiani, Glen Ellen, Korbel, Jordan, and Simi wineries — not exactly small time operations! And Gallo is moving into Sonoma, in a *big* way. We have the sneaking impression that if we visit Sonoma in 15 or 20 years, it will bear a striking resemblance to Napa. But we hope not; we like it the way it is.

Sonoma is larger and more spread out than Napa. Its climate is similar to Napa's, except that some areas near the coast are definitely cooler. Although there is plenty of Chardonnay, Cabernet Sauvignon, and Merlot in Sonoma, the region's varied microclimates and terrain have allowed three other varieties to excel — Pinot Noir, Zinfandel, and Sauvignon Blanc.

The viticultural areas (AVAs) of Sonoma County and their principal grape varieties (and wines) are the following:

- **Sonoma Valley:** Chardonnay (to a lesser extent, Pinot Noir, Cabernet Sauvignon, Zinfandel)

- **Sonoma Mountain:** Cabernet Sauvignon

- **Russian River Valley:** Pinot Noir, Chardonnay, sparkling wine, Zinfandel

- **Sonoma-Green Valley** (within Russian River Valley): Sparkling wine, Chardonnay

- **Chalk Hill** (within Russian River Valley): Chardonnay, Sauvignon Blanc

- **Dry Creek Valley:** Zinfandel, Cabernet Sauvignon

- **Alexander Valley:** Cabernet Sauvignon, Chardonnay, Sauvignon Blanc

- **Knights Valley:** Cabernet Sauvignon, Sauvignon Blanc

Sonoma County has two more AVAs: Northern Sonoma, a patchwork area encompassing Russian River Valley, Alexander Valley, Dry Creek Valley, and Knight's Valley; and Sonoma Coast, a hodgepodge of land in western Sonoma, along the coast.

Pinot Noir lovers should look for wine from Russian River Valley producers, such as Williams & Selyem, Rochioli, Gary Farrell, and Dehlinger. We agree with the many wine critics who say that the Russian River Valley is the source of some of the best Pinot Noir in the entire New World.

Recommmended Sonoma producers and wines

The following list includes some of Sonoma's better producers along with their best wines, listed alphabetically. It's *slightly* less staggering than the Napa list.

- **Alexander Valley Vineyards:** Cabernet Sauvignon, Merlot

- **Arrowood Vineyards:** Chardonnay, Cabernet Sauvignon, Late Harvest Riesling

- **Davis Bynum Winery:** Pinot Noir, Zinfandel, Merlot

- **Carmenet Vineyard:** Meritage (mainly Cabernet Sauvignon)

- **Chalk Hill Winery:** Sauvignon Blanc, Chardonnay

- **Château Souverain:** Cabernet Sauvignon, Merlot, Chardonnay, Zinfandel

- **Cline Cellars:** Oakley Cuvée (Rhône blend), Zinfandel

- **Clos du Bois:** Chardonnay, Cabernet Sauvignon, Marlstone (Cabernet-based blend)

- **Dehlinger Winery:** Pinot Noir, Chardonnay

Make my Zinfandel *red*

In most wine stores, not a day goes by without the following scene taking place.

Customer: Where is your Zinfandel?

Sales Person: Do you want red or white?

Customer (with puzzled look and hesitation): Er, white, you know, the pink one! (Pause) You mean it comes in red, too?

When Bob Trinchero of Napa's Sutter Home Winery decided to make a pink wine out of his Red Zinfandel grapes in 1972 and call it White Zinfandel, he made a brilliant marketing decision. Red Zins were not selling well at the time. Few Americans had developed a taste for dry red wine — and those who *did* drink dry red wine drank Cabernet Sauvignon or European reds. But millions of Americans drank Coke, Pepsi, and other sweet soft drinks. The slightly sweet, fruity taste of White Zinfandel suited their taste just right. White Zinfandel became the hottest wine in the U.S.

Actually, Red Zinfandel is *the* California wine. The Zinfandel grape variety hardly exists outside of California. Red Zin is a wonderful, exuberant wine, one of our favorites. It smells and tastes of berry-cherry fruit, it's rich, and it has a velvety texture. Red Zinfandel is at its best when it's young (in its first six years), but it's also capable of aging. And Zinfandel is not expensive. The best examples come from Dry Creek and Russian River Valleys in Sonoma, especially from the old Zinfandel vines that Italian immigrant farmers planted 80 to 100 years ago (see the list of recommended producers).

- ✔ **De Loach Vineyards:** Chardonnay, Gewurztraminer, Zinfandel
- ✔ **Dry Creek Vineyards:** Fumé Blanc, Cabernet Sauvignon, Zinfandel
- ✔ **Gary Farrell Wines:** Pinot Noir, Chardonnay
- ✔ **Ferrari-Carano:** Chardonnay, Fumé Blanc, Merlot
- ✔ **Field Stone Winery:** Petite Sirah
- ✔ **Fisher Vineyards:** Chardonnay, Cabernet Sauvignon
- ✔ **Foppiano Vineyards:** Petite Sirah
- ✔ **Geyser Peak Winery:** Cabernet Sauvignon, Merlot, Semchard (75 percent Sémillon)
- ✔ **Gundlach-Bundschu Winery:** Zinfandel, Cabernet Sauvignon
- ✔ **Hanna Winery:** Chardonnay, Sauvignon Blanc, Cabernet Sauvignon
- ✔ **Hanzell Vineyards:** Chardonnay
- ✔ **Jordan Vineyard:** Cabernet Sauvignon
- ✔ **Kenwood Vineyards:** Cabernet Sauvignon, Zinfandel
- ✔ **Kistler Vineyards:** Chardonnay (considered by many to be America's best); Pinot Noir

- ✓ **Landmark Vineyards:** Chardonnay (especially Two Williams)
- ✓ **Laurel Glen Vineyard:** Cabernet Sauvignon
- ✓ **Limerick Lane Cellars:** Zinfandel
- ✓ **Marcassin:** Chardonnay (small production; mailing list only)
- ✓ **Marietta Cellars:** Cabernet Sauvignon, Zinfandel, Old Vine Red Lot 12 (Zin blend)
- ✓ **Matanzas Creek Winery:** Chardonnay, Sauvignon Blanc, Merlot
- ✓ **Peter Michael Winery:** Chardonnay
- ✓ **Murphy-Goode Estate Winery:** Fumé Blanc
- ✓ **Nalle Winery:** Zinfandel
- ✓ **Preston Vineyards:** Sauvignon Blanc, Zinfandel, Barbera
- ✓ **Quivera Vineyards:** Zinfandel, Cabernet Cuvée (mainly Cabernet Sauvignon)
- ✓ **A. Rafanelli Winery:** Zinfandel, Cabernet Sauvignon
- ✓ **Ravenswood:** Zinfandel (especially single-vineyards), Merlot, Pickberry (Bordeaux blend)
- ✓ **Rochioli Vineyards:** Pinot Noir, Sauvignon Blanc
- ✓ **St. Francis Winery:** Chardonnay, Merlot
- ✓ **Sausal Winery:** Zinfandel, White Zinfandel
- ✓ **Seghesio Winery:** Zinfandel, Chianti Station (85 percent Sangiovese)
- ✓ **Simi Winery:** Chardonnay, Sauvignon Blanc, Cabernet Sauvignon
- ✓ **Sonoma-Cutrer Vineyards:** Chardonnay
- ✓ **Joseph Swan Vineyards:** Zinfandel
- ✓ **Trentadue Winery:** Zinfandel, Petite Sirah, Old Patch Red (Carignane blend)
- ✓ **Williams & Selyem Winery:** Pinot Noir, Zinfandel
- ✓ **Z. Moore Winery:** Gewurztraminer (dry)

Mendocino and Lake Counties

If you have a chance, it's worth your while to drive up the beautiful California coastline from San Francisco on Route 1 to the quaint, old town of Mendocino — perhaps with a side trip to view the magnificent, giant redwoods of the Pacific

Coast. There aren't as many tourists up here as in Napa or Sonoma, but that makes it all the nicer: You'll be genuinely welcomed at the wineries.

Lake County, dominated by Clear Lake, is Napa's neighbor to the north, while Mendocino County is directly north of Sonoma. Prohibition hit both Mendocino and Lake Counties quite hard. As recently as 1967, the only operating winery in Mendocino was Parducci; none were left in Lake County. But the following year, Fetzer opened its doors in Mendocino, and the wine boom was on. Fetzer went on to become the dominant winery in that county, and Kendall-Jackson, which started selling wine in the early 1980s, became the dominant Lake County winery (although most of the grapes are from elsewhere).

The cool Anderson Valley in Mendocino is ideal for the production of Chardonnay, Pinot Noir, Gewurztraminer, Riesling, and sparkling wine. The wily Roederer Champagne house bypassed Napa and Sonoma to start its sparkling wine operation here and has been doing extremely well in a short time — as have Scharffenberger and Handley, two other successful sparkling wine producers in Anderson Valley.

The following list includes recommended producers and their best wines. Producers are listed alphabetically by county (sparkling wine producers are covered in the California section of Chapter 13).

Mendocino County

- ✔ **Fetzer Vineyards:** Cabernet Sauvignon Reserve, Chardonnay Reserve
- ✔ **Greenwood Ridge Vineyards:** Riesling, Merlot, Zinfandel
- ✔ **Handley Cellars:** Chardonnay, Gewurztraminer, Sauvignon Blanc
- ✔ **Hidden Cellars:** Zinfandel, Alchemy (Sémillon-Sauvignon Blanc blend)
- ✔ **Husch Vineyards:** Gewurztraminer, Pinot Noir
- ✔ **Lazy Creek Vineyards:** Gewurztraminer
- ✔ **Lolonis Winery:** Chardonnay, Fumé Blanc (especially Reserve)
- ✔ **McDowell Valley Vineyards:** Syrah
- ✔ **Navarro Vineyards:** Gewurztraminer (regular and Late Harvest)
- ✔ **Parducci Wine Cellars:** Zinfandel, Petite Sirah
- ✔ **Whaler Vineyard:** Zinfandel

Lake County

- ✔ **Guenoc Winery:** Zinfandel, Cabernet Sauvignon, Petite Sirah, Chardonnay
- ✔ **Kendall-Jackson Vineyards:** Chardonnay, Zinfandel
- ✔ **Konocti Cellars:** Fumé Blanc, White Meritage (Sauvignon Blanc-Sémillon blend)
- ✔ **Steele Wines:** Chardonnay, Zinfandel

San Francisco Bay Area

The urban spread, from Palo Alto to San Jose (Silicon Valley) and extending eastward, has taken its toll on vineyards in both Livermore and Santa Clara Valleys. Livermore, directly east of San Francisco, is quite warm, with some ocean breezes. Sauvignon Blanc and Sémillon have always done well there. Santa Clara Valley, south of San Francisco with the Santa Cruz Mountains on its western side, is cooled by breezes from the San Francisco Bay. Chardonnay, Cabernet Sauvignon, and Merlot are the three big grape varieties (and wines) there.

In the following listing of recommended producers, we've included one winery actually located in Marin County — Kalin Cellars. The winemaker, Terry Leighton, gets his grapes from many diverse areas, including Livermore. We've also included a winery located near San Francisco — Rosenblum Cellars. (We'll treat the wineries of the Santa Cruz Mountains separately in the next section.)

The following list includes some recommended producers in Livermore and Santa Clara Valleys (listed alphabetically, by locality):

- ✔ **Marin County**

    Kalin Cellars: Sauvignon Blanc, Sémillon, Chardonnay
- ✔ **Alameda**

    Rosenblum Cellars: Zinfandel (especially single-vineyards)
- ✔ **Livermore Valley**

    Concannon Vineyard: Sauvignon Blanc, Petite Sirah

    Wente Bros.: Chardonnay, Late Harvest Riesling
- ✔ **Santa Clara Valley**

    J. Lohr Winery: Cabernet Sauvignon (Paso Robles)

    Jory Winery: Red Zeppelin (Zinfandel, Carignane, Cabernet Franc), Merlot

    Mirassou Vineyards: White Burgundy (Pinot Blanc)

Santa Cruz Mountains

Standing atop one of the isolated Santa Cruz Mountains, you forget that you are only an hour's drive south of San Francisco. The rugged, wild beauty of this area has spawned quite a few wineries, including some of the best in the state. The climate is basically cool, especially on the ocean side, where Pinot Noir thrives. On the San Francisco Bay side, Cabernet Sauvignon is the important red variety. But Chardonnay is the dominant grape on both sides. There are also some important winemakers in this region — Paul Draper of Ridge Vineyards and Randall Grahm of Bonny Doon being but two.

The following is a list of recommended producers in the Santa Cruz Mountains, along with their best wines (listed alphabetically):

- **Ahlgren Vineyard:** Chardonnay, Cabernet Sauvignon

- **Bargetto:** Chardonnay, Cabernet Sauvignon

- **Bonny Doon Vineyard:** Le Sophiste, Le Cigare Volant (white and red Rhône-types)

- **David Bruce Winery:** Pinot Noir

- **Cinnabar Vineyards:** Chardonnay, Cabernet Sauvignon

- **Thomas Fogarty Winery:** Chardonnay, Pinot Noir, Gewurztraminer

- **Kathryn Kennedy Winery:** Cabernet Sauvignon

- **Mount Eden Vineyards:** Chardonnay (estate bottled), Cabernet Sauvignon

- **Page Mill Winery:** Chardonnay (Santa Clara), Pinot Noir, Sauvignon Blanc

- **Ridge Vineyards:** Cabernet Sauvignon (especially Monte Bello), Geyserville (Zin blend), Zinfandel, Chardonnay

- **Santa Cruz Mountain Vineyard:** Pinot Noir, Cabernet Sauvignon

- **Storrs Winery:** Chardonnay, White Riesling

- **Sunrise Winery:** Zinfandel, Pinot Noir

- **Woodside Vineyards:** Cabernet Sauvignon, Chardonnay

Down in old Monterey

Monterey County has a little bit of everything — a beautiful coastline, the *chic* town of Carmel, some very cool vineyard districts, some very warm areas, mountain wineries and Salinas Valley wineries, a few gigantic wine firms, and lots of small ones. The wineries have had their growing pains, such as learning how to avoid vegetal flavors in their wines, where the best areas for the various grape varieties are located, and (presently) how to cope with the phylloxera louse (see the "Of genus and species" section in Chapter 9).

Chardonnay leads the way here — as it does in most of the state. But the cooler parts of Monterey are also principal sources for Riesling and Gewurztraminer. Cabernet Sauvignon and Pinot Noir (in the mountains) are the leading red varieties.

The following is a list of recommended producers in Monterey County (and one producer from neighboring San Benito County), along with their best wines (listed alphabetically):

- **Bernardus:** Chardonnay
- **Calera (San Benito):** Pinot Noir, Viognier
- **Chalone Vineyard:** Chardonnay, Pinot Blanc
- **Durney Vineyard:** Cabernet Sauvignon
- **Estancia:** Chardonnay
- **Jekel Vineyard:** Riesling
- **Lockwood:** Riesling, Chardonnay Reserve, Cabernet Sauvignon, Pinot Blanc
- **Morgan Winery:** Cabernet Sauvignon
- **Smith & Hook Winery:** Merlot
- **Robert Talbott Vineyard:** Chardonnay
- **Ventana Vineyards:** Riesling, Sauvignon Blanc

Thar's wine in them there Foothills

No wine region in America has a more romantic past than the Sierra Foothills. The Gold Rush of 1849 carved a place in history for the Foothills. It also brought vineyards to the area to provide wine for the thirsty miners. That wine was undoubtedly Zinfandel — still the region's most famous wine. In fact, very little has changed in the Sierra Foothills over the years. This is clearly the West Coast's most rustic wine region — perhaps the country's. Therein lies its charm: A visit to the Foothills is like a trip into the past, when life was simple.

The Sierra Foothills is a sprawling wine region east of Sacramento, centered in Amador and El Dorado Counties, but spreading north and south of both. Two of its best-known viticultural areas are Shenendoah Valley and Fiddletown. Summers can be hot, but many vineyards have been planted in high altitudes, such as around Placerville in El Dorado. Soil throughout the region is mainly volcanic in origin.

The following is a listing of recommended producers in the Sierra Foothills, along with their best wines (listed alphabetically):

- ✔ **Amador Foothill Winery:** Zinfandel
- ✔ **Boeger Winery:** Merlot, Zinfandel, Barbera
- ✔ **Granite Springs Winery:** Zinfandel, Petite Sirah
- ✔ **Karly:** Zinfandel, Sauvignon Blanc
- ✔ **Madrona Vineyards:** Riesling, Gewurztraminer, Zinfandel
- ✔ **Nevada City Winery:** Zinfandel
- ✔ **Renaissance Vineyard:** Riesling (dry and late harvest), Sauvignon Blanc
- ✔ **Santino Winery:** Zinfandel, Barbera, Late Harvest Riesling
- ✔ **Sierra Vista Winery:** Zinfandel, Cabernet Sauvignon
- ✔ **Sobon Estate:** Syrah
- ✔ **Stevenot Winery:** Zinfandel, Chardonnay (Grand Reserves)

San Luis Obispo: Mountain meets maritime

San Luis Obispo County is another region made up of vastly diverse viticultural areas ranging from warm, hilly Paso Robles (north of the town of San Luis Obispo) where Zinfandel and Cabernet Sauvignon reign, to cool, maritime Edna Valley and Arroyo Grande (south of the town), home of some very good Pinot Noirs and Chardonnays. The areas are so different that we have grouped the producers separately below.

The following producers, along with their best wines, are recommended in San Luis Obispo (listed alphabetically):

- ✔ **Paso Robles**

    Creston Vineyards: Pinot Noir, Zinfandel
    Eberle Winery: Cabernet Sauvignon, Zinfandel
    Justin Winery: Cabernet Sauvignon, Chardonnay
    Mastantuono: Zinfandel
    Meridian Vineyards: Chardonnay, Syrah
    Peachy Canyon Winery: Zinfandel
    Wild Horse Winery: Pinot Noir, Chardonnay, Merlot

- ✔ **Edna Valley and Arroyo Grande**

    Alban Vineyards: Viognier
    Corbett Canyon Vineyards: Pinot Noir Reserve (and other good value wines)
    Edna Valley Vineyards: Chardonnay
    Saucelito Canyon Vineyard: Zinfandel
    Talley Vineyards: Pinot Noir, Chardonnay

Santa Barbara, paradise in southern California

Clearly, the most exciting new viticultural areas in California — if not in the entire country — are in Santa Barbara County. We say *new* even though we are aware that the Spanish missionaries had vineyards planted here 200 years ago. But in modern times, it was as late as 1975 before the first major winery (Firestone Vineyards) opened for business. In light of what we now know — that is, how well-suited Santa Barbara is for winemaking — 1975 was a late start.

The cool Santa Maria, Santa Ynez, and Los Alamos Valleys, which lie north of the city of Santa Barbara, run east to west, opening towards the Pacific Ocean and chanelling in the cool ocean air. The climate is ideal for Pinot Noir and Chardonnay. In the Santa Maria Valley, one of the main sources of these varieties, the average temperature during the growing season is a mere 74°F. Further south, in the Santa Ynez Valley, Riesling also does well.

The Pinot Noir grape has earned Santa Barbara much of its acclaim as a wine region. Santa Barbara is now generally recognized as one of the four great American viticultural areas for the difficult to grow Pinot Noir — the other three being Carneros, the Russian River Valley, and the Willamette Valley (in Oregon). In Santa Barbara, Pinot Noirs seem to burst with luscious strawberry fruit, with herbal tones. Pinot Noirs tend to be precocious, delicious in their first four or five years — not the *keepers* that the sturdier, wilder-tasting Russian River Pinot Noirs seem to be. But why keep them when they taste so good?

Mini-trends in California wine

Experimentation is a constant in California. Although Chardonnay and Cabernet are the annointed grape varieties at the moment, winemakers can never know whether they're missing the boat on some other important grape — unless they try growing it.

Some producers have become enchanted with the grape varieties from France's Rhône Valley — the red grapes Syrah, Grenache, Mourvèdre, and Cinsault and the white Viognier. These producers are collectively referred to as the Rhône Rangers, an unofficial term. Other producers are growing Italian grapes like Sangiovese and Nebbiolo. (Some Italian grapes, like Barbera, have been grown in California since the days of the Italian immigrants in the last century.) And next year — who knows? — the new grape could be Spain's Tempranillo. Stay tuned.

The following is a list of some recommended producers in Santa Barbara, along with their best wines (listed alphabetically):

- **Au Bon Climat:** Pinot Noir, Chardonnay (especially single-vineyard bottlings of both)
- **Babcock Vineyards:** Chardonnay (Grand Cuvée), Sauvignon Blanc
- **Byron Vineyard:** Chardonnay, Sauvignon Blanc
- **Cambria Winery:** Chardonnay, Pinot Noir
- **J. Carey Cellars:** Cabernet Sauvignon, Merlot, Sauvignon Blanc
- **Cottonwood Canyon:** Pinot Noir, Chardonnay
- **Fiddlehead Cellars:** Pinot Noir
- **Firestone Vineyard:** Riesling, Cabernet Sauvignon Reserve
- **Foxen Vineyard:** Pinot Noir, Chardonnay
- **Gainey Vineyard:** Riesling, Sauvignon Blanc (estate), Pinot Noir (Sanford & Benedict Vineyard)
- **Fess Parker Winery:** Riesling, Syrah
- **Qupé Cellars:** Syrah, Chardonnay Reserve, Los Olivos Cuvée (Syrah, Mourvèdre)
- **Sanford Winery:** Pinot Noir (especially Sanford & Benedict Vineyard), Chardonnay, Sauvignon Blanc
- **Santa Barbara Winery:** Pinot Noir Reserve, Chardonnay Reserve
- **Lane Turner:** Pinot Noir (Sanford & Benedict Vineyard)

Oregon, A Tale of Two Pinots

Because Oregon is north of California, most people rightfully assume that Oregon's wine regions are cool. The *real* reason for Oregon's cool climate, though, is that there are no mountains standing between the Pacific Ocean and the vineyards. Along with cool temperatures, the ocean influence brings rain. Grape growing and winemaking are thus completely different in Oregon than they are in California.

Oregon first became recognized in wine circles for its Pinot Noir, a grape that needs cool climates to perform at its best (see "Red Grape Varieties" in Chapter 9). Although The Eyrie Vineyards released the state's first Pinot Noir in 1970, Oregon really only began to grab national attention for its wines after the excellent 1983 vintage. Today Pinot Noir is still Oregon's flagship wine. Oregon has had a string of good vintages, beginning with 1988 (especially 1990) on up to 1993. And 1994 is promising to be one of the best yet!

Neither Chardonnay nor Riesling — Oregon's two leading white grape varieties in terms of acreage — has received the acclaim of Pinot Noir. Because Chardonnay is the companion grape to Pinot Noir in the Burgundy region, however, and because the grape is so popular in America, Chardonnay has been considered important in Oregon.

Oregon's other Pinot

Now a white variety is emerging to challenge Chardonnay's domination — Pinot Gris, Oregon's other Pinot. It's too early to tell if Pinot Gris (a mutated descendant of Pinot Noir) will become a permanent fixture in Oregon, but it has sold very well during the last five years.

David Lett, founder and winemaker of The Eyrie Vineyards, is the man who made Oregon's first Pinot Gris in the early 1970s, followed by Ponzi Vineyards and Adelsheim Vineyards. Today, more than 30 wineries in Oregon are making Pinot Gris. While there are a few wineries in California and Washington making this variety, so far Pinot Gris has been an Oregon story in the U.S.

Pinot Gris has many things going for it. Because it doesn't particularly need oak aging to give it complexity (but it takes to oak well when that's the winemaker's preference), Pinot Gris can be ready to drink six months after the vintage. Pinot Gris is medium-bodied; its color ranges from a light golden yellow to a copper-pink, its aromas are reminiscent of pears and apples, sometimes of melon, and it has surprising depth and complexity. It's an excellent food wine, especially with seafood and salmon, just the kind of food that it's paired with in Oregon. And the best news is the price. Most of Oregon's Pinot Gris are in the $11 to $13 range.

Who's who in Willamette Valley

The main home of Pinot Noir and Pinot Gris in Oregon is the Willamette (will AM ett) Valley. Lying directly south of the city of Portland in northwest Oregon, the cool Willamette Valley has established itself in the last 25 years as the most important wine region in Oregon.

The Willamette Valley wine region is a convenient wine destination to visit because the wonderful city of Portland, with all its fine restaurants, hotels, and shops, is barely twenty minutes away.

The huge Willamette Valley encompasses several counties. Yamhill County, directly southwest of Portland, has the greatest concentration of wineries, all of which produce Pinot Noir (most of them now have Pinot Gris as well). But many wineries are located in Washington County, west of Portland, and in Polk County, south of Yamhill. In fact, one of Oregon's pioneer wineries, Tualatin, is located in Washington County. This winery has become a white wine specialist, with Riesling, Gewurztraminer, and Chardonnay as its standard-bearers.

The most important producers in the Willamette Valley, primarily for Pinot Noir and Pinot Gris (but sometimes also Chardonnay or Riesling), are listed alphabetically below:

Acme Wineworks (John Thomas)
Adelsheim Vineyard
Amity Vineyards
Archery Summit
Argyle (for sparkling wines)
Beaux Frères
Bethel Heights Vineyard
Broadley Vineyards
Cameron Winery
Chehalem Vineyards
Cooper Mountain Vineyards
Cristom Vineyards
Domaine Drouhin (owned by the famed Burgundy négociant, Joseph Drouhin)
Domaine Serene
Elk Cove Vineyards
Eola Hills Wine Cellars
Evesham Wood Vineyard

The Eyrie Vineyards
Hinman Vineyards (Silvan Ridge)
King Estate Winery (located just south of Willamette Valley)
Knudsen-Erath (Erath Winery)
Kramer Vineyards
Lange Winery
Laurel Ridge Winery
Montinore Vineyards
Oak Knoll Winery
Panther Creek Cellars
Ponzi Vineyards
Redhawk Vineyard
Rex Hill Vineyards
St. Innocent Winery
Sokol Blosser Winery
Tualatin Vineyards
Willamette Valley Vineyards
Yamhill Valley Vineyards

King of Oregon

Oregon's wineries have mainly been small, family-run operations. But King Estate, which opened in 1992, is a major exception. Owned by multimillionaire Ed King, Jr., King Estate is located southwest of Eugene — about a three-hour drive from Portland. King has built a state-of-the-art winery; he has already become Oregon's largest producer, primarily of Pinot Noir and Pinot Gris, but with some Chardonnay. Furthermore, the quality of the wines has been quite good in its first two vintages, 1992 and 1993. Everyone in the Oregon wine industry hopes that King Estate's well-financed marketing efforts will help increase awareness of all of Oregon's wines — just as Chateau Ste. Michelle has done for Washington's wines.

Two other Oregon wine regions

Two other wine regions of note in Oregon are both in the southwest part of the state: the Umqua Valley (around the town of Roseburg) and farther south, next to California's northern border, the Rogue River Valley.

Considerably warmer than Willamette, the Umqua Valley is the site of Oregon's first winery, Hillcrest Vineyards, founded in 1962. The main grape varieties in Umqua are the Pinot Noir, Chardonnay, Riesling, and Cabernet Sauvignon. Besides Hillcrest Vineyards, which is known primarily for its Riesling, the other major wineries are Henry Estate and Girardet Wine Cellars, known for their Pinot Noir and Chardonnay.

The Rogue River Valley is warmer still; therefore, Cabernet Sauvignon and Merlot often perform better than Pinot Noir. Chardonnay is the leading white wine, but Pinot Gris is becoming popular. Bridgeview Vineyards, the region's largest winery, is doing an admirable job with Pinot Gris as well as Pinot Noir. Three other vineyards to watch are Ashland Vineyards, Valley View Vineyard, and Foris Vineyards — the latter a specialist in Merlot and Cabernet Sauvignon.

Wine on the Desert: Washington State

Although Washington and Oregon are neighboring states, their wine regions have vastly different climates due to the Cascade Mountains, which cut through both states from north to south.

On Washington's western side, the climate can be described as maritime — cool, plenty of rain, and lots of vegetation. (In Oregon, almost all the vineyards are located on the coastal side.) East of the mountains, the climate in Washington is continental, with hot, very dry summers, and harsh, almost desertlike conditions. Most of Washington's vineyards are situated in this area.

Washington's winemakers have found that many grapes, but certainly not Pinot Noir, flourish in this environment. Here, in the Washington "desert," the Bordeaux varieties — Merlot, Cabernet Sauvignon, Sauvignon Blanc, and Sémillon — are the name of the game, along with the ever present Chardonnay. Washington has become particularly well-known for the quality of its Merlots. One brand, Columbia Crest, is the largest-selling Merlot in the United States.

Washington does have a few vineyards west of the Cascades, around Puget Sound, where Riesling does well. And, in fact, many of the larger wineries, such as Chateau Ste. Michelle and Columbia Winery, are located in the Puget Sound area, near the thriving city of Seattle. Selling wine in Seattle is a bit easier than in the desert! Chateau Ste. Michelle (along with Columbia Crest, its subsidiary winery) is the giant in the state; it accounts for 50 percent of all of Washington's wines at present.

Like Oregon, Washington got off to a late start in the wine business. Not until the early 1980s did wineries, recognizing the state's potential for growing vinifera varieties (see Chapter 9), really begin to develop.

Vintage-wise, the two great years for Washington have been the 1983 and 1989 (the 1983 Cabernet Sauvignons, in fact, could use more time). In recent vintages, 1992 has been fine for both white and red wines.

Washington's wine regions

Washington has three major viticultural areas, two very large regions and one tiny one (just getting started but huge with potential). The three regions are

- ✔ **Columbia Valley:** The largest in terms of acreage, this region accounts for about 58 percent of Washington's *vinifera* varieties. Eleven wineries are located here, and many Puget Sound wineries use grapes from this area.

- ✔ **Yakima Valley:** The second largest in acreage (about 40 percent of Washington's vinifera acreage), but with the largest number of wineries (22).

- ✔ **Walla Walla Valley:** Less than one percent of the state's vinifera grapes and only six wineries here, but this region includes two of the state's premium names, Leonetti and Woodward Canyon.

A Washington oddity

When was the last time you had a Lemberger? No, we don't mean cheese! Lemberger is a little-known grape variety from Germany that's also grown in Austria, where it's called Blaufrankish. Don't feel bad if you haven't heard of it, because few people in the United States — outside of Washington — have tasted it.

Lemberger is a hardy red variety that does well in the Yakima Valley; it makes a fruity but dry, inexpensive wine in the Beaujolais or Dolcetto school but is uniquely its own. Hoodsport Winery, Covey Run, and Hogue Cellars are three good producers of Lemberger — the wine!

Who's who in Washington

No, we're not talking about cabinet members and senators here! The following are recommended producers in Washington, grouped according to location of the winery (listed alphabetically within each group):

Columbia Valley and Yakima Valley

Blackwood Canyon Vintners
Gordon Brothers Cellars
Chinook Wines
Columbia Crest Winery
Covey Run Vintners
Barnard Griffin Winery

The Hogue Cellars
Hyatt Vineyards
Preston Wine Cellars
Quarry Lake Winery
Staton Hills Winery
Stewart Vineyards

Walla Walla Valley

L'Ecole #41
Leonetti Cellar (outstanding Cabernet Sauvignon; mailing list is your best bet)
Seven Hills (technically in Oregon, but a Walla Walla Valley producer)

Waterbrook Winery
Woodward Canyon (the other star in Walla Walla; Cabernet and Chardonnay)

Puget Sound Producers

Château Ste. Michelle
Columbia Winery
Hedges Cellars
Hoodsport Winery
McCrea Cellars
Mount Baker Vineyards

Quilceda Creek Vintners (small but excellent producer of Cabernet Sauvignon)
Snoqualmie Winery
Paul Thomas Winery

You can buy some wines (usually from small wineries whose wines are sought after — such as Leonetti Cellar) only directly from the winery. In the "Directly From the Source" section of Chapter 16, we provide the necessary information for you to put yourself on these wineries' mailing lists.

The Empire State

New York City may be the capital of the world in many ways, but its state's wines do not get the recognition they deserve, perhaps because of California's overwhelming presence in the U.S. market. The oldest continuously operating winery in the United States, Brotherhood Winery, opened its doors in New York's Hudson Valley in 1839. And the second largest winery in the United States, Canandaigua Wine Company, has its headquarters in the Finger Lakes. In fact, New York is the second largest wine producer in the country.

New York's most important region by far is the Finger Lakes in western New York, where four large lakes temper the climate. This AVA produces approximately 85 percent of New York's wines. The other two important regions are the Hudson Valley, along the Hudson River north of New York City, and Long Island, which has two AVAs — North Fork of Long Island (the more important) and the Hamptons, on the island's south fork.

In the early days (prior to 1960), most of New York's wines were made from local *Vitis labrusca* (see Chapter 9) varieties, such as Concord, Catawba, Delaware, and Niagara. The phylloxera louse never did develop a taste for these vines. Unfortunately, most wine drinkers didn't develop a taste for the wines, either (they are mainly sweet, grapey beverages). One step in the right direction for New York grape growers was the 1930s introduction of French-American hybrid grapes (see Chapter 9) such as Seyval Blanc, Baco Noir, and Marechal Foch by the pioneering French winemaker, Charles Fournier. The hybrids can withstand the difficult winters of New York's Finger Lakes region, like the grapes from the *labrusca* species vines, but their wines are more mainstream in taste.

Common wisdom held that New York climate could not support *Vitis vinifera* varieties. But a Russian immigrant, the late, great Dr. Konstantin Frank, proved all the naysayers wrong when he succeeded in growing Riesling (followed by many other vinifera varieties) in 1953 in Hammondsport, part of the Finger Lakes region. (The first wines from vinifera grapes were actually made in 1961 at his winery, Dr. Frank's Vinifera Wine Cellars.) Today, son Willy Frank runs one of the most successful wineries in the state, with an entire line of fine vinifera wines and an excellent sparkling wine.

The Long Island story

The newest wine success story in New York is Long Island. In 1973, Alec and Louisa Hargrave got the idea that Long Island's North Fork (about a two-hour drive east of New York City) had the ideal climate and soil for vinifera grapes. Today, Long Island is 17 wineries strong and growing! Like Washington state, Long Island seems particularly suited to Merlot, but Chardonnay, Riesling, Cabernet Sauvignon, and Sauvignon Blanc are also grown. An excellent Long Island vintage was the 1991, which was actually a good vintage throughout the state.

Who's who in New York

The New York wine industry has grown from 19 wineries in 1976 to over 100 today — half of them in the Finger Lakes region and most of them small, family-run operations. Following is a list of recommended producers in New York's three major wine regions.

The Finger Lakes Region

Casa Larga Vineyards
Fox Run Vineyards
Glenora Wine Cellars (especially for sparkling wines)
Heron Hill Vineyards
Hunt Country Vineyards
Knapp Vineyards
Lamoreaux Landing Wine Cellars
Lucas Vineyards

McGregor Vineyard Winery
Prejean Winery
Standing Stone Vineyards
Swedish Hill Vineyard
Vinifera Wine Cellars (and its affiliate, Chateau Frank, for sparkling wines)
Wagner Vineyards
Widmer's Wine Cellars
Hermann J. Wiemer Vineyard

Hudson River Valley Region

Adair Vineyards
Baldwin Vineyards
Benmarl Vineyard
Brotherhood America's Oldest Winery, Ltd.

Cascade Mountain Vineyards
Clinton Vineyards
Magnanini Winery
Millbrook Vineyard & Winery
Walker Valley Vineyards

Long Island Region

Bedell Cellars
Gristina Vineyards
Hargrave Vineyard
Lenz Winery
Palmer Vineyards
Paumanok Vineyards, Ltd.

Peconic Bay Vineyards
Pelligrini Vineyards
Pindar Vineyards
Sagpond Vineyards (South Fork)

Oh, Canada

Ask just about any wine lover in the U.S. about Canadian wines, and you'll probably get a blank stare in response. Canada's wines are known mainly to Canadians, who consume the bulk of their country's production.

Wine is made in four of Canada's provinces, but Ontario has bragging rights as the largest producer by far, with 80 percent of the national production. British Columbia ranks second. Quebec and Nova Scotia also produce wine.

Following the same path as other New World countries, Canada's wine industry has shifted away from sweet, fortified wines and toward dry wines (although naturally sweet wines such as icewine are a specialty). Canada has also moved away from native grape varieties — mainly *Vitis labrusca* vines — toward hybrids (see chapter 9) and now *Vitis vinifera* grapes.

To identify and promote wines made entirely from local grapes (some Canadian wineries import wines from other countries to blend with local production), the provinces of Ontario and British Columbia have established an appellation system called VQA, Vintners' Quality Alliance. This system regulates the use of provincial names on wine labels, establishes which grape varieties can be used (vinifera varieties and certain hybrids), regulates the use of the terms *Icewine, Late Harvest,* and *Botrytised,* and requires wines to pass a taste test.

Ontario

Ontario's vineyards are cool-climate wine zones, despite the fact that they lie on the same parallel as Rioja and Chianti Classico, warmer European wine regions discussed in Chapter 11. Sixty percent of the production is white wine, from Chardonnay, Riesling, Gewurztraminer, Pinot Blanc, Auxerrois, and the hybrids Seyval Blanc and Vidal. Red wines come from Pinot Noir, Gamay, Cabernet Sauvignon, Cabernet Franc, Merlot, and the hybrids Marechal Foch and Baco Noir.

Ontario's VQA rules permit the use of the appellation Ontario and also recognize three *Designated Viticultural Areas* (DVAs):

- ✔ **Niagara Peninsula:** Along the south shore of Lake Ontario
- ✔ **Pelee Island:** Eleven miles south of the Canadian mainland, in Lake Erie, Canada's most southerly vineyards
- ✔ **Lake Erie North Shore:** The sunniest of Canada's viticultural areas

Because winter temperatures regularly drop well below freezing, icewine is a specialty of Ontario, one that is gradually earning the Canadian wine industry a modicum of international attention.

British Columbia

The small but rapidly growing wine industry of British Columbia now boasts 33 wineries. Production is 84 percent white — from Auxerrois, Bacchus, Chardonnay, Ehrenfelser, Gewurztraminer, Pinot Gris, and Riesling — and 15 percent red, from Pinot Noir and Merlot. Bacchus and Ehrenfelser are vinifera crossings developed in Germany.

The Okanagan Valley in southeast British Columbia, where the climate is influenced by Lake Okanagan, is the center of wine production. VQA rules recognize four Designated Viticultural Areas:

- Okanagan Valley
- Similkameen Valley
- Fraser Valley
- Vancouver Island

History and Change in Chile

Chile's wine industry wears the designation *New World* somewhat uncomfortably. Vineyards were first established in Chile in the mid-16th century by the Spanish, and the country has maintained a thriving wine industry for several centuries, producing traditional wines for the home market from the common, red Pais grape. What is "new" about Chile, however, is the growth of its wine industry since the mid-1980s; what's "worldly" is her sudden development of a strong export market, and the strong shift of her viticulture toward French grape varieties like Cabernet Sauvignon, Sauvignon Blanc, and Chardonnay.

Blessed isolation

With the Pacific Ocean on one side and the Andes Mountains on the other, Chile is an isolated country. Viticulturally, this isolation has its advantages: Phylloxera doesn't exist in Chile, and vinifera vines can therefore grow on their own roots. Chile's other viticultural blessings include a coast range of mountains, which blocks the damp ocean air and rain from most vineyards, and the ocean's general cooling influence to moderate what might otherwise be a hot climate (considering Chile's fairly northerly latitude within the Southern Hemisphere).

Most of Chile's vineyards occupy the Central Valley, which lies between the coastal range and the Andes. The vineyards are specialized according to latitude. In the warmer north, table grapes (as opposed to wine grapes) grow, as well as grapes for Chile's brandy, *Pisco*. In the middle area — about 50 miles north of Santiago to 150 miles south of the city — the best wine grapes grow. And in the damper, southern part, the grapes for the domestic wine market — mainly Pais and Moscatel — grow. Growing conditions vary from east to west in the middle area of the Central Valley, the eastern area near the Andes being sunnier and drier, and the western area being damper.

From north to south within the Central Valley, the wine regions are:

- ✓ **Aconcagua:** North of Santiago, the warmest area for fine grapes
- ✓ **Maipo:** A small region where many of the major wineries are based
- ✓ **Rapel:** Where the Colchagua district is located, a cooler region than Maipo
- ✓ **Maule:** Where the Curicó district is located, cooler and less dry than Rapel; parts of this region grow Pais

The southern region of Bió Bió is planted mainly with Pais and Moscatel.

Another of Chile's wine regions, Casablanca, is slightly north of Santiago, close to the coast, and not in the Central Valley. This cool region has new vineyards of white grapes, mainly Chardonnay.

Foreign flavor

Half of Chile's wine-grape acreage is still planted with the Pais grape, and Moscatel acreage is significant, too. But Chile's natural resources and the popularity of her wines on export markets have spurred foreign investment in new vineyards. These new vineyards are mainly Cabernet Sauvignon, Merlot, and Chardonnay. Some of these grape varieties have existed in Chile for more than 100 years, but their plantings have increased dramatically in the past decade. Two white grapes, so-called Sauvignon and Sémillon, are also well established in Chile's vineyards, but the true identity of these grapes is uncertain.

Chile's wines are named for their grape varieties and generally carry a regional (or sometimes a district) indication, too. Stylistically, Chile's wines lack the exuberant fruitiness of Californian and Australian wines. The whites can be quite dilute and watery — probably the result of very high yields or perhaps the grapes' doubtful pedigree. The reds are finer and offer excellent value, ranging in price from $4 to $12. But Chilean reds have yet to prove themselves at the high end of the quality spectrum, with the possible exception of Concha y Toro's Cabernet Sauvignon, Don Melchor. Considering the rapid growth of Chile's wine industry, though, the style and quality of the wines could change within the course of just a few years.

Wineries and winemakers from France, Spain, and the U.S. have become part of the action in Chile. Château Lafite-Rothschild, for example, is an owner of the Los Vascos winery. Two other prominent Bordeaux producers, Bruno Prats of Château Cos d'Estournel, and Paul Pontallier, the brilliant winemaker of Château Margaux, have collaborated on a Chilean winery called Viña Aquitania. The Miguel Torres winery in Curicó is Spanish owned. And Augustin Huneeus of Franciscan Vineyards in California is developing a property in the Casblanca region.

Chile's most important wineries for the export market, in addition to those mentioned above, include Concha y Toro, Santa Rita, Santa Carolina, Cousiño Macul, Undurraga, Carmen, and Casa Lapostolle.

Argentina, a Major Player

Argentina produces about four times as much wine as Chile does, which is approximately as much as the U.S. It boasts the largest wine production in South America, the fifth largest wine production in the world, and one of the highest levels of wine consumption per capita in the world. Considering what a major player these statistics make Argentina on the international wine scene, the country's wine industry is very old-fashioned, and her wines are little known on export markets.

Vineyards have grown in Argentina since the mid-16th century, as they have in Chile. But Argentina's source of vines has been more diverse. For example, many vines were brought over by Italian immigrants.

Argentina's wine production centers on the Criolla grape, a pink-skinned version of Chile's Pais, and another pink grape called Cereza, which together account for half the grape plantings in Argentina. Most of the wine made from these grapes is a simple beverage for the domestic market.

White grapes include a grape called Pedro Giminez, Moscatel, the Spanish Torrontés, Chenin Blanc, Sémillon, Riesling, Chardonnay, and others. The most important red grape has traditionally been Malbec, a French variety credited with making Argentina's best reds, but the Italian Bonarda is now slightly more common. Other red grapes include Tempranillo, Barbera, Lambrusco, Cabernet Sauvignon, Pinot Noir, Syrah, and others.

Argentina's vineyard regions are situated mainly in the country's interior, where the Andes mountains divide Argentina from Chile. High altitude tempers the climate, but the vineyards are still very warm by day, cool by night, and desert dry. Rivers originating in the Andes flow through the area and provide water for irrigation.

The vast majority of Argentina's vineyards are in the state of Mendoza, roughly at the same latitude as Santiago, Chile. (One of Mendoza's wine districts is Maipú, not to be confused with Maipo in Chile.) San Juan, a hotter and drier state to the north, is the next most important vineyard area, with approximately one-third the acreage of Mendoza. North of San Juan is La Rioja.

The huge Penaflor winery — one of the largest in the world — dominates wine production in Argentina and is leading the country's movement toward modernization of winemaking. Penaflor now runs the smaller Trapiche winery, whose wines are commonly seen abroad. Other wineries that export include Santa Ana, Weinert, Catena, Etchart, Finca Flichman, Pasquale Toso, Navarro Correas, Bianchi, and Canale. Argentina's wines are generally even less expensive than Chile's.

Winemaking Thunder Down Under

Make no mistake about it: Australia is one of the World Powers of wine. In the course of just a few decades, the wine industry of Australia has catapulted itself from purveyor of mainly sweet and fortified wines into perhaps the most technologically-advanced, forward-thinking wine nation on earth.

Vinifera grapevines came to Australia from the Cape of Good Hope and Europe in the late 18th and early 19th centuries (the country has no native vines). As recently as 1960, the wines of Australia were rich, sweet wines, many of them fortified (styles typical of a warm climate) — a far cry from the fresh red and white table wines of today. In 1980, Chardonnay production was negligible; now Chardonnay is Australia's top white grape for fine wine. The fruity, well-priced, well-made wines that Australia has forged in the past two decades have rapidly earned fans as far away as the U.S., the U.K., and Sweden.

A country approximately the same size as the continental U.S., Australia has about 700 wineries but produces less than 30 percent as much wine as California. (Yet per capita wine consumption in Australia is double that of the U.S.) Australia's wine regions are, for the most part, all in the southern, cooler, half of the country, with many of them clustered in the state of Victoria, the southern part of South Australia, and the cooler parts of New South Wales (three states often lumped together as South Eastern Australia).

Winemaking, grapes, and terroir

Australia's number one grape for fine wine is Syrah, locally called *Shiraz*, followed by Cabernet Sauvignon, Chardonnay, Riesling, and Semillon. The wines are generally labeled with the name of their grape variety, which must constitute at least 85 percent of the wine. An Australian peculiarity is to blend two grapes and name a wine after both, with the dominant variety first as in Shiraz/Cabernet Sauvignon or Cabernet Sauvignon/Shiraz.

Shirazes are particularly interesting because they are made in numerous styles, from very light, quaffable wines brimming with fresh strawberry fruit (delicious but simple) to serious, complex wines that need time to evolve. Another very interesting variety is Semillon (pronounced *SEM eh lon* in Australia, as opposed to the French *sem ee yon* elsewhere in the world), especially from the Hunter Valley. Some are aged in oak, similar to Chardonnay, while a few unoaked Semillons, simple when young, take on fascinating nutty/honey flavor with age.

The success of Australia's wines stems from her warm, dry climate (which provides winemakers with excellent raw material for their work) and from the winemakers' embrace of technology to achieve wines that preserve the intense flavors of their grapes and are soft and pleasant to drink from an early age. Australian wines epitomize user-friendliness.

The European concept that a wine should reflect its *terroir* (see Chapter 7) seems to hold little importance in Australia at this stage. The country is just now defining the boundaries of all its wine regions. Meanwhile, winemakers freely blend wines or grapes from different regions — often regions as far as 900 miles away from each other — as if to suggest that regional flavor in the wine is secondary to the fruit.

Those close to Australian wine can describe the country's wine regions in great detail, differentiating stylistic nuances from one area to the next the way that Francophiles distinguish the villages of the Côte de Nuits. But for wine drinkers outside of Australia, the whole discussion of Australian wine regions is academic. The vast majority of wines from Australia are labeled simply *South Eastern Australia*, meaning that the grapes could have come from any of three states, a huge territory. It's the taste that you drink, not the place, mate.

Odd couples

Although winemakers all over the world make blended wines — wines from more than one grape variety — generally the grape combinations follow the classic French models: Cabernet Sauvignon with Merlot and Cabernet Franc, for example, or Sémillon with Sauvignon Blanc. Unencumbered by foreign tradition, Australia has invented two completely original formulas:

- ✔ Shiraz with Cabernet Sauvignon
- ✔ Semillon with Chardonnay

The grape in the majority is listed first on the wine label, and the percentages of each grape are usually indicated.

We mention some of the more famous regions of Australia, state by state, below. If you're interested in learning about these regions — and the many others that we don't mention — in more detail, read James Halliday's excellent "Wine Atlas of Australia and New Zealand" (Angus & Robertson, 1991).

Australia's wine regions

Australia's most important state for wine production is South Australia, whose capital is Adelaide (see Figure 12-2). South Australia makes 58 percent of Australia's wine, and its vineyards are phylloxera-free. The state has a split winemaking personality: Vineyards in the Riverlands region produce inexpensive wines for the thirsty home market (much of it sold in 4.5 liter boxes), while vineyards closer to Adelaide make wines that are considered among the country's finest. Among these fine wine regions are

- **Barossa Valley:** North of Adelaide, one of Australia's oldest areas for fine wine; it's a warm area famous especially for its Shiraz and Cabernet Sauvignon.

- **Clare Valley:** Farther north, a climatically diverse area that makes everything from crisp Rieslings to full-bodied red wines.

- **McLaren Vale:** South of Adelaide, a cool climate influenced by the sea, and particularly admired for its Chardonnay and Sauvignon Blanc.

- **Coonawarra:** 300 miles southeast of Adelaide, a cool region famous for its red soil and its Cabernet Sauvignon.

- **Padthaway:** North of Coonawarra, a cool area known for its white wines.

Adjoining South Australia is Victoria, a smaller state but important viticulturally, making 14 percent of Australia's wines. While South Australia is home to most of Australia's largest wineries, Victoria has *more* wineries; most of them are small. Nonetheless, Victoria does make its share of everyday wines, mainly in the northwestern area along the Murray River. Victoria's fine wine production ranges from rich, fortified dessert wines to delicate Pinot Noirs. Principal regions include:

- **Rutherglen, Glenrowan,** and **Milawa:** In the northeast; long-established, warm climate zones that are outposts of traditional winemaking and home of an Australian specialty, fortified Muscats and Tokays.

- **Goulburn Valley:** In the center of the state, known especially for its Marsanne as well as Shiraz.

- **Great Western:** Site of Australia's largest sparkling wine production.

- **Yarra Valley:** A region close to Melbourne, the capital, with a cool climate suitable for fine Pinot Noir, Chardonnay, and Cabernet.

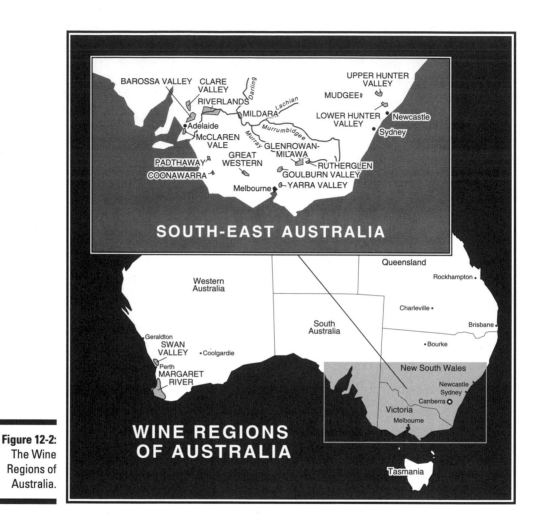

Figure 12-2:
The Wine
Regions of
Australia.

The first Australian state to grow vines was New South Wales, which today makes 27 percent of Australia's wine. High-volume production of everyday wines comes from an interior area called the Riverina (we prefer its alternative name, the Murrumbidgee Irrigation Area). Fine wine comes from three other areas:

✔ **Lower Hunter Valley:** An historic grape-growing area less than 100 miles north of Sydney with a very warm, damp climate and heavy soils; Semillon, Shiraz, and Chardonnay are important.

> ✔ **Upper Hunter Valley:** A drier climate north of the Hunter River and farther from the coast where good Chardonnay and Semillon are produced.

> ✔ **Mudgee:** An interior area near the mountains, specializing in Chardonnay, Merlot, and Cabernet Sauvignon.

Western Australia makes little wine compared to the previous three states. Swan Valley is the state's historic center of wine production, but cool climate regions such as Margaret River are becoming increasingly important. Australia's *true* cool climate region is Tasmania, an island south of Victoria, where a few producers have begun to prove what potential exists for delicate Pinot Noirs and Chardonnays.

New Zealand

New Zealand wines are riding into export markets on the coattails of the very successful wines of Australia. But the wines of the two countries are actually quite different.

New Zealand, situated farther south than Australia, is a cooler wine area, whose climate is greatly influenced by the ocean. Of the two large islands that comprise New Zealand, the North Island is the warmer, producing red wines around Auckland and Hawkes Bay (especially known for its Cabernet Sauvignon), as well as inexpensive wines from the Muller-Thurgau grape. On the South Island, Marlborough has become the largest of New Zealand's wine regions. This region is an important production zone for Chardonnay and, especially, Sauvignon Blanc.

New Zealand whites are generally unoaked wines with big, rich flavor and high acidity. New Zealand Sauvignon Blanc is so distinctive — pungent and intense, with a flavor that could be compared to asparagus — that it has become recognized almost overnight as a new prototype of Sauvignon Blanc.

New Hope in South Africa

With the democratic election of President Nelson Mandela in 1994, and the abolition of *apartheid* a few years before, South Africa is emerging with new energy and a positive outlook. Its wine industry's future, in particular, has never looked better, especially for its table wines.

Vines came to South Africa in the 1650s with the Dutch, the first European settlers. Less than 40 years later, French Huguenots, driven out of their mother country, arrived in South Africa with much-needed winemaking knowledge. By the end of the 18th century, South Africa was producing a world famous, luscious, dessert wine called Constantia, which became sought after in European royal courts.

But politics, wars, and phylloxera took their toll on wine in South Africa in the 19th century. By 1918, the quality of wine was so poor (due to overproduction and a general lack of regulation) that the government approved the formation of a regulating body, the KWV — actually a giant, semi-national wine cooperative — that to this day controls South Africa's wine industry. Many people in the wine business have accused the KWV of overregulation. As recently as 1992, the KWV finally suspended its tight quota system, allowing independent wineries to make more wine (over 80 such wine estates exist in South Africa).

South Africa has only recently begun focusing on table wine production. Traditionally, most of the country's 5000 grape growers would take their grapes to one of the 70 cooperatives run by the KWV, where over half of the crop would be turned into distilled alcohol or grape concentrate (still true today); the remaining grapes were used mainly for sherry or port. Today, in response to a worldwide demand for table wines, more of those grapes are being used to make dry, unfortified wine.

The South African wine industry continues to be dominated by large firms. In addition to the KWV, the Stellenbosch Farmers' Winery Group (SFW) is a conglomerate that is the leading producer of table wines in the country. The highly regarded Nederburg Estate is part of SFW. Another important table wine firm is the Bergkelder Group; eighteen wine estates, including some of South Africa's best, are affiliated with the Bergkelder Group.

Today, South Africa ranks eighth in the world in wine production. It exports about 20 percent of its wine, mainly to the U.K.

South Africa's principal wine regions

Although there are some cooler microclimates, especially around the southern coast (near the Cape of Good Hope) and in higher altitudes, the climate in most of South Africa's wine regions is warm and dry. Irrigation is often necessary.

South Africa's Wine of Origin legislation in 1973 created ten wine districts (and a number of subdistricts). Almost all the vineyards are near the southwestern coast, in Cape Province (within 90 miles of Cape Town, the country's most fascinating and picturesque city). These vineyards are referred to as the Coastal District vineyards.

The five major districts — including one subdistrict — are

- ✔ **Constantia:** The oldest wine producing area in the country (located south of Cape Town).
- ✔ **Durbanville:** Noted for its rolling hills and well-drained soils; north of Cape Town.
- ✔ **Stellenbosch:** East of Cape Town; the most important wine district in quantity and quality.
- ✔ **Paarl:** North of Stellenbosch; home of the KWV and the beautiful Nederburg Estate.
- ✔ **Franschhoek Valley:** (Subdistrict of Paarl); many innovative winemakers here.

About ten percent of South Africa's wines qualify as Wine of Origin (WO). Wine of Origin regulations are based on the French *Appellation Contrôlée* laws. These laws strictly designate vineyards, allowable grape varieties, vintage-dating, and so on. Varietal wines must contain at least 75 percent of the named variety; exported wines (complying with the stricter European Union regulations) must contain 85 percent of the named variety.

Steen, Pinotage, and company

The dominant grape variety in South Africa is Chenin Blanc. Often called *Steen*, this grape accounts for about one-third of total plantings. Chenin Blanc is very versatile. Primarily used to make medium-dry to semi-sweet wines, it also makes dry wines, sparkling wines, late harvest botrytis wines, and rosés. Cinsaut (the same as Cinsault, the Rhône variety), formerly called the Hermitage in South Africa, is still the leading red variety.

But things are starting to change. Cabernet Sauvignon and Merlot (and, to a lesser extent, Pinot Noir and Shiraz) are becoming increasingly important among the red varieties, while Sauvignon Blanc and Chardonnay are becoming the popular white varieties. Cabernet Sauvignon and Sauvignon Blanc do particularly well in South Africa's climate. (A very assertive version of Sauvignon Blanc is produced here.)

And then you have Pinotage. Uniquely South African, Pinotage is a hybrid grape born when Pinot Noir was crossed with Cinsaut back in 1925. However, Pinotage didn't appear as a wine until 1959. Pinotage combines the cherry fruit of a Pinot Noir with the earthiness of a Rhône wine. It can be a truly delicious, light- to medium-bodied red wine that makes for easy drinking (especially suitable as a warm-weather red wine). Good examples of Pinotage can be found in the $8 to $11 price range.

South Africa's best bets

While Pinotage is a pleasant wine, certainly worth trying, we believe South Africa's future is with Cabernet Sauvignon and Merlot (and blends of these grapes) for its red wines and Sauvignon Blanc and Chardonnay for its whites. Some of the producers that we recommend, along with their wines and districts, are the following (listed according to preference).

Red wines

- **Meerlust (Stellenbosch):** Especially the Rubicon (mainly Cabernet Sauvignon blend); but also, the Cabernet Sauvignon and Merlot

- **Rust En Vrede (Stellenbosch):** Cabernet Sauvignon, Estate (Cabernet blend), Shiraz

- **Zonnebloem (Stellenbosch):** Lauréat (Bordeaux-type blend), Merlot

- **Rozendal (Stellenbosch):** Mainly Merlot blend

- **Klein Constantia (Constantia):** Marlbrook (Bordeaux-type blend), Cabernet Sauvignon

- **Villera Estate (Paarl):** Cru Monro (60/40 Cabernet Sauvignon/Merlot blend)

- **La Motte (Franschhoek Valley):** Cabernet Sauvignon/ Merlot blend

- **Groot Constantia (Constantia):** Cabernet Sauvignon

- **Middelvlei (Stellenbosch):** Pinotage

White wines

- **Klein Constantia (Constantia):** Especially Sauvignon Blanc; also, Chardonnay

- **Louisvale (Stellenbosch):** Chardonnay

- **Boschendal (Paarl):** Sauvignon Blanc

- **Thelema (Stellenbosch):** Sauvignon Blanc, Chardonnay

- **Neil Ellis (Stellenbosch):** Sauvignon Blanc, Chardonnay

- **Mulderbosch (Stellenbosch):** Sauvignon Blanc

- **Backsberg (Paarl):** Chardonnay

- **Nederburg (Paarl):** Sauvignon Blanc (Private Bin D234); Prelude (a 70/30 bend of Sauvignon Blanc and Chardonnay, which is unusual, but it works)

- **L'Ormarins (Franschhoek Valley):** Chardonnay

The red wines listed above are in the $10 to $20 price range; the white wines are in the $8 to $14 price range. Sauvignon Blancs and Pinotages are best values.

Recent Vintages in South Africa

As in other predominantly warm-climate regions, vintages are rather consistently good in South Africa. You do find some variability in the Coastal Districts, however. The best recent vintages for red wines have been the 1992, 1991, 1989, 1987, and 1986. For white wines, 1993, 1992, and 1991 all have been quite good.

The best wines in South Africa have been made from the 1986 vintage on.

Ten red wines you should try at least once

Wine	Grape Varieties	Country of Origin	Approximate Price
1. **Chianti, Cetamura,'90 (Badia a Coltibuono)**	Sangiovese	Italy (Tuscany)	$7 to $8
2. **Barolo, '89/'90 (Le Terre del Barolo)**	Nebbiolo	Italy (Piedmont)	$11 to $12
3. **Barbera d'Alba,'93** (Vietti)	Barbera	Italy (Piedmont)	$11 to $13
4. **Zinfandel, '92/'93 (Ridge Vineyards)** (any Ridge Zin)	Zinfandel Carignane; Petite Sirah	U.S. – California (Sonoma)	$15 to $16
Zinfandel, '92/'93 (Ravenswood) (any Ravenswood Zin)	Zinfandel	U.S. – California (Sonoma)	$15 to $20
5. **Bordeaux, '88 – '91 (Ch. Léoville Las – Cases)**	Cabernet Sauvignon; Merlot; Cab Franc	France (Bordeaux – St. Julien)	$22 to $45 (depending on vintage)
6. **Burgundy, '90/'91 (Dom. Leroy, Bourgogne)**	Pinot Noir	France	$15 to $17 (Burgundy)
7. **Pinot Noir, '91/'94 (Williams – Selyem)**	Pinot Noir	U.S. – California (Sonoma – Russian River)	$25 to $45
8. **Cabernet Sauvignon, '90/'91 (Hess Collection)**	Cabernet Sauvignon; Merlot; Cab.Franc	U.S. – California (Napa – Mt. Veeder)	$15 to $20 (Reserve $32)
Cabernet Sauvignon, '89 – '92 (Cakebread Cellars)	Cabernet Sauvignon; Merlot;	U.S. – California	$23 (Napa)

(continued)

(continued from preceding page)

Wine	Grape Varieties	Country of Origin	Approximate Price
9. Pinot Noir, '92 (Ponzi Vineyards)	Pinot Noir	U.S. – Oregon (Willamette Valley)	$17 to $18 (Reserve $28)
10. Rubicon, '87 (Meerlust) also, other vintages	Cabernet Sauvignon; Merlot; Cab Franc	South Africa (Stellenbosch)	$16

Chapter 13

Bubbling Beauties

. . . .

In This Chapter

▶ When *extra dry* means sweeter

▶ Judging quality in a sparkling wine

▶ The difference between Champagne and *champagne method*

▶ Sparkling wines from $6 to $150

. . . .

*I*n the universe of wine, sparkling wines are a solar system unto themselves. Sparkling wines are produced in just about every country that makes wine, and they come in a wide range of flavors, quality levels, and prices. Champagne, the sparkling wine from the Champagne region of France, is the brightest star in the sky, but by no means the only one.

Sparkling wines are distinguished (and distinguishable) from other wines by the presence of bubbles — *carbon dioxide* — in the wine. In the eyes of most governments, these bubbles must occur as a natural result of fermentation in order for a wine to be officially considered a sparkling wine. If a wine has bubbles thanks to a canister of carbon dioxide — the way carbonated soft drinks do — then it is called *carbonated wine* (USA) or *aerated wine* (EU countries) rather than sparkling wine.

Where Sparkling Wines Grow

Sparkling wines are made all over the wine world, wherever there is a market for them and the know-how to make them. In most of the regions where they are made, sparkling wines are merely an adjunct to the production of table wines or light wines, a diversification of local wine styles.

But in a few places, sparkling wines *grow* — that is, they are an integral expression of a region's agricultural reality. In those places, if sparkling wines didn't already exist, the winemakers would have to invent them, because their grapes are ideally suited to sparkling wine.

At the top of that list is France's Champagne region (where, in many ways, sparkling wine *was* invented). Italy's Asti wine zone is another such region, as is the Loire Valley in France, northeastern Spain, and parts of California.

Many of the regions where sparkling wines grow are very cool areas, where grapes don't ripen sufficiently for still wine production. Vinified normally, the wines of these regions would be extremely high in acid, disagreeably tart, and very thin; the reds would lack color. But the elaborate process of sparkling wine production (the *traditional method* of production, described later in the text, as practiced in the Champagne region) turns the deficits of such grapes into virtues.

All that glitters is not Champagne

In other places where sparkling wine is made, the wines merely represent an application of the technology born of necessity in the regions where sparkling wines grow.

While technology can create wines that mimic the general style of the classic wine regions, it cannot re-create what the grapes contribute to the wine. Thus most sparkling wines are shadows of the classic models they aspire to resemble.

Champagne, the sparkling wine of Champagne, France, is the classic model for most sparkling wines, for a number of reasons:

- Champagne is the most famous sparkling wine in the world; the name has immediate recognition for the general population, not just for wine drinkers.

- A particular technique for making sparkling wine was invented in the Champagne region.

- The wines of Champagne are considered not only the finest sparkling wines in the world, but also among the finest wines in the world of any type.

For these reasons, the name *champagne* has been applied to all sorts of sparkling wines that don't come from the Champagne region. Wine producers who want to make their product more salable name their wine champagne; wine drinkers themselves use the word champagne indiscriminately to refer to all wines that have bubbles.

Ironically, most sparkling wine sold in the U.S. that's called champagne is not even made using the same technology as true Champagne. Most imitation-Champagnes are made by a technique that takes only a few months from beginning to end (compared to a few years to make Champagne), costs less to the producer, and works more effectively on an industrial scale.

Within the European Union, only the wines of the Champagne region in France can use the name Champagne.

Whenever we use the word Champagne, we'll be referring to true Champagne, from the region of the same name; we'll use the generic term *sparkling wine* to refer to bubbly wines collectively, as well as for sparkling wines other than Champagne.

Sparkling wine styles

All sparkling wines have bubbles and nearly all of them are either white or pink (far less common than white). That's about as far as broad generalizations will take us in describing sparkling wines.

Some sparkling wines are downright sweet, some are bone dry, and many fall somewhere in the middle, from medium-dry to medium-sweet. Some have toasty, nutty flavors and some are fruity; among those that are fruity, some are just nondescriptly grapey, while others have delicate nuances of lemons, apples, cherries, berries, peaches, and so on.

The sparkling wines of the world fall into two broad types, according to how they're made:

- ✔ Wines that express the character of their grapes; these wines tend to be fruity and straightforward, without layers of complexity.

- ✔ Wines that express complexity and flavors (yeasty, biscuity, caramel-like, honeyed) that derive from winemaking and aging, rather than direct fruitiness.

Each of these styles corresponds to a particular method of making sparkling wine, described in the section, "How Sparkling Wine Happens," later in this chapter.

How sweet is it?

Nearly all sparkling wines are sweet in the sense that they contain measurable amounts of residual sugar, usually as the result of sweetening added at the last stage of production. But all sparkling wines don't necessarily *taste* sweet. The perception of sweetness depends on two factors: the actual amount of sweetness in the wine (which varies according to the wine's style) and the wine's balance between acidity and sweetness.

Here's how the balance factor operates. Sparkling wines are usually very high in acidity. The wine's carbon dioxide compounds the acidic impression in the mouth. But the wine's sweetness counterbalances its acidity and vice versa. Depending on the particular acid/sugar balance a sparkling wine strikes, the wine might taste dry, very slightly sweet, medium sweet, or quite sweet.

Champagne is made in a range of sweetness levels, the most common of which is a dry style called *brut* (see "Sweetness categories" later in this chapter). Sparkling wines made by the *traditional method* used in Champagne (see "How Sparkling Wine Happens" later in this chapter) are made in the same range of styles as Champagne.

Inexpensive sparkling wines tend to be medium sweet in order to appeal to a mass market that enjoys sweetness. Wines labeled with the Italian word *spumante* tend to be sweet. (See the section on Italian Spumante later in this chapter.)

How good is it?

When you taste a sparkling wine, the most important consideration is whether you like it — just as for a still wine. If you want to evaluate a sparkling wine the way professionals do, however, you have to apply a few criteria that don't apply to still wines (or are less critical in still wines than in sparkling wines). Some of those criteria are

✔ **The visual appearance of the bubbles.** In the best sparkling wines, the bubbles are tiny and float upward in a continuous stream from the bottom of your glass. If the bubbles are large and random, you have a clue that the wine is a lesser-quality sparkler. If you don't see many bubbles at all, you could have a bad bottle, or the wine could be too old.

Tiny variations in the glassware can drastically affect the flow of bubbles, though. If your glass looks almost flat, but another glass from the same bottle is lively with bubbles, blame the glass and not the wine. (In this case, you should be able to *taste* the bubbles, even if you can't *see* many of them.)

✔ **The feel of the bubbles in your mouth.** The finer the wine, the less aggressive the bubbles will feel in your mouth. (If the bubbles remind you of a soft drink, we hope you didn't pay more than $5 for the wine.)

✔ **The balance between sweetness and acidity.** Even if you decide that a wine is too sweet or too dry for your particular taste, you should consider its sweetness/acid balance and decide whether these two elements seem reasonably balanced.

✔ **The texture.** Traditional-method sparkling wines should be somewhat creamy in texture as a result of their extended lees aging. (See the section, "How Sparkling Wine Happens" for an explanation of *traditional method* and *lees*.)

✔ **The finish.** Any impression of bitterness on the finish of a sparkling wine is a sign of low quality.

✔ **What style the wine is intended to be.** Above all, consider this factor. If you are tasting a sparkling wine made to be overtly fruity, don't criticize it for failing to have toasty flavors that come only at the expense of fruit!

How Sparkling Wine Happens

Wine becomes sparkling when fermentation takes place in a closed container and the carbon dioxide created by the yeasts cannot escape into the air. With nowhere else to go, the carbon dioxide (CO_2) becomes trapped in the wine and takes the form of bubbles.

When yeasts convert sugar into alcohol, carbon dioxide is a natural by-product.

Most sparkling wines actually go through *two* fermentations: one to turn the grape juice into still wine (without bubbles) and a subsequent one to turn the still wine into bubbly wine (conveniently called the *second fermentation*). The winemaker has to instigate the second fermentation by adding yeasts and sugar to the base wine. The added yeasts convert the added sugar into alcohol and CO_2 bubbles.

Methods of trapping the CO_2 vary — and with them, the style and quality of the wine. Basically, the longer and slower the winemaking process, the more complex and expensive the sparkling wine will be. Some sparkling wines are ten years in the making; others are produced in only a few months. The former can cost more than $100 a bottle, while bubblies at the opposite end of the spectrum can sell for as little as $3.

Although you find many variations on the theme, most sparkling wines are produced in one of two ways: through *second fermentation in a tank*, or through *second fermentation in the bottle*. Wine people usually use the terms *tank-fermented* and *bottle-fermented* for these two processes, without specifying that they're referring to the *second* fermentation, not the first one.

Economy of scale

The quickest, most efficient way of making a sparkling wine involves conducting the second fermentation in large, closed, pressurized tanks. This method is called the *bulk method, tank method, cuve close* (meaning *closed tank* in French), or *charmat method,* after a Frenchman named Eugene Charmat, inventor of the process.

Sparkling wines that are made in the charmat (pronounced *shar mah*) method are usually the least expensive because they are ready for sale soon after harvest and are usually made in large quantities.

The following occurs in the charmat method:

  ✔ A base wine is *seeded* with sugar and yeast and ferments.

  The carbon dioxide created by the fermentation becomes trapped in the wine, thanks to the closed tank, the pressure within the tank, and the cold temperature.

- ✔ The wine — now a dry sparkling wine with higher alcohol than the base wine had — is filtered (under pressure) to remove the solid deposits from the second fermentation (the *lees*).

- ✔ Before bottling, some sweetness is added to adjust the wine's flavor, according to the desired style of the final wine.

The whole process can take just a few weeks. In some exceptional cases, it might be extended to a few months, allowing the wine to rest between the fermentation and the filtration.

Small is beautiful

The charmat method is a fairly new method of producing sparkling wines, dating back less than 100 years. The more traditional method is that of conducting the second fermentation in the individual bottles in which the wine is later sold.

Champagne has been made in this way for approximately 300 years and according to French law can be made in no other way. Many other French sparkling wines are made in the same way, as are the best sparkling wines from Spain, California, and other countries.

The technique of conducting the second fermentation in the bottle is called the *classic* or *traditional method* in Europe; in the U.S., it's called the *champagne method* or *method champenoise*.

Bottle fermentation (or, more correctly, second fermentation in the bottle) is an elaborate process in which every single bottle becomes an individual fermentation tank, so to speak. This process requires a minimum of one year and usually takes three years or more. Invariably, sparkling wines made in this way are more expensive than those made by tank fermentation.

The elements of bottle fermentation are

- ✔ Each bottle is filled with a mixture of base wine and a sugar-and-yeast solution, closed securely, and laid to rest in a cool, dark cellar.

- ✔ Inside each bottle, the second fermentation occurs, producing carbon dioxide and leaving its fermentation lees inside the bottle.

- ✔ As the bottles continue to lie in the cellar, the wine gradually undergoes changes through interaction of the lees and the wine.

- ✔ Eventually — nine months to several years after the second fermentation — the bottles are put through a process of shaking and turning so that the solid lees fall to the neck of each upside-down bottle.

> ✔ The lees are flash-frozen in the neck of each bottle and expelled from each bottle as a frozen plug, leaving clear sparkling wine behind.
>
> ✔ A sweetening solution (called a *dosage*) is added to adjust the flavor of the wine, and the bottles are corked and labeled for sale.

The beauty of blending

Actually, the classic method as practiced in Champagne involves several steps that occur way before the second fermentation. For example, the pressing to extract the juice for the first fermentation must be conducted with meticulous care to prevent the grapeskins' bitter flavors — and their color, in the case of black grapes — from passing into the juice. Another step crucially important to the quality of the sparkling wine is the production of the base wine for the second fermentation.

Following the first fermentation, the wines of different grape varieties and different vineyards are kept separate. To create his base wine, or *cuvée*, the winemaker blends these separate wines in varying proportions, often adding some *reserve wine* (older wine purposely held back from previous vintages). From 100 to 200 different wines may go into a single base wine, each bringing its own special character to the blend. What's particularly tricky about blending the base wine — besides the sheer volume of components in the blend — is that the winemaker has to see into the future and create a blend *not* for its flavor today but for how it will taste in several years, after it has been transformed into a sparkling wine. The men and women who blend sparkling wines are the artists of the wine world.

Taste: The proof of the pudding

Tank-fermented sparklers tend to be fruitier than traditional-method sparkling wines. This difference occurs because in tank-fermentation, the route from grape to wine is shorter and more direct than that of bottle-fermentation. Some winemakers use the *charmat*, or tank, method because their goal is a fresh and fruity sparkling wine. Asti (formerly called Asti Spumante), Italy's most famous sparkling wine, is a perfect example. Charmat-method sparklers should be consumed young, when their fruitiness is at the max.

Sparkling wines produced through second fermentation in the bottle tend to be less overtly fruity than charmat-method wines. Chemical changes that take place as the wine develops on its fermentation lees diminish the fruitiness of the wine and contribute aromas and flavors such as toastiness, nuttiness, caramel, and yeastiness. The texture of the wine can also change as a result of prolonged aging on the lees, becoming smooth and creamy. The bubbles themselves tend to be tinier, and they feel less aggressive in your mouth than the bubbles of tank-fermented wines. Although classic-method sparkling wines can be enjoyed when you buy them, they can usually also age well, provided that you store them in a cool place (see Chapter 15).

The technical term for the decomposition of yeast cells after the second fermentation, and the chemical changes that occur as a result, is *autolysis*. The flavors and aromas contributed through autolysis are referred to as *autolysed* aromas. The presence of autolysed character is one of the important differences between bottle-fermented and tank-fermented sparkling wines. The *degree* of autolysed character is also a key difference between bottle-fermented sparkling wines that spend many years of aging on the lees (like a *prestige cuvée* Champagne, described later in this chapter) and those that spend less time on the lees (like a non-vintage Champagne) because autolysed aromas become increasingly intense the longer the wine ages on its lees.

Champagne and Its Magic Wines

Champagne. Does any other word convey such a sense of celebration? Think of it: Anytime that anyone, in any country in the world, wants to celebrate, he or she says, "This calls for Champagne!" ("This calls for iced tea!" just isn't quite the same.)

Champagne, the real thing, comes only from the region of Champagne (*sham pahn yah*) in northeast France. Dom Pérignon, the famous monk who was cellar master at the Abbey of Hautvillers, didn't invent Champagne, but he did achieve a number of breakthroughs that are key to making Champagne as we now know it. He perfected the method of making white wine from black grapes, for example, and, most importantly, he mastered the art of blending wines from different grapes and different villages to achieve a complex base wine.

Champagne is the most northerly vineyard area in France. Most of the important Champagne *houses* (as Champagne producers are called) are located in the cathedral city of Rheims — where 17-year-old Joan of Arc had Prince Charles crowned King of France in 1429 — and in the town of Epernay, south of Rheims. Around Rheims and Epernay are the main vineyard areas, where three permitted grape varieties (two black and one white) for Champagne flourish:

- The Montagne de Reims (south of Rheims), where the best Pinot Noir grows
- The Côte des Blancs (south of Epernay), home of the best Chardonnay
- The Vallée de la Marne (west of Epernay), most favorable to Pinot Meunier (a black grape) although all three grape varieties grow here

Most Champagne is made from all three grape varieties. Pinot Noir contributes body, structure, and longevity to the blend; Chardonnay offers delicacy, freshness, and elegance; and Pinot Meunier provides precocity, floral aromas, and fruitiness.

What makes Champagne special

The climate for grape growing in Champagne is marginal. With cold winters and warm (but not hot) summers, the grapes struggle to ripen sufficiently in some years. Even in warmer years, the climate dictates that the grapes will always be high in acidity (see "Worst case ripening scenarios" in Chapter 9) — a sorry state for table wine but perfect for sparkling wine. The cool climate — combined with chalky, limestone soil — are the leading factors contributing to Champagne's excellence.

Three other elements help distinguish Champagne from all other sparkling wines:

1. The number and diversity of vineyards (about 300 *crus*) provide a huge range of individual wines for blending.

2. The cold, deep, chalky cellars (many built during Roman times) in which Champagnes age for many years.

3. The 300 years of experience the Champenois have in making sparkling wine.

The result is an elegant sparkling wine with myriad tiny, gentle bubbles, complexity of flavors, and a lengthy finish. Voilá! Champagne!

Non-vintage Champagne

Non-vintage (NV) Champagne — any Champagne without a vintage year on the label — accounts for 85 percent of all Champagne produced. The typical blend is two-thirds black grapes (Pinot Noir and Pinot Meunier) and one-third white (Chardonnay). Wine from three or more harvests goes into the blend. And remember, the wines from as many as 30 to 40 different villages from each year may also go in. The Champagne winemaker is by necessity a master blender.

Each Champagne house controls its own blend, thus creating its own *house style* for its non-vintage Champagne. (For example, one house may seek elegance and finesse in its wine, another might opt for fruitiness, and a third might value body, power, and longevity.) Maintaining a consistent house style is vital for Champagne producers because wine drinkers get accustomed to their favorite Champagne's style and expect to find that style in that non-vintage wine year after year.

Most major Champagne houses age their non-vintage Champagne for two and one-half to three years, even though the legal minimum for non-vintage is one year. The extra aging prolongs the *marrying time* for the blend and enhances the wine's flavor and complexity. If you have good storage conditions (see Chapter 15), aging your non-vintage Champagne for a year or two after you purchase it will usually improve the flavor.

Don't leave your Champagne — or any other good sparkling wine — in your refrigerator for more than a few days! Its flavor will become numb and flat from the excessively cold temperature; also vibrations of the refrigerator motor going on and off are not good for any wine — especially sparkling wine (see Chapter 15).

Most non-vintage Champagnes sell for $15 to $30 a bottle. Often, a large retailer will buy huge quantities of a few major brands, obtaining a good discount that he passes on to his customers. Seeking out stores that do a large-volume business with Champagne is worth your while.

Vintage Champagne

In four or five of every ten years, the weather in Champagne is good enough to make a vintage Champagne — that is, the grapes are ripe enough that some wine can be made entirely from the grapes of that year without being blended with reserve wines from previous years. (The 1980s had exceptional weather, enabling most houses to make vintage Champagne every year from 1981 to 1990, with the exception of 1984 and 1987.)

Vintage Champagnes fall into two categories:

✔ Regular vintage, with a price range of $25 to $50 a bottle; these wines simply carry a vintage date in addition to the name of the house; see "Recommended Champagne producers" later in this chapter

✔ Premium vintage (also known as a *prestige cuvée* or *tête de cuvée*), such as Moët & Chandon's Dom Pérignon, Roederer's Cristal, or Veuve Clicquot's La Grande Dame; the typical price for prestige cuvées ranges from $50 to $100 per bottle

Vintage Champagne is *invariably* superior to non-vintage for the following reasons:

1. The best grapes from the choicest vineyards are put into vintage Champagne (this is *especially* so for prestige cuvées).

2. Usually, only the two finest varieties (Pinot Noir and Chardonnay) are used in vintage Champagne. Pinot Meunier is saved for NV Champagne.

3. Most Champagne houses age vintage Champagnes at least two more years than the non-vintage variety. The extra aging assures more complex flavors.

4. The grapes all come from one year — an above average year at least, a superb one at best.

Vintage Champagne is more intense in flavor than non-vintage Champagne. It is more full-bodied, more complex, and longer-lasting on the palate. Being fuller and richer, these Champagnes are the ones to have with food. Non-vintage Champagnes — being lighter, fresher, and less complicated — are suitable as apéritifs; and they are good values. Whether a vintage Champagne is worth its extra cost or not is a judgment you have to make for yourself.

The 1990 vintage in Champagne (just as in most other wine regions in Europe) is super, and the 1989 is almost as good. 1988 is also good, yet not quite up to the '89 or '90 (but Roederer's Cristal is great). 1986 is inconsistent, but Pol Roger, Roederer, and Billecart-Salmon were fine. 1985 is quite good, especially for Bollinger, Dom Pérignon, and Laurent-Perrier. 1982 is a super vintage, if you can still find it; Krug and Dom Pérignon did especially well.

Blanc de blancs

A small number of Champagnes are made from just one of the three permitted grapes. That grape is Chardonnay, and that type of Champagne is called *blanc de blancs* (literally, white from white). A *blanc de blancs* can be a vintage Champagne or a non-vintage. It usually costs a few dollars more than other Champagnes in its category. Because they are lighter and more delicate than other Champagnes, *blanc de blancs* make ideal apéritifs. Not every Champagne house makes a *blanc de blancs*. Two of the best are Taittinger's Comte de Champagne and Billecart-Salmon's Blanc de Blancs.

Blanc de noirs Champagne (made from 100 percent black grapes, often just Pinot Noir) is rare but does exist. Bollinger's Blanc de Noirs *Vieilles Vignes Francaises* (old vines) is absolutely the best, but it is *very* expensive ($185 to $200). The 1985 Bollinger Blanc de Noirs was one of the two best Champagnes we ever had; the other was the 1928 Krug.

Who's drinking Champagne

France leads the world in Champagne consumption, drinking almost twice as much as the rest of the world put together. The UK and Germany are the leading export markets for Champagne, each with sales of about 15 million bottles a year. The U.S. is third (about 11 million bottles), followed by Switzerland, Belgium, and Italy. But the U.S. buys the most *prestige cuvée* Champagne, especially Dom Pérignon.

Rosé Champagne

Rosé Champagnes — pink Champagnes — can also be vintage or non-vintage. Usually, only Pinot Noir and Chardonnay are used, in proportions that vary from one house to the next.

Rosés are made primarily by including some red Pinot Noir wine in the base wine blend, although a few houses actually vinify some of their red grapes into pink wines for rosé Champagne. Colors range from pale onion skin to salmon to rosy pink (the lighter-colored ones are usually better quality). Rosés are fuller and rounder than other Champagnes and are best had with dinner. (Because they have become associated with romance, they're popular choices for wedding anniversaries and Valentine's Day.)

Like *blanc de blancs* Champagnes, rosés cost a few dollars more than regular Champagnes and not every Champagne house makes one. Some of the best rosés are made by Roederer, Billecart-Salmon, Gosset, and Moët & Chandon (their Dom Pérignon Rosé).

For some people, rosé Champagne has a bad connotation because of the tons of sweet, insipid (inexpensive) pink wines — sparkling and otherwise — that are sold. But rosé Champagne is just as dry and has the same high quality as regular (white) Champagne.

Sweetness categories

Champagnes always carry an indication of their sweetness on the label, but the words used to indicate sweetness are cryptic: "extra dry" is not really dry, for example. In ascending order of sweetness, Champagnes are labeled:

- **Extra Brut, Brut Nature, or Brut Sauvage:** Totally dry
- **Brut:** Dry
- **Extra Dry:** Medium dry
- **Sec:** Slightly sweet
- **Demi-Sec:** Fairly sweet
- **Doux:** Sweet

The most common style of Champagne and other serious bubblies is brut. However, the single best-selling Champagne in the U.S., Moët & Chandon White Star, falls into the extra dry category. The first and the last styles in the preceding listing are now very rare.

Producers of classic-method sparkling wines from other areas use the same words to describe their wines. But while the terms are defined legally in Champagne, they are not necessarily defined elsewhere.

Madame Lily Bollinger's advice on drinking Champagne

When Jacques Bollinger died in 1941, his widow, Lily Bollinger, carried her famous Champagne house through the difficult years of the German occupation of France. She ran it until her death in 1977. Bollinger prospered under her leadership, doubling in size. She was a beloved figure in Champagne, where she could be seen bicycling through the vineyards every day. In 1961, when a London reporter asked her when she drank Champagne, Madame Bollinger replied:

"I only drink Champagne when I'm happy, and when I'm sad. Sometimes I drink it when I'm alone. When I have company I consider it obligatory. I trifle with it if I am not hungry and drink it when I am. Otherwise I never touch it — unless I'm thirsty."

The redoubtable Madame Lily Bollinger died at the age of 78, apparently none the worse for all that Champagne.

Recommended Champagne producers

The Champagne business — especially the export end of it — is dominated by about 25 or 30 large houses, most of whom purchase the majority of grapes they need to make their Champagne from independent growers. Of the major houses, only Roederer and Bollinger own most of the vineyards from which they get their grapes — a definite economic and quality-control advantage for them.

Moët & Chandon is by far the largest Champagne House. In terms of worldwide sales, the next-largest producers are Mumm, Veuve Clicquot, Laurent-Perrier, Pommery, and Lanson. The following lists indicate some of our favorite producers in rough order of preference, grouped according to the style of their Champagne: light-bodied, medium-bodied, or full-bodied.

✔ **Light, elegant styles**

Laurent-Perrier	Perrier-Jouët
Billecart-Salmon	Delamotte*
Taittinger	de Castellane
Ruinart	Jacques Selosse*
Philipponnat	Charles de Cazanove
Jacquesson	Batiste-Pertois*
Bruno Paillard	J. Lassalle*

✔ **Medium-bodied styles**

Charles Heidsieck	Heidsieck Monopole
Pol Roger	Pommery
Moët & Chandon	Deutz
Mumm	Joseph Perrier

✔ **Full-bodied styles**

Krug	Veuve Clicquot
Louis Roederer	Alfred Gratien*
Bollinger	Henriot
Salon*	Paul Bara*
Gosset	

* small producer; may be difficult to find

The following list names, in rough order of preference, the houses whose vintage and prestige cuvées have been in top form lately. (If you're going to lay out big bucks for a top-of-the-line Champagne, you might as well go for the best!)

✔ **Krug:** Vintage (1982, 1985, 1973 Collection)

✔ **Louis Roederer:** Cristal (1988, 1986, 1985)

✔ **Bollinger:** Vintage (1988, 1985); Blanc de Noirs Vielles Vignes (1985)

✔ **Moët & Chandon:** Dom Pérignon (1988, 1985, 1982)

✔ **Veuve Clicquot:** La Grande Dame (1988, 1985, 1983)

✔ **Mumm:** René Lalou (1985, 1982); Grand Cordon white and rosé (1985)

✔ **Pommery:** Cuvée Louise Pommery (1988, 1987, 1985)

✔ **Gosset:** Grand Millesime and Rosé (1985)

✔ **Heidsieck Monopole:** Diamant Bleu and Rosé (1985, 1982)

✔ **Philipponnat:** Clos des Goisses (1986, 1985, 1982)

✔ **Pol Roger:** Cuvée Sir Winston Churchill (1986, 1985)

✔ **Salon:** Vintage (1983, 1982, 1979)

✔ **Taittinger:** Comtes de Champagne white and rosé (1988, 1985)

✔ **Billecart-Salmon:** Blanc de Blancs (1986, 1985)

✔ **Laurent-Perrier:** Grand Siècle (1988, 1985)

- **Cattier:** Clos du Moulin (a non-vintage)
- **Jacquesson:** Signature (1985)
- **Ruinart:** Dom Ruinart Blanc de Blancs (1988, 1986)
- **Charles de Cazanove:** Stradivarius (1989)
- **Charbaut:** Certificate Blanc de Blancs (1985)
- **Charles Heidsieck**: Blanc des Millenaires (1983)

Other Sparkling Wines

France makes many other sparkling wines besides Champagne, especially in the Loire Valley, around Saumur, and in the regions of Alsace and Burgundy. When sparkling wine is made by the traditional method (second fermentation in the bottle), it is often called *Cremant*, as in Cremant d'Alsace, Cremant de Bourgogne, and so on. Grape varieties are those typical of each region. Most of it sells in the $10 to $15 price range and is of decent quality (but for a few dollars more, you can buy a good NV Champagne, such as Charles Heidsieck).

American sparkling wine

Sparkling wine is made in the United States in almost as many states as still wine is, but the two states most famous for it are California and New York. Two fine examples of New York State sparkling wines made in the traditional method are Chateau Frank and Glenora, both selling in the $12 to $14 range.

Having run out of vineyard space in their home region, Champagne producers have set up wineries all over the world — in California (Moët & Chandon began the French invasion there in 1973), New York, Australia, New Zealand, Brazil, India, and Korea. Sparkling wines made by Champagne houses have been particularly successful in California.

California bubbly is definitely a different wine from Champagne, even when made by a Champagne house using the same methods as in Champagne and the same grape varieties (it tastes fruitier). Good California sparkling wine can be purchased for as low as $9 to $10 on up to $25 and more.

Most of California's finest sparkling wines do not call themselves *Champagne*, while the less-expensive, best-selling wines do. Among the best-selling sparkling wines in the U.S. that use the name Champagne, Korbel, at about $9, is the only one that is *bottle-fermented*.

We recommend the following California sparkling wines:

U.S.-owned

- ✔ **J:** Not content with making one of America's most popular Cabernet Sauvignons and Chardonnays, the Jordan winery in Sonoma is now making one of the best sparkling wines in the country. And it keeps getting better each year. Quite fruity and fairly delicate, the wine comes in a knock-out bottle, and costs $20 to $25.

- ✔ **Iron Horse:** In Green Valley, the coolest part of Sonoma, Iron Horse is clearly making some of California's finest sparkling wine. Especially good are their better cuvées, such as the Wedding Cuvée and Vrai Amis, which cost $20 to $25.

- ✔ **Schramsberg:** The oldest quality producer of California sparkling wine and still one of the best, Schramsberg has a diversified line of wines priced between $22 and $25. They now make California's most expensive sparkler, the J. Schram Tête de Cuvée ($45 to $50).

- ✔ **Handley Cellars:** Up in Anderson Valley near Mendocino, Milla Handley is making some excellent, quite dry sparkling wine; her Rosé Brut is a beauty, at $14 to $16.

French- or Spanish-owned

- ✔ **Domaine Chandon:** This winery, in the Napa Valley, is a must-stop for its restaurant alone. Winemaker Dawnine Dyer continues to make solid, consistent sparkling wine at reasonable prices ($12 to $14). Their premium sparkler, Etoile ($23 to $25), deserves to be better-known: It is one of the most elegant sparkling wines in the U.S.

- ✔ **Mumm Cuvée Napa:** Mumm has established itself as one of California's best sparkling wine houses. Much of its production comes from the cool Carneros District. The price range is $15 to $18, and its new premium cuvée, called DVX, is especially fine.

- ✔ **Domaine Carneros:** Taittinger's California winery makes elegant, quality wines in cool Carneros, with a price range from $18 to $20.

- ✔ **Roederer Estate:** This Anderson Valley winery is a relative newcomer, but some critics think it's already California's best. Wines include a good-value Brut ($14), a delicate rosé that's worth seeking out, and an outstanding new premium cuvée, L'Ermitage ($33 to $35).

- **Maison Deutz:** Down in cool Santa Barbara, Maison Deutz has lived up to the Deutz Champagne name. They produce some good-value sparklers at $14 to $18.

- **Scharffenberger:** Now part of LVMH (Moët & Chandon's corporate group), Scharffenberger, in Anderson Valley, continues to make some of California's best sparkling wines, selling for $15 to $20.

- **Piper-Sonoma:** These wines are in a very dry, light style and are good values at $12 to $14.

- **Codorniu Napa:** This Spanish-owned winery located in Carneros has made some impressive, good-value ($12 to $14) sparklers under winemaker Janet Pagano.

- **Gloria Ferrer:** Spain's Freixenet company has built a beautiful winery in windswept Carneros. Its wines are priced right ($12 to $16) and are widely available.

Spanish sparkling wines (Cava)

What if you want to spend less than $10 for a sparkling wine? The answer is Spain's sparkling wine, Cava, almost all of which is produced in Penedés, near Barcelona. Many of these wines sell for $6 to $8 a bottle.

Cava is made in the traditional method, fermented in the bottle. Most Cavas use local Spanish grapes. As a result, they taste distinctly different from California bubblies and from Champagne although some of the more expensive cuvées do contain Chardonnay. Two gigantic wineries dominate Cava production — Freixenet (pronounced *fresh net*) and Codorniu. Freixenet's black-frosted *Cordon Negro* bottle has to be one of the most recognizable bottles in the world. Two of our favorite Cavas are Marques de Monistrol, a great value at $7 to $8, and Juve y Camps, a vintage-dated Cava at $12 to $13.

German sparkling wines (Sekt)

Germany makes an enormous amount of sparkling wine (called *Sekt),* most of which is consumed in Germany. The charmat (tank) method is used; the style of the wine is fresh and fruity. The grapes are the Riesling (for the better wines) and Muller-Thurgau. Two of the largest brands, which are widely available, are Henkell, priced at $12 to $14, and Dienhard Brut, at $8 to $9.

Italian spumante: dry and sweet

Spumante is simply the Italian word for "sparkling," but it has come to refer to sweet, fruity imitations of Italy's classic Asti Spumante made in Italy and elsewhere.

The real Asti (producers have dropped the second word) is a delicious, exuberantly fruity sparkling wine made in Piedmont from Moscato grapes using the tank method. It's one bubbly that you can drink with dessert. Because freshness is essential in Asti, buy a good brand that sells well (Asti is a non-vintage wine). We recommend Cinzano, Gancia, and Martini & Rossi (all priced around $10 to $12). You can also find a really fine Fontanafredda Asti at $12 to $14.

For Asti flavor with fewer bubbles, try Moscato d'Asti, a delicate and delicious medium-dry wine. Vietti makes a good one for about $12. Again, freshness is essential. With Moscato d'Asti, let the vintage date guide you; buy the youngest one you can find.

Using the traditional method, Italy produces a good deal of dry sparkling wine in the Oltrepó-Pavese and Franciacorta wine zones of Lombardy. Italy's dry sparkling wines are very dry with little or no sweetening *dosage*. They come in all price ranges, from the affordable Castello Gancia at about $10, to the medium-priced Ferrari Brut ($17 to $20), to three upscale (and very good) Bruts: Bellavista ($20 to $30), Ca' del Bosco ($35), and Bruno Giacosa Brut ($38 to $40). Giacosa, well-known for his outstanding Barbarescos and Barolos, makes his 100 percent Pinot Noir Brut in his spare time, for kicks. Like everything else he produces, it's superb.

Serving Champagne and Sparkling Wines

Sparkling wine is at its best when it is cold, about 45°F (7° to 8°C), although some people prefer it less cold (52°F; 11°C). We prefer the colder temperature because the wine holds its effervescence better when cold, and it warms up so quickly in the glass. Older Champagne and vintage Champagne, being more complex, can be chilled less than young, non-vintage Champagne or sparkling wine.

Never leave an open bottle of sparkling wine on the table unless it's in an ice bucket (half cold water, half ice) because it will warm up quickly. Use a sparkling wine stopper to keep leftover bubbly fresh for a couple of days (in the fridge, of course).

If you're entertaining, you should know that the ideal bottle size for Champagne is the magnum, which is equivalent to two bottles. The wine ages more gently in the larger bottle.

Magnums are the largest bottles in which Champagne is usually fermented. All the other larger bottles have Champagne poured into them, and the wine is not as fresh as it is in a magnum or a regular bottle.

Avoid half-bottles (375 ml) and splits (187 ml) — Champagne in these small bottles is often not too fresh. (If you're given a small bottle of Champagne or any sparkling wine as a wedding favor, for example, open it at the first excuse; do not keep it around for a year waiting for the right occasion!)

Champagne and other good, dry sparkling wines are extremely versatile with food — and the essential wine for certain kinds of foods. For example, no wine goes better with egg dishes than Champagne. Indulge yourself next time that you have brunch. And the next time you're having spicy Asian cuisine, try sparkling wine. No wine goes better with spicy Chinese or Indian food!

Turkey is excellent with sparkling wine. If you're having lamb (pink, not well done) or ham, try rosé Champagne with it. For aged Champagne, chunks of aged Asiago, aged Gouda, or Parmesan cheese go extremely well.

Do not serve a dry Brut (or Extra-Dry) sparkling wine with dessert. These styles are just too dry and won't taste good with dessert. With fresh fruit, try a demi-sec Champagne. With sweeter desserts (or wedding cake!), we recommend Asti.

Ten excuses to drink Champagne (or another good sparkling wine)

1. You have a bottle on hand.

2. The boss just left for vacation.

3. The noisy neighbors next door finally moved out.

4. You finished doing your income taxes.

5. It's Saturday.

6. The kids left for summer camp.

7. You won a tee shirt and a coffee mug on the radio.

8. You didn't get a single telephone solictation all day.

9. The wire muzzle over the cork makes a great cat toy.

10. You have just finished writing a wine book!

Chapter 14

Wine Roads Less Traveled: Apéritif, Dessert, and Fortified Wines

· ·

In This Chapter

▶ The world's most versatile wine

▶ 48 grapes for one wine

▶ A wine that lasts 200 years

▶ Liquid gold from rotted grapes

· ·

*T*he wines we lump together as *apéritif wines, dessert wines,* and *fortified wines* aren't mainstream beverages that you want to drink every day. Some of them are much higher in alcohol than regular wines, and some of them are extremely sweet (and rare and expensive!). They're the wine equivalent of really good candy — delicious enough that you could get carried away if you let yourself indulge daily. So you treat them as treats, a glass before or after dinner, a bottle when company comes, a splurge to celebrate the start of your diet — tomorrow.

Pleasure aside, you owe it to yourself to try these wines from a purely academic point of view. Seriously. Learning about wine is hard work, but somebody's got to do it.

Timing Is Everything

Many wines enjoyed before dinner, as apéritif wines, or after dinner, as dessert wines, fall into the category of *fortified wines* (called *liqueur wines* by the EU). These wines all have alcohol added to them at some point in their production, giving them an alcohol content that ranges from 16 to 24 percent.

The point at which alcohol is added determines whether the wines are sweet or dry. When fortified with alcohol *during* fermentation, the wines become sweet. The added alcohol stops fermentation, leaving natural, unfermented sugar in the wine (see Chapter 1). When fortified *after* fermentation (after all the grape sugar has been converted to alcohol), the wines become dry (unless they are subsequently sweetened).

Some of the wines we call dessert wines don't have added alcohol. Their sweetness occurs because the grapes are at the right place at the right time — when noble rot strikes (see the discussion of German wines in Chapter 11). Occasionally, winemakers pick very ripe (but not rotten) grapes and dry them before fermentation to concentrate their juice, which is another method of turning grape juice into the nectar of the gods.

Sherry: The World's Most Misunderstood Wine

The comedian Rodney Dangerfield built a career around the line, "I get no respect!" His wine of choice should be Sherry, because it shares the same plight. We avoided Sherry like the plague — until we found out how good it can be. We thought it was just a sweet, cheap wine that our elderly aunts and the British fancied. Now we realize that the British (and our elderly aunts) were on to something: Sherry is a wine of true quality and diversity; but it remains undiscovered by most of the world. In a way, we're not sorry, because the price of good Sherry is pleasantly low.

The Jerez triangle

Sherry is produced in the Andalucía region of sun-baked southwestern Spain. The wine is named after Jerez *(her ETH)* de la Frontera, an old town of Moorish and Arab origin where many of the Sherry *bodegas* are located. *(Bodega* can refer to the actual building in which Sherry is matured or to the Sherry firm itself.)

Actually, Jerez is just one corner of a triangle that is the Sherry region. Puerto de Santa María, a beautiful, old coast town southwest of Jerez, has a number of large bodegas. The sea air is thought to enhance the making of dry *fino (FEE noh)* Sherry (discussed in the following section). The third corner of the triangle, Sanlúcar de Barrameda (also on the coast but northwest of Jerez), is so famous for its sea breezes that the lightest and driest of Sherries, *Manzanilla,* can legally be made only there. Aficionados of Sherry swear that they can detect the salty tang of the ocean in Manzanilla *(mahn zah NEE yah).*

Paradise found

If you ever watch the sun set over the Atlantic Ocean from the terrace of a restaurant in Sanlúcar, sipping Manzanilla with *tapas* (little morsels of food such as olives, cheese, prawns, ham, sausages, potatoes), you may feel that you are close to heaven.

Traveling from Sanlúcar to Jerez, you pass vineyards with dazzling white soil. This soil is *albariza,* the region's famous chalky earth, rich in limestone from fossilized shells. Summers are hot and dry, but balmy sea breezes temper the heat.

The Palomino grape — the main variety used in Sherry — thrives only here in the hot Sherry region on *albariza* soil. Palomino is a complete failure for table or light wines because it makes neutral, low-acid wine, but it's perfect for Sherry production. Two other authorized grape varieties, the Pedro Ximénez (*PAY dro he MAIN ehz*) and the Moscatel (Muscat), are also used for dessert types of Sherry.

The phenomenon of the flor

All Sherry is fortified with alcohol after fermentation, but from that point the diversity begins. Sherry consists of two basic types: *fino* (light, very dry) and *oloroso* (rich and full, but also dry). Sweet Sherries are made by sweetening either type.

After fermentation, the winemaker decides which Sherries will become *finos* or *olorosos* (*oh loh ROH sohs*) by judging the appearance, aroma, and flavor of the young, unfortified wines. If a wine is to be a *fino*, the winemaker fortifies it lightly (until its alcohol level reaches about 15.5 percent). He strengthens future *olorosos* to 18 percent alcohol.

At this point, the special Sherry magic begins: A yeast called the *flor* grows spontaneously on the surface of the wines destined to be *finos*. The flor eventually covers the surface of the wine, preventing the wine from oxidizing. The flor feeds on oxygen from the air and on alcohol and glycerin in the wine. As it lives on the wine, the flor changes the wine's character, contributing a distinct aroma and flavor and rendering the wine thinner and more delicate.

Flor doesn't grow on wines destined to become *olorosos* because of their higher alcohol content. Without the protection of the flor (and because the barrels are never filled to the brim) these wines are exposed to oxygen as they age.

Communal aging

Both the *fino* and *oloroso* types of Sherry age in a special way that is unique to Sherry making.

The young wine is not left to age on its own but is added to casks of older wine that are already maturing. To make room for the young wine, some of the older wine is emptied out of the casks and is added to casks of even older wine. To make room in *those* casks, some of the wine is transferred to casks of even older wine, and so on. At the end of this chain, four to nine generations away from the young wine, finished Sherry is taken from the oldest casks and is bottled for sale.

This system of blending wines is called the *solera* system. It takes its name from the word *solera* (floor), the word also used to identify the oldest casks of wine. Earlier generations are referred to as *criaderas,* suggesting that the wine is still in nursery school.

As wines are blended — younger into older, into yet-older, and eventually into oldest — each cask is emptied less than halfway to make room for the younger wine. In theory, then, each cask contains small (and ever-decreasing) amounts of very old wine. As each wine mingles with older wine, it takes on the characteristics of the older wine; within a few months, the wine of each generation is totally indistinguishable from what it was before being refreshed with younger wine. Thus, the solera system maintains infinite consistency of quality and style in Sherry.

Of course, no vintage-dated sherries can be made in the solera system. A Sherry labeled "Solera 1890," for example, merely indicates the year that particular solera began. A small quantity of vintage Sherry — wines matured for as much as thirty or forty years without blending — is produced by some firms. These wines are called *añada,* pronounced *ah NYAH dah,* (vintage) Sherries.

Because the casks of Sherry age in dry, airy bodegas above ground (rather than humid, underground cellars like most other wines), some of the water in the wine evaporates, and the wine's alcoholic strength increases. Some *olorosos* kept for more than ten years can have as much as 24 percent alcohol.

Two makes twelve

So far, so good: two types of Sherry — delicate *fino* aged under its protective flor, and fuller *oloroso*, aged oxidatively — and no vintages. But now Sherry begins to get a bit confusing. Those two types are about to branch into at least twelve. Sometimes the natural course of aging changes the character of a Sherry so that its taste no longer conforms to one of the two categories. Deliberate sweetening of the wine can create different styles as well.

Among dry Sherries, these are the main styles:

- **Fino:** Pale, straw-colored Sherry, light in body, dry and delicate. Fino Sherries are always matured under flor, either in Jerez or Puerto de Santa María. They have 15.5 to 17 percent alcohol. Once they lose their protective flor (by bottling), *finos* become very vulnerable to oxidation spoilage, and must therefore be stored in a cool place, drunk young, and refrigerated after opening. They're best served chilled.

- **Manzanilla:** Pale, straw-colored, delicate, light, tangy, and very dry *fino*-style Sherry made only in Sanlúcar de Barrameda. (Although various styles of Manzanilla are produced, Manzanilla Fina, the *fino* style, is by far the most common.) The temperate sea climate causes the flor to grow thicker in this town, and Manzanilla is thus the driest and most pungent of all the Sherries. Handle it similarly to a Fino Sherry.

- **Manzanilla Pasada:** A Manzanilla that has been aged about seven years and has lost its flor. It's more amber in color than a *Manzanilla Fina* and fuller-bodied. It's close to a dry amontillado (see the next item) in style, but still crisp and pungent. Serve cool.

- **Amontillado:** An aged *fino* that has lost its flor. It is deeper amber in color and richer and nuttier than the previous styles. *Amontillado* (*ah moan tee YAH doh*) is dry but retains some of the pungent tang from its lost flor. True *amontillado* is fairly rare, while cheaper Sherries labeled *amontillado* are common, so be suspicious if it costs less than $6 a bottle. Serve *amontillado* slightly cool.

- **Oloroso:** Dark gold to deep brown in color (depending on its age), full-bodied with rich, raisiny aroma and flavor, but dry in the finish. *Olorosos* lack the sharp pungency of *fino* (flor) Sherries. They are usually between 18 and 20 percent alcohol and can age indefinitely because they have already been oxidized in their aging. Serve them at room temperature.

- **Palo Cortado** (*PAH loe cor TAH doh*): The rarest of all Sherries. It starts out as a *fino* with a flor and develops as an *amontillado*, losing its flor. But then, for some unknown reason, it begins to resemble the richer, more fragrant *oloroso* style, all the while retaining the elegance of an *amontillado*. In color and alcohol content, *palo cortado* is similar to an *oloroso*, but its aroma is quite like an *amontillado*. Like Amontillado Sherry, beware of cheap imitations. Serve at room temperature.

The bouquet, or aroma, of *fino* Sherry is often compared with almonds. *Amontillados* are said to smell like hazelnuts, and *olorosos* smell like walnuts.

Sweet Sherry is made by adding sweetening to dry Sherry. The sweetening can come in many forms, such as the juice of Pedro Ximénez grapes that have been dried like raisins. All the following sweet styles of Sherry should be served at room temperature.

- **Medium Sherry:** Amontillados and light olorosos that have been slightly sweetened. They are light brown in color.

- **Pale Cream:** Made by blending *fino* and light *amontillado* Sherries and lightly sweetening the blend. They have a very pale gold color. Pale Cream is a fairly new but popular style that now accounts for 25 percent of all Sherry worldwide.

- **Cream Sherry:** Cream and the lighter "milk" Sherries are rich *amorosos* (term for sweetened *olorosos*). They vary in quality, depending on the *oloroso* used, and can improve in the bottle with age. These Sherries are a very popular style today.

- **Brown Sherry:** Very dark, rich, sweet, dessert Sherry, usually containing a coarser style of *oloroso*.

- **East India Sherry:** A type of Brown Sherry that has been deeply sweetened and colored.

- **Pedro Ximénez** and **Moscatel:** Extremely sweet, dark brown, syrupy dessert Sherries. Low in alcohol, the Sherries are made from raisined grapes of these two varieties. They are as rare as straight Sherries today. Delicious over vanilla ice cream (really!).

Wines from elsewhere in the world, especially in the U.S. and Australia, also call themselves "Sherry." Many of these are inexpensive wines in large bottles. Occasionally you can find a decent one, but usually they're sweet and not very good. Authentic Sherry is made only in the Jerez region of Spain and carries the official name, *Jerez-Xeres-Sherry* (the Spanish, French, and English names for the town) on the label (either front or back).

Serving and storing Sherry

The light, dry Sherries — *fino* and *manzanilla* — must be fresh. Buy them from stores with large-volume turnover; a *fino* or *manzanilla* that has been languishing on the shelf for several months will not give you the true experience of these wines. We find that half-bottles are the practical size to buy, eliminating the problem of the wine's getting oxidized in the open bottle.

Although fino or manzanilla can be an excellent apéritif, be wary when ordering a glass in a restaurant or bar. Never accept a glass from an already-open bottle unless the bottle has been refrigerated. Even then, ask how long it has been open — more than a couple of days is too much. Once you open a bottle at home, refrigerate it and finish it within a couple of days.

Unlike table wines, which you should always store on their sides, Sherries can be stored standing up. Try not to hold bottles of *fino* or *manzanilla* more than three months, however. The higher alcohol and oxidative aging of other Sherries permits you to hold them almost indefinitely.

Manzanilla and Fino Sherry are best accompanied by almonds, olives, shrimp or prawns, all kinds of seafood, and those wonderful tapas in Spanish bars and restaurants. Amontillado Sherries can accompany tapas before dinner but are also fine at the table with light soups, cheese, ham, or sausage (especially the Spanish type, *chorizo*). Dry *olorosos* and *palo cortados* are best with nuts, olives, and hard cheeses (such as the excellent Spanish sheep-milk cheese, Manchego). All the sweet Sherries can be served with desserts after dinner or enjoyed on their own.

Recommended Sherry producers

Sherries are among the great values in the wine world: you *can* buy decent, authentic Sherries of all types for five or six dollars. But if you want to try the best wines, you might have to spend $10 to $12. The following are some of our favorite producers, according to type.

Manzanilla

▸ Vinícola Hidalgo's **La Gitana** (a great buy at $7 to $8), or their **Manzanilla Pasada**

Fino

▸ González Byass's **Tío Pepé** *(TEE oh PAY pay)*

▸ Pedro Domecq's **La Ina** *(EEN ah)*

▸ Emilio Lustau's **Jarana** *(har AHN ah)*

▸ Osborne's **Fino Quinta** *(KEEN tah)*

Amontillado

You will find a great deal of cheap imitations in this category. For a true *amontillado*, stick to one of the brands below.

▸ González Byass's **Del Duque** (the *real thing* at a reasonable $17 to $18)

▸ Emilio Lustau (any of his *amontillados* labeled **Almacenista**)

▸ Vinícola Hidalgo

▸ Osborne's **Old, Rare Amontillado** (available in a 10-year-old or 30-year-old version; an expensive Sherry at $20-plus, and hard to find)

Oloroso

▸ González Byass's **Apostoles**

▸ Emilio Lustau (any of his *olorosos* labeled **Almacenista**)

- Osborne's **Old, Rare Oloroso** (from a 40-year-old Solera; about $30)
- Sandeman's **Royal Corregidor** and **Imperial Corregidor** (rich, but a bit sweet)

Palo Cortado

You'll find many imitations in this category, too. True *palo cortados* are quite rare.

- Emilio Lustau (any of his palo cortados labeled **Almacenista**)
- Sandeman's **Royal Ambrosante** (has been sweetened a bit)
- Vinícola Hidalgo's **Jerez Cortado**
- Osborne's **Old, Rare** (30 years old and costs about $30)

Cream

- González Byass's **San Domingo** (a pale cream — delicate, not too sweet)
- Sandeman's **Armada Cream**
- Pedro Domecq's **Celebration Cream**
- Emilio Lustau's **Rare Cream Reserva** or **Vendimia Cream**

East India, Pedro Ximénez, Moscatel

- Emilio Lustau (a quality brand for all of these Sherries)
- González Byass's **Pedro Ximénez "Noe"**
- Osborne's Pedro Ximénez **Old, Rare** or **India Oloroso** (42 years old)

Montilla: A Sherry look-alike

Northeast of the Sherry region is the Montilla-Moriles region (commonly referred to as Montilla), where wines very similar to Sherry are made in *fino, amontillado,* and *oloroso* styles. The two big differences between Montilla *(moan TEE yah)* and Sherry are:

- Pedro Ximénez is the predominant grape variety in Montilla.
- Montillas usually reach their high alcohol levels naturally (without fortification).

Alvear is the leading brand. Reasonably priced ($8 to $9), this wine is widely available.

Marsala and the Gang

Italy has a number of interesting dessert and fortified wines, of which Marsala is the most famous. Marsala (named after a town in western Sicily) has been through hard times leaving its image reduced to a mere cooking ingredient. However, serious producers in the zone are intent on reviving Marsala as an important fortified wine.

Marsala is made in numerous styles, all of which are fortified after fermentation, like Sherry, and aged in a form of the solera system. You can find dry, semi-dry, or sweet versions and amber, gold, or red versions, but the best Marsalas have the word *Superiore* or — even better — *Vergine,* on the label. Marsala Vergine is unsweetened and uncolored and is aged longer than other styles. Marco De Bartoli is the most acclaimed producer of Marsala. His 20-year-old Vecchio Samperi is an excellent example of a dry, apéritif Marsala. Pellegrino, Rallo, and Florio are larger producers of note.

Two fascinating Sicilian dessert wines are made from dried grapes on small islands that are part of Sicily. One is Malvasia delle Lipari from Carlo Hauner. This wine has a beautiful, orange-amber color and an incredible floral, apricot, and herb aroma. The other is Moscato di Pantelleria, a very rich dessert wine; De Bartoli is one of the best producers of this brand.

Tuscany is very proud of its Vin Santo, a golden amber wine made from dried grapes and barrel-aged for several years. Vin Santo is made in dry, medium-dry, or sweet versions. We prefer the first two, the dry style as an apéritif and the medium-dry version as an accompaniment to the wonderful Italian almond cookies called *biscotti*. Two outstanding producers of Vin Santo (conveniently available in half-bottles as well as full bottles) are Avignonesi and Badia á Coltibuono.

Port: The Great Fortified Wine of Portugal

Thanks to one of the many wars between the British and the French, Port was "discovered" by the Brits, and subsequently the rest of the world.

In the late 17th century, when the English could not obtain French wine, they turned to Portugal. To insure that Portuguese wines were stable enough for shipment, a small amount of brandy was added to the finished wine. The first English Port house, Warre, was established in the city of Oporto in 1670 and was followed by several others.

But Port as we know it was not made until the 19th century. At that point, producers in Portugal (mainly British by now) began fortifying their wine with brandy during fermentation in response to English consumers' requests for sweeter wine. This increase in alcohol stopped the fermentation, leaving the wine with some residual sugar. Port — as we now know it — had been created.

Actually, until 1900, dry and medium-dry styles of Port continued to be made, along with the rich, sweet style of today's Port, but only the sweeter style has survived. Port today, made with a combination of four parts wine and one part spirits, usually contains about 20 percent alcohol.

Ironically, the French, who drove the British to Portugal, today drink three times as much Port as the British!

Home, home on the Douro

Although Port takes its name from the city of Oporto, situated where the northerly Douro River empties into the Atlantic Ocean, its vineyards are far away in the hot, mountainous Douro Valley. (In 1756, this region became one of the first wine regions in the world to be officially recognized.) You can find some of the most dramatically beautiful vineyards in the world on the slopes of the upper Douro — an area so rugged and unspoiled that much of it can still be traveled only by canoe or mule.

Most Port wine travels from the Douro Valley to the coast after it is made. The wine is finished and matured in the Port lodges of Vila Nova de Gaia, a suburb of Oporto. From Oporto, the wine is shipped all over the world.

To stop your wine-nerd friends in their tracks, ask them to name the 48 authorized grape varieties for Port. In truth, most wine lovers — even Port lovers — can't name even one variety. These grapes are mostly local and unknown outside of Portugal. For the record, the five most important varieties are *Touriga Nacional*, *Tinta Roriz* (Tempranillo), *Tinta Barroca*, *Tinto Cão*, and *Touriga Francesca*.

Many Ports for a storm

Think Sherry is complicated? In some ways, Port is even trickier. Although all Port is sweet, and most of it is red, a zillion styles exist. The styles vary according to the quality of the base wine (ranging from ordinary to exceptional), how long the wine aged in wood before bottling (ranging from 2 to 40-plus years), and whether the wine is from a single year or blended from wines of several years.

Following is a brief description of the main styles:

- ✔ **White Port:** Made from white grapes, this gold-colored wine can be almost dry (and drunk as an apéritif) or sweet. We can't quite figure out why it exists. Sherries and Sercial Madeiras (discussed later in this chapter) are far better as apéritifs and red Ports are far superior as sweet wines.

- ✔ **Ruby Port:** This young, non-vintage style is aged in wood for about three years before being sold. Fruity, simple, and inexpensive (around $9 or $10), it's the best-selling type of Port. If labeled *Reserve* or *Special Reserve*, the wine has aged about six years and costs a few dollars more. Ruby Port provides a good introduction to the Port world.

- ✔ **Tawny Port:** Garnet or brownish-red in color, simple tawnies are lighter wines that age in casks for about three years before bottling. (Some are even blends of ruby Port and white Port.) The best tawny Ports are good-quality wines that acquire their pale color through long wood aging, which causes browning. They cost about $15, compared to $6 or $8 for cheaper tawnies. The very best tawnies have an indication of their average age (the average age of the wines from which they were blended) on their labels — 10, 20, 30, or 40 years. Ten-year-old tawnies cost about $20 to $25, and 20-year-olds sell for $40. We consider 20-year-tawnies the best; the older ones aren't worth the extra bucks. A serious Tawny Port can be enjoyed in warm weather when a Vintage Port would be too heavy and tannic.

- ✔ **Vintage Character Port:** Despite its name, this wine is not single-vintage Port — it just tries to taste like one. Vintage Character Port is actually premium ruby blended from higher-quality wines of several vintages and matured in wood for about five years. Full-bodied, rich, and ready-to-drink when released, these wines are a good value at about $15. Of course, the labels don't always say Vintage Character: They have proprietary names like Boardroom (made by Dow), Six Grapes (made by Graham), or Bin 27 (made by Fonseca). As if Vintage Character wouldn't have been confusing enough!

- ✔ **Late Bottled Vintage Port (LBV):** This type *is* from a specific vintage, but usually not from a very top year. The wine is aged in wood four to six years before bottling and is ready to drink when released — unlike Vintage Port itself. Quite full-bodied, it sells for about $18 to $20.

- ✔ **Colheita Port:** Often confused with Vintage Port because it's vintage-dated, Colheita is actually a tawny from a single vintage. In other words, it has aged (and softened and tawnied) in wood for many years. Unlike a 20-year-old tawny, though, this is the wine of a single year.

- ✔ **Vintage Port:** The pinnacle of Port production, Vintage Port is the wine of a single year blended from several of the best vineyards. It's bottled during its "Terrible Twos," before the wine has much chance to shed its tough tannins. It therefore requires an enormous amount of bottle aging; Vintage Port is usually not ready to drink for 20 years after the vintage.

Very rich, very tannic, and long-lived (70 or more years in good vintages), this wine throws a heavy sediment and *must* be decanted, preferably several hours before drinking (it needs the aeration). Most good Vintage Ports sell in the $35 to $45 range when they are young (and years away from drinkability). Producing a Vintage Port in a particular year amounts to a *declaration* of the vintage on the part of an individual Port house.

✔ **Single Quinta Vintage Port:** These are Vintage Ports from a single estate *(quinta)* that is usually a producer's best property (such as Taylor's Vargellas and Graham's Malvedos). They're made in good years, but not in declared vintages — when their grapes are needed for the Vintage Port blend. Priced at about $25 to $35, they have the advantage of being readier to drink than declared Vintage Ports. They should be decanted and aerated, however. (Some Port houses, incidentally, are single estates, such as Quinta do Noval and Quinta do Infantado. When such a house makes a vintage-dated Port, it's a Vintage Port, as well as a single quinta Port.)

The term *Port* has been borrowed even more extensively around the world than Sherry has. Many countries outside the EU make a sweet, red wine in the Port style and label it as Port. Some of it can be quite good, but, usually, it's not as good as the genuine article that is only made in Portugal.

Storing and serving Port

Vintage Ports should be treated like all other fine red wines: stored on their sides in a cool place. Other Ports may be stored on their sides or standing up because they are no longer developing. All Ports, except white and ruby, can be kept for several weeks after opening.

You can now find Vintage Ports in half-bottles — a brilliant development for Port lovers. Opening a bottle after dinner is far easier to justify when it's just a half-bottle. The wine evolves slightly more quickly in half-bottles, but considering the wine's longevity, that may even be a bonus!

Port should be served at cool room temperature, 64° to 66° F (18° C), although Tawny Port can be a bracing pick-me-up when served chilled during warm weather. The classic complements to Port are walnuts and strong cheeses, such as Stilton, Gorgonzola, Roquefort, mature Cheddar, and aged Gouda.

Recommended Port producers

In terms of quality, with the exception of a few clinker producers, Port is one of the most consistent of all wines. We've organized our favorite Port producers into two categories — outstanding and very good — each in rough order of preference. As you may expect, producers in the first group tend to be a bit more expensive. Our rating is based mainly on Vintage Port but can be generally applied to all the various Port styles of the house.

Outstanding

- Taylor (also known as Taylor-Fladgate)
- Fonseca
- Graham
- Quinta do Noval "Nacional" (made from ungrafted, pre-phylloxera vineyards; see Chapter 9)
- Dow
- Cockburn *(COH burn)*

Very Good

- Smith-Woodhouse
- Warre
- Ramos Pinto
- Quinta do Noval
- Croft
- Sandeman
- Niepoort
- Quarles Harris
- Quinta do Infantado
- Quinta do Vesuvio
- Ferreira
- Cálem
- Churchill
- Gould Campbell
- Martinez
- Offley Boa Vista
- Rebello Valente

Declarations of quality

On the average, only three or four years out of every ten are good enough to be declared *vintage years* by the Port houses. Following is a list of the top declared vintages since 1945:

- **1992:** Looks outstanding but only a few houses, such as Taylor and Fonseca, declared
- **1991:** Very good
- **1985:** Good to excellent
- **1983:** Very good
- **1977:** Good to excellent
- **1970:** Very good
- **1966:** Good to excellent; underrated; ready to drink
- **1963:** Outstanding, especially Quinta do Noval Nacional
- **1955:** Good to excellent; perfect now
- **1948:** Outstanding, especially Taylor, Fonseca, and Graham; aging well
- **1945:** Classic; still needs time, especially Taylor and Graham

Madeira M'dear

The legendary wine called Madeira is produced on the island of the same name, which sits nearer to Africa than Europe in the Atlantic Ocean. Madeira is a subtropical island whose precarious vineyards rise straight up from the Atlantic on hillsides. The island is a province of Portugal, but its wine trade has always been run by the British. Historically, Madeira could even be considered an American wine, for this is the wine that American colonists drank.

Although Madeira's fortified wines were quite the rage 200 years ago, the island's vineyards were devastated last century, first by mildew and then by the phylloxera louse. Most vineyards were replanted with lesser grapes. Madeira has been recovering a long time from these setbacks. The best Madeiras are still those from the old days, vintage-dated wines from 1920 back to 1795. Surprisingly, you can still find many Madeiras from the last century. The prices are reasonable, too, ($100 to $200) considering the wine's age. Refer to Chapters 15 and 16 for sources of old Madeira.

Timeless and indestructible

You never have to worry about Madeira getting too old. It's indestructible. The enemies of wine — heat and oxygen — have already had their way with Madeira during the winemaking and maturing process. Nothing you do once it's bottled can make it blink.

Madeira comes in four styles, two fairly dry and two sweet. The sweeter Madeiras generally have their fermentation halted somewhat early by the addition of high-alcohol spirit. Drier Madeiras have alcohol added after fermentation. A curiosity of Madeira production is a baking process called the *estufagem (es too FAH jem),* which follows fermentation. The fact that Madeira improves by heating was discovered back in the 17th century. When trading ships crossed the equator with casks of Madeira as ballast in their holds, the wine actually improved with the voyage! Today, baking the wine at home on the island is a bit more practical than sending it around the world in a slow ship.

Madeira spends a minimum of three months, often longer, in heated tanks, in *estufas* (heating rooms), or exposed to the sun (the weather stays warm year round). Any sugars in the wine become caramelized, and the wine becomes thoroughly *maderized* (oxidized through heating) without developing any unpleasant aroma or taste.

Endless finish

Technically a white wine, Madeira has an amber color with a pale green rim, a tangy aroma and flavor that is uniquely its own, and as long a finish on the palate as you'll find on the planet. When Madeira is made from any of the four noble grapes of the island (see the following list), the grape name indicates the style. When Madeira doesn't carry a grape name — and most younger Madeiras don't — the words *dry, medium-dry, medium-sweet,* and *sweet* indicate the style.

Some of the most memorable wines we've ever tasted were old Madeiras, so we're afraid we might get carried away a bit, beginning any time now. Their aroma alone is divine, and you keep on tasting the wine long after you've swallowed it. (Spitting is out of the question.) Words truly are inadequate to describe this wine.

If you can afford to buy an old bottle of vintage-dated Madeira (the producer's name is relatively unimportant), you'll understand our enthusiasm. And maybe some day when Madeira production gets back on its feet, every wine lover will be able to experience vintage Madeira. In the meantime, for a less expensive Madeira experience, look for wines labeled *Special Reserve,* which means that the wines in the blend are about ten years old. *Reserve* Madeira has half that age with some shortcuts in winemaking. Don't bother with any other type, because it will be unremarkable, and then we'll look crazy.

Vintage Madeira must spend at least 20 years in a cask, but for the old wines, the wood-aging was even longer. Vintage Madeira is made from one of the four noble grape varieties following (once there were six) and varietally labeled. Each grape variety corresponds to a specific style of wine.

- **Sercial:** The Sercial grape grows at the highest altitudes. Thus the grapes are the least ripe and make the driest Madeira. The wine is high in acidity, very tangy, and fairly dry. Sercial Madeira is an outstanding apéritif wine with almonds, olives, or light cheeses. Unfortunately, true Sercial is quite rare today.

- **Verdelho:** The Verdelho grape makes a medium-dry style, with nutty, peachy flavors and a tang of acidity. Good as an apéritif or with consommé.

- **Bual (or Boal):** Darker amber in color, Bual is a rich, medium-sweet Madeira with spicy flavors of almonds and raisins and a long, tangy finish. Bual should be consumed after dinner. Like Sercial, true Bual is rare today.

- **Malmsey:** Made from the Malvasia grape, Malmsey is dark amber, sweet, and intensely concentrated with a very long finish. Drink it after dinner.

Two disappearing varieties, whose names you may see on some very old bottles, are

- **Terrantez:** Medium-sweet, between Verdelho and Bual in style, a powerful, fragrant Madeira with lots of acidity. Drink after dinner.

- **Bastardo:** The only red grape of the noble varieties. Old Bastardos from the last century are mahogany-colored and rich, but not so rich as the Terrantez.

Another Portuguese classic

One of the great dessert wines produced from the white Muscat grape is Setúbal *(SHTOO bahl).* Produced in Azeitão, just south of Lisbon, Setúbal is made similarly to Port with grape spirit added to stop fermentation. Like Port, it is a rich, long-lasting wine. The most important producer is J. M. da Fonseca.

Sauternes and the "Nobly Rotten" Wines

Warm, misty autumns encourage the growth of a fungus called *botrytis cinerea* in vineyards. Nicknamed *noble rot*, botrytis concentrates the juice and sugar in the grapes, giving the winemaker amazingly rich juice to ferment. The best wines from botrytis-infected grapes are among the greatest dessert wines in the world with intensely concentrated flavors and plenty of acidity to prevent the wine from being excessively sweet.

The greatest "nobly rotten" wines are made in the Sauternes district of Graves (Bordeaux) and in Germany (see Chapter 11), but they are also produced in Austria and California, among other places.

Sauternes: Liquid gold

Sauternes is a very labor-intensive wine. Grapes must be picked by hand; workers pass through the vineyard several times — sometimes over a period of weeks — selecting only the botrytis-infected grapes. Yields are low. Harvests sometimes linger until November, but now and then bad weather in October dashes all hopes of making botrytis-infected wine. Often, only two to four vintages per decade yield decent Sauternes (the 1980s decade was exceptional).

Consequently, good Sauternes is expensive. Prices range from $20 or $25 on up to $200 or $250 (depending on the vintage) for Château d'Yquem (d'ee kem). The greatest and most labor-intensive Sauternes, d'Yquem has always been prized by collectors (see Chapters 15 and 20). It was the only Sauternes given the status of *first great growth* in the 1855 Bordeaux Classification (explained in Chapter 10).

Sauternes is now widely available in half-bottles, reducing the cost somewhat. A 375 ml bottle is a perfect size for after dinner, and you can buy a decent Sauternes like Château Doisy-Daëne *(dwahs ee dayne)* in that size for $11 to $12.

Mining the gold

The Sauternes wine district includes five communes in the southernmost part of Graves (one of them named Sauternes). One of the five, Barsac, makes wines that are slightly lighter and less sweet than Sauternes and are entitled to their own appellation. The Garonne River and the Ciron, an important tributary, produce the mists that encourage the formation of *botrytis cinerea* on the grapes.

The three authorized grape varieties are Sémillon, Sauvignon Blanc, and Muscadelle — although the latter is used by only a few châteaux, and even then in small quantities. Sémillon is the king. Most producers use at least 80 percent Sémillon in their blend.

Wine that is called "Sauterne" (no final *s*) is produced in California and other places. This semi-sweet, rather insipid wine is made from inexpensive grapes and usually sold in large bottles. *This wine bears absolutely no resemblance to true, botrytis-infected Sauternes, from Sauternes, France.* California does make late-harvest, botrytis-infected wines, mainly Rieslings, and while they are far better than Sauterne (even worth trying), they are generally not as fine as the botrytis wines of Sauternes or Germany.

Recommended Sauternes

All of the Sauternes below range from outstanding to good. In Sauternes, vintages are just as important as in the rest of Bordeaux. Check our vintage recommendations later in this chapter.

Outstanding

- **Château d'Yquem:** Can last for 100 years or more

- **Château de Fargues:** Owned by d'Yquem; almost as good as d'Yquem, at one-third the price

- **Château Climens (Barsac):** At $45 to $55, a value; near d'Yquem's level

- **Château Coutet (Barsac):** Especially the rare Cuvée Madame

Excellent

- **Château Suduiraut:** Only its inconsistency from vintage to vintage denies it an outstanding rating

- **Château Rieussec:** Rich, lush style

- **Château Raymond-Lafon:** Located next to d'Yquem; owned by d'Yquem's manager

Very Good

- Château Lafaurie-Peyraguey

- Château Guiraud

- Château Rabaud-Promis

- Château Latour Blanche

- Château Doisy-Dubroca (Barsac)

- Château Doisy-Daëne (Barsac)

- Château Doisy-Védrines (Barsac)

- Château Sigalas-Rabaud

Good

- ✔ Château Lamothe-Guignard
- ✔ Château Rayne Vigneau
- ✔ Château Clos Haut-Peyraguey
- ✔ Château Bastor-Lamontagne
- ✔ Château d'Arche
- ✔ Château Filhot
- ✔ Château de Malle
- ✔ Château Nairac (Barsac)

Letting baby grow

Sauternes has such balance of natural sweetness and acidity that it can age well (especially the better Sauternes mentioned here) for an extraordinarily long time. Unfortunately, because Sauternes is so delicious, it is often consumed in its early years when it is very rich and sweet. But Sauternes is really at its best when it loses its baby fat and matures.

After about ten to fifteen years, Sauternes's color changes from light gold to an old gold-coin color, sometimes with orange or amber tones. At this point, the wine loses some of its sweetness and develops flavors reminiscent of apricots, orange rind, honey, and toffee. This time is the best to drink Sauternes. The better the vintage, the longer Sauternes takes to reach this stage, but once there, it stays at this plateau for many years — sometimes decades — and very gradually turns dark amber or light brown in color. Even in these final stages, Sauternes retains some of its complex flavors.

In good vintages, Sauternes can age for 50 to 60 years or more. Château d'Yquem and Château Climens are particularly long-lived. (We recently had a half-bottle of 1893 Château d'Yquem, which was glorious!)

Sauternes is at its best when served cold, but not ice cold, at about 52° to 53° F (11° C). Mature Sauternes can be served a bit warmer. Because the wine is so rich, Sauternes is an ideal companion for *foie gras* although, ordinarily, the wine is far more satisfying after dinner than as an apéritif. As for desserts, Sauternes is excellent with ripe fruits, lemon-flavored cakes, or pound cake.

The years to buy

The 1980s were truly exceptional for Sauternes. Following are the best vintages of Sauternes since 1959:

- ✔ **1990:** Great
- ✔ **1989:** Very good to great
- ✔ **1988:** Outstanding (best since 1959)
- ✔ **1986:** Great
- ✔ **1983:** Very good to great
- ✔ **1976:** Good (ready to drink)
- ✔ **1975:** Great
- ✔ **1971:** Good (ready to drink)
- ✔ **1967:** Very good to great
- ✔ **1962:** Very good (ready to drink)
- ✔ **1959:** Outstanding

Sauternes look-alikes

There are many sweet, botrytis-infected wines similar to Sauternes that sell for considerably less money than Sauternes or Barsacs. These wines are not as intense or as complex in flavor, but they are fine values (in the $10 to $15 price range).

Directly north and adjacent to Barsac is the often overlooked Cérons wine region. You can probably convince many of your friends that a Cérons, served blind, is a Sauternes or Barsac. In the Entre-Deux-Mers district of Bordeaux, look for the Cadillac, Loupiac, or Sainte-Croix-du-Mont appellations for less expensive versions of Sauternes.

Part III
When You've Caught the Bug

The 5th Wave — By Rich Tennant

@RICHTENNANT

"LOOK KIDS, MOMMY AND DADDY NEED A THERMOSTATICALLY CONTROLLED ENVIRONMENT FOR THEIR WINE UNTIL THE CELLAR IS FINISHED – WE'RE TALKING BORDEAUXS HERE, KIDS – OVER 60 YEARS OLD."

In this part...

The incubation period of the wine bug is unpredictable. Some people no sooner express interest in wine than they become engrossed in the subject. Other people exhibit mild symptoms for many years before succumbing to the passion. (Lots and lots of people never get bitten by the bug at all.)

But once you've been smitten by the wine bug, you know it. You find yourself subscribing to magazines that your friends never heard of, making new friends with whom you have little in common other than an interest in wine, boycotting restaurants with substandard wine lists, and planning vacations to wine regions.

However quickly you got to this stage, the following chapters will provide fuel for your fire.

Chapter 15

To Have and To Hold — or To Sell

· ·

· ·

*W*hen we first started buying wine, we operated from the gut. Carried away with the excitement of a wine-tasting, we'd decide to buy 4 or 6 — or even 12 — bottles of our favorite wine of the evening. Sometimes, browsing the shelves of retail stores, we'd buy 12 different Zinfandels (see Chapter 12) with the intention of setting up our own comparative tasting, but we didn't always get around to it. Sometimes, we'd buy wines just because they got exceedingly high scores from critics — 4 bottles of something expensive purchased on blind faith (with a little help from VISA).

Our wine consumption couldn't keep pace with our curiosity to try new wines and our passion to possess wines we had tried and liked. Before we knew it, we had become wine collectors.

Luckily for us, we didn't make *too* many mistakes along the way. Nonetheless, we came to appreciate the wisdom of having a plan for our wine purchases. Wine, we decided, has something in common with rabbits: The population of bottles can very easily get out of hand.

Wine Collecting Just Happens

Most wines are consumed very quickly after they have been purchased — a bottle or two to drink on Saturday evening when the neighbors drop by, Champagne for the anniversary toast, something red for the lasagna on Sunday. If this is your custom, you've got plenty of company.

But many people who enjoy wine operate a bit differently. Oh, sure, they buy wine because they intend to *drink* it; they're just not exactly sure *when* they'll drink it. And until they do drink it, they'll get pleasure out of knowing that the bottles are waiting for them.

If you count yourself in this second group, you are probably a wine collector at heart. The chase, to you, is every bit as thrilling as the consummation.

If you are a closet wine collector, a little forethought will help steer you toward an organized inventory of wines that you are pleased to own. But *even if you never intend to have a wine collection,* it's worthwhile to put at least a little thought into your wine purchases. Developing a strategy of wine buying can prevent a haphazard collection of uninteresting or worthless bottles from happening to you.

Formulating a wine-buying strategy involves assessing

 ✔ How much wine you drink

 ✔ How much wine you want to own

 ✔ How much money you are prepared to spend on wine

 ✔ The types of wine you enjoy drinking

Unless you strike a balance on these issues, you could end up either broke, bored, or frustrated, or in the salad dressing and vinegar business!

The avowed non-collector

You are enthusiastic about wine and you enjoy buying it. But you have no intention of becoming a wine collector — you don't have the space, or you have better things to spend your money on.

In your circumstances, the only way to prevent a wine collection from happening is strict personal discipline. Determine how many bottles of wine you consume in a month (don't forget to take entertaining into account) and never have more than that number of bottles on hand. If you drink wine at home two nights a week, for example, and entertain once a month, the number could be somewhere around 12 bottles.

When you buy wine, avoid purchasing robust, red wines that improve with age. Avoid buying more than two bottles of any one wine unless you don't mind drinking the same wine frequently. Don't buy any bottle of wine that is so extraordinary or expensive that you might be tempted to hold it for a special occasion.

Resist the urge to subscribe to wine magazines; cut up all your credit cards except the *one* with the lowest line of credit.

The small collector

Moderation in wine collecting is as challenging as it is commendable.

Say you decide that a six-month inventory of wine seems reasonable for you. (That's probably about 75 bottles, given the same scenario of entertaining once a month and drinking wine two nights a week at home.)

You've just given yourself license to collect, because with 75 bottles, you could surely manage to devote a *case* (12 bottles) or two to wines that require long-term aging. You could also rationalize a full-case purchase of a wine you particularly like, figuring that you'd drink it twice a month for six months (but will you really?).

Your challenge is to maintain the proper balance between maturing wines and drinkable wines and enough diversity among your drinkable wines that you are not bored with your choices. To accomplish these two goals, you probably have to keep records of your inventory. You also need to think about the storage conditions of your wine — especially those long-term keepers.

The serious collector

Congratulations! Most wine collectors don't ever really *decide* to become wine collectors; they just keep buying and buying until they *are* wine collectors. By making a calculated decision to own a few hundred bottles of wine, you have the opportunity to develop a collection that truly suits your palate and your goals, and to avoid common pitfalls of wine collecting.

Your challenge is to define your goals clearly, diversify your collection appropriately, and exercise patience in your wine buying. You'll also want to make sure that your wine is stored under optimal conditions, or many of your purchases will never bring you the pleasure you anticipate from them.

Is the sky the limit?

There are some wine collectors who have extensive cellars of over 10,000 bottles! This might be called taking one's hobby to the extreme. We believe that a collection of 1,000 to 1,500 bottles is definitely sufficient to handle *anyone's* needs nicely. Then again, 100 bottles isn't so bad, either!

Likely Suspects

Unless your intention is to fill your cellar with wines that bring you the greatest return when you later sell them (in other words, unless you aren't interested in actually *drinking* the wines you own), you should like a wine before buying it. (We're not talking about all those bottles you buy while you're playing the field and experimenting with new wines — just those that you're thinking of making a commitment to, by buying in quantity.)

We remember hearing a story about a Hollywood starlet who stocked her new wine cellar only with wines that scored 95 to 100 points from the major critics. We wish we could be there on the day she realizes that she doesn't actually *like* many of the wines she owns!

Balance in your inventory

A well-planned wine inventory features a range of wines: it can be heavy in one or two types of wine that you particularly enjoy, but it has other types of wine, too. Your inventory should also strike a balance between wines that are ready to drink and wines that require additional aging, inexpensive wines that can be enjoyed on simple occasions, and important wines that demand a special occasion.

If you like California Chardonnays or Cabernet Sauvignons, for example, you may decide to make them your specialty. But consider that you might grow weary of them if you had nothing else to drink night after night. By purchasing other wines as well, you can have the fun of exploring different types of wine — a pleasant way to educate your palate.

Table wines (or light wines), of course, constitute the bulk of most wine collections. But it's a good idea to build in a little diversity with apéritif wines — such as Champagne or dry Sherry — and dessert wines — such as Port or sweet white wines — so that you'll be prepared when the occasion arises. (If you're like us, you'll invent plenty of occasions to open a bottle of Champagne!)

In planning your own wine inventory, you'd be prudent to include some age-worthy wines that you buy in their youth when their prices are lowest. Many of the better red wines, such as Bordeaux, Barolo, and Brunello di Montalcino, often are not at their best for at least ten years after the vintage — and some of them are difficult to find once they are ready to drink (see Chapter 20 for more information on wines that need to be aged). Aging is also the rule for some fine white Burgundies (such as Corton-Charlemagne), white Bordeaux, Sauternes, German late-harvest wines, and vintage Port (the latter usually requires about 20 years of aging before it matures!).

But don't limit yourself to wines so important that you are discouraged from opening anything when you just feel like having a glass of wine. Your selection should cover both ends of the seriousness spectrum:

- ✔ Everyday wines, best enjoyed in their youth, which do not need extensive aging — usually fairly inexpensive wines, in the $4 to $15 a bottle price range

- ✔ Age-worthy wines, richer and more complex, to enjoy after they (and you) have matured gracefully over a period of years — usually costing more than $15 a bottle

Everyday wines

Our candidates for everyday white wines include

- ✔ Simple white Burgundies, such as Mâcon-Villages, St. Veran, or Chablis

    (White Burgundies are made from the Chardonnay grape; for further information, see "Burgundy: The Other Great French Wine" in Chapter 10)

- ✔ Sauvignon Blancs (from California, France, and so on)

- ✔ Chardonnays (from California, Australia, and so on)

- ✔ Pinot Gris (or the Italian equivalent, Pinot Grigio)

- ✔ Alsace Pinot Blancs

For everyday red wines, we like

- ✔ Barbera (from Italy)

- ✔ Red Zinfandel (from California)

These two wines are enjoyable young, versatile enough to go well with the foods many people eat on an everyday basis (simple, hearty, flavorful foods), and sturdy enough to age for a couple of years if you don't get around to them (that is, they won't deteriorate quickly).

Other everyday red wines we recommend include

- ✔ Beaujolais

- ✔ Côtes du Rhône

- ✔ Pinot Noir

- ✔ Merlot

- ✔ Dolcetto (from Italy)

- ✔ Simple, lighter-bodied Bordeaux (under $15)

Age-worthy wines

Age-worthy whites we recommend include

- Above all, *grand cru* and *premier cru* white Burgundies — such as Corton-Charlemagne, Batard- and Chevalier-Montrachets, Meursault, and Chablis *Grand Crus*

- Also, the better white Bordeaux, some great German Rieslings, and Alsace Rieslings or Gewürztraminers (see Chapters 10 through 12 for an explanation of these wines)

Among the many long-lived red wines, some likely candidates for keeping (or *cellaring* — the term for letting wines mature) are

- Fine Bordeaux

- *Grand Cru* and *Premier Cru* Burgundies

- Big Italian reds, such as Barolo, Barbaresco, Chianti Classico Riserva, Brunello di Montalcino, Taurasi, and Super-Tuscan Cabernet/Sangiovese blends

- From Spain, Rioja and Vega Sicilia

- From California, better Cabernet Sauvignons (and Cabernet blends)

- From the Rhône, Hermitage and Côte Rôtie

- Portugal's Barca Velha

- Australia's Grange Hermitage

The finer Champagnes (usually vintage Champagnes and *prestige cuvées;* see Chapter 13) and oloroso Sherries (see Chapter 14) are very age-worthy. So are the finest dessert wines, such as French Sauternes, late-harvest German Rieslings, sweet Vouvrays from the Loire Valley, Vintage Port, and Madeira.

Where to Draw the Line

One of the toughest decisions you'll have to make is *how much* of a particular wine you should buy. When you believe that a certain wine is really exceptional (you love it, it's just received a great rating, and/or the vintage year is reputedly terrific), you'll probably have a natural tendency to buy large quantities.

We know a fellow who refinanced his house in order to buy 60 cases of 1982 Château Mouton-Rothschild! Actually, that decision wasn't as crazy as it sounds because a First Growth Bordeaux (see Chapter 10) from a great vintage like

1982 was a sound investment. Our friend will most likely make a fine profit on that purchase (when he sells the wine), as the Mouton probably cost him no more than $600 a case in 1985, possibly less, and its value is now $2,400 a case!

If you are about to buy a large quantity of a particular wine — say, two or more cases — the first question that you should ask yourself is, "Will I be able to sell this wine in the future, if I decide to do so?" (Check our investment wine list later in this chapter or consult with a wine-knowledgeable acquaintance if you're not sure of a wine's resale potential.)

If the wine that you are planning to buy in a large quantity has no proven track record for resale, we advise restraint. There are several reasons:

- ✔ You may grow tired of the wine and end up with a case or more of it (borrr-ing!).

- ✔ Your tastes may change, or (as your palate gains experience) you may find that the wine you thought was so great doesn't live up to your expectations.

- ✔ The wine may get old more quickly than you expected (which happens often), leaving you with several bottles of a wine that is past its prime.

Except for investment purposes, we would suggest that you never buy more than one case of a particular wine, *at the most*. We save "buying by the case" for just a very few of our proven favorite wines; most of the time, we limit ourselves to three or six bottles of particular wines that we know we like and we know have potential for long life. If we haven't tasted a particular wine before (or we're uncertain whether to buy a wine) and are curious about its potential, we'll buy just one bottle first — and try it.

Be careful not to overbuy sought-after wines for fear that they will sell out. There is always more wine to buy! You might regret not buying more bottles of a few particular wines when you had the opportunity, but the truth is that more good wine is being made every year. You can manage to let a few big fish get away now and then.

Orderliness Is Next to Peace of Mind

Whether you ever intended to collect wine or not, there might come a time when you realize that you are not only a wine drinker but also a wine collector. Maybe you'll realize that you are a wine collector when you've accumulated your first 90 or 100 bottles.

With this realization comes the awareness that you need to keep track of all your wine so that

- You can find a bottle quickly when you're looking for it.

- You know what you own (many a bottle has gone *over the hill* because the owner forgot that he had it!).

- You can show off your wine collection to your friends (something like showing your baby's pictures).

Orderly organization of your wine

There are many ways to keep track of your wine. One way is simply to arrange your wines in a logical order in their storage space — keeping all the wines from each country or region together, for example. You'll find that this type of organization will save you lots of time when you need to locate a particular bottle. It sure beats opening up case after case to find what you're looking for when you're in a hurry.

If all of your wine is crammed into a tiny, dark corner of your basement with little room for maneuvering, of course, orderly physical arrangement of your wines is impossible.

Cellar book or other paper inventory

Another way to keep track of your wines is to keep a record of the specific wines in your collection, the number of each, and the location.

When we first started cataloging our wines, we used a large loose-leaf book (affectionately, if somewhat pompously, referred to as our cellar book). Whenever we purchased a wine, we would write the wine's name and vintage in pencil on the appropriate page of the book (one page per country or major wine region). Whenever we consumed a wine, we'd use an eraser to change the quantity of that wine remaining or to eliminate the wine completely. With time, the book got pretty ragged-looking. (The pages representing our favorite wines actually were worn through from all the eraser activity.) We thought that we were upgrading our cellar book quite a bit when we bought plastic sleeves for each page!

Then one of us got the bright idea of using our computer to keep track of our wine.

Computerized record-keeping

Cataloging our wine collection by computer turned out to be a lot easier than we expected. We used a database program (Filemaker, specifically) on our Macintosh to create the file. We set up a field for each of the following items:

- ✔ Vintage
- ✔ Producer
- ✔ Wine name
- ✔ Appellation
- ✔ Vineyard name
- ✔ Region
- ✔ Country
- ✔ Type (red, white, rosé, sparkling, apéritif, or dessert)
- ✔ Quantity owned
- ✔ Price paid (per bottle)
- ✔ Value (the latest estimated worth, per bottle)
- ✔ Size of bottle (to indicate 1.5-liter magnums)

Two summary fields provide the total number of bottles in our inventory at any one moment (or the total of any *segment* of our inventory, such as our red Bordeaux) as well as the current value of our inventory.

The work of entering all our wines into the database was considerable. But with that task accomplished, we were thoroughly pleased with the results. We discovered that we could enter and delete wines or bottles more easily than on a paper inventory, could sort the inventory any way that we liked, could print out lists in any fashion we wanted, and would always have up-to-date records when it came time to renew our insurance.

One of these days, we intend to make the file even more useful by adding a few more fields, such as

- ✔ Best drinking period
- ✔ Where purchased
- ✔ When consumed

A Healthy Environment for Your Wines

If you are an avowed non-collector who never has more than a one- or two-month supply of wine on hand *and* who is careful to deplete his inventory systematically, you do not need to worry about how your wines are stored. You can keep your bottles lying down on a rack in the den or the dining room or any other room, as long as they are not right next to the radiator or in direct sunlight. Even if they're standing upright, they'll survive for a few months.

If you've decided to collect a few bottles, however — or if you discover that a wine collection is happening to you — please take heed. If your wines are stored poorly, disappointment after disappointment is the inevitable outcome of all your efforts.

If you plan to keep wines indefinitely, you really need a wine storage facility that offers controlled temperature and humidity. This is especially important if you live in an area where the temperature exceeds 70° F (21° C) for any length of time.

Good wine storage can not only protect your fine wines from early demise, but also can give you the courage to age young wines that need to be aged. Without proper storage, fine wine is either consumed long before it reaches its best drinking period (known in wine circles as *infanticide*), or it dies an untimely death in some closet, garage, or warm cellar.

The passive wine cellar

You might be fortunate enough to have what is called a *passive* wine cellar (if you've recently inherited a castle in Scotland, for example).

If the place where you store your wine is very cool (below 60° F, 15.5° C) and very damp (75 percent humidity or higher) *all year round,* you are the lucky owner of a passive cellar. (It's called *passive* because you don't have to do anything to it, such as cool it or humidify it.) Usually, only deep cellars completely below ground level with thick stones or comparable insulation can be completely passive in most temperate climates.

Passive cellars are certainly the ideal way to store wines. And you can save a lot of money on their upkeep, to boot.

If you don't have a passive cellar, you might discover that you are able to build one. For instructions on building your own passive wine cellar, see Richard M. Gold's authoritative book, *How and Why To Build a Passive Wine Cellar* (Sand Hill Publishing, 1983, Box 461, North Amherst, MA 01059).

If you can't be passive, be bullish on wine storage

Most of us are neither fortunate enough to have a passive wine cellar nor fortunate enough to be able to create one without extraordinary expense and trouble (bulldozers, wrecking crews, and so on). But second best — an artificially cooled and/or humidified area — is still far better than nothing.

The following are key features of a good wine storage area:

- A good storage area should be cool — ideally, in the 53° to 59° F range (12° to 16° C).

- The temperature should be fairly constant — wide swings in temperature are not good for the wine.

- The area should be damp or humid — with a minimum of 75 percent humidity and a maximum of 95 percent (mold sets in above 95 percent).

- It should be free from vibrations, which can travel through the wine; heavy traffic and motors going on and off — such as refrigerators or washers/dryers — are all detrimental to your wine.

- The area should be free from light, *especially direct sunlight;* the ultraviolet rays of the sun are especially harmful to wine.

- The storage area should be free from chemical odors, such as paints, paint remover, and so on.

Buy a *hygrometer* (an instrument that measures atmospheric humidity) for your wine storage facility. Our hygrometer gives us both the percentage of humidity and a digital reading of the temperature — information so valuable that we check it almost daily. (Hygrometers are advertised in wine accessory catalogs, such as *The Wine Enthusiast,* Pleasantville, NY; telephone: 1-800-356-8466.)

Avoid refrigerators for wine storage. Don't leave good wine or champagne in the refrigerator for indefinite periods of time — say, more than a few days; not only is the refrigerator motor harmful, but the excessively cold temperature (as low as 35° F, 1.6° C) tends to numb and flatten the flavors of the wine.

In summary, your wine storage area should be cool (without big variations in temperature), damp, dark, and vibration free.

CAUTION!

The issue of humidity

Some wine collectors are not particularly concerned with the humidity levels of their cellars. High humidity causes mold, they argue, and it disfigures the labels. But dry air can cause your wine to either evaporate or leech out through the cork, causing *ullage* (space between the wine and the cork). The greater the ullage, the greater the chance of your wine becoming oxidized. Because we recommend humidity between 75 percent and 95 percent, we believe that *air conditioners, which dehumidify the air to about 50 percent, should not be used* to cool your wine storage area.

Keeping it cool and damp

Professional cooling units are available. (You'll find them advertised in wine accessory catalogs and wine magazines.) These are climate-controlled units that humidify the air of a room as well as cool it. These units come in various capacities to suit rooms of different dimensions. They require professional installation and cost from $500 to $1,950, depending on their capacity.

Depending on where you live, you might not need to run your cooling unit all year. We keep ours going from about late May to late September. The additional expense for electricity comes to about $15 a month (in our area, northeastern U.S.) for four months — well worth it when you consider the value of the wine you are protecting. During the winter months when the air usually gets dry, we run a humidifier in our wine room, which is a lot cheaper than running the cooling unit.

Wine racks

Racking systems vary from elaborate redwood racks to simple metal or plastic ones. The choice of material and configuration really hinges on how much you want to spend. Large, diamond-shaped wooden (or synthetic composition) racks are popular because they efficiently store up to eight bottles per section and make maximum use of space. Such racks also permit the easy removal of individual bottles (see Figure 15-1).

A configuration of racks that gives each wine its own cubbyhole is more expensive; if you're checking out such racks, consider whether any of your oversized bottles (such as bulbous champagne bottles) might be too large to fit the racks (and your half-bottles might be too small!).

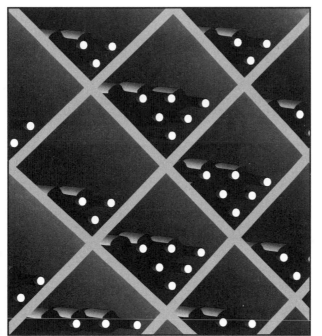

Figure 15-1:
Diamond-
shaped
wine rack.

Some wine collectors prefer to store their wine in the original wooden crates in which the wine was sold. (Many classic wines, such as Bordeaux and Vintage Port, come in these crates; you can usually pick up empty wooden crates in most wine stores.) The wooden crates are beneficial for storing wine because the wine remains in a dark environment inside the case, and the temperature changes very slowly thanks to the mass of wine bottles packed together in the closed case. Retrieving a bottle from the bottom row of the case can really be inconvenient, though.

Cardboard boxes, on the other hand, are not recommended for wine storage. The chemicals used in the manufacture of the cardboard can eventually affect the wine. Also, the cardboard boxes become damaged, in time, from the moisture in the air, assuming that you are maintaining a proper humidity in your cellar.

Insulation

Far more important than your choice of racks is your choice of insulation.

We definitely *do not recommend* fiberglass insulation because it will absorb the moisture from your cooling unit. We've heard of cases in which the weight of the moisture inside the insulation actually caused parts of ceilings to come tumbling down, creating quite a mess.

The ideal insulation is a 3-inch thick, thermoplastic resin called *polyurethane*. It is odorless, does not absorb moisture, and makes a fine seal. Even when a cooling unit is not running, temperatures will change extremely slowly in most wine rooms with this kind of insulation.

Wine caves

If you live in a house that has either a cellar or a separate area for your wine, consider yourself fortunate. What if you have no space — for instance, if you live in an apartment?

As an apartment dweller, you have three choices:

- ✔ Leave your wine in a friend's or relative's house (provided that *he* has adequate storage facilities — and that you trust him not to drink your wine!).
- ✔ Rent storage space in a refrigerated public warehouse.
- ✔ Buy a *wine cave* — also known as a wine vault — a self-contained, refrigerated unit that you plug into an electrical outlet.

We find the first two options barely acceptable because they don't give you immediate access to your wine. It's downright inconvenient to make a trip every time you want to get your hands on your own wine. And both of these options rob you of the pleasure of having your wines readily available in your home where you can look at them, fondle the bottles, or show them off to your friends.

If we lived in an apartment, we'd definitely own a wine cave. They come in all varieties — some are made of wood, some of metal, and some are a combination of both. Many of the nicer-looking wine caves resemble attractive pieces of furniture, either vertical or horizontal credenzas. Some have glass doors, and all of them can be locked.

Wine caves range in size and capacity from a tiny unit that holds only 24 bottles to the really large units that hold up to 2,800 bottles, with many sizes in between. Prices range from $400 to about $5,000. You'll find wine caves advertised extensively in wine accessory catalogs and in the back pages of wine magazines.

If you're planning to build a wine cellar or buy a wine cave, allow for expansion in your wine collection. Like most waistlines, wine cellars inevitably grow larger with the passing years.

Are You a Drinker or an Investor?

If you're like most people, you buy wine for one purpose only — to drink it, either immediately or sometime in the future. Bravo! Winemakers don't put their hearts and souls into their wines just so that people can admire the outside of the bottles.

But some wines do become rarer and more valuable with age, and selling them for profit can be a temptation that's difficult for even the most dedicated wine lover to resist. In many places nowadays, individuals may legally sell their wines either to a retail store or to an auction house. As a result, more and more people are selling wines that they no longer want or purchasing wines with the specific intention of reselling them.

Personality traits of good investment wines

It is definitely true that (a very small percentage of) wines are great invest-ments. Certain wines are even safer to invest in than stocks or real estate because they only increase in value — they never decline in value. Even when the economy is shaky, some people always have enough money to buy fine wine.

Investment wines have certain attributes:

- ✔ They have been universally acknowledged by the wine press and the wine trade to be outstanding.
- ✔ They have potential for longevity.
- ✔ They are from very good to excellent vintages.
- ✔ They become even more valuable with every passing year.

They also have one important requirement: They must have been well stored so that they are in good condition.

Some investment wines also share a *rarity factor* — not many bottles were produced in the first place.

The best bets for investing or keeping

French wines certainly have the monopoly on the wine investment market world-wide. They have a well-established reputation, especially with the British, who more or less *invented* the wine investment market. Therefore, while Portugal, Spain, the United States, and Australia are represented in the following list by only one wine (or category), France has five large categories of investment wines.

Fine Red Bordeaux — with pedigree and reputation for longevity:

Château Petrus
Château Lafite-Rothschild
Château Mouton-Rothschild
Château Latour
Château Margaux
Château Haut-Brion

Château Cheval-Blanc
Château Lafleur (Pomerol)
Château Trotanoy
Château Palmer
Château La Mission-Haut-Brion
Château Ausone

(The chateaux in the first column are *especially* good investments.)

Fine White Bordeaux — with pedigree and reputation for longevity:

Château Haut-Brion (Blanc)
Château Laville Haut Brion
Domaine de Chevalier

Fine Red Burgundy — the most highly respected:

Domaine de la Romanée-Conti wines
    (especially Romanée-Conti, La Tache, Richebourg)
Domaine Leroy wines
    (especially Grand Crus, such as Musigny and Chambertin)
Henri Jayer wines (especially Grand Crus)

Fine White Burgundy — the most highly sought after:

Montrachet (Domaine de la Romanée-Conti; Ramonet)
Ramonet (his other Grand Cru White Burgundies)
Domaine des Comtes Lafon (Premier Cru Meursaults)
Coche-Dury (Grand and Premier Crus)
Raveneau (Grand and Premier Cru Chablis)

Sauternes — the crème de la crème:

Château d'Yquem (clearly the *big gun,* investment-wise)
Château Climens
Château Coutet (Cuvée Madame, only)
Château de Fargues

Vintage Port — the Big Four of Portugal:

Taylor-Fladgate
Graham
Fonseca
Quinta do Noval (Nacional, only)

Spain's Most Prized Wine:

Vega Sicilia Unico

Certain California Cabernet Sauvignons — the Rarity Factor:

Grace Family Vineyards Cabernet Sauvignon (any vintage)
Beaulieu Vineyards Private Reserve Cabernets (1970 vintage and older)
Heitz Martha's Vineyard Cabernet Sauvignon (1974 vintage and older)

The Big One from Down Under:

Grange Hermitage (especially, older vintages)

The mortality factor

The inevitable question of your life expectancy, of course, must enter into the equation when you are considering how much wine to buy — unless you don't mind leaving your wine to your heirs.

If, in your twilight years, you find that you own too much wine, one option is to sell the stuff. If you have bought wisely, you'll make a killing in profits. You might even live long enough to spend it all!

Our hero is the late, great wine writer, André Simon. When he died at the age of 94, André reputedly had only *two* magnums of wine left in his once extensive cellar. Now *that's* good planning!

Selling Your Wine

Because wine is a regulated beverage, you can't necessarily sell your wine without complications. But it is getting easier all the time.

Selling your privately owned wine is now completely legal in many states of the U.S. — California, New York, and Illinois included. In other places, you might be permitted to sell it to a store only, or through a charity auction only. Check with your local beverage control authorities to learn what rules apply in your area.

New York is currently one of the hottest wine auction markets around, thanks to the recent legalization of wine auctions. (You can either sell or buy wines at these auctions.) The crusade is led by four large retail stores, Morrell & Company (212-688-9370); Sherry-Lehmann, in conjunction with Sotheby's Auction House (212-606-7207); Zachy's, together with Christie's Auction House (914-723-0241); and Acker, Merrall & Condit (212-787-1700).

In Illinois, The Chicago Wine Company (708-647-8789), John Hart Fine Wine Limited (312-944-5385), and Davis & Company (312-587-9500) are three leading buyers of privately owned wine.

In California, Butterfield & Butterfield Auction House (415-861-7500, extension 307) and The Rare Wine Company (800-999-4342) will happily buy your well-stored wine.

Most large retail wine stores (in places where it is legal to do so) will also buy wine from you. Usually quite a few classified advertisements are listed in the back of wine magazines from stores and wine companies looking to buy wine.

When selling your wine, bear in mind a few factors about most auction houses, wine companies, and retail stores:

- ✔ They are interested mainly in valuable, prestigious, or rare wines; they're not looking to buy some bomb you might be trying to unload.

- ✔ Wines in good condition are what they really want; some places won't buy wines that aren't at their best — but some will.

- ✔ All, of course, charge a premium for their services, ranging from 10 to 25 percent of the sale price. Some auction houses pass most of the premium on to the buyer rather than to the seller.

- ✔ Some outlets will only pay you after they sell your wine; others will pay you up front. Shop around for the best deal.

Insuring your precious investment

If your wine collection increases in size to the point that it becomes one of your most valuable assets, you should definitely think about insurance coverage. *Normal* homeowners' policies do not cover wine in case of fire, theft, breakage, and so on (some policies might cover up to a few thousand dollars' worth). You can purchase a *rider* on your homeowner's policy covering such items as wine or crystal, however, which will give you peace of mind.

Figure the annual cost of wine insurance to be about 40 to 50 cents per $100 of wine insured. For instance, if your wine inventory is worth $75,000, your annual premium might be about $315.

You can appraise your own collection — especially for older wines — simply by looking at auction prices in the catalogues of the various auction houses listed earlier in this chapter; prices for younger wines are readily available in newspaper and magazine advertisements. Or, if you prefer, check the wine magazine classifieds for wine appraisers, who will do the job for you when you mail them a copy of your inventory.

Most insurance companies will issue riders to your homeowner's policy covering wine and other precious items. The Chubb Group of Insurance Companies and Sedgwick James are two such insurance firms that are familiar with wine insurance coverage.

Chapter 16

Insider's Guide to Wine Buying

• •

In This Chapter

▶ Playing hardball with hard-to-get-wines

▶ Building your own black book of wine retailers

▶ Joining wine-buying clubs

▶ Buying directly from the winery

▶ Putting time in a bottle

• •

*Y*ou read about a wine that sounds terrific. Your curiosity is piqued; you want to try it. But your local wine shop doesn't have the wine. Neither does the store in the next town.

Or you decide to balance out your wine collection with several mature wines. The few older wines you can find in wine shops aren't really what you want — and besides, they're so expensive!

How do other wine lovers manage to get their hands on special bottles of wine when you can't?

Wines That Play Hard to Get

There's a Catch-22 for wine lovers who have really caught the bug: The more desirable a wine is, the harder it is to get. And the harder it is to get, the more desirable it is.

Several forces conspire to frustrate consumers who want to get their hands on special bottles. First, some of the best wines are made in ridiculously small quantities. We wouldn't say that quantity and quality are necessarily incompatible in winemaking, but at the very highest echelons of quality, there usually isn't much quantity to go around.

We once bought six bottles of a grand cru red Burgundy produced by a small grower/winemaker, Hubert Lignier. The importer told us that Lignier made only 150 cases of that wine, and 50 of those cases came to the U.S. We found it incredible that we could buy half a case of such a rare wine for ourselves, leaving only 49.5 cases to satisfy the whole rest of the country! Right time, right place.

This brings us to the second factor conspiring against equal opportunity in wine buying: Wine buying is a competitive sport. If you're there first, you get the wine, and the next guy doesn't. (We've been on the short end of that deal plenty of times, too.)

These days, buying highly rated wines is especially competitive. When a wine receives a very high score from critics, wine lovers have just got to get the wine. A feeding frenzy results, not leaving much for Johnny-come-latelies.

Finally, most wines are sold by the winery — or by the importer in the case of imported wines — just once, when the wine is young. Most store owners cannot bear the capital investment of storing some fine wines to sell at a later date. This means that properly aged wines are usually hard to get.

Playing Hardball

When the wine plays hard-to-get, you have to play hardball. You have to look beyond your normal sources of supply. Your allies in this game are wine auction houses, wine shops in other cities, and the wineries themselves.

Pros and cons of buying wines at auctions

The clear advantage of buying wine through auction houses is the availability of *older* and *rarer* wines. In fact, auction houses are the principal source of mature wines — their specialty. You can buy wines at auctions that are practically impossible to obtain in any other way. (Many of these wines have been off the market for years, sometimes decades!) In general, you can obtain younger wines at better prices elsewhere.

The main disadvantage of buying wine at auction houses is that you frequently don't know the storage history of the wine you are thinking about buying. The wine may have been stored in somebody's warm basement for years. And if the wine *does* come from some well-known wine collector's temperature-controlled cellar, and thus has impeccable credentials, it will sell for a very high price.

Also, at an auction house, you have to pay a *buyer's premium,* a tacked-on charge of 10 or 15 percent of your bid. In general, prices of wine at auctions range from fair (sometimes you even find bargains) to exorbitant.

Don't catch auction fever if you're personally present at an auction. The desire to win can motivate you to pay more for the wine than it's worth. Carefully planned, judicious bidding is in order. To plan your attack, you can obtain a catalog for the auction ahead of time, usually for a small fee. The catalog lists wines for sale by *lots* (usually groupings of three, six, or twelve bottles) with a suggested minimum bid per lot.

(Phone numbers for all U.S. auction houses are listed in the "Selling Your Wine" section of Chapter 15.)

Pros and cons of buying wine by catalog

A real plus of perusing wine shop catalogs and ordering wine from your armchair is, of course, the convenience (not to mention the time savings). Other advantages of buying wine long-distance include the availability of scarce wines and (sometimes) lower prices than you might pay in your home market.

Sometimes, the *only* way to buy certain wines is by catalog. The sought-after wines made in small quantities are definitely not available in every market. If a wine you want *is* available locally, but you don't live in a market where pricing is competitive, you might decide that you can save money by ordering the wine from a retailer in another city — even after the added shipping costs.

One minor disadvantage of buying wine by catalog is that an adult usually must be available to receive the wine. Also, because wine is perishable, you have to make certain that it's not delivered to you during hot (above 75° F/24°C) or cold (below 28°F/-2°C) weather. Spring and autumn are usually the best times for wine deliveries in most parts of the world.

A final, more important disadvantage is that wine is a legally controlled substance whose free commerce is not permitted everywhere. The transportation of wine from one state to the next or from one province to the next — not to mention across national borders — is not necessarily legal. If you're not sure what's permissible where you live, ask the store you intend to purchase from or check with your local (state or provincial) liquor authorities.

The penalty box

Many local governments have laws that prohibit the shipment of wine directly to consumers. If consumers want a wine, local governments figure that they should just purchase it in their own state; that way, the local government can be sure that state liquor taxes have been paid on the wine (by the state-licensed retailer) — not to mention local sales tax, too. As if every wine is available everywhere!

But wine enthusiasts know that most wine shops and wineries will ship wine to them anyway without any problems. If a store (or a winery) is willing to ship to you, you can usually rely on the company's experience and trust that the wine will arrive without complication. (California, for example, has established agreements with several other states legalizing shipments to consumers.) But now and then, when local governments crack down on illegal shipments, entire truckloads of wine are confiscated. It's a risk. Address the issue with the shop or winery if you are uncertain.

Some U.S. wine stores worth knowing

We can't possibly list *all* the leading wine stores that sell wine by catalog or newsletter. But the following purveyors are some of the best. Each of them either specializes in catalog sales or in certain kinds of fine wine that can be very difficult to obtain elsewhere.

- Bel-Air Wine Merchant, West Los Angeles, CA; 310-474-9518 — Bordeaux (especially rare, old)
- Brookline Liquor Mart, Allston, MA; 617-734-7700 — Italian, Burgundy, Rhone
- Burgundy Wine Company, New York, NY; 212-691-9092 — Burgundy, Rhone
- D & M Wines & Liquors, San Francisco, CA; 1-800-637-0292 — Champagne (great prices)
- John Hart Fine Wine, Chicago, IL; 312-944-5385 — Bordeaux, Burgundy
- Kermit Lynch Wine Merchant, Berkeley, CA; 510-524-1524 — French country wines, Burgundy, Loire, Rhone
- MacArthur Liquors, Washington, D.C.; 202-338-1433 — California, Bordeaux, Italian, Burgundy, Rhone, Alsace
- Marin Wine Cellar, San Rafael, CA; 415-459-3823 — Bordeaux (especially fine, rare, old)

- Mills Wine & Spirit Mart, Annapolis, MD; 410-263-2888 — Bordeaux, German, Italian

- Pop's Wines & Spirits, Island Park, NY; 516-431-0025 — Bordeaux, Italian, German

- Rosenthal Wine Merchant, New York, NY; 212-249-6650 — Burgundy

- Royal Wine Merchants, New York, NY; 212-689-4855 — French (especially rare Bordeaux)

- The Chicago Wine Company, Niles, IL; 708-647-8789 — Bordeaux, Burgundy, California

- The Party Source, Bellevue, KY; 606-291-4007 — German, Alsace, Burgundy

- The Rare Wine Company, Sonoma, CA; 1-800-999-4342 — Italian, French, Port, Madeira

- Twenty-Twenty Wine Co., West Los Angeles, CA; 310-447-2020 — Bordeaux (especially rare, old)

Wine-of-the-month clubs

A rather recent phenomenon is the proliferation of wine-buying *clubs*. (They're not really clubs in the true sense of the word; they're just people trying to sell you wine.) It seems that a week doesn't go by without our receiving a solicitation from one of these groups trying to sign us up.

Most wine-buying clubs work on the principle of "The Book of the Month" club, except that the merchandise is wine. Wine-buying clubs are worthwhile if you don't want to take the time and trouble to select your own wines. You know the old advertisement: "Let Greyhound do the driving!"

But there is one inherent problem with these companies — you have to like the wine that they select for you. Usually, the clubs expect you to buy 6 (sometimes 12) bottles of a particular wine — that they, of course, describe in glowing terms. If you don't like their selection after tasting the first bottle, you're stuck with the rest of 'em. But the wines are usually reasonably priced. It's your decision — convenience versus choice.

One of the largest and most successful mail-order "personal wine services" (as they like to call themselves) is the Massachusetts-based Geerlings & Wade, founded in 1987. For more information about them, call 1-800-782-WINE (9463).

Wine online

You can buy wine online, although the field is in its infancy. For example, Northside Wine & Spirits, a wine shop in Ithaca, NY, has established itself on America Online's Food and Drink Network to offer an electronic catalog of wines it imports exclusively (NsideWine@aol.com). The Napa Valley Wine Exchange offers "micro-production" California wines through the same online service (Nvwex@aol.com). On the Internet, operations such as Virtual Vineyards (http://www.virtualvin.com) offer wines for sale where legal, as do wineries such as Sterling Vineyards (http://www.napavalley.com/sterling.html).

Directly from the source

You can buy directly from wineries in two ways:

- ✔ You can visit the winery in person and carry away the wine.
- ✔ You can call and ask the winery to ship wine to you.

Many smaller wineries sell a fairly large percentage of their wines to visitors. In New York state, for instance, some wineries sell as much as half of their annual production at their doorsteps!

It's a common fallacy that you save money by buying from the winery. You don't. To avoid undercutting the retailers who also sell their wines, wineries usually charge visitors standard retail-store prices for their wine. But you get two bonuses: the excitement of buying the wine where it's made and the good feeling of supporting the people behind the wine, who are trying hard to please you.

Most wineries will also happily ship you their wine if it is legal for them to do so. If you live too far away to visit a particular winery, or if the winery's production is small or in high demand, ordering wine from the winery may be the only way to get a certain wine.

A few small wineries in California and Washington state, for example, produce wines that have been so praised by wine critics that they are available only to those people on the winery's mailing list. (In some cases, the availability of the wines is *so* tight that there's a waiting list to get on the mailing list, or a lottery decides who actually gets the wines from all those on the mailing list.)

Some wineries whose mailing lists we suggest you join (and the wines to get) include the following:

Williams & Selyem Winery, Healdsburg, CA; 707-433-6425: In the Russian River Valley (Sonoma), Burt Williams and Ed Selyem are producing some of the finest Pinot Noirs in North America — practically impossible to get without being on their mailing list; they're making some darn good red Zinfandels, too! But there's a waiting list for the mailing list.

Ravenswood, Sonoma, CA; 707-938-1960: Winemaker/proprietor Joel Peterson's talent for making outstanding red Zinfandels from special single-vineyard sites is almost legendary; you cannot get them without being on the mailing list.

Ridge Vineyards, Cupertino, CA; 408-867-3233: Located in the Santa Cruz Mountains, one hour south of San Francisco, Ridge Vineyards is actually one of Calfornia's veteran wineries today. And winemaker/CEO Paul Draper, one of the nicest guys in the business, has been at the helm most of the way. Although you can sometimes find Ridge's Cabernets and Zinfandels in retail stores, they do sell out quickly. And the winery has a "limited-release program" of some wines available only by mail.

Grace Family Vineyards, St. Helena, CA; 707-963-0808: Dick Grace's intensely flavored Cabernet Sauvignons are undoubtedly the hardest to get, most sought-after wines in North America (if not the world). After all, he only makes 200 cases a year! Put yourself on his mailing list . . . if you're patient. It may be a while before you get any wine!

Rafanelli Winery, Healdsburg, CA; 707-433-1385: Dave Rafanelli's Dry Creek Valley (Sonoma) red Zinfandels set the standard for this variety. Unfined, unfiltered — and just about unavailable unless you get on the mailing list — these naturally made wines are worth the effort.

Rosenblum Cellars, Alameda, CA; 510-865-7007: Veterinarian Kent Rosenblum makes some mighty fine single-vineyard red Zinfandels on the side, when he's not treating sick cats, dogs, and horses! Although some of his wines are available in stores, you can get Rosenblum's best Zins only via the mailing list or by visiting the winery.

Leonetti Cellar, 1321 School Avenue, Walla Walla, WA 99362: Definitely Washington state's most sought-after Cabernet Sauvignons and Merlots. It is impossible to obtain these classic, well-balanced wines unless you're on the mailing list. (The winery requests that you write instead of telephoning.)

Quilceda Creek Vintners, Snohomish, WA; 206-568-2389: Only about 1,000 cases are made of this rich Cabernet Sauvignon. Getting on the mailing list is definitely your best (if not your only) bet! The 200 cases of the winery's Reserve Cabernet Sauvignon are just about impossible to get nowadays.

Woodward Canyon Winery, Lowden, WA; 509-525-4129: Although producer Rick Small's rich, oaky Chardonnays and Cabernet Sauvignons are occasionally available in stores, you're much safer being on the mailing list of this popular Washington winery.

Buying time

Every so often you might notice ads in the newspaper or in wine store catalogs urging you to buy *futures* of certain wines (usually Bordeaux, but sometimes California wines). The ads suggest that, to insure getting a particular wine at the lowest price, you should buy it now for future delivery. In other words, "Give us your money now; you'll get the wine in due course, probably some time next year when the winery releases it."

Generally, we recommend that you don't buy futures. Often the same wine will be the same price, or only slightly higher, when it hits the market. To save little or nothing, you will have tied your money up for a year or more, while the store has made interest on it or spent it. And stores *have* gone bankrupt. During the recent recessionary economy, in fact, some people who bought wine futures actually paid *more* for their wine than they would have paid if they had waited for the wine to arrive before purchasing it.

The only time that it's worth your while to buy wine futures is when you want to guarantee getting a certain wine that's made in small quantities (say, 3,000 cases or less annually), and you're pretty sure that the wine will be sold out before it reaches the stores.

For example, there are many small châteaus in the Pomerol section of Burgundy — and a few wineries in California and Washington state and in Piedmont, Italy — whose wines normally sell out on pre-orders, especially in the good (hyped) vintage years. Also, if a wine receives an extraordinarily high rating in the wine press (for example, the highly rated 1990 Château Montrose), its price could double and even triple by the time the wine reaches the market; in those situations, you have to act fast to be able to buy the wine — even on futures.

The 1982 Bordeaux vintage was one glaring exception to our rule of avoiding wine futures. Because of the early, almost universal hype over the vintage, those who bought 1982 Bordeaux futures purchased them at a considerable savings. The wines' prices were 30 to 50 percent higher than the early offerings when the wines arrived on the market in 1985. This scenario has not recurred since the 1982 vintage, however.

Here is the bottom line: Buy futures only when you must have a particular wine and buying futures might be the only way you can buy it. For most wines, though, keep your wallet in your pocket until the wine is actually available.

Chapter 17

You Never Graduate from Wine School

. . . .

In This Chapter

▶ School was never such fun

▶ Physical education for your palate

▶ The magical places behind the labels

▶ Wine publications to keep you current

. . . .

*L*earning about wine is like space travel: When you get going, there's no end in sight. Fortunately for those who choose to be educated wine drinkers, learning about wine is a fascinating experience, full of new flavors, new places, and new friends.

Although we teach others about wine, we are avid students of wine. We can't imagine that we'll ever reach the point of saying, "Now we know enough about wine. We can stop here." So off we go to another vineyard, to another wine tasting, or deep into the pages of another wine magazine. Every step brings not only more knowledge but also more appreciation of this amazing beverage.

Let Me Count the Ways . . .

Virtual wine school has no walls and no fixed location. It takes the form of liquid, paper, and people. It exists wherever you are.

Your own continuing education in wine is shaped by your budget, disposition, and free time. You can literally go back to school by taking wine classes; you can attend wine tastings or winemaker dinners; you can take field trips to wineries; or you can become an armchair student, reading about the wine regions of the world.

Back to the classroom

For many people, the best way to learn more about wine and to improve wine-tasting skills is to take a wine course. Wine classes provide an ideal combination of authoritative instruction and immediate feedback on tasting impressions.

If you live in a medium-sized or large city, you're sure to find several wine courses available — offered either by private individuals, by universities, as adult-education extension programs of local school districts, or by local wine shops or restaurants. If you're lucky enough to live near a wine-producing district, you might find a wine course offered by a winery itself.

Most wine courses are referred to as *wine appreciation courses* because they don't teach you how to make wine, they're not usually intended to provide professional credentials, and they're not accredited. (Courses offered at an actual university can be an exception.) The purpose of most wine courses is to provide both information about wine and practice in tasting wine.

Wine courses can cover a wide range of topics and levels of expertise. Introductory classes deal with how to taste wine, while more advanced classes discuss in depth the various wine regions of the world or the wines of a particular district. The instructors in wine schools usually are experienced professionals who work in the wine trade or who write about wine.

One wine school in action

The following announcement is a shameless plug: We run a wine school in New York City called International Wine Center. Because we believe that it's the perfect wine school, we are convinced that a description of its programs can give you an accurate idea of what wine school is all about.

The Center offers two types of studies:

- ✔ **Wine appreciation courses for consumers:** These classes range from beginner-level to advanced and from a single-evening to three sessions. (Some wine schools offer courses up to twelve sessions long.)

- ✔ **Professional courses:** These classes are more comprehensive, and the information covered is more technical. Professional courses are for members of the wine trade (or keenly interested consumers) who wish to become particularly proficient in their wine knowledge. Courses range from 7 to 28 sessions in length, come with a textbook, and have an examination.

A typical class usually lasts about two hours; students listen to a lecture on a particular topic and taste six to eight wines related to the subject at hand. The instructor encourages questions. Slide shows, references to maps of wine regions, or sketches on the blackboard punctuate the discussion.

Each student sits before a place-setting of wine glasses. Water and crackers are available to help students clear their palates between tastes of wine. Next to each student is a large plastic cup that he can use for dumping his leftover wine. Each student receives printed information about the topic of the class and a list of the wines tasted that evening.

Most wine programs follow a similar format. For the name of a wine school or individuals who offer wine programs in your area, get in touch with the Society of Wine Educators, East Longmeadow, MA (413-567-8272), which has members throughout the U.S., Canada, and some other countries.

Wine tastings of all shapes and sizes

Wine tastings are events designed to give wine enthusiasts the opportunity to sample a range of wines. The events can be very much like classes (seated, seminar-like events), or they can be more like parties (tasters milling around informally). Compared to a wine class, the participants at a wine tasting are more likely to have various levels of knowledge. Tastings don't come in beginner, intermediate, and advanced levels — one size fits all.

Wine tastings are popular because they override the limitations of sampling wine alone, at home. How many wines can you taste on your own (unless you don't mind throwing away nine-tenths of every bottle)? How many wines are you willing to buy on your own? And how much can you learn tasting wine in isolation — or with a friend whose expertise is no greater than yours?

At wine tastings, you can learn from your fellow tasters, as well as make new friends who share your interest in wine. Most importantly, you can taste wine in the company of some individuals whose palates are more experienced than yours, which is a real boon in training your palate.

We have led or attended literally thousands of wine tastings in our lives — so far. And it is fair to say that *we have learned something about wine at almost all of them.*

The learning curve for the novice wine taster is *especially* amazing. In our Wine Club (at the International Wine Center), we've seen new members who knew very little about wine become experienced and knowledgeable tasters in about two years. Being exposed to ten or fifteen wines (many of which you might be tasting for the first time) is a marvelous way to learn about wine!

Naturally, some people learn faster than others. A few variables can affect the rate of learning, such as

- Enthusiasm, or desire to learn
- Palate memory (an inborn, fairly uncommon talent of remembering specific flavors)
- Sensory acuity (taste, smell, and sight)

But everyone who attends wine tastings gains *some* degree of knowledge.

When in Rome . . .

If you've never been to a wine tasting, we should warn you that a few matters of etiquette are in operation at most tastings. Familiarizing yourself with this etiquette will help you feel more comfortable. Otherwise, you're likely to be appalled by what you see or hear. Why are these people behaving like that?

To spit or not to spit?

Remember we mentioned a large, plastic cup that each student in a wine class has for dumping out his leftover wine? Well, we lied. (We wanted to ease you into what we realize might be a shocking concept.) The cup is really for students to *spit out each mouthful of wine* after tasting it.

Professional wine tasters long ago discovered that if they swallowed every wine they tasted, they'd be far less thoughtful tasters by the time they reached wine nine or ten. So spitting became acceptable. In wineries, professional tasters sometimes spit right onto the gravel floor or into the drains. In more elegant surroundings, they spit into a *spittoon,* usually a simple container like a large plastic cup (one per taster) or an ice bucket that two or three tasters share.

At first, some tasters, naturally, are loath to spit out wine. Not only have you been brought up to believe that spitting is uncouth, but you've also paid your good money for the opportunity to taste the wines. Why waste them?

Well, you *can* drink all of your wine, of course, if you wish — and some people do. But we don't advise that you do, for the following reasons:

- Evaluating the later wines clearly will be difficult if you swallow the earlier ones. The build-up of alcohol in your body will cloud your judgment.

- ✔ Swallowing is not really necessary in order to taste the wine fully. If you leave the wine in your mouth for eight to ten seconds (see Chapter 2), you'll be able to taste it thoroughly — without having to worry about the effects of the alcohol.

- ✔ If you are driving to the tasting, you're taking a risk in driving home after ingesting all that alcohol — that is, if you're drinking instead of spitting. The stakes are high — your life and health, others' lives, and your driver's license. Why gamble?

The simple solution — spit out the wine. Just about all experienced wine tasters do. Believe it or not, spitting will seem to be the very normal thing to do at wine tastings after a while. (And, in the meantime, it's one sure way to appear more experienced than you are!)

If you know that you can't bring yourself to spit, be sure to have something to eat before going to a wine tasting. You absorb alcohol *much* more slowly on a full stomach — and the simple crackers or bread at most wine tastings are not sufficient to do the trick.

What's with the sound effects?

Do you have to make that loud, slurping or gurgling noise that you hear "serious" wine tasters make at tastings?

Of course you don't. But the drawing of air into your mouth does enhance your ability to taste the wine (as explained in Chapter 2). With a little practice, you can gurgle without making loud, attention-getting noises.

Horizontal or vertical?

Two of the goofiest expressions in the world of wine are applied to wine tastings. Depending on the nature of the wines featured, wine-tasting events can be categorized as *vertical tastings* or as *horizontal tastings*. Nothing to do with the position of the tasters themselves — they are usually seated, and they're *never* lying down (that went out of fashion after the Romans).

A vertical tasting is a wine tasting featuring several vintages of the same wine — Château Latour in each vintage from 1982 to 1990, for example. A horizontal tasting examines the wines of a single vintage from several different wineries, usually of a similar type, such as 1991 Napa Valley Cabernets.

There's no particular name for tastings with less disciplined themes, but we'd like to suggest *paisley*.

Blind man's bluff

One of the favorite diversions of wine tasters is tasting wines *blind*. Before you conjure up thoughts of darkened rooms, blindfolded tasters, or other forms of hanky-panky, let us explain that the tasters are not blind, the bottles are. Or anyway, the bottles are wearing blindfolds.

In *blind tastings*, the identities of the wines are not known to the tasters. The theory behind this exercise is that knowing the identities might prejudice the tasters to prefer (or dislike) a particular wine for its reputation rather than for "what's in the glass," as they say. Sometimes, extremely skilled tasters taste wines blind and try to identify them (if they can!), in an effort to sharpen their tasting skills even further.

If you don't know enough about wine to be prejudiced by the labels, there's little point in tasting blind. Nevertheless, there's something about blind tasting that really helps you focus your concentration on what you're tasting — and that's always good practice.

More fine points of wine etiquette

Because smell is such an important aspect of wine tasting, courteous tasters will try not to interfere with other tasters' ability to smell. This means

- ✔ Smoking (anything) is a complete *no-no* at any wine tasting.
- ✔ Using any scent (perfume, after-shave lotion, scented soap, and so on) is undesirable. These *foreign* odors can really interfere with your ability to detect the wine's aroma. Guys, that means you, too!

Dining with the winemaker

A popular type of wine event in recent years has been the *winemaker dinner*, a multicourse dinner at which a winemaker or winery owner is the guest of honor. Wine drinkers pay a fixed price for the meal and samples of the winery's wines are matched to each course.

As far as learning goes, winemaker dinners rank below seminar-style wine-tastings, but above many informal, reception-style tastings. These dinners offer the chance to taste wines under ideal circumstances — with food — but we find that very little information of any value is disseminated, and there's little opportunity to ask questions.

In considering potential for fun, winemaker dinners are right up there at the top of the list. Even if you don't get to sit next to the winemaker.

Courteous wine tasters also do not volunteer their opinion about a wine until *after* other tasters have had a chance to taste the wine. Serious tasters like to form their opinions independently and are sure to throw dirty looks at anyone who interrupts their concentration prematurely.

Other rules of etiquette are the simple courtesies extended at any gathering. For instance, you shouldn't talk (above a whisper) to your neighbor if a speaker is lecturing. Not talking becomes more difficult as the wine tasting goes on because the alcohol loosens inhibitions. For this reason, experienced lecturers at wine tastings get most of their talking done in the early part of the evening.

Most of these guidelines regarding wine-tasting etiquette apply to wine classes as well — and are also relevant when you visit wineries around the world.

The People and Places behind the Labels

One of the best — and most fun-filled — ways to learn about wine is to actually go to the region where the wine is made, and, if possible, speak to the winemakers and producers about their wine. There's nothing like learning about some of your favorite wines from the source!

You'll discover that there's something special about the people who devote their lives to making wine: Maybe it's their creativity or their commitment to bringing so much pleasure to the world through their labor. Whatever the reason, they are exceptional people. We have found some of our dearest friends in the wine regions throughout the world.

You'll benefit from multiple sensory impressions on visits to wine regions — experiencing the climate firsthand, seeing the soil and the hills, touching the grapes, and so on. You can walk through the vineyards if you wish, visit nearby villages, eat the local food, and drink the wine of the region.

Here are some examples:

- ✔ Walking through the back roads of the cool, Russian River Valley in Sonoma, California, speaking to the winemakers — some of whom seldom leave the Valley — you come away with a feeling for, and an understanding of, their remarkable Russian River Pinot Noirs.

- ✔ Seeing the incredibly steep slopes along the Mosel River in Germany — slopes too steep for tractors or horses — where the Riesling grapes grow and the soil must be worked and the grapes picked, by hand, gives you a new appreciation the next time you drink a delightful glass of Riesling from the Mosel.

> ✔ Wandering up and down the Langhe hills around Alba in Piedmont, Italy, visiting the markedly individualistic producers of the Barolo region, you finally come to understand the nature of the elusive Nebbiolo grape from which Barolo is made.
>
> ✔ Visiting the Romanée-Conti vineyard in Vosne-Romanée, Burgundy, seeing the little 4.4-acre plot of land, and pondering the fact that the legendary Romanée-Conti wine can be made only here, gives you a visceral appreciation of *terroir* (see Chapter 7).

Don't know the language? No problema

Don't let your limited (or nonexistent) ability to speak the local language prevent you from visiting wine regions. These days, English is becoming the universal language of the wine world. Even if the person you're visiting doesn't speak English, he'll invariably have someone available (his wife, his son, or his dog) who does. Besides, wine itself is a universal language. A smile and a handshake go a long way towards communicating!

Junior year abroad

While in wine regions, you often have the opportunity to combine some formal learning with travel. You can take courses on wine and/or food.

If wanderlust carries you to the Chianti Classico region in Tuscany, for example, you can take either a five-day wine course taught by Italian wine expert Nick Belfrage, MW, or a one-week food course given by the proprietress of the magnificent Badia a Coltibuono estate, Lorenza de' Medici (of the historic Medici family). Both are given at the Coltibuono estate, and include meals and accommodations. Contact either: The Villa Table, Badia a Coltibuono, 53013 Gaiole in Chianti (SI), Italy, Telephone: 577-749498, Fax: 577-749235; or Judy Terrell Ebrey, P.O. Box 25228, Dallas, TX 75225, Telephone: 214-373-1161, Fax: 214-373-1162; America Online: villatable@aol.com.

In Germany, the German Wine Academy offers either six-day courses or four-day weekend courses at various times throughout the year. The courses include travel to wine-growing regions, visits to private estates and castles, wine tastings, and a cruise on the Rhine River. The courses are centered in historic Kloster Eberbach, near the city of Frankfurt, and are conducted in English. Meals and accommodations are provided. For further information, get in touch with the German Trade Promotion Office wherever you live. In the U.S., contact the German Wine Information Bureau, 79 Madison Avenue, New York, NY 10016, Telephone: 212-213-7028; Fax: 212-213-7042.

Similar courses on wine and/or food are available in other wine regions. Just consult the local tourist office of the country you are planning to visit.

What do the initials MW mean?

You might have noticed that Nick Belfrage (the Italian wine expert mentioned earlier) and one of the co-authors of this book have *MW* after their names. MW stands for Master of Wine. You receive this title after passing a grueling written and tasting exam. The title is awarded by the Institute of Masters of Wine in London; preparatory programs are offered by the Institute in Australia, the U.S., the U.K., and continental Europe. A high level of preliminary knowledge is required.

For more information, write to: Institute of Masters of Wine, Five Kings House, 1 Queen Street Place, London EC4R 1QS England. By the way, there are only 195 Masters of Wine in the world. Most of them are in the U.K.; there are only 13 MWs in America.

Helpful tourist agencies

Government tourist agencies, whose function is to promote tourism to their own countries, will be more or less helpful in the planning of your trip, depending on the season and the extent to which each country's wine regions are organized for tourists. Contact them well in advance and ask for maps, brochures, and any material they have that is specifically related to wine districts you wish to visit. Most governments also have wine promotional bureaus, often as part of their trade promotion offices in foreign cities. (In the U.S., most of these wine bureaus are located in New York.)

France (Bordeaux)

Bordeaux, arguably the world's most famous wine region, has several tourism offices that can provide you with maps and local information. Contact any (or all) of the following organizations:

- ✔ **Conseil Interprofessionnel du Vin de Bordeaux:** Maison du Vin, 3, cours du XXX Juillet, 33075 Bordeaux. Telephone: (33) 56 00 22 66; Fax: (33) 56 00 22 77

- ✔ **Conseil des Vins du Médoc:** 1, cours du XXX Juillet, 33075 Bordeaux. Telephone: (33) 56 48 18 62; Fax: (33) 56 79 11 05

- ✔ **Comité Départemental du Tourisme de la Gironde:** 21, cours de L'Intendance, 33000 Bordeaux. Telephone: (33) 56 52 61 40; Fax: (33) 56 81 09 99

- ✔ **Office de Tourisme:** 12, cours du XXX Juillet, 33000 Bordeaux. Telephone: (33) 56 44 28 41

- ✔ **Wine Tours of Burgandy:** Hixson Lefils, 6, Rue de Tamnes, 21700 Nuits-St. George. Telephone: (33) 80 61 48 39.

Italy

Only recently has Italy begun encouraging tours of its plentiful, rich wine regions. The new tourism movement called *agritourismo* (farm tourism) helps visitors vacation at working farms and wineries. Much of the tourism effort has focused on the Chianti Classico region in Tuscany, but Piedmont, the Veneto, Trentino-Alto Adige, and Umbria are also involved in the program. Contact the following three organizations:

- **Movimento Del Turismo Del Vino:** c/o Fattoria dei Barbi, 53024 Montalcino (SI), Italy, Telephone: 39 577 849421; Fax: 39 577 849356. This organization is made up of more than 200 estate owners throughout Italy, with an emphasis on Tuscany. Programs include cultural heritage and nature, as well as wine.

- **Stagioni Del Chianti:** Via di Campoli 142, 50024 Mercatali VdP (FI), Italy, Telephone: 39 55 821481; Fax: 39 55 821449. Contact Katharina Trauttmansdorff. This organization provides accommodations at any of the following five wine estates in Tuscany: Castello di Brolio, Castello di Cacchiano, Castello di Fonterutoli, Rocca delle Macie, and Villa Vistarenni.

- **Butterfield & Robinson:** 70 Bond Street, Toronto Ontario, Canada M5B 1X3, Telephone: 416 864 1354; Fax: 416 864 0541. This organization specializes in biking and walking holidays in a number of wine regions, with an emphasis on Italy.

Calling ahead

When you do plan to visit a winery, you usually need to call or write ahead of time for an appointment.

The major exceptions are the many large wineries in Napa, California, where regular tours are conducted, or self-guided tours are available. Many wineries in the United States do have tasting rooms that are open every day during the busy tourism months and on weekends during the winter. In these tasting rooms, you can sample wines (sometimes for a small fee), buy wine, and buy souvenirs such as T-shirts or sweatshirts with the logo of the winery imprinted on them.

If you visit wineries that are not so formally geared toward tourism — which is most of the rest of the wine world — you can simply sample the wines, talk to the winemaker or proprietor when he's available (you *have* made an appointment, right?), take an informal tour of the winery, and buy some wine if you wish (an especially nice idea if the wine is not available back home).

DUMMIES APPROVED

California, here I come

The essential guidebook to use if you are planning to make a wine trip to California is The Wine Spectator's annual guide, *Wine Country Guide to California.* It's available for $6.95 plus $2.25 postage and handling (outside the U.S., $5.50 postage and handling). This guide has a directory of all California wineries with tasting and tour information, telephone numbers, each winery's hours, and an indication as to whether appointments are needed. There are also maps of each of California's wine regions. Call 1-800-752-7799 for order information.

The guide also includes a listing of restaurants in California's various wine regions along with reviews of the restaurants and a listing of lodging available — inns, bed and breakfasts, hotels, and motels. It also provides information on other activities and attractions in the California wine country.

Armchair Travel

It takes time and money to travel around the world. Alternatively, you can travel through the wine world from the comfort of your living room, letting the written word carry you to faraway wine regions.

Many retail wine stores keep extensive libraries of wine magazines, newsletters, and books available for sale. Retail wine stores are the best places to look. Most major book stores have a separate section for food and wine books, also.

Recommended reading

The following books will take you into greater depth on particular aspects of wine.

General knowledge

Hugh Johnson, *World Atlas of Wine* (fourth edition), New York, Simon & Schuster, 1994. England's Hugh Johnson is probably the world's best known and most respected wine writer. This is his seminal book, complete with detailed maps of all of the world's wine regions. (*Modern Encyclopedia of Wine* and *Pocket Encyclopedia of Wine* are two additional worthwhile books by Hugh Johnson.)

Oz Clarke, *Oz Clarke's Wine Advisor* (formerly *Wine Handbook,* a new edition every year), New York, Simon & Schuster, 1994. Oz Clarke, another Brit, is undoubtedly the wine world's most prolific wine writer — the Stephen King of winedom. It's difficult to keep up with all of his wine books. We like his *Advisor* because it's an easy-to-use, A to Z reference on all of the important wine places, wine terms, and so on in one convenient pocketbook.

Jancis Robinson, MW (editor), *The Oxford Companion to Wine,* Oxford, Oxford University Press, 1994. An encyclopedic reference book that sets the standard in the wine field. We would expect no less from England's Jancis Robinson, one of the truly brilliant wine writers in the world. (Also check out Robinson's *Vines, Grapes, and Wines,* published by Alfred A. Knopf.)

Bordeaux

Robert M. Parker, Jr., *Bordeaux* (second edition), New York, Simon & Schuster, 1991. Robert Parker is certainly America's — if not the world's — most famous wine writer. He established his reputation on his knowledge of Bordeaux; he was also the first writer to use the 100-point rating system of wines. His second edition covers all major Bordeaux wines from 1961 to 1990 — an essential book for any Bordeaux lover. (Other books by Parker worth having include *Parker's Wine Buyer's Guide, The Wines of the Rhône Valley and Provence,* and *Burgundy).*

David Peppercorn, MW, *Bordeaux* (second edition), London, Faber and Faber, 1991. Peppercorn's and Parker's books on arguably the most important wine region in the world are so well done that we had to include them both. England's David Peppercorn is rightfully regarded as one of *the* great Bordeaux experts in the world. Peppercorn's *Bordeaux* goes into more detail than Parker's book, but without the ratings.

Burgundy

Matt Kramer, *Making Sense of Burgundy,* New York, William Morrow & Company, 1990. France's other great wine region is given a brilliant, understanding treatment by Oregon's Matt Kramer. Burgundy is so complex a region that any wine lover of this fabled region will cherish this insightful tome. (Another recommended book by Kramer is *Making Sense of California Wine).*

Remington Norman, MW, *The Great Domaines of Burgundy,* New York, Henry Holt, 1992. Although Kramer's book is more opinionated, Britain's Remington Norman's is more factually oriented. Both are excellent works on this very complicated wine region.

Champagne

Serena Sutcliffe, MW, *Champagne,* New York, Simon & Schuster, 1988. For Champagne lovers, few books will be as enjoyable to read and to look at as this wonderfully well-written book by the U.K.'s Serena Sutcliffe, one of the great ladies of the wine world.

Tom Stevenson, *Champagne*, London, Sotheby's Publications, 1986. England's Tom Stevenson knows more about Champagne than the Champenoise themselves! A truly sage, authentic guide to this wonderful beverage and region (also recommended by Stevenson: *Alsace*).

Old and rare wines

Michael Broadbent, MW, *The New Great Vintage Wine Book,* New York, Alfred A. Knopf, 1991. No one has tasted more great wines, especially old and rare ones, than England's Michael Broadbent. His guide to vintage wines going back to the 19th century concentrates on Bordeaux, Sauternes, and Burgundy. This is a book for the advanced wine buff.

Italy

Burton Anderson, *The Wine Atlas of Italy*, New York, Simon & Schuster, 1990. Anderson, originally from Minnesota but now living in Tuscany, is probably the world's most highly regarded writer on Italian wines. This atlas does for Italy, in more detail, what Hugh Johnson's does for the world. Complete and thorough, this is an essential book for Italian wine lovers.

California

James Halliday, *Wine Atlas of California*, New York, Viking (Penguin), 1993. The erudite and affable James Halliday, an Australian writer and winemaker, has written a brilliant atlas on California's wines. (Also recommended by Halliday is *Wine Atlas of Australia and New Zealand.*)

Bob Thompson, *The Wine Atlas of California and the Pacific Northwest,* New York, Simon & Schuster, 1993. California's own Bob Thompson has long been recognized as one of the true experts on the wines of his region. This atlas also covers the Oregon and Washington state wine regions.

Wine and food

David Rosengarten and Joshua Wesson, *Red Wine with Fish*, New York, Simon & Schuster, 1989. One of the few books totally devoted to the difficult topic of wine and food pairings, *Red Wine with Fish* is controversial, but food (and wine) for thought.

Wine magazines

Wine magazines can provide more topical information about wine than books can. They keep you up-to-date on the current happenings in the wine world, give you recent tasting notes on currently released wines, profile the hot, new wines and winemakers, and so on. The classified ads in the back of most wine magazines are a good way to hear about equipment for sale, wine tours, and other useful offers.

Some magazines that we recommend include:

- *Decanter* — One of the oldest and one of the best, this magazine covers the world, but is especially strong on French and Italian wines. It's published monthly in London. Telephone: 800-875-2997 (U.S.) or 0181-646-6672 (U.K.).

- *Wine* — England's other major wine magazine, this one provides good coverage of Europe's wine regions, without attitude. It's published monthly in the U.K. Telephone: 01483-776345 (U.K.) or 914-735-8083 in North America.

- *Wine Spectator* — A lot of current news happenings are in the *Spectator,* including rather extensive coverage of the world's major wine regions, with plenty of tasting notes. This magazine originated in California, but is currently published in New York, twice monthly. Telephone: 800-752-7799.

- *Wine Enthusiast* — An experienced staff of wine writers covers the wine world in an authentic fashion. The magazine is an off-shoot of a large wine accessories (glasses, wine storage units, and so on) company and includes an extensive wine-buying guide. It is published monthly in Pleasantville, New York. Telephone: 914-345-8463.

- *The Wine News* — This very attractive magazine covers the world's major wine regions and includes tasting notes in its Buyline section. It's published bimonthly in Coral Gables, Florida. Telephone: 305-444-7250.

- *Wine & Spirits* — As the name suggests, this magazine covers spirits as well as major wine regions. Extensive tastings notes are always included. It's published seven times a year in San Francisco, California, but the business office is in Princeton, New Jersey. Telephone: 609-921-1060.

Wine newsletters

Wine newsletters are an important part of the information pipeline in the wine world. They usually express the personal opinion of one writer, who has established himself as an authority in wine. They contain mainly wine-tasting notes, as opposed to magazines, which contain feature-length articles as well as tasting notes.

One nice thing about newsletters is that they accept no advertising; thus, they can maintain (in theory, at least) more impartiality than magazines. Most wine newsletters are intended for the intermediate to advanced wine buff.

✔ *The Wine Advocate* — Robert M. Parker, Jr., is a practicing attorney-turned-wine critic. His approach to wine is methodical and thorough, complete with ratings of wine on a 100-point scale. Clear and easy-to-read with lots of charts and wine-buying tips, *The Wine Advocate* is a must read for all serious wine lovers (not for the complete beginner); it covers the world's major wine regions, but is especially strong on French wines. Published bimonthly in Monkton, Maryland. Telephone: 410-329-6477.

✔ *International Wine Cellar* — Steve Tanzer combines thoughtful articles, interviews with major wine figures, and extensive tasting notes — an intelligent guide for the advanced wine buff. Published bimonthly in New York; Tanzer Business Communications, Incorporated, P.O. Box 20021, New York, NY 10021.

✔ *The Vine* — England's Clive Coates, MW, is an authority on the wines of Burgundy and Bordeaux. So, as you might expect, *The Vine* (more of a booklet than a newsletter in design) focuses mainly on these two major wine regions; in fact, many of his issues provide in-depth coverage devoted solely to several leading producers of one region — reds from Burgundy, for example. This newsletter is for the advanced wine lover. Published monthly in London. Telephone: 081-995-8962.

✔ *The Wine Journal* — This newsletter uses a staff of writers, although much of the work is done by editors Christine R. Graham and John Tilson. It offers a well-rounded approach to the world's major wine regions; it is especially strong on Burgundy, Germany, California, Oregon, and Washington state. Published bimonthly in Malibu, California. Telephone: 310-457-8111.

Wine on the Internet

Wineries and wine importers all over the U.S. are turning to the Internet to publicize their companies and their wines to consumers. Some have their own home pages, and others participate in larger web sites that focus on wine. Here are just a few of the places you can turn to learn about wine while you're online. (Each of the major online services has its own wine corner, too, of course.)

✔ **Wine Country Virtual Visit (http://www.freerun.com):** Visit two dozen Napa Valley and Sonoma County wineries

✔ **The Grapevine (http://www.valuenet.com):** Profiles and information from approximately 12 wineries

✔ **Wine on the Internet (http://www.wines.com):** Features information from 24 wineries, a calendar of events, wine gifts, and so on

✔ **Wine Web (http://www.wineweb.com/wine):** Features information on five charter wineries and their wines

- ✔ **Wine Net (http://www.wine.net/wine):** Has a directory of winery addresses and telephone numbers, some information about grape varieties, and a forum for messages.

- ✔ **VineNet (http://kbt.com/vinenet/welcome.html):** Specializes in information about wine events, wine shops, and wineries in the northeast U.S.

Before embarking on your search for wine on the Internet, check out Wine Site Links at http://www.webcreations.com/wines/index.htm for a listing of the wine sites that are currently the most informative. At this site, you can read a "report card" of users' opinions of the various wine sites and voice your opinion of the sites you visit.

The 5th Wave   By Rich Tennant

"THIS ONE'S EARTHY BUT LIGHT, WITH UNDERTONES OF BLACKBERRY, VANILLA, AND SCOTCH-GUARD."

Chapter 18

What Does a Rainbow Taste Like?

*W*hen we first got excited about wine, we tried to share our enthusiasm with a relative who appeared to have some interest in the subject (well, he drank a glass now and then). Each time we served a wine, we'd talk about it, comparing it in great detail to the wine we drank the week before. But he wasn't interested. He brought our proselytizing to an abrupt halt by proclaiming, "I don't want to talk about wine — I just want to drink it."

On some fundamental level where wine is just a generic beverage, it's certainly possible to drink wine without talking about it. But if you're the kind of person who likes to talk about food, or if you've been bitten by the wine bug, you know that it's difficult (if not impossible) to enjoy wine without talking about it. Wine is a social pleasure that is enhanced by sharing with others.

Ironically, the experience of a wine is highly personal. If you and three other people are tasting the same wine at the same time, each of you will have your own impression of that wine based on personal likes and dislikes, physiology, and experience. Maybe some day, if humans learn how to do a "Vulcan mind-meld," someone else will be able to experience your experience of a wine — but until then, your taste is singular. The only way you can share your impressions with others is through conversation — talking about it.

Words Cannot Describe . . .

Language is our main vehicle for communicating our entire experience of life. We use language to tell the doctor where it hurts, to describe how radiant the bride looked, and to inform the bozo who almost sideswiped us what we think of his driving ability. When we taste something, language — words — communicates to others what we tasted and what our impression is.

Words describing a wine enable us to imagine what a wine tastes like before we spend our money, open a bottle, and find out for ourselves. Words also help us to make decisions about which wine to serve with which food.

Our vocabulary of taste is undeveloped, however. When we were young, we were taught a visual vocabulary: what is green, yellow, gold, and orange — and for that matter, what is pine green, jungle green, olive green, forest green, and sea green (thanks, Crayola!). No one ever taught us precisely what *bitter, astringent,* and *tart* are. Yet to talk about wine taste, we use these words as if we all agree on what they mean.

Any discussion of wine's taste is particularly complicated, because wine is a complex beverage that gives us multiple taste sensations:

- Olfactory sensations (all those *flavors* we perceive by smelling them in our mouths — as we discuss in Chapter 2)

- Basic taste sensations (sweetness, sourness, and bitterness)

- Tactile sensations (the bite of astringency, for example, as well as the prickliness, roughness, smoothness, or other textural impressions of a wine in our mouths)

- Sensations on the holistic level, a synthesis of all the wine's characteristics taken together

Say we just tasted an oaked Sauvignon Blanc from California. We might perceive the wine as *oaky and herbaceous, with melon-like fruit* (olfactory impressions), *very slightly sweet yet with firm acidity* (basic taste impressions), *smooth and rich* (tactile impressions), *a delicious, vibrant wine with personality to spare* (holistic impression). What sounds like some insufferable wine snob showing off is actually just some poor slob of a wine lover trying his best to report the taste data the wine is sending him.

You've probably gotten many a laugh from wine descriptions you've read. At face value, they sound preposterous: *Unctuous, with butter and vanilla flavors that coat the sides of your mouth. Fleshy, with rich and deep velvety texture, suppleness, and smoothness. Some fatness in the mouth, with a long finish.* (Wait! They forgot to say wet and "liquidy.")

Reading wine descriptions (or *tasting notes*, as they're often called) in wine newsletters or magazines can be as difficult as writing them. We must admit that our eyes often glaze over when we try to read tasting notes. And we're not alone. Frank Prial, wine columnist of *The New York Times,* once wrote that ". . . a stranger's tasting notes, to me anyway, are about as meaningful as a Beijing bus schedule."

Different strokes for different folks

To help us communicate about wine more effectively, scientists have attempted to standardize the language of wine. Traditional wine descriptors, they say, lack specific definitions and are meaningful only to insiders familiar with wine.

Being scientific, they propose that we use only words that are a) objective and b) have the same meaning to the entire population. Words like *apricot, green olive, honey,* or *tar* are acceptable in describing wine because the words represent specific substances that can be identified in repeated testing. Words like *rich, young, balanced,* or *smooth* are inappropriate, in the scientists' opinion, because they are too subjective and indefinite.

Most of the acceptable words end up being aroma/flavor descriptors, because aromatic compounds lend themselves to reproducible testing. The basic tastes — sweetness, acidity, and bitterness — are also objective and measurable, but their perception in wine is subjective due to personal thresholds and the interaction of the tastes (sweetness diminishing the perception of acidity, for example; see the discussion of balance in Chapter 2). Tactile and holistic impressions of a wine are likewise subjective.

SNOB ALERT

What the words are worth

Once, we engaged in a humbling yet fascinating exercise. Several wine writers were given a wine to taste, along with eight published tasting notes from other writers. (Only one tasting note corresponded to the wine that we were tasting — the others described similar wines.) We were asked to identify the tasting note that corresponded to the wine we were tasting as well as the note that seemed the most inappropriate for the wine. The description we all voted *least* appropriate for the wine turned out to be the description taken from the back label of the wine bottle! Not one of us had correctly matched the description's words to our taste experience. Again, with another wine, we each discovered that *our* taste and *their* words failed to correspond. Our only possible conclusions were either that we can't taste very well, the writers can't write very well (present company included), or that communicating taste is a hopeless exercise.

Scientifically-acceptable Winespeak

An objective wine vocabulary is thus heavily skewed toward olfactory sensations (aromas and flavors). An example? Here's the winery's description of the 1993 Fetzer Sundial Chardonnay: *Tropical citrus-pineapple aromas lead to green-apple and toasty oak flavors.* This description tells you what flavors to expect in the wine, in simple words that anyone can understand — but it doesn't describe the whole wine. (It tells you what the wine's flavors are, but not what the wine tastes like — a subtle but meaningful difference.) Using this scientific system to describe wine is like describing a house only as *pale yellow with forest green trim and a brown roof,* because *big* is too indefinite and not enough people know what *mock Tudor* means.

This scientific approach has the support of professors at the University of California at Davis, one of the leading institutions in the world for the scientific study of wine. We've noticed that a lot of wine producers from California use objective, olfactory-skewed language, maybe because they learned it in school, or maybe because it works well for their wines, which are aromatically rich (that is, they have lots of flavors to describe).

When this objective language is applied to a European wine with understated flavors, though, there is almost nothing to say about the wine. A full-bodied Meursault with excellent concentration, creamy texture, and enormous depth becomes just *hazelnut and smoky oak with suggestions of honey.*

Traditional Winespeak

Many of the established British writers, whose subject is more often European wines than New World wines, use aroma/flavor (olfactory) descriptors sparingly in tasting notes. They're more likely to mention a wine's *harmony, balance, youthfulness, ripeness, harshness, vigor, power, silkiness, dullness, vitality,* and so on (the scientists cringing with every word). These writers might give us only a vague idea of what color the house is, but they describe its bricks and mortar, its size, and its style.

Language like theirs could derive from the style of the wines these writers are describing: wines that have more to say on the level of basic taste (sweetness, acidity, bitterness), tactile impressions, and holistic impressions than on an olfactory level. Unlike scientific language, the traditional wine language of these writers is judgmental. Harshness is bad, power is good, dullness is bad, harmony is good, and so on.

The methods of both the scientific school and the traditional school have their virtues. Objective language works well for fruity, flavorful wines and when communicating with people who know less about wine than you do. Traditional wine language can actually communicate the complete taste of a wine (as opposed to just its flavors). But because the words being used are personal to wine tasters (and not even all tasters use the words similarly) they are meaningless dribble to anyone with limited wine experience.

Most tasting notes that you read will have elements of both schools, meaning that they'll have enough words to make your eyes glaze over.

Language without words

When a wine critic writes a tasting note, he usually accompanies it with a point score, a judgment of the wine's quality on a scale of 20 or 100. You'll see these numbers plastered all over the shelves in your wine shop and in wine advertisements.

Because words are such a difficult medium for describing wine, the popularity of numbers has spread like wildfire. Many wine lovers don't even try to read the descriptions — they just run out to buy the wines with the highest scores. (Hey, they're the best wines, right?)

We saw a customer storm out of a wine shop because the salesperson had the audacity to suggest that a Cabernet rated at 94 points might be a good substitute for the particular 95-point Cabernet that the customer requested. Thank heavens IQs and SAT scores aren't interpreted so literally!

Numbers provide a convenient shorthand for communicating a critic's opinion of a wine's quality, but they tell you absolutely nothing about what the wine tastes like. You might hate a wine that's rated highly — and not only that, but you might end up feeling like a hopeless fool who can't recognize quality when it's staring him in the face. Save your money and your pride by deciding what kinds of wine you like and then trying to figure out from the words whether or not a particular wine is your style — regardless of the number rating.

Like everyone else, critics have their own taste preferences that inevitably influence the ratings, no matter how objective the critic is trying to be. Your taste might not agree.

When It's Your Turn to Speak

Describing your experience or impression of a wine involves two steps: first, you have to form the impression; second, you have to communicate it. When you're drinking wine with friends purely for enjoyment and appreciation — over dinner, for example — there's absolutely nothing wrong with simple impressions and silly comments. If a wine strikes you as unusually full and voluptuous, why *not* say it's like Marilyn Monroe? If a wine seems tight and unyielding, go ahead and call it Ebenezer Scrooge. Everyone will know exactly what you mean.

In other circumstances, though, like when you're attending a wine-tasting event, you might want to form more considered impressions of each wine so that you can participate in the discussion and gain the most from the event (unless you relish the role of class clown). To form a considered impression you need to taste thoughtfully.

Talking to yourself

The language you use to describe a wine starts with your own thoughts as you taste the wine. Thus, the process of tasting a wine and the process of describing it are intertwined.

Although wine tasting involves examining wine visually and smelling it as well as tasting it, those first two steps are a breeze compared to the third. When the wine is in your mouth, the multiple taste sensations — flavors, texture, sweetness or dryness, acidity, tannin, balance, length, body — occur practically all at once. In order to make sense of the information you receive from the wine, you have to impose some order on the impressions.

One way of organizing the impressions a wine sends you is to classify the wine's input, according to the nature of the "taste":

- The wine's *aromatics* (the olfactory data, all the flavors you smell in your mouth)

- The wine's *structure* (its alcohol/sweetness/acid/tannin makeup and its basic tastes — the wine's bricks and mortar, so to speak)

- The wine's *texture* (the tactile data, how the wine feels in your mouth; texture is a function of the wine's structural components; a high acid, dry, low-alcohol white wine might feel thin or sharp, while a high-alcohol red wine with low tannin might feel soft and silky)

Another way of organizing the impressions a wine sends you is by the sequence of your impressions, as we describe in Chapter 2. The words that tasters use to describe the sequence are

- ✔ **Attack:** The first impression of sweetness, dryness, or viscosity as the wine enters your mouth

- ✔ **Evolution:** The development of the wine in your mouth, a stage when the wine's acidity registers — and subsequently, its tannin

- ✔ The **finish** or **aftertaste:** Flavors or impressions that register after the wine has been spat or swallowed; both the duration of the aftertaste and the nature of the flavors are considered noteworthy (a long finish is commendable, for example, and a bitter one is not)

Similarly, some tasters organize their impressions of a wine according to

- ✔ **Fore-palate:** Front-of-the mouth impressions, usually sweetness, dryness, or viscosity

- ✔ **Mid-palate:** Subsequent impressions, usually concerning the wine's acidity

- ✔ **Rear-palate:** Final impressions of a wine while it's in your mouth, usually relating to its tannin as well as its length across the tongue; see Chapter 2 regarding length

- ✔ **Finish**

Writing tasting notes

Some people have a special ability to remember tastes. But other people need to take notes in order to remember *what* they tasted, let alone what they thought of it. If you have the slightest difficulty remembering the names of wines, jot down the names of wines you try and like so that you can enjoy them — or similar wines — again.

It's a good idea to write *comments* about wines that you taste, too. Even if you're one of those lucky few who can remember everything you taste, we recommend that you write tasting notes now and then because the exercise of taking notes helps discipline your tasting methods.

By all means, you should note the appearance and aroma of each wine. Then jot down your mouth impressions of the wine, according to the thoughts you formed as you tasted the wine. You can and should give the wine a score to indicate your impression of its quality; ratings are very meaningful when *you* are the taster.

We automatically write the letters *C* (for color and appearance in general), *N* (for nose), and *T* (for taste), one below the other, under the name of each wine, leaving space to record our impressions. When we taste, we take each wine as it comes: If a wine is very aromatic, we write lots of things next to *N*, but if the aroma is understated we might just write *subtle* or even *not much*. When we taste the wine, we approach it sequentially, noting its attack and evolution, but we hold the wine long enough to note its balance and texture, too. Then (having spat), we taste the wine again to determine what else it might be saying. Sometimes at that point we arrive at a summary description of the wine, like *a huge wine packed with fruit that's ready to drink now,* or *a lean, austere wine that will taste better with food than alone.* Our tasting notes are a combination of fragmented observation — *high acid, very tart* — and summary description.

At first, your own notes will be brief. Just a few words, like *soft, fruity* or *tannic, hard* are fine to remind you later what the wine was like. And as an evaluation of overall quality, there's absolutely nothing wrong with *yum!*

Sometimes, if a wine is really a great wine, you might stumble into the most dangerous realm of wine description: poetry. We never *try* to come up with picturesque metaphorical descriptions for wines, but sometimes a wine just puts the words in our mouths. One memorable wine in our early days of tasting was a 1970 Brunello di Montalcino that we described as *a rainbow in the mouth, its flavors so perfectly blended that each one is barely perceptible individually.* Recently a friend of ours described a glass of young Port as *like rubbing a cat in the right direction.*

If a wine inspires you to such fanciful description, by all means go with it; only a cold-blooded scientist would resist. The experience of that wine will become memorable through the personal words you use to name it.

But beware of anyone who is moved to poetry over every wine. The vast majority of wines are prosaic, and their descriptions should be, too.

And when you do lapse into metaphor over a wine, don't necessarily expect others to understand what you mean or to even approve. Literal types will be all over you, demanding to know what a rainbow tastes like and how a wine can possibly resemble a cat.

In the end, the experience of wine is so personal that the best any of us can do is to *try* to describe the experience to others. Your descriptions will be meaningful to people who share your approach and your language, especially if they are tasting the wine along with you. But someone else picking up your notes will find them incomprehensible. Likewise, you'll find many wine descriptions you read incomprehensible — which they are.

Chapter 19

Marrying Wine with Food (and Other Entertaining Issues)

. . . .

In This Chapter

▶ Predictable reactions between wines and foods

▶ Guiding principles for matchmakers

▶ Classic combos that still work

▶ How much wine to serve your guests

. . . .

*E*very now and then, we encounter a wine that stops us dead in our tracks. It's so sensational that we lose all interest in anything but that wine. We drink it with intent appreciation, trying to memorize the taste. We wouldn't dream of diluting its perfection with a mouthful of food.

But 999 times out of 1,000, we drink our wine with food. Wine is meant to go with food. And good food is meant to go with wine.

Matchmaker, Matchmaker, Make Me a Match...

Good. We've settled that. Wine goes with food, and food goes with wine. Any questions?

Of course we're being facetious. There are thousands of wines in the world, and every one is different. And there are thousands of basic foods in the world, each different — not to mention the infinite *combinations* of foods in prepared dishes (what we really eat). In reality, food-with-wine is about as simple an issue as boy-meets-girl.

A quick history of food-with-wine

Once upon a time, in the days of arranged marriages, food and wine pairings were automatic. You drank the wine of your village with your local cuisine. The two went together well, probably because they evolved together — farmers favoring the grapes whose wines went well with the foods available to eat and vice versa.

Progress gave us choices. People who lived in places where wine was not made, such as large cities, could choose several types of wines with their food. A handy rule evolved: Drink white wine with white meats and fish; drink red wines with red meats; drink sweet wines with dessert. (Didn't anyone ever eat vegetables?) Everyone followed the rule and managed just fine until someone suggested that we all lacked imagination, which of course we did.

Now the Age of Imagination in wine-and-food pairing is upon us. The old rules are out the window, and our choices in pairing wine with food are wide open. We wouldn't go so far as to actually say *anything goes;* but, in theory, anything *could* go (taste is subjective), so you can't rule anything out. All this freedom in pairing wine with food is supposed to make life easier, but somehow the issue seems more complicated than ever.

At least there's a silver lining. For one thing, a few guidelines have evolved to channel our imaginations in the right direction. Also, we all now accept that matching food and wine is so complex — the choices are so staggering — that there's no point in worrying about choosing the perfect wine every time. You win some, you lose some, and you have fun in the process. Only someone as compulsive as Felix Unger of "The Odd Couple" would get uptight.

The dynamics of food and wine

Every dish is dynamic — it's made up of several ingredients and flavors that interact to create a (more or less) delicious whole. Every wine is dynamic in exactly the same way. When food and wine combine in your mouth, the dynamics of each change; the result is completely individual to each dish-and-wine combination. (Dare we also mention that we each *use our individual palates* to judge the success of each combination? No wonder there are no rules! For more information on the individuality of each person's taste, please see Chapter 2.)

When wine meets food, several things can happen:

- The food can exaggerate a characteristic of the wine. For example, if you eat walnuts (which are tannic) with a tannic red wine, such as a Bordeaux, the wine tastes so dry and astringent that most people would consider it undrinkable.

✔ The food can diminish a characteristic of the wine. Protein diminishes tannin, for example, and an overly-tannic red wine — unpleasant on its own — could be judged delightful when it is drunk with a rare steak.

✔ The flavor intensity of the food can obliterate the wine's flavor or vice versa. If you've ever drunk a big, rich red wine with a delicate filet of sole, you've had this experience first-hand.

✔ The wine can contribute new flavors to the dish. For example, a red Zinfandel that's gushing with berry fruit can bring its berry flavors to the dish, as if another ingredient had been added.

✔ The combination of wine and food can create an unwelcome third-party flavor that wasn't in either the wine or the food originally; we get a metallic flavor when we eat plain white meat turkey with red Bordeaux.

✔ The food and wine can interact perfectly, creating a sensational taste experience that is greater than the food or the wine alone. (This scenario is what we hope will happen every time we eat and drink, but it's as rare as a show-stopping dish.)

Certain elements of food react in predictable ways with certain elements of wine, giving us a fighting chance at making successful matches. The principle whereby the major components of wine (alcohol, sweetness, acid, tannin) relate to the basic tastes of food (sweetness, sourness, bitterness, and saltiness) is rather like the principle of wine balance; some of the elements exaggerate each other, and some of them compensate for each other (see "Balance" in Chapter 2).

Here are some ways that food and wine interact, based on the components of the wine. Remember, each wine and each dish has more than one component, and the simple relationships we describe can be complicated by other elements in the wine or the food. Whether a wine is considered *tannic, sweet, acidic,* or *high-alcohol* depends on its dominant component. (See "Describing Taste" in Chapter 2.)

Tannic wines

✔ Can diminish the perception of sweetness in a food

✔ Can taste less tannic when served with protein-rich, fatty foods, such as steak or cheese

✔ Can taste more tannic when paired with salty foods

Sweet wines

✔ Can taste less sweet, but fruitier, when matched with salty foods

✔ Can make salty foods more appealing

✔ Can go well with sweet foods

Acidic wines

- ✔ Can taste less acidic when served with salty foods
- ✔ Can taste less acidic when served with slightly sweet foods
- ✔ Can make foods taste slightly saltier
- ✔ Can counterbalance oily or fatty heaviness in food
- ✔ Can go well with acidic foods

High-alcohol wines

- ✔ Can overwhelm lightly flavored or delicate dishes
- ✔ Can go well with slightly sweet foods

Birds of a feather, or opposites attract?

These days, wine and food people acknowledge that two principles can help in matching wine with food: the complementary principle and the contrast principle.

The complementary principle involves choosing a wine that is similar in some way to the dish you are planing to serve. Generally, you shoot for similarity of flavor.

Think about the flavors in a dish the same way you think about the flavors in wine — as types, or families, of flavors. If a dish has mushrooms, that's an earthy flavor; if it has citrus or other elements of fruit, that's a fruity flavor (and so on). Then consider which wines would offer their own earthy flavor, fruity flavor, herbal flavor, spicy flavor, or whatever.

The complementary principle can also work with textures of wine and food or with structural components of wine, such as acidity. For example, a California Chardonnay with a creamy, rich texture could match the rich, soft texture of lobster. If the wine tastes slightly buttery and you dip the lobster in butter, all the better for your taste buds (just don't tell your cardiologist).

One of our favorite combinations is Italian Barbera, a high-acid, red wine, with just about any dish made with tomatoes. The acidic tomatoes don't make the wine taste astringent, probably because their acidity is no match for the wine's. Similarly, a hearty meat dish like a stew would be at home with a high-alcohol, hearty, full-bodied wine, especially if the wine had earthy flavors like the root vegetables in the stew.

Let freedom ring?

Freedom of choice has its downside. Now that there are no rules to restrict our creativity, the perfectionists are loose, fine-tuning every wine-and-food pairing ever more precisely. We once attended a lunch at which all the wines — three per dish — had been chosen just to complement the food. But the featured wines didn't work perfectly with one particular dish (they were fine, if you ask us). The expert who planned the lunch rose to apologize. It seems that the chef had altered the recipe: Instead of sprinkling cayenne pepper around the rim of the plate, for color, he (gasp!) sprinkled the pepper *on the food!* The pepper changed the entire food/wine interaction.

For those who feel comfortable with rules, there's a lesson here: Be supremely attentive not just to the ingredients of a dish, but also to where they're situated!

You probably use the complementary principle often without realizing it: You choose a light-bodied wine to go with a light dish, a medium-bodied wine to go with a fuller dish, and a full-bodied wine to go with a heavy dish.

The contrast principle seeks to find flavors or structural elements in a wine that are not in a dish but that would enhance it. A dish of fish or chicken in a rich cream and butter sauce, for example, might be matched with a dry Vouvray, a white wine whose uplifting, high acidity would counterbalance the heaviness of the dish.

A dish with earthy flavors such as portobello mushrooms and fresh fava beans (or potatoes and black truffles) might contrast nicely with the pure fruit flavor of an Alsace Riesling. We also apply the contrast principle every time we decide to serve simple food, like unadorned lamb chops or hard cheese and bread, with a gloriously complex aged wine.

 In order to apply either principle, of course, you have to have a good idea of what the food is going to taste like and what various wines taste like. That second part can be a real stumbling block for people who don't devote every ounce of their free energy to learning about wine. The solution is to ask your retailers. They might not have the world's greatest knack in wine and food pairings (then again, they might), but at least they should know what their wines taste like.

The wisdom of the ages

No matter how much you value imagination and creativity, there's no sense in reinventing the wheel. In wine-and-food terms, it pays to know the classic pairings because they work, and they're a sure thing. They didn't become classics by being mediocre.

Here are some famous and reliable combinations. Every wine region of the world has its own magic pairing, no doubt; but now that you ask, we realize that when we travel to wine regions, we're usually so busy writing notes on the wines and just enjoying the food that we fail to record most of the local food wisdom. Anyway, what good would it do you to know that Chianti is just fabulous with Tuscan wild boar?

- Oysters and Chablis

- Lamb and red Bordeaux (we like Chianti with lamb, too, when we can't get wild boar)

- Port with walnuts and Stilton cheese

- Amarone with Gorgonzola cheese

- Foie gras with Sauternes or with late-harvest Gewürztraminer

- Dry *amontillado* Sherry with soup

- Salmon with Pinot Noir

- Toasted almonds or green olives with *fino* or *manzanilla* Sherry

- Grilled fish with Vinho Verde

- Braised beef with Barolo

- Grilled chicken with Beaujolais

- Goat cheese with Sancerre or Pouilly-Fumé

- Beef bourguignonne with red Burgundy

- Chocolate with California Cabernet Sauvignon

Look for various additional suggestions on wine and food pairings scattered throughout Chapters 10 through 14.

Why stop there? Create your own list of favorite reliables. Here are a few to start you off:

- Buttered popcorn with Sauternes

- Hot dogs (mustard and sauerkraut) with white Zinfandel

> ✔ Spicy nachos with red Zinfandel
>
> ✔ Pizza with Italian Barbera
>
> ✔ Breakfast with Moscato d'Asti (goes with whatever orange juice does)

Entertaining with Wine

It's natural to become a little concerned about rules and conventions when company is coming. What if one of your guests knows more about wine than you do? What if you serve the wrong wine or run out of wine?

We first went to Venice, we then played Verona

When you're hosting a dinner party, you'll probably serve more wines than you would in the course of a normal dinner; instead of just one wine all through the meal, you might want to serve a different wine with every course. Many people serve two wines at the table, a white with the first course and a red with the entree (and if they love wine, they'll use a cheese course as an excuse to serve a second, knockout red).

Because you want every wine to taste even better than the one before it — besides blending perfectly with the food you're serving — you should give some thought to the sequence in which the wines will be served. One set of rules that no one has abolished yet (at least no one ever told us) suggests the following sequence:

> ✔ White wine before red wine
>
> ✔ Light wine before heavy wine
>
> ✔ Dry wine before sweet wine
>
> ✔ Simple wine before complex, richly flavored wine

Each of these principles operates independently. You needn't go crazy trying to follow all of them together, or you'll be able to drink nothing but light, dry simple whites and heavy, complex, sweet reds! A very light red wine served before a rich, full-bodied white can work just fine.

If the food you're serving calls for only white wine, though, there's really no reason that both wines couldn't be white: a simpler, lighter white first and a richer, fuller-bodied white second. Likewise, both wines could be red, or you could serve a dry rosé followed by a red.

First things first

Even if you don't plan to serve hors d'oeuvres, you'll need to offer your guests a drink when they arrive (unless all your guests are as punctual as Felix Unger). White wine is the usual choice, and in our experience, it's usually forgettable white wine.

Before we offend any of our friends who think that we've just insulted their taste in wine, we hasten to clarify that remark. When you're a guest, you walk in (hello, hello, has it been *that* long?), meet new people, and then there's a glass of white wine in your hand. To focus very much on the wine would be rude; people are the point. So we sip it, and half the time we don't know what we're sipping and don't care.

We prefer to serve Champagne (notice the capital *C*) instead of white wine as the apéritif because opening the bottle of Champagne is a ceremony that brings together everyone in the group. Champagne honors your guests. And a glass of Champagne is compelling enough that to spend a thoughtful moment tasting it doesn't seem rude; even people who think it's absurd to talk about wine understand that Champagne is too special to be ignored. Unlike many white wines, Champagne stands alone just fine, without food.

How much is enough

The necessary quantity of each wine depends on all sorts of issues:

- ✔ The number of wines being served (if there are several, you'll need less of each)

- ✔ The pace of service (if you plan a long, leisurely meal, you'll need more of each wine)

- ✔ The size of your wine glasses (if you're using oversized glasses, you might gauge each pour incorrectly and end up running out of a wine; better have extra on hand)

Assuming a full-blown dinner that includes an apéritif wine, two wines with dinner, and another with cheese — and guests who all drink moderately — we recommend that you plan to have one bottle of each wine for every four people. That gives each person four ounces of each wine, with plenty left over in the 25-ounce bottle for refills. If you plan to serve only two wines, expect to go through one bottle for every two guests.

- ✔ When serving two wines, plan one bottle of each wine per couple.

- ✔ When serving four wines, plan one bottle of each wine per every four people.

One simpler rule of thumb is to figure, in total, *a full bottle of wine per guest (total consumption).* That quantity might sound high, but if your dinner is spread over several hours and you're serving a lot of food, it really isn't immoderate. If you're concerned that your guests might overindulge, be sure that their water glasses are always full so that they have an alternative to automatically reaching for the wine.

If your dinner party is special enough to have several food courses and several wines, we recommend giving each guest a separate glass for each wine. The glasses can be different for each wine, or they can be alike. All those glasses really look festive on the table. And with a separate glass for each wine, no guest feels compelled to empty each glass before going on to the next wine. (You also can tell at a glance who is drinking the wine and who isn't really interested in it, and you can adjust your pouring accordingly.)

Which wines to serve

The choice of wines to serve your guests brings us back to the issue of matching wine with food. When company's coming, though, you probably want to be a little less adventuresome in your pairings than you might be otherwise — unless you know your guests love to experiment.

We don't believe that you have to impress your guests by serving great or expensive wines. Unless you're entertaining a serious wine crowd, the most important aspect of the wine is its readiness to drink and its compatibility with the food. (Most great wines are unlikely to be ready to drink unless they're older vintages.)

If you *are* entertaining a serious wine crowd, your guests will care less about the food-wine combination than they will about the wine alone — which gives you license to make the following suggestion: Each guest or couple brings two bottles of a wonderful wine for a particular course. (You choose one course to cover yourself, and coordinate who is covering every other course.) The selection of wines will probably be varied and fascinating, and everyone can learn a little something about each wine from the person who brought it.

With company or not, sooner or later you're bound to experience food-and-wine disaster — when the two taste miserable together. We've had many opportunities to test our solution to food-and-wine disaster, and it works: As long as the wine is good and the food is good, eat one first and drink the other afterwards — or vice versa.

Chapter 20

The Sweet Seduction of an Older... Wine

Compare a teenager with a fully mature woman or man. The young person may be bursting with energy, perhaps sensually appealing, and may possess enormous potential. But something is missing. The word *immature* comes to mind — a lack of complexity in the personality. Everything is up-front, obvious; subtlety is lacking. But with care and nourishment, *some* young people turn into magnificent adults.

The same is true of wine. *Some* young wines, those with potential for greatness, just need time and a little TLC to mature well and reach a wonderful old age.

The Many and the Few

Wine is such a complex field that it defies rigid thinking and simple categorizations. But here's a simple categorization anyway. Say that all the wines of the world can be divided into two groups: commercial wine and fine wine. The line between the two categories is very fuzzy, but it falls somewhere around the $15 per bottle mark.

Commercial wines range in quality from decent to very good. They are more or less ready to drink when they are released from the winery for sale, anywhere from a few months to three years after the harvest. They will not benefit from extended aging — in fact, they'll deteriorate. The category includes most of the wines that most people drink: fruity Chardonnays and Cabernets, Beaujolais and Côtes de Rhônes, Zinfandels and soft Merlots, Valpolicellas and light Chiantis, and so on. (Chapters 10 through 14 discuss the wines covered in this chapter in detail.)

Fine wines range from good to extraordinary in quality, and they generally require additional aging before they are ready to drink. Their taste will change considerably depending on how long they age before being consumed (always assuming good storage conditions, as described in Chapter 15). The wine's taste will gradually improve until it reaches a plateau of maturity (its *peak*), where it stays for an indefinite period. Then gradually it declines (*goes downhill*). At a certain point it can be considered "over the hill," as they say. Kaput.

Any individual's perception of whether a wine is improving, just right, or declining will depend, of course, on that person's subjective taste. Some people enjoy drinking wines younger than others.

Naturally, you find fewer fine wines than commercial wines; fine wine accounts for less than ten percent of all wines. By definition, only fine wines have the potential to improve with age.

The Charm of an Aged Wine

Fine wines don't just have the potential to age; they usually *need* to age. Try drinking a highly-acclaimed red Bordeaux, say a 1986 Château Mouton Rothschild. You may wonder what all the fuss is about. You taste a mouthful of tannin and acidity, and although the wine has concentrated fruit, its elements don't seem to be in sync. Try it in ten to fifteen years; the aggressive tannins and acidity will have softened, a wonderful bouquet of cedar and blackcurrants will emerge from the glass, and a natural sweetness of flavor will have developed.

As a fine wine matures in the bottle, a series of chemical changes occur. These changes are poorly understood, but their effects are evident in the style of a mature red wine:

- ✔ The wine becomes paler in color.
- ✔ Its aroma evolves from the fruit aromas (and often oakiness) it had when young to a complex leathery and earthy bouquet.
- ✔ Its tannin diminishes.
- ✔ Its texture becomes silky.

Fine wines are easier to digest when they are mature because they lack bitter tannins and astringent acidity. Besides visceral pleasure, they offer a special emotional satisfaction, too. Tasting an aged wine can be like traveling back in time, sharing a connection with people who have gone before in the great chain of humanity.

If you've only experienced young wines — commercial wines, and fine wines of, say, less than ten years' age — you're in for a treat when you taste your first older wine. Of course, taste is personal: You might prefer the big fruitiness and firm tannin of young red wine. The French, as generalizations go, are said to enjoy their wines young, while the British much prefer older wines. A common joke in wine circles, when everyone agrees that a wine is too old, is to comment that the British would love it.

Buy young or buy cautiously

You may ask yourself (if you talk to yourself), "Why should I bother collecting wines? I can always buy whatever I need."

However, even if money is no object, it's not so easy to buy mature wines — in good condition. The only *sure* way to know that your mature wine has been well stored is to *buy it when it is young (and relatively inexpensive) and age it yourself.* To assure ourselves a supply of aged, mature beauties to enjoy in *our* maturity, that's exactly what we do. In a nutshell, this is the raison d'etre for collecting wines!

How do you know when a wine has been poorly stored? First, look at the *ullage* (the space between the top of the wine and the cork). Ullage of an inch or more can be a danger sign indicating that evaporation has occurred, either from excessive heat or lack of humidity — both of which can spoil the wine. On a very old wine, say 35 or more years old, an inch of ullage is quite acceptable, though. A certain amount of evaporation occurs naturally, even with good storage. Another sign of poor storage is leakage or stickiness at the top of the bottle, suggesting that wine has seeped out through the cork.

Then consider the color. A white wine that is excessively darkened or dulled, or a red wine that has become quite brown, can be oxidized and too old. (Shine a penlight flashlight through the bottom of the bottle to check the color of red wines.) But colors for red wines and Sauternes can be tricky sometimes; the wines can show quite a bit of brown and still be very much alive. If you're not sure about the color, get advice from someone who knows about older wines before plunking down your money.

Is it soup yet?

One question we frequently face in wine classes is, "How do I know when I should drink my older wine?" Unfortunately, no precise answer to this question exists because all wines age at a different pace. Even two bottles that appear to be exactly the same (name, vintage, and so on.) and are stored under the same conditions can age differently.

When you have a specific wine in mind, you can get advice in several different ways:

- ✔ Consult the comments of critics like Robert Parker, Michael Broadbent, or Clive Coates, who almost always list a suggested drinking period for wines they review in their newsletters and books (see Chapter 17); their educated guesses are usually quite reliable.

- ✔ If you're not in a hurry for an answer, send a letter to a wine magazine (see Chapter 17). These magazines consult their staff experts and answer reader questions in the "Letters to the Editor" section.

- ✔ Call or write to the winery; the winemaker and his staff are usually happy to give you their opinion on the best time to drink their wine — and they typically have more experience with the wine than anyone else.

- ✔ If you have several bottles of the same wine, try one from time to time to see how it is developing. Your own palate is really the best guide — you may enjoy the wine younger, or older, than any of the experts who are writing about it.

The Wines That Age Best

Following are some specific examples of wines that have proven their longevity to us over the years. (For a general listing of red, white, apéritif, and dessert wines that age well, see Chapter 15.)

Red wines go the distance

In general, concentrated red wines, which are too tannic and powerful to drink in their youth, are the red wines that age the best. Many of these wines are from France and Italy, although we have some contenders for long life from Spain, California, and Australia represented in the following sections.

Bordeaux

Among dry red wines, Bordeaux, especially the classified growths (see Chapter 10), certainly has the finest track record. Of these, the first growths — Lafite-Rothschild, Margaux, Latour, Mouton-Rothschild, and Haut-Brion — have all produced many bottles still in good condition from vintages dating back to the 19th century. We can't forget the tasting we did of 1874 Bordeaux in 1984: Château Lafite stood out like a beacon, simply outstanding, still at its peak. Similarly, the 1870 Château Latour is still drinking beautifully, showing no signs of excessive age!

Three second growths that also have remarkable records for longevity are Montrose, Cos d'Estournel, and Gruaud-Larose. We had the 1870 Château Montrose in 1994 at a vertical tasting of 44 vintages. Many vintages were outstanding, but the 1870 was voted the best by 11 of the 14 tasters! The 1921, 1961, and 1959 Montroses were also memorable.

Bordeaux vintages of the last 100 years that have proven to possess the greatest longevity are the 1899, 1900, 1928, 1945, 1959, and 1961. Of recent Bordeaux vintages, 1986 promises the most age worthiness, especially for wines from the Médoc, on the left bank.

Red Burgundies

Although red Burgundies generally don't age as long as Bordeaux, you will find some notable exceptions — certainly the Grand Cru Burgundies of Domaine Leroy, such as Musigny and Chambertin, and the leading Grand Crus of the Domaine de la Romanée-Conti (Romanée-Conti, La Tache, and Richebourg) have proven longevity.

The recent vintage of red Burgundy that promises longevity (for *all* of the finer Burgundies) is the 1990.

Rhône

Côte-Rôties and Hermitages of the northern Rhône, both based on the Syrah grape, can sometimes age 20 years or more. Look for Guigal's Côte Rôties (especially his single-vineyard La Mouline, La Landonne, or La Turque); his 1978s, especially, still need time. Paul Jaboulet Aine's Hermitage, La Chapelle, is a justifiably world-famous wine. His 1961 is a classic, still at its peak, while his 1978 and 1983 La Chapelles still need more time. Jean Louis Chave's Hermitages have also proven to be long lived. From the southern Rhône two Châteauneuf-du-Papes, renowned for their age worthiness are Château Rayas and Château de Beaucastel. The 1978 vintage of either of these wines is a real treat today. The 1989 and 1990 vintages show promise as long-lived years for Rhône wines.

Italy

Italy has four great red wines that have proven their longevity: Barolo and Barbaresco from Piedmont, Brunello di Montalcino from Tuscany, and Taurasi from Campania.

Giacomo Conterno, Giuseppe Mascarello, Vietti, Bartolo Mascarello, Giuseppe Rinaldi, and Bruno Giacosa are some of the producers making the greatest and longest-lived Barolos. Conterno's Monfortino is especially good. Any 1971 well-stored Barolo from these winemakers is still fine today; 1978s may need additional aging. Top Barbarescos for aging include Gaja (especially his single-vineyard Sori San Lorenzo and Sori Tildin), Bruno Giacosa (especially his Santo Stefano Riserva), and Marchesi di Gresy. 1982, 1985, 1988, 1989, and 1990 are all very good to great vintages for both Barolo and Barbaresco.

The producer with the greatest track record for Brunello di Montalcino is Biondi-Santi, whose family invented the wine in the 19th century. Try the 1975 Biondi-Santi Brunello. This wine is awesome today, and it will only get better with more years of aging. Biondi-Santi Brunellos have lasted over 100 years. 1985, 1988, and especially 1990 are great recent vintages for Brunello di Montalcino.

Taurasi, made from the Aglianico grape in southern Italy, is probably the least-known great Italian red wine. In the hands of a masterful producer such as Mastroberardino, this wine can be wonderfully long lived. His 1958 and 1968 Taurasi are still drinking well today. The best recent vintages for Taurasi have been the 1985, 1987, 1988, and 1990.

Spain

Spain's most prized red wine is Vega Sicilia's Unico. The 1968 and 1970 Unico and the Unico Riserva Especiale (a blend of '59, '60, and '61) are three of the great wines from this producer. We've tasted vintages of Unico going back to the 1950s, and we can certainly attest to the wine's longevity.

California Cabernet

California Cabernet Sauvignons don't have a long track record because most of the wineries in California were founded after 1970. But Beaulieu Vineyards (BV) is an exception. Their Georges de Latour Private Reserve Cabernet Sauvignon dates back to 1936. We are astonished at how well most vintages, including the 1936, have aged. The 1951 BV Private Reserve is simply the finest American wine that we have ever tasted! Inglenook and Simi also made some very fine Cabs in the '30s and '40s. The 1941 Inglenook is legendary.

Of the post-World War II wineries, Ridge, Mayacamas, Robert Mondavi, and Heitz have produced some wonderful Cabernets from the 1960s and '70s. Especially memorable are the 1970 and 1974 Ridge Monte Bello and Mayacamas

Cabs, the 1971 and 1974 Robert Mondavi Reserve Cabs, and the 1974 Heitz Martha's Vineyard Cabernet Sauvignon.

Australia

Australia's great red wine is Penfold's Grange Hermitage (now known simply as Grange). Grange was "invented" by the legendary Australian winemaker, the late Max Schubert, in 1951. This magnificent, world-class wine can age 30 years or more in some vintages.

White wines for the long haul

Most of the white wines that have proven their ability to age come from France and Germany. White Burgundy heads our list of age-worthy white wines.

White Burgundies

Among white Burgundies, look especially for Ramonet's Montrachet, Bâtard-Montrachet, or his Bienvenues-Bâtard-Montrachet. Coche-Dury's Corton-Charlemagne and Meursault Les Perriéres are his two greatest white Burgundies. Comtes Lafon's three best Meursaults are the Les Perriéres, Les Genevrieres, and the Les Charmes. And he makes a small quantity of a magnificent Le Montrachet.

Three other producers of white Burgundy whose wines are worth seeking out — and more readily available — are Domaine Leflaive, Michel Niellon, and Verget. And two other outstanding white Burgundies from large négociant firms (and, consequently, made in good quantities) are Louis Latour's Corton Charlemagne and Louis Jadot's Chevalier Montrachet "Les Demoiselles." The last two wines are particularly long lived. Recent good vintages for white Burgundy are the 1992, 1990, 1989, 1986, and 1985.

Before we leave white Burgundy, we must mention Chablis, a lighter, crisper Chardonnay. Actually, nothing is really light-bodied about the two Chablis producers we recommend, both of whom still use oak barrels in fermenting and aging their wine.

No one makes longer-lasting Chablis than Raveneau. Any of his Grand or Premier Cru wines are terrific and can age 20 years or more. We recently attended a dinner that included many great wines, but the one that everyone talked about was Raveneau's 1983 Chablis Les Clos (a Grand Cru). His great vintages have been the 1964, 1969, 1978, 1983, 1986, and 1989. (We haven't tried the 1992 yet — Raveneau's Chablis needs a minimum of 4 or 5 years to even begin its development.) The other producer making monumental Chablis is René et Vincent Dauvissat. These wines don't take as long as Raveneau's to develop, but they will last 15 to 20 years and are more readily available. Dauvissat's Les Clos is generally regarded as his greatest Chablis.

White Bordeaux

Dry white Bordeaux, at least the outstanding ones, can be surprisingly long lived. The three truly age-worthy Bordeaux blancs are *Château Haut-Brion Blanc*, *Château Laville-Haut-Brion*, and *Domaine de Chevalier*. In good vintages, these wines can age 25 to 30 years or more. Recent good vintages of dry Bordeaux blanc are the 1994, 1993, 1990, 1989 (outstanding), 1985 (very good), and 1983.

Riesling

The Riesling grape ages extremely well. The best examples of age-worthy Rieslings can be found in Germany and Alsace. In Germany, look for Rieslings (Kabinett, Spätlese, or Auslese) in such great vintages as 1992, 1990, 1989, 1983, 1976, 1971, or 1959. Alsace Rieslings or Gewurztraminers (another noble, age-worthy variety) from 1990, 1989, 1985, 1983, 1976, 1971, or 1967 are the ones to keep.

Just one note on a special Alsace Riesling — *Clos Sainte Hune*. It is a single-vineyard wine made by Trimbach in small quantities. This dry wine is outstanding and complex, Riesling at its best. Clos St. Hune can easily age 20 years or more. Difficult to find but worth the search for one of the great white wines of the world.

Champagnes that sparkle with age

We don't know who started the myth to the contrary, but Champagne *does* age well! If it's the product of a very good year, vintage Champagne can age especially well. We have enjoyed two outstanding 1928 vintage Champagnes, Krug and Moët & Chandon's Dom Pérignon, neither of which showed any sign of decline. The oldest Champagne that we've ever tasted, a 1914 Pol Roger, was also in fine shape.

But Champagne, perhaps more than any other wine, demands excellent storage. Magnums (1.5 l) do generally age better than regular size (750 ml) bottles. If kept in a cool, dark, damp place, many Champagnes can age for decades, especially in the great vintages. They lose some effervescence with the years but take on a complexity of flavor somewhat similar to a fine white Burgundy.

If you want to try some very fine, reliable, older bottles of vintage Champagne, look for either the Krug or Salon in the 1964, 1969, 1973, or 1976 vintage. If stored well, they will be magnificent. Dom Pérignon is also reliable — the 1961 and 1969 DPs are legendary.

Following are the houses that produce Champagnes known to age well:

- **Krug:** All their Champagnes are remarkably long lived
- **Pol Roger:** Especially Cuvée Sir Winston Churchill
- **Moët & Chandon:** Cuvée Dom Pérignon, ageless when well stored

- **Louis Roederer:** Cristal, Cristal Rosé, and Vintage Brut all age well
- **Jacquesson:** Signature and Vintage Blanc de Blancs
- **Bollinger:** All their Champagnes, especially the Grande Année
- **Gosset:** Grand Millésime and Grande Reserve
- **Salon:** This remarkable Blanc de Blancs needs to age at least 15 years before you try it
- **Veuve Clicquot:** La Grande Dame and the Vintage Brut
- **Taittinger:** Their Blanc de Blancs, the Comtes de Champagne
- **Billecart-Salmon:** Their Blanc de Blancs
- **Pommery:** Especially Cuvée Louise Pommery
- **Alfred Gratien:** Their Vintage Brut (seen mainly in England and France)

Recent great vintages for Champagne are the 1990, 1989, 1988, 1985, and 1982.

Dessert wines: true golden oldies

Sauternes not only ages extremely well, but it also improves remarkably with age. Unfortunately, much Sauternes is consumed young. A mature Sauternes (when it's turned to an old-gold coin color) can have all sorts of wonderful honeyed, apricot, toffee flavors. Even when the color has become a golden brown, Sauternes can still be delicious.

The great Château d'Yquem, of course, is the one Sauternes in a class by itself. It can age as well, or better, than any red wine. Many vintages of d'Yquem from the 19th century are still drinking well. But you can find many other good Sauternes that age well and aren't nearly so expensive as d'Yquem, starting with Château de Fargues (also owned by the proprietors of d'Yquem, the Lur-Saluces family). Others include Château Climens, Château Coutet, Château Suduiraut, and Château Lafaurie-Peyraguey. Recent great vintages for Sauternes are 1990, 1989, 1988, 1986, 1983, 1976, 1975, 1967, 1962, and 1959. Put away any one of these vintages in honor of someone's birth year, and it will last a lifetime.

Vintage Ports remind us of old soldiers: They never die, they just fade away. Even when the color of a vintage Port has turned to a light tawny and it is 70 years old or more, it can still be enjoyed for its spicy, sweet, rich flavor and lengthy finish. Ports from a good vintage require at least 20 years of age before they begin to soften and lose their tannins. Like Sauternes, too many bottles of vintage Port are consumed way too young. The vintage Ports showing admirable longevity have been the Taylor, Graham, Fonseca, Quinta do Noval "Nacional," Dow, and Cockburn. The best years for vintage Port since World War II have been the 1945, 1948, 1955, 1963, 1966, 1970, 1977, 1983, 1985, 1991, and 1992 (for Taylor and Fonseca).

The late-harvest Rieslings of Germany, the BAs and TBAs (see Chapter 11), are amazingly long lived, certainly comparable to Sauternes. Alsace's late-harvest Rieslings, Gewürztraminers, and Tokay-Pinot Gris — called *vendage tardives* (VT) and *sélection de grains nobles* (SGN) — can all be magnificent and long lived in the great vintage years. (See our comments on Riesling, earlier in this chapter.

How Long Will Modern Wines Age?

Most wines produced today are made to be consumed earlier than the wines of 50 or 100 years ago. Life styles are different today. Not many people have patience for the delayed gratification of laying down wines for 20 years or more.

If you *are* planning to save wines for your mature years, here are a few general guidelines to follow:

- ✔ Modern red Bordeaux may not have the longevity of the 1928s or 1945s, but you can usually count on 20 to 30 years of life from them, in good vintage years such as 1982, 1986, 1988, 1989, or 1990.

- ✔ Most of today's red Burgundies, with the possible exception of the 1990 vintage, should be consumed within 10 to 15 years (the less expensive ones even earlier).

- ✔ Barolos, Barbarescos, and Brunello di Montalcinos can age for 20 to 25 years in good vintages. (See Appendix B.)

- ✔ The best white Burgundies and white Bordeaux will age — and improve — with 10 to 15 years of aging or more, in good vintage years, if well stored.

Old wines for sale

If you want to experience really old wines, you can still buy vintage Madeiras from the last century. They are often available at wine auctions (at surprisingly reasonable prices, considering their age). Also, the Rare Wine Company in Sonoma and the Chicago Wine Company (see Chapter 16) always have some vintage Madeira for sale, sometimes as old as the 1790s!

Red Bordeaux from the 19th century and early 20th century are available at wine auctions, but they are invariably very expensive. In terms of longevity, the 1928, 1945, and 1961 vintages of Bordeaux are your safest bets for vintages of this century.

Kid Gloves for Handling the Aged . . . and Nearly Senile

For proper storage conditions for your older wines, see Chapter 15.

Like people, wine can become somewhat fragile as it advances into its later stages. For one thing, it doesn't like to travel. If you *must* move old wine (probably shaking it up in the process), give it a good rest of several days or more after the travel before opening the bottle. (Red Burgundies and other Pinot Noirs are especially disturbed by journeys.)

Older wine, with its delicate bouquet and flavors, can be easily overwhelmed by strongly flavored foods and sauces. Simple cuts of meat or just hard cheeses and good, crusty bread are usually fine companions for mature wine.

If you're going to drink an older wine, don't over-chill it (whether it's white or red). Older wines show their best at moderate temperatures. Temperatures below 60° F (15.5° C) inhibit development in the glass.

Decant red wines or vintage Ports. (For a review of decanting, see Chapter 6.) Stand the bottle up two or three days before you plan to open it so that the sediment can drift to the bottom. An important concern in decanting an old wine is giving the wine *too* much aeration: A wine in its last stages will deteriorate rapidly upon exposure to air, often within a half hour — sometimes in 10 or 15 minutes. (We knew one fellow who checked his watch constantly as he tasted very old wines, to note how long each wine lasted in the glass before fading.)

When you decant an old wine, taste it immediately and be prepared to drink it rapidly if it shows signs of fading.

Tips for Improving Your Odds of Getting a "Good, Old Bottle" of Wine

Acquiring and drinking old wines requires you to be a bit of a gambler. But you *can* reduce the odds against coming up with a bottle well past its peak by following a few easy tips:

  ✔ Buy from reputable wine merchants. The best wine retailers usually know something about the history of their older wines. (See Chapter 16 for stores that specialize in older wines.) They most likely acquired the wines from sources that they trust. Moreover, they often will stand behind the wine; if it is not good, they frequently will give you credit towards another purchase or refund your money. Verify this guarantee before you buy the wine.

✔ Trade with knowledgeable wine friends who know the storage history of their wines.

✔ Stick to well-known wines with a proven history of longevity.

✔ Inspect the wine if you can. If you buy by telephone or fax, ask your wine merchant to physically look at the bottle and describe its fill level.

✔ Be wary if the price of the bottle seems too low. Often, what appears to be a bargain is a damaged or over-the-hill wine being unloaded on unsuspecting customers.

✔ Ask wine-knowledgeable friends or wine merchants about the particular wines that you are considering buying. Frequently, someone will be familiar with them.

Say a prayer, take out your corkscrew, and plunge in. Live dangerously!

Part IV
The Part of Tens

The 5th Wave   By Rich Tennant

Wines to Avoid

©RICHTENNANT

LIMITED RELEASE
11,000 BARRELS

CONDE DE PETRO

OIL RIG RIOJA
AGED 6,000,000 YEARS

CONTAINS SULFITE
MAGMA RESIDUE AND
METAMORPHIC ROCK

BOTTLING
EXXON
ESTATE

VERSION 1.0 RELEASE 1993
OR 1994 BUT MORE LIKE LATE
1995

VIRTUAL VINE

16MB MERLOT
SILICON VALLEY VINEYARDS

CONTAINS ONE CD-ROM FOR
FULL MOTION VIDEO 3D STEREO
HIGH PERFORMANCE OPTIMIZED
WINE DRINKING EXPERIENCE.

Silo Aged
Farmers Reserve
1994

Nebraska White
Pitchfork Vineyards

CONTAINS SULFITE, ALFALFA
SORGHUM AND HAYSEED

In this part...

This is the place to turn for quick answers and easy solutions. The next time a friend tells you that expensive wines are always better, the next time you're looking for something new to try, the next time you're tempted to take a point score seriously — check out the advice in this part.

Chapter 21

Answers to Ten Common Questions about Wine

● ●

*I*n our years of teaching about wine and helping customers in wine shops, we've noticed that the same questions about wine pop up again and again. Here are our answers.

What's a good wine?

This is probably the question most frequently asked by customers in wine shops. When they ask this question, they usually mean, "Please recommend a good wine to me," to which the retailer will usually respond with a barrage of questions:

- ✔ "Do you prefer red wines or white wines?"
- ✔ "How much are you willing to spend for a bottle?"
- ✔ "Are you planning to serve the wine with any particular dish?"

Hundreds of good wines are in every wine shop. Twenty or thirty years ago, there were far fewer — but winemaking and grape growing know-how has progressed dramatically to the point that there are few poor wines now (especially on retail shelves in competitive markets like the U.S.). But you won't necessarily like everyone of them.

There is simply no getting around the fact that taste is personal. If you want to drink the good wine that's right for you, you have to decide what the characteristics of that wine may be.

When should I drink this wine?

Wine retailers frequently hear this question from customers, too. The answer might disappoint some customers who think that they're not buying a bottle of a beverage but a precious and special commodity. The answer, for most wines, is "Anytime now."

The great majority of wines are ready to drink when you buy them. Some of them might improve marginally if you hold them for a year or so (and many of them will maintain their drinkability), but they won't improve enough for you to notice, unless you're a particularly thoughtful and experienced taster.

Is wine fattening?

A glass of dry wine contains about 85 percent water, 12 percent ethyl alcohol, and small quantities of tartaric acid and various other components. Wine contains no fat.

A four-ounce serving of dry white wine has about 104 calories, and four ounces of red wine has about 110 calories. Sweeter wines contain about ten percent more calories depending on how sweet they are; fortified wines that are higher in alcohol than table wines also contain additional calories because of the higher alcohol.

Wine contains various vitamins and minerals, including B vitamins, iodine, iron, magnesium, zinc, copper, calcium, and phosphorus.

Which vintage should I buy?

Nearly every wine that you find in your wine shop is available in only one vintage, which is referred to as the *current* vintage.

Most wineries don't ship a new vintage of their wines out to their customers until their own stocks of the old vintage are depleted. Likewise, local wholesalers in your market won't ship that new vintage to wine shops until they've sold out on the old vintage. And retailers usually won't order the new vintage until they run out of *their* stock of the current vintage.

For white wines, the current vintage represents grapes that were harvested as recently as nine months ago (in the case of wines that are supposed to be drunk very young) or as long as three years ago; for red wines, the current vintage is a date one to four years ago.

Classified-growth red Bordeaux wines (see Chapter 10) are the notable exception to the above rule: most wine shops feature several vintages of these wines simultaneously. A few other fine wines — such as Burgundies, Barolos, or Rhône wines — might also be available in multiple vintages, but often they're not because the quantities produced are small and the wines sell out.

A red Rioja or a Chianti Classico might appear to be available in multiple vintages, but if you read the label carefully, you'll see that one vintage of the Rioja could be a *crianza* (aged two years before release), another might be a *reserva* (aged three years), and another might be a *gran reserva* (aged five years) — so they are each actually different wines, not multiple vintages of the same wine. Likewise, a Chianti might be available in an aged *riserva* version as well as a *non-riserva* style.

Most of the time, for most wines, the vintage to buy is the vintage you *can* buy, the current vintage. For the exceptional cases, consult our Vintage Chart in Appendix B.

What grape variety is this wine made from?

Many wines today tell you what grape variety they're made from right on the front label — it's often the very name of the wine — or on the back label. Traditional European wines blended from several grape varieties usually don't give you that information: a) because the winemakers consider the name of the place more important than the grapes anyway, and b) because the grapes they use are local varieties whose names few people would recognize.

If you really want to know what grape varieties make a Soave, Valpolicella, Châteauneuf-du-Pape, Rioja, Côtes du Rhône, or other blended European wines, you'll have to look it up (see our charts in Chapters 10 and 11).

Are there any wines without sulfites?

Sulfur dioxide exists naturally in wine as a result of fermentation. It also exists naturally in other fermented foods, such as bread, cookies, and beer. (Various sulfur derivatives are used regularly as preservatives in packaged foods.)

Winemakers use sulfur dioxide at various stages of the winemaking process because it stabilizes the wine (preventing it from turning to vinegar or deteriorating from oxygen exposure), and it safeguards the flavor of the wine. Sulfur has been an important winemaking tool since Roman times.

Very few winemakers refrain from using sulfur dioxide; most use it out of concern that their wine will change after it is bottled or that its shelf life will be shortened. Depending on where you live, your wine shop might carry two or three wines whose sulfite content is so low that their labels do not have to carry the phrase *Contains Sulfites* (which the U.S. government requires on the label of any wine that contains more than 10 parts per million of sulfites).

If you wish to limit your consumption of sulfites, dry red wines should be your first choice, followed by dry white wines. Sweet wines contain the most sulfur dioxide. For more information, turn to "Contains Sulfites" in Chapter 1.

Are there any organic wines?

Yes, there are — depending on what you mean by organic.

If you mean wines that are made from organically grown grapes, there are dozens of brands now. Many more winemakers are in the course of making their vineyards organic (it's a gradual process that can't happen overnight), switching from chemical fertilizers, herbicides, and pesticides to compost and natural pest prevention and seeking to restore the soil's microbial activity. In dry climates such as California, where mildew and rot are not concerns for the growers, enthusiasm for organic viticulture (sometimes called *sustainable viticulture)* is particularly keen. Many vineyards that practice organic farming are not officially *certified* as organic, however.

Organic winemaking has traditionally meant the production of wine from organically grown grapes without the use of chemical additives in the winemaking. Use of the term *organic wine* has therefore been limited to those producers who do not use sulfur dioxide — a very limited group. (See "Contains Sulfites" in Chapter 1 and "Are there any wines without sulfites?" in this chapter.) The National Organic Standards Board, a U.S. federal advisory group, has recently decided to permit a fairly liberal amount (up to 100 parts per million) of sulfur dioxide in organic wines. At that level, lots of wineries could qualify as organic. But the board's recommendations are not final.

What is the bottom line? Depending on what you mean by organic wine, you can probably find it, but not without doing a little digging. Try asking your wine merchant.

What's new oak?

You don't have to read very many wine columns before realizing that many winemakers use *new oak* for their wines and are proud of it. The term refers to 60-gallon oak barrels (usually French oak but sometimes American oak) that winemakers use to either ferment or age their better white wines and to age their better red wines.

The amount of oaky aroma and flavor that a barrel is able to give to a wine — and the amount of tannin — is a function of how often the barrel has been used. In some parts of Europe, winemakers have traditionally used oak casks (many times bigger than barrels) or large oak barrels for their wines for twenty years or even longer before replacing them. After a few years the insides of the casks or barrels become encrusted with crystalline acid deposits from the wine so that the wood itself might not even come in contact with each new wine that's put into it. Such oak is usually referred to as *old oak.*

Most winemakers who use new oak barrels replace them after just three to five vintages. To avoid being hit with a big expense all at once, for example, winemakers might replace 20 percent of their barrels each year. Their *new oak* is therefore 20 percent brand new, 20 percent one year old, 20 percent two years-old, and so on. (Using barrels that aren't all brand new is a good idea for most white wines, which would be overwhelmed by the amount of oakiness the fresh barrels would give.) When a winemaker replaces 20 percent of his oak barrels every year, he might say that he practices a *five-year rotation* for his oak. If he replaces one-third of his barrels every year, he uses a *three-year* rotation.

What is a wine expert?

A wine expert is someone with a high level of knowledge about wine in general (including grape growing and winemaking) and the various wines of the world. A wine expert also has a high degree of skill in tasting wine.

More often than not, wine experts gain their expertise through informal study, work experience, or experience gained as *amateurs* (lovers) of wine. The only official, state-accredited programs in wine are *enology* (winemaking) and *viticulture* (grape growing) programs offered by universities. These programs are valuable for people who plan to become winemakers or grape growers, but they represent scientific overkill for people whose goal is breadth of knowledge about wine.

Because wine experts gain their expertise through informal study and experience, it can be difficult to know whether someone is really a wine expert. In fact, if someone *claims* to be a wine expert and knows more about wine than you do, the only way you can determine that he's *not* a wine expert is by becoming more of an expert yourself.

Few people who do know a great deal about wine actually call themselves wine experts, because they know enough to realize how vast the field is and how much they don't know. But some of these people are considered experts by their peers or by their readers, students, or customers.

Gifted winemakers are not automatically considered wine experts. They are acclaimed for their skill, craftsmanship, or artistic talent but not necessarily for their breadth of knowledge of the world's wines.

What's that funny name for the study of wine?

That's *enology* (sometimes spelled as *oenology*). Either way, the term is pronounced *ee NOL oh gee.*

Enology is the study of wine (as in winemaking), and the dictionary will tell you that an *enologist* is someone involved in the study of wine. (If you read three or four pages of this book, that could be you — but the cartoons don't count.) In *real life,* however, we reserve the term enologist for people who have studied *winemaking.*

People who love wine can call themselves *oenophiles*, but they usually never do because they're entirely too down-to-earth for such fancy language; they call themselves winos, wine-ies (as opposed to foodies), or just wine lovers.

Another term that's used a fair amount in reference to people who know or love wine is *connoisseur*. That's our favorite term because it suggests an understanding and appreciation of wine, not an encyclopedic knowledge of facts and figures. We hope that's what you become when you read this book. You can go back and look up the facts and figures later.

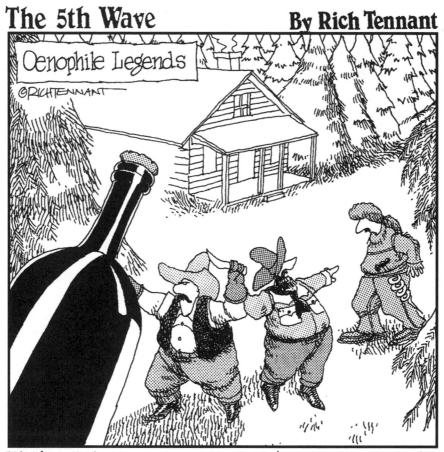

The 5th Wave   By Rich Tennant

Oenophile Legends

@RICHTENNANT

"Hold on Luke, here comes Jim Bowie's cousin, Maurice Bowie. Let him have a go at that Mountain Red Cabernet with that Bowie corkscrew of his."

Chapter 22

Ten Wine Myths Demystified

● ●

*A*s you leaf through the pages of this chapter, you will probably recognize several of the wine myths mentioned here. They are common thinking — and common misinformation — about wine. We set the record straight.

Wine is for experts

True, wine is for experts. Wine involves so much detailed information — vintages, winemakers, winemaking techniques, history, tradition, new trends — that there's plenty of stuff for experts to sink their teeth into. Wine is definitely for them.

But wine isn't *only* for experts. Wine is for anyone who likes the taste of wine.

Wine is a beverage, one of the oldest beverages in history. Millions of people all over the world drink wine without knowing anything about the wine they're drinking other than the fact that it's the local wine of their region, it's the wine their brother-in-law recommended, or it tastes good.

Wine is a beverage, plain and simple. It is fermented grape juice, the product of a simple, natural process.

The next time you worry that maybe you don't know enough to be a wine lover, consider this: If people in the wine business had to rely on experts to drink their wines, they'd have been out of business long ago!

Wine has to be expensive to be good

For wine, as for any other product, the more you pay for a bottle, the better the quality generally is. But the best quality doesn't always mean the best wine.

- ✔ Your taste is personal, and you might not like a wine that everyone else says is great.
- ✔ All wines are not suitable for all situations.

You certainly can enjoy even a $4 wine under many circumstances. At large family gatherings, picnics, at the beach, and so on, an expensive, top-quality wine would be out-of-place — too serious and important.

Expensive wines are seldom the best choice in restaurants — considering typical restaurant prices. Instead, we either look for the best value on the wine list (keeping in mind what we are eating) or experiment with some moderately priced wine that we haven't tried before. (There will *always* be some wines that you haven't tried.)

Quality isn't the only consideration in choosing a wine. Often, the very best wine of all — for your taste, or for a certain situation — will be inexpensive.

Imported wines are better

First of all, imported from where? If you live in Europe, California wine is imported wine; if you live in the U.S., European wine is imported wine. How can they both be better than each other?

We have a friend in the U.S. who only drinks French wine. He insists that all California wine is inferior. We love to serve him a good California wine *blind* (that is, with the label covered), and watch his reaction when he discovers it's from California — after he has praised the wine!

Nowadays, every principal winemaking country is making some excellent wine. The "Imported wines are better" myth is just a bit of snobbery, let's face it.

Here's a daring suggestion that flies in the face of the imported wine myth: Discover your own local wines. If you live in southern Pennsylvania, New England, Ohio, Texas, Idaho, Vancouver, or Toronto, for example (not to mention Sydney, Melbourne, and Santiago), people are making wine practically in your own backyard. Try them. How do you think the Burgundians discovered that Burgundy is worth drinking?

White wine with fish, red with meat

As guidelines go, this isn't a bad one. But we said *guideline*, not rule. Anyone who slavishly adheres to this generalization as if it were a rule deserves the boredom of eating and drinking exactly the same thing every day of his life!

Do you want a glass of white wine with your burger? Go ahead, order it. *You're* the one who's doing the eating and drinking, not your friend and not the server who's taking your order.

Even if you're a perfectionist who's always looking for the perfect food and wine combination, you'll find yourself wandering from the guideline. The best wine for a grilled salmon steak is probably red — like a Pinot Noir or a Bardolino — and not white at all. Veal and pork do equally well with red or white wines, depending on how the dish is prepared. And what could be better with hot dogs on the barbecue than a cold glass of rosé?

No one is going to arrest you if you have white wine with everything, or red wine with everything, or even Champagne with everything! There are no rules.

Numbers don't lie

It's natural to turn to critics for advice. We do it all the time, when we're trying to decide which movie to see, when we're choosing a new restaurant to try, or when we want to know what someone else thinks of a particular book.

In most cases, we weigh the critics' opinions against our own experience and tastes. Say a steak house just got three stars and a fabulous review from the dining critic. Do we rush to the telephone to make a reservation? Not if we don't like red meat! When the movie critics give two thumbs up, do we automatically assume that we'll like the movie — or do we listen to their commentary and decide whether the movie might be too violent, silly, or serious for us? You know the answer to that.

Yet many wine drinkers, when they hear that a wine just got more than 90 points, go out of their way to get that wine. The curiosity to try a wine that scores well is understandable. But the rigid belief that such a wine a) is necessarily a great wine, and b) is a wine you will like, is simply misguided.

The critics' scores are nothing more than the critics' professional opinion — and opinion, like taste, is always personal.

Oaked wines are better

If political correctness existed for wine, people who made statements like this would end up holding press conferences to apologize for their thoughtlessness. After all, unoaked wines have feelings, too!

The association between wine and oak goes way back to the days when oak containers (or other types of wood) were the only types of containers available to hold wine. But today, oak is more than just a container for wine; it's a status symbol.

No doubt, oak barrels can help some wines achieve greatness. Oak barrels interact with developing wine in many ways, influencing the wine's texture, tannin level, and aroma/flavor (turn to "Winemaking wonder words" in Chapter 3 for more about oak). The effect can be a sensationally good wine — if what went into the oak in the first place was already good and if the winemaker is skilled. Put a light or feeble wine into oak — and all you'll get is an oaky-tasting light and feeble wine. Some of our greatest disappointments in wine lately have been over-oaked wines that tasted more like wood than like grapes.

Oak barrels are expensive, so generally they're used only for the best wines (and even then, only for certain types of wine), or for wines that have delusions of grandeur. To simulate the effect of oak barrels in their less expensive wines, winemakers can use oak chips or oak flavoring — a far cry from the complex changes that occur with barrel-aging.

Whether or not you like oaky wines is a matter of personal taste. We like the effects of oak in some wines, but we also enjoy wines that have no oak at all — just bright, fresh, vibrant flavors of wine.

Vintages always matter/vintages don't matter

The difference between one vintage and the next of the same wine is the difference between the weather in the vineyards from one year to the next (barring extenuating circumstances such as new ownership of the winery). The degree of vintage variation is thus equivalent to the degree of weather variation.

In some parts of the world the weather varies a lot from year to year, and *for wines from those regions*, vintages certainly do matter. In Bordeaux, Burgundy, Germany, and most of Italy, for example, problems (frost, hail, ill-timed rain, or insufficient heat) can affect one vintage for the worse, while the next year there may be no such problems. Where there is a lot of weather variation, the quality of the wine can swing from mediocre to outstanding.

In places where the weather is more predictable year after year (like much of California, Australia, and South Africa), vintages can still vary, but the swing is narrower. Serious wine lovers who care about the intimate details of the wines they drink will find the differences meaningful, but most people won't.

Another exception to the "Vintages always matter" myth is inexpensive wine. Top-selling wines that are produced in large volume are usually blended from many vineyards in a fairly large area. Swings in quality from year to year are not important.

Wine authorities are experts

Wine is an incredibly vast subject. It involves biochemistry, botany, geology, chemistry, climatology, history, culture, politics, laws, and business. How can anyone be an expert in all of that?

Different aspects of wine appeal to different people. Depending on what they particularly like about wine, people tend to specialize in some of wine's disciplines at the expense of others. (Now you know why it takes two of us to write this book.)

Don't expect any one person to be able to answer all your questions about wine in the most accurate and up-to-date manner. Just like doctors and lawyers, wine professionals specialize. They have to.

Old wines are good wines

The idea of rare old bottles of wine being auctioned off for tens of thousands of dollars apiece, like fine art, is fascinating enough to capture anyone's imagination. But valuable old bottles of wine are even rarer than valuable old coins because, unlike coins, wine is perishable.

The great majority of the world's wines don't have what it takes to age for decades. Most wines are meant to be enjoyed in the first one to five years of their life (see "The Many and the Few" in Chapter 20).

Even those wines that have the potential to develop slowly over many years will achieve their potential only if they are properly stored (see Chapter 15 for information on storing wines).

The purpose of wine is to be enjoyed — usually, the sooner the better.

Great wines are supposed to taste bad when they're young

If this myth were true, wouldn't that be convenient for anyone who made poor wine! "It's a great wine," the winery owner could argue. "It's *supposed* to taste bad when it's young."

In the past, some of the great wines of the world, like red Bordeaux, were so tough and tannic that you really couldn't drink them until they had a few decades under their belts. As recently as the 1975 vintage of Bordeaux, some collectors believed that the undrinkability of the young wines was proof positive of their age-worthiness.

Winemakers today believe that a great wine must be in balance when it's young in order to be a balanced wine when it's old. Although wines will shed some of their tannins as they age, most wines that are extraordinarily tannic when young do not have enough fruit to last until their tannins fade.

Of course for a wine to be in balance doesn't mean that it's ready to drink. A great wine can have enormous tannin when it's young, along with its enormous fruit. It might be balanced, even if it's still embryonic. You may be able to appreciate the wine's balance when it's young; you may even enjoy the wine to some degree, but its true greatness is years away.

Part V
Appendixes

The 5th Wave   By Rich Tennant

"I'll have the `85 Dribble Creek Zinfandel and a glass of white wine for my fish—nothing too dry."

In this part...

Here we give you some useful tools of the trade, like a vintage chart and a listing of all the wines in the famous 1855 classification of Bordeaux. We were going to include a listing of every winery in the world that makes Chardonnay, but we ran out of space.

Appendix A

The 1855 Classification of the Great Growths of the Gironde

(The Bordeaux region of France is in the département of the Gironde.)

Table A-1 — Haut-Médoc Wines: First Growths

Estate	Commune	Average Annual Production (Cases*)
Château Lafite-Rothschild	Pauillac	26,000 – 33,000
Château Latour	Pauillac	20,000
Château Margaux	Margaux	30,000 – 35,000
Château Haut-Brion**	Pessac (Graves)	12,000 – 18,000

* *A case is 12 750 ml bottles, or 6 1.5 l bottles*

** *This wine, although a Graves, was universally recognized and classified as one of the four First Growths.*

Table A-2 — Haut-Médoc Wines: Second Growths

Estate	Commune	Average Annual Production (Cases)
Château Mouton-Rothschild*	Pauillac	25,000 – 30,000
Château Rausan-Ségla	Margaux	15,000
Château Rauzan-Gassies	Margaux	11,000
Château Léoville-Las Cases	St-Julien	25,000
Château Léoville-Poyferré	St-Julien	25,000
Château Léoville-Barton	St-Julien	20,000
Château Durfort-Vivens	Margaux	8,000
Château Lascombes	Margaux	35,000 – 40,000

(continued)

Table A-2 (continued)

Estate	Commune	Average Annual Production (Cases)
Château Gruaud-Larose	St-Julien	32,000
Château Brane-Cantenac	Cantenac-Margaux	30,000 – 35,000
Château Pichon-Longueville Baron	Pauillac	14,000
Château Pichon-Lalande	Pauillac	20,000 – 25,000
Château Ducru-Beaucaillou	St-Julien	16,500
Château Cos d'Estournel	St-Estèphe	28,000 – 32,000
Château Montrose	St-Estèphe	27,000

* This wine was decreed a First Growth in 1973.

Table A-3 Haut-Médoc Wines: Third Growths

Estate	Commune	Average Annual Production (Cases)
Château Giscours	Labarde-Margaux	30,000
Château Kirwan	Cantenac-Margaux	8,000 – 12,000
Château d'Issan	Cantenac-Margaux	10,000 – 12,000
Château Lagrange	St-Julien	20,000
Château Langoa-Barton	St-Julien	7,500
Château Malescot St. Exupéry	Margaux	17,000
Château Cantenac-Brown	Cantenac-Margaux	15,000
Château Palmer	Cantenac-Margaux	13,000
Château La Lagune	Ludon (Haut-Médoc)	25,000
Château Desmirail	Margaux	4,500
Château Calon-Ségur	St-Estèphe	20,000
Château Ferrière	Margaux	3,000
Château Marquis d'Alesme-Becker	Margaux	5,000
Château Boyd-Cantenac	Cantenac-Margaux	8,000

Table A-4   Haut-Médoc Wines: Fourth Growths

Estate	Commune	Average Annual Production (Cases)
Château St.-Pierre	St-Julien	8,000
Château Branaire-Ducru	St-Julien	20,000
Château Talbot	St-Julien	38,000
Château Duhart-Milon-Rothschild	Pauillac	15,000 – 20,000
Château Pouget	Cantenac-Margaux	4,500
Château La Tour-Carnet	St. Laurent (Haut-Médoc)	15,000
Château Lafon-Rochet	St-Estèphe	12,000 – 14,000
Château Beychevelle	St-Julien	30,000
Château Prieuré-Lichine	Cantenac-Margaux	23,000 – 30,000
Château Marquis-de-Terme	Margaux	12,000

Table A-5   Haut-Médoc Wines: Fifth Growths

Estate	Commune	Average Annual Production (Cases)
Château Pontet-Canet	Pauillac	25,000 – 40,000
Château Batailley	Pauillac	23,000
Château Grand-Puy-Lacoste	Pauillac	13,000 – 14,000
Château Grand-Puy-Ducasse	Pauillac	18,000
Château Haut-Batailley	Pauillac	7,500 – 8,500
Château Lynch-Bages	Pauillac	40,000 – 45,000
Château Lynch-Moussas	Pauillac	13,000
Château Dauzac	Labarde-Margaux	20,000
Château Mouton D'Armhailac	Pauillac	16,000
Château du Tertre	Arsac-Margaux	18,000 – 20,000
Château Haut-Bages-Libéral	Pauillac	12,000
Château Pédesclaux	Pauillac	7,500

(continued)

Table A-5 *(continued)*

Estate	Commune	Average Annual Production (Cases)
Château Belgrave	St. Laurent (Haut-Médoc)	25,000
Château Camensac	St. Laurent (Haut-Médoc)	26,000
Château Cos Labory	St-Estèphe	7,000
Château Clerc-Milon	Pauillac	10,000
Château Croizet-Bages	Pauillac	9,500
Château Cantemerle	Macau (Haut-Médoc)	20,000

Table A-6 **Sauternes and Barsac: First Great Growth**

Estate	Average Annual Production (Cases)
Château d'Yquem	5,000 – 6,000

Table A-7 **Sauternes and Barsac: First Growths**

Estate	Average Annual Production (Cases)
Château Guiraud	8,500
Château La Tour Blanche	4,000
Château Lafaurie-Peyraguey	5,000
Château de Rayne-Vigneau	7,500
Château Sigalas-Rabaud	2,500
Château Rabaud-Promis	5,000
Clos Haut-Peyraguey	5,000
Château Coutet	7,000
Château Climens	6,000
Château Suduiraut	8,500
Château Rieussec	7,000

Table A-8	Sauternes and Barsac: Second Growths
Estate	*Average Annual Production (Cases)*
Château d'Arche	4,000
Château Filhot	10,000
Château Lamothe-Despujols*	1,700
Château Lamothe-Guignard*	2,900
Château de Myrat**	**
Château Doisy-Védrines	2,500
Château Doisy-Daëne	4,200
Château Suau	1,500
Château Broustet	2,000
Château Caillou	4,500
Château Nairac	2,000
Château de Malle	1,300
Château Romer du Hayot	4,200

* *The original Château Lamothe is now two estates.*

** *This Estate has been inactive, but is now in the process of being replanted.*

Appendix B
Vintage Wine Chart: 1975 – 1993

· ·

*A*ny vintage wine chart must be regarded as a rough guide — a general, average rating of the vintage year in a particular wine region. Remember that many wines will always be exceptions to the vintage's rating. For example, some wine producers will manage to find a way to make a decent — even fine — wine in a so-called *poor* vintage.

WINE REGION	1975	1976	1977	1978	1979	1980	1981	1982	1983
Bordeaux:									
Médoc, Graves	85b	75c	70d	80c	80c	75c	80c	95b	85b
Pomerol, St-Emil	90c	80c	65d	80c	80c	70d	80c	95b	85b
Burgundy:									
Côte de Nuits-Red	50d	85c	60d	90c	80c	85c	65d	75c	85b
Côte Beaune-Red	50d	85d	55d	85c	80c	80c	70d	75d	80b
Burgundy, White	65d	85d	75d	90c	85c	75d	85c	80d	80d
Rhône Valley:									
Northern Rhône	70d	80c	70c	100b	85c	80c	75d	85c	90b
Southern Rhône	60d	70d	65d	95b	85c	75d	85c	70d	85c
Alsace	80d	90c	70d	75d	80c	75d	85c	75d	95c
Champagne	85c	85c	NV	70d	85c	NV	85b	90c	80c
Sauternes	90b	85c	55d	70c	75c	80c	80c	70c	90a
Germany	85c	90c	60d	60d	80c	65d	80c	75d	90c
Rioja (Spain)	85c	80c	70d	85c	75c	75c	85c	90c	80c
Vintage Port	75c	NV	90a	NV	NV	80b	NV	80b	85b
Italy:									
Piedmont	65d	65d	65d	90a	80c	75c	70c	90b	75c
Tuscany	85c	60d	85c	75d	80c	70d	80d	85c	80c
California North Coast:									
Cabernet Sauvignon	85c	85b	85c	85b	80c	80c	75c	75c	70d
Chardonnay	85d	80d	80d	85d	80d	85d	85d	75d	80d

WINE REGION	1984	1985	1986	1987	1988	1989	1990	1991	1992	1993
Bordeaux:										
Médoc, Graves	70c	90b	90a	75c	85a	90a	95a	75b	75b	80a
Pomerol, St-Emil	65d	85b	85a	75c	85a	90a	95a	65c	75b	80a
Burgundy:										
Côte de Nuits-Red	75c	85c	75d	85c	90b	85b	95a	85a	75b	85a
Côte Beaune-Red	70d	85c	70d	80d	90b	85b	90b	70b	80b	85a
Burgundy, White	75d	85c	90c	80c	80c	90b	85c	70c	90b	70c
Rhône Valley:										
Northern Rhône	75c	90c	80b	75c	90c	90b	90a	90b	75c	65c
Southern Rhône	70d	80c	75c	60d	85c	95a	95b	70c	75c	80b
Alsace	70d	90b	80c	75c	85c	95b	95b	75c	85b	80b
Champagne	NV	85b	80b	NV	85b	90b	95a	NV	NV	NV
Sauternes	70c	80c	90a	70c	95a	90b	95a	70c	70c	65c
Germany	65d	85c	75c	65c	85c	90b	95b	80c	85c	85c
Rioja (Spain)	70c	80c	80c	80c	85b	90b	85b	75c	85b	85b
Vintage Port	NV	90a	NV	NV	NV	NV	NV	90a	95a	NV
Italy:										
Piedmont	65d	95b	85c	80c	90a	95a	95a	75c	70c	85b
Tuscany	60d	95c	85c	75c	90a	70c	90b	75c	70c	75c
California North Coast:										
Cabernet Sauvignon	85c	90b	80c	85c	75c	80b	95b	90a	90b	90a
Chardonnay	80d	85c	90c	75d	85c	75d	90c	85c	90c	90b

Key:

100	= Outstanding	75	= Average	a = Too young to drink
95	= Excellent	70	= Below Average	b = Can be consumed now, but will improve with time
90	= Very Good	65	= Poor	
85	= Good	50 – 60	= Very Poor	c = Ready to drink
80	= Fairly Good			d = May be too old
				NV = Non-vintage year

WINE REGION	*Recent Past Great Vintages*
Bordeaux:	
Médoc, Graves	1959, 1961, 1970
Pomerol, St-Emil	1961, 1964, 1970
Burgundy:	
Côte de Nuits-Red	1959, 1964, 1969, 1972
Côte Beaune-Red	1959, 1969
Burgundy, White	1962, 1966, 1969, 1973
Rhône Valley:	
Northern Rhône	1959, 1961, 1966, 1969, 1970, and 1972 (Hermitage)
Southern Rhône	1961, 1967, 1971
Alsace	1959, 1961, 1967, 1971
Champagne	1964, 1969, 1971
Sauternes	1959, 1962, 1967
Germany	1959, 1971
Rioja (Spain)	1964, 1970
Vintage Port	1963, 1966, 1970
Italy:	
Piedmont	1964, 1971
Tuscany	1967, 1970 (Brunello di Montalcino), 1971
California North Coast:	
Cabernet Sauvignon	1951, 1958, 1968, 1970, 1974
Chardonnay	---

Index

●●●

• *G* •

•S•

(continued)

1/26/95

Fun, Fast, & Cheap!

CorelDRAW! 5 For Dummies™ Quick Reference
by Raymond E. Werner

ISBN: 1-56884-952-4
$9.99 USA/$12.99 Canada

Windows "X" For Dummies™ Quick Reference, 3rd Edition
by Greg Harvey

ISBN: 1-56884-964-8
$9.99 USA/$12.99 Canada

Word For Windows 6 For Dummies™ Quick Reference
by George Lynch

ISBN: 1-56884-095-0
$8.95 USA/$12.95 Canada

WordPerfect For DOS For Dummies™ Quick Reference
by Greg Harvey

ISBN: 1-56884-009-8
$8.95 USA/$11.95 Canada

Title	Author	ISBN	Price
DATABASE			
Access 2 For Dummies™ Quick Reference	by Stuart A. Stuple	1-56884-167-1	$8.95 USA/$11.95 Canada
dBASE 5 For DOS For Dummies™ Quick Reference	by Barry Sosinsky	1-56884-954-0	$9.99 USA/$12.99 Canada
dBASE 5 For Windows For Dummies™ Quick Reference	by Stuart J. Stuple	1-56884-953-2	$9.99 USA/$12.99 Canada
Paradox 5 For Windows For Dummies™ Quick Reference	by Scott Palmer	1-56884-960-5	$9.99 USA/$12.99 Canada
DESKTOP PUBLISHING / ILLUSTRATION/GRAPHICS			
Harvard Graphics 3 For Windows For Dummies™ Quick Reference	by Raymond E. Werner	1-56884-962-1	$9.99 USA/$12.99 Canada
FINANCE / PERSONAL FINANCE			
Quicken 4 For Windows For Dummies™ Quick Reference	by Stephen L. Nelson	1-56884-950-8	$9.95 USA/$12.95 Canada
GROUPWARE / INTEGRATED			
Microsoft Office 4 For Windows For Dummies™ Quick Reference	by Doug Lowe	1-56884-958-3	$9.99 USA/$12.99 Canada
Microsoft Works For Windows 3 For Dummies™ Quick Reference	by Michael Partington	1-56884-959-1	$9.99 USA/$12.99 Canada
INTERNET / COMMUNICATIONS / NETWORKING			
The Internet For Dummies™ Quick Reference	by John R. Levine	1-56884-168-X	$8.95 USA/$11.95 Canada
MACINTOSH			
Macintosh System 7.5 For Dummies™ Quick Reference	by Stuart J. Stuple	1-56884-956-7	$9.99 USA/$12.99 Canada
OPERATING SYSTEMS / DOS			
DOS For Dummies® Quick Reference	by Greg Harvey	1-56884-007-1	$8.95 USA/$11.95 Canada
UNIX			
UNIX For Dummies™ Quick Reference	by Margaret Levine Young & John R. Levine	1-56884-094-2	$8.95 USA/$11.95 Canada
WINDOWS			
Windows 3.1 For Dummies™ Quick Reference, 2nd Edition	by Greg Harvey	1-56884-951-6	$8.95 USA/$11.95 Canada
PRESENTATION / AUTOCAD			
AutoCAD For Dummies™ Quick Reference	by Ellen Finkelstein	1-56884-198-1	$9.95 USA/$12.95 Canada
SPREADSHEET			
1-2-3 For Dummies™ Quick Reference	by John Walkenbach	1-56884-027-6	$8.95 USA/$11.95 Canada
1-2-3 For Windows 5 For Dummies™ Quick Reference	by John Walkenbach	1-56884-957-5	$9.95 USA/$12.95 Canada
Excel For Windows For Dummies™ Quick Reference, 2nd Edition	by John Walkenbach	1-56884-096-9	$8.95 USA/$11.95 Canada
Quattro Pro 6 For Windows For Dummies™ Quick Reference	by Stuart A. Stuple	1-56884-172-8	$9.95 USA/$12.95 Canada
WORD PROCESSING			
Word For Windows 6 For Dummies™ Quick Reference	by George Lynch	1-56884-095-0	$8.95 USA/$11.95 Canada
WordPerfect For Windows For Dummies™ Quick Reference	by Greg Harvey	1-56884-039-X	$8.95 USA/$11.95 Canada

FOR MORE INFORMATION OR TO ORDER, PLEASE CALL ▶ 800. 762. 2974

For volume discounts & special orders please call
Tony Real, Special Sales, at 415. 655. 3048

IDG BOOKS®

Order Center: **(800) 762-2974** *(8 a.m.–6 p.m., EST, weekdays)*

12/20/94

Quantity	ISBN	Title	Price	Total

Shipping & Handling Charges

	Description	First book	Each additional book	Total
Domestic	Normal	$4.50	$1.50	$
	Two Day Air	$8.50	$2.50	$
	Overnight	$18.00	$3.00	$
International	Surface	$8.00	$8.00	$
	Airmail	$16.00	$16.00	$
	DHL Air	$17.00	$17.00	$

*For large quantities call for shipping & handling charges.
**Prices are subject to change without notice.

Ship to:

Name _____

Company _____

Address _____

City/State/Zip _____

Daytime Phone _____

Payment: ☐ Check to IDG Books (US Funds Only)

☐ VISA   ☐ MasterCard   ☐ American Express

Card # _____ Expires _____

Signature _____

Subtotal _____

CA residents add
applicable sales tax _____

IN, MA, and MD
residents add
5% sales tax _____

IL residents add
6.25% sales tax _____

RI residents add
7% sales tax _____

TX résidents add
8.25% sales tax _____

Shipping _____

Total _____

Please send this order form to:

IDG Books Worldwide
7260 Shadeland Station, Suite 100
Indianapolis, IN 46256

Allow up to 3 weeks for delivery.
Thank you!

IDG BOOKS WORLDWIDE REGISTRATION CARD

Title of this book: Wine For Dummies

My overall rating of this book: ❑ Very good [1]   ❑ Good [2]   ❑ Satisfactory [3]   ❑ Fair [4]   ❑ Poor [5]

How I first heard about this book:

❑ Found in bookstore; name: [6]

❑ Advertisement: [8]

❑ Word of mouth; heard about book from friend, co-worker, etc.: [10]

❑ Book review: [7]

❑ Catalog: [9]

❑ Other: [11]

What I liked most about this book:

What I would change, add, delete, etc., in future editions of this book:

Other comments:

Number of computer books I purchase in a year: ❑ 1 [12]   ❑ 2-5 [13]   ❑ 6-10 [14]   ❑ More than 10 [15]

I would characterize my computer skills as: ❑ Beginner [16] ❑ Intermediate [17] ❑ Advanced [18] ❑ Professional [19]

I use ❑ DOS [20]   ❑ Windows [21]   ❑ OS/2 [22]   ❑ Unix [23]   ❑ Macintosh [24]   ❑ Other: [25]_____
(please specify)

I would be interested in new books on the following subjects:
(please check all that apply, and use the spaces provided to identify specific software)

❑ Word processing: [26]

❑ Data bases: [28]

❑ File Utilities: [30]

❑ Networking: [32]

❑ Other: [34]

❑ Spreadsheets: [27]

❑ Desktop publishing: [29]

❑ Money management: [31]

❑ Programming languages: [33]

I use a PC at (please check all that apply): ❑ home [35] ❑ work [36] ❑ school [37] ❑ other: [38] _____

The disks I prefer to use are ❑ 5.25 [39]   ❑ 3.5 [40]   ❑ other: [41]_____

I have a CD ROM: ❑ yes [42]   ❑ no [43]

I plan to buy or upgrade computer hardware this year: ❑ yes [44]   ❑ no [45]

I plan to buy or upgrade computer software this year: ❑ yes [46]   ❑ no [47]

Name: Business title: [48]   Type of Business: [49]

Address (❑ home [50] ❑ work [51] /Company name: _____)

Street/Suite#

City [52]/State [53]/Zipcode [54]:   Country [55]

❑ **I liked this book!** You may quote me by name in future
IDG Books Worldwide promotional materials.

My daytime phone number is _____

IDG BOOKS

THE WORLD OF
COMPUTER
KNOWLEDGE

❏ YES!

Please keep me informed about IDG's World of Computer Knowledge.
Send me the latest IDG Books catalog.